War and Public Health

EDITED BY

Barry S. Levy
Victor W. Sidel

AUG 1 9 2004

American Public Health Association
800 I St., NW
Washington, DC 20001-3710

Mohammad N. Akhter, MD, MPH
Executive Vice President

2.5 M 10/00
Library of Congress Card Number: 00-106713

ISBN 0-87553-249-7

Printed and bound in the United States of America
Epilogue Typesetting: Susan Westrate
Cover Design: Joseph R. Loehle
Cover Photo: David L. Parker, MD
Printing and Binding: Kirby Lithographic

This book is dedicated to the memory of
the late James P. Grant, Executive Director
of the United Nations Children's Fund (UNICEF),
1980–1994, in honor of his contributions
to the health and well-being of children
and to the prevention of war.

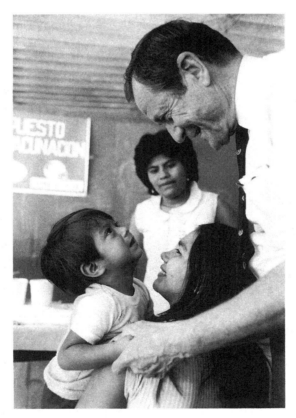

UNICEF's Executive Director, James P. Grant, at a
temporary vaccination post in El Salvador, where
400,000 children were inoculated (Source/Photographer:
UNICEF/1091/Dennis Budd Gray).

Foreword

War and militarism have catastrophic effects on human health and well-being. These effects include casualties during war, long-lasting physical and psychological effects on noncombatant adults and children, the reduction of human and financial resources available to meet social needs, and the creation of a climate in which violence is a primary mode of dealing with conflict.

War and Public Health is a milestone in documenting the impact of war and militarism on human health. It also demonstrates how health professionals, working through organizations like the American Public Health Association, the Centers for Disease Control and Prevention, the International Rescue Committee, and the International Physicians for the Prevention of Nuclear War, can reduce the impact of war and contribute to its prevention.

The participation of respected and trustworthy intermediaries and the willingness of parties to communicate with each other are two key elements in preventing war and resolving conflicts through nonviolent means. Through our work at The Carter Center, I have personally seen the importance of these and other factors in preventing or resolving conflicts in Africa and Latin America, as well as here in the United States.

Because they promote healing, most health professionals are respected and trusted. They should be leaders in constantly working to prevent the pain and suffering that result from war, which has an unconscionable impact on human health. It is commendable that the editors and contributing authors of this book have addressed issues of war and militarism in a public health context. But as the editors state in the final chapter, we, as a global society, need to devote considerably more resources to improving our ability to prevent war. We need to gather and analyze information systematically, and then we need to ensure that this information is used to educate national leaders and others.

Public health workers led the fight to eradicate smallpox. They are now working to eliminate other diseases. We should all strive for a time when, through the efforts of public health workers and others, war too will be eliminated.

JIMMY CARTER

Preface to the Paperback Edition

The first edition of *War and Public Health* was published in early 1997. In the three years since then, the book has had a warm reception, has been extensively reviewed, and has been used in a number of courses in schools of public health, in schools of medicine, and in other schools of other health professions around the world. We are pleased that the book is now available in this paperback edition so that its content and overall message can be available to a much wider audience and we are grateful to the American Public Health Association and Oxford University Press for making its publication possible.

Some of the topics covered in the first edition of *War and Public Health* have undergone significant change over the past three years. These changes are summarized in the Epilogue to this edition.

We are grateful to the authors of the chapters in *War and Public Health* for their support and their suggestions over the years since the publication of the first edition. We are especially grateful to Ellen Meyer, APHA Director of Publications, for her help in the preparation of the paperback edition and to Hillel Cohen, Lachlan Forrow, Richard Garfield, Jack Geiger, Robert Gould, Darryl Kimball, Omar Khan, Steven Meyer, and Carolyn Mikanowicz for their comments on drafts of the Epilogue.

Bronx, New York   Victor W. Sidel, MD
Sherborn, Massachusetts   Barry S. Levy, MD, MPH
July, 2000

Preface

War has an enormous and tragic impact—both directly and indirectly—on public health. War accounts for more death and disability than many major diseases combined. It destroys families, communities, and sometimes whole cultures. It directs scarce resources away from health and other human services, and often destroys the infrastructure for these services. It limits—and often totally eliminates—human rights. War leads many people to think that violence is the only way to resolve conflicts, a mindset that contributes to domestic violence, street crime, and many other kinds of violence in the world. War contributes to the destruction of the environment. In sum, war threatens large elements of the fabric of our civilization.

Yet, despite all of the effects of war on human health and well-being, up until now war and its prevention have not been seen as integral parts of the work of public health professionals and have not been adequately covered in their professional education.

A number of public health workers are already being called on to provide services in war-torn areas on a short-term or long-term basis; they would benefit from systematic background information on war, its effects, and its prevention. Other public health workers are involved in the prevention of domestic or street violence in their communities and would benefit from systematic background information on the attempts to prevent international violence and its consequences. Most, if not all, public health workers are concerned with helping to set political agendas in their communities and would benefit from information on the ways in which the military budget diverts resources from health and social services, the ways in which arms sales contribute to violence and war in other nations, and the ways in which expanded economic development aid could lead to prevention of violence and war internationally.

This book has two primary purposes.

The first is to provide a systematic survey of information about the direct and indirect effects of war and militarism on public health, and the roles that public health professionals can play in preventing the effects of war and in preventing war itself. This compendium is intended for use by a wide spectrum of individuals and organizations, not only health professionals—and students in the health professions—and their organizations, but also economists, politicians, sociologists, and all those who may play a role in the prevention of war and its effects, and the organizations to which they belong.

The second purpose of this book is to help make war and its prevention an integral part of public health, placing these issues in the mainstream of public health education, research, and practice. Like other public health problems, war is preventable. The same, or similar, approaches that have been used successfully to prevent or totally eliminate major public health problems—ranging from smallpox to lead poisoning, from lack of health services for mothers and children to contaminated water and air— can be used to prevent war and its public health consequences.

The prevention of war needs to become an integral part of public health education, research, and practice. It needs to be integrated into the curricula of schools of public health, other schools for health workers, and other academic institutions. It needs to become a focus for research into ways that war and its effects on public health can be prevented. And it needs to become a greater part of the practice of public health professionals. National public health associations should have peace sections just as they have sections on maternal and child health or health administration.

This book arose from a session that we organized at the 1991 Annual Meeting of the American Public Health Association. That session focused primarily on the manifold impacts on public health of the then-recent Persian Gulf War. The strong support of many participants during and after that session and the encouragement of our colleagues in the leadership of the American Public Health Association and on its Publications Board and staff led us to pursue the development of this book.

The book is divided into seven parts. The first part places war in the context of the public health agenda. The second part deals with the impact of war on health, human rights, and the environment. The third part focuses on the effects of weapons systems on public health. The fourth part deals with the effects of war and other military activities on populations, including children, women, and displaced persons. The fifth part deals with the impact on public health of specific military conflicts in Vietnam, Central America, and the Persian Gulf. The sixth part discusses the roles of public health professionals and organizations during war. The seventh part addresses the prevention of war and its public health consequences.

The views expressed in this book are those of the contributors and editors, and are not necessarily those of the organizaitons with which they are affiliated.

We intend that this book be used not only to provide necessary information about war and its impact, but also to motivate and inspire public health professionals, students, and others to work for sustainable peace throughout the world, for nonviolent approaches to conflict resolution, and for freeing the resources and energies that have been used for war and other military activities to address the other serious public health issues that threaten humankind.

Sherborn, Massachusetts   B.S.L.
Bronx, New York   V.W.S.
May 1996

Acknowledgements

Developing and producing a book like *War and Public Health* takes the combined skills and resources of many people, to whom we are profoundly grateful.

We deeply appreciate the guidance, assistance, and support of Jeffrey House, Vice-President and Executive Editor, Medicine; Charles Annis, production editor for this book; and Sean Finnegan, editorial assistant; and their colleagues at Oxford University Press.

We are indebted to all of the contributors to this book, who worked tirelessly in writing and revising their chapters and in identifying references and illustrative materials.

We thank the following individuals who reviewed earlier revisions of the manuscript and made many helpful suggestions: Mary-Wynne Ashford, Richard Garfield, Jack Geiger, Robert Gould, Sabine Beisler, Dorothy Oda, and Berttina Wentworth. We are especially grateful to Ms. Beiser, Dr. Oda, and Dr. Wentworth for nurturing the development of this book and for facilitating the co-publication arrangement with the American Public Health Association.

We are grateful to Robert Cohen of UNICEF for his devoted and expert contributions to the chapter written by James P. Grant.

We express our appreciation to Rosalyn Cooper for her excellent secretarial assistance.

Finally, we express our deepest gratitude and appreciation to Nancy Levy and Ruth Sidel for their continuing encouragement and support.

Sherborn, Massachusetts   B.S.L.
Bronx, New York   V.W.S.
May 1996

Contents

Contributors

Myron Allukian, Jr., DDS, MPH
Director, Bureau of Community Dental
  Programs
Boston Department of Health and
  Hospitals
Boston, MA

Mary-Wynne Ashford, MD
University of Victoria
Victoria, British Columbia
Canada

Paul L. Atwood, PhD
William Joiner Center for the Study of
  War and Social Consequences
University of Massachusetts, Boston
Boston, MA

Paula Braveman, MD, MPH
Departments of Family and Community
  Medicine and of Epidemiology and
  Biostatistics
School of Medicine
University of California, San Francisco
San Francisco, CA

Jimmy Carter
The Carter Presidential Center
Atlanta, GA

James C. Cobey, MD, MPH
Founder, Health Volunteers Overseas
Washington, DC

Nancy D. Connell, PhD
Department of Microbiology and
  Molecular Genetics
UMDNJ—New Jersey Medical School
Newark, NJ

Jonathan Fine, MD
Cambridge, MA

Annette Flanagin, RN, MA
Associate Senior Editor
*Journal of the American Medical
  Association*
Chicago, IL

William H. Foege, MD, MPH
The Carter Presidential Center
Atlanta, GA

Lachlan Forrow, MD
Division of General Medicine
Beth Israel Hospital
and Division of Medical Ethics
Harvard Medical School
Boston, MA

Richard M. Garfield, RN, DrPH
Professor of Clinical Nursing
and Henrik H. Bendixen Chair in
  International Nursing
Columbia University School of Nursing
New York, NY

H. Jack Geiger, MD, MSciHyg
Arthur C. Logan Professor of
    Community Medicine
City University of New York Medical
    School
New York, NY

Robert M. Gould, MD
Department of Pathology
Santa Teresa Community Hospital
San Francisco, CA

James P. Grant
Late Executive Director
United Nations Children's Fund
New York, NY

Eric Hoskins, MD, DPhil, MPH,
    FRCPC
Center for International Health
McMaster University
Hamilton, Ontario, Canada

Yolanda Huet-Vaughn, MD
Family Practice Program
Trinity Lutheran Hospital
Kansas City, MO

Ernesto Kahan, MD, MPH
Department of Epidemiology
Institute of Occupational Health
Tel Aviv University
Tel Aviv, Israel

Nanao Kamada, MD
Professor, Department of Cancer
    Cytogenetics
Research Institute for Nuclear Medicine
    and Biology
Hiroshima University
Hiroshima, Japan

Chen Lee, DipEd, MA
Seoul, Republic of Korea

Barry S. Levy, MD, MPH
Director
Barry S. Levy Associates
Sherborn, MA
and Adjunct Professor
Department of Family Medicine and
    Community Health
Tufts University School of Medicine
Boston, MA
and President
American Public Health Association

Nick Lewer, BDS, PhD
Centre for Conflict Resolution
Department of Peace Studies
University of Bradford
Bradford, West Yorkshire,
    United Kingdom

Alan H. Lockwood, MD
Professor of Neurology and Nuclear
    Medicine
School of Medicine and Biomedical
    Sciences
SUNY/University of Buffalo
Buffalo, NY

Leland Miles, PhD
President Emeritus, International
    Association of University Presidents
Southport, CT

Alan Meyers, MD
Assistant Professor of Pediatrics
Boston City Hospital
Boston, MA

Alfred I. Neugut, MD
Associate Clinical Professor of Public
    Health and Medicine
Columbia University School of Public
    Health
New York, NY

Michael Renner
Senior Researcher
Worldwatch Institute
Long Island City, NY

Joanna Santa Barbara, MB, BS
Centre for Peace Studies and
    Department of Psychiatry
McMaster University
Hamilton, Ontario, Canada

Thomas Schlenker, MD, MPH
Executive Director
Salt Lake City-County Health
    Department
Salt Lake City, UT

Gurinder S. Shahi, M.B.B.S.,
    Ph.D., M.P.H.
Coordinator, Operations Development
International Vaccine Institute Project
United Nations Development
    Programme
Seoul, Republic of Korea

Victor W. Sidel, MD
Distinguished University Professor of
    Social Medicine
Montefiore Medical Center
Albert Einstein College of Medicine
Bronx, NY
and Co-President
International Physicians for the
    Prevention of Nuclear War

Barbara Smith, Ph.D.
Director of Programs
International Rescue Committee
New York, NY

Eric Stover
Human Rights Program
Townsend Center for the Humanities
University of California at Berkeley
Berkeley, CA

Elizabeth Temkin, RN
New Haven, CT

Michael J. Toole, MD
International Health Unit
MacFarlane Burnet Center for Medical
    Research
Fairfield, Victoria, Australia

Curt Wands
National Coordinator, National
    Coordinating Office on Refugees and
    Displaced Persons of Guatemala
Chicago, IL

Kenjiro Yokoro, MD
Senior Consultant, Radiation Effects
    Research Foundation
Professor Emeritus,
    Hiroshima University
Secretary General, Japanese Physicians
    for the Prevention of Nuclear War
c/o Hiroshima Prefectural Medical
    Association
Hiroshima, Japan

I

War as a Part of the
Public Health Agenda

1

Arms and Public Health:
A Global Perspective

WILLIAM H. FOEGE

What is the most wonderful thing in the world? asks Yama Man after man dies; seeing this, men still move about as if they were immortal, replies Yudishthira.[1]

We have the capacity to ignore the obvious, to become fatalistic about what we do not understand, and to accept, because of familiarity, what should not be acceptable. The unlimited expansion of arms, the continuing and even increasing level of conflict, and the frightening volume of violence are not acceptable ingredients in a quality level of human existence.

Throughout history, the leading causes of premature death have been infectious diseases and violence. For two centuries, the world has made gains against infectious diseases, and despite the problems of emerging infections, as well as the development of resistance to antibiotics and insecticides, the world is a much safer place when it comes to microorganisms than ever before in history. The same is not true of violence. The age of science has provided more efficient methods of inflicting violence, and it has changed the ethics of violence. People can now kill and maim without confronting the effects of their actions due to the distance, time, and filters placed between them and the victims. Many forces in society have made it possible for arms to be acquired by almost anyone regardless of age, wealth, or propensity for violence. What is the cost of this situation, and is there real hope for changing the equation?

The Problem

Arms are Deadly

Violence has always had a public health impact because of the direct effects of injury and death. But it also has an indirect effect on health. The violence seen in households,

3

for example, beyond the direct effects, results in psychological scars that become part of the complex of forces involved in the struggle for health. Likewise, organized violence, as seen in small or large conflicts, has direct and indirect effects on health as it leads to famines, epidemics, social dislocations, and the disruption of public health programs in general.

In addition to these impacts, violence is now seen as a public health problem in itself, and epidemiological methods are being used to characterize the problems, to define the risk factors involved, to develop interventions, and to measure the impact of those interventions. Early work on unintentional violence has indicated the power of such an approach and has led to major reductions in the death rate from highway injuries. If the United States still had the fatalities per million miles recorded six decades ago, we would experience a staggering half million deaths a year on our highways. Now public health workers at the Centers for Disease Control and Prevention, at many schools of public health, and in city, county, and state health departments are characterizing the risk factors leading to morbidity and death from arms in the civilian population. As a public health approach to individual violence develops, there is merit in asking whether the discipline of public health could play a role in moderating violence in the aggregate.

DIRECT IMPACT OF ARMS ON MORBIDITY AND MORTALITY. Several "crossovers" appear to have taken place in recent history. The first concerns trauma versus infectious diseases in time of war. Throughout history, infectious diseases have killed more soldiers than have weapons. In the American Civil War, twice as many casualties were recorded for infectious diseases as for weapons. Public health practices make it safer to be a soldier today, because the risk of infectious diseases, including infections following trauma, have decreased. Yet that crossover may be misleading since the impact of conflict on infectious diseases in the civilian population remains significant but insufficiently studied.

The other crossover involves deaths due to conflicts. It has always been very hazardous to be a soldier. It still is, but in recent decades the greatest risk seems to be carried by civilians. In recent conflicts, it has been reported that nine civilians have died for every soldier killed, and UNICEF[2] reports that in the past decade two million children have died because of conflicts, more deaths in children than in soldiers.

Following the 50 million or more deaths in World War II, millions more have died in a continuous stream of conflicts. All parts of the world have been involved, but much of the publicity in recent years has concentrated on conflicts in Africa—Zaire, Nigeria, Ethiopia, Sudan, Angola, Zimbabwe, South Africa, Mozambique, Liberia, Rwanda. It has always been difficult to obtain complete figures on the total death rate or the burden of suffering. In 1993,[3] the World Bank provided one of the first attempts to combine both death and suffering into a single number to represent the burden of disease (Disability Adjusted Life Years, or DALYs), and to compare war with other pathological conditions. They found in 1990 a total of 1.4 billion DALYs lost in the

Table 1-1.   Burden of disease–global, 1990

Specific Conditions	Total DALYs Lost (in millions)
Respiratory diseases	123
Violence	102
Perinatal conditions	100
Diarrhea	99
Neuropsychiatric disorders	93
Cancer	79
Vaccine-preventable diseases	68
Tropical diseases	66
Maternal conditions	59
Nutritional diseases	54

world. Twenty-four different conditions each accounted for more than one percent of that total. Five of these 24 conditions involved violence: automobile injuries, falls, homicide, suicide, and war. The burden of war was equivalent to the total global burden of homicide or suicide. The five violence conditions were second only to respiratory diseases as a disease burden in the world. (Table 1-1.)

RISK OF CONFLICT. A decade ago there was little understanding that a gun in the house might actually increase the risk of homicide and suicide for the members of that house. Dr. Art Kellerman, at the Emory University School of Public Health, has shown that the risk of suicide increases five times and the risk of homicide increases three times for persons living in homes with guns, even though most of these people are law-abiding citizens who acquired guns to protect themselves and their families, thinking they were actually decreasing their risks.[4]

Can similar techniques characterize the risks associated with arms in the aggregate? Do countries increase their risk of violent death by acquiring arms even if for self-defense? It is possible that the same relationship is operative for nations. That is, countries and groups that stockpile weapons may actually increase the chances that those weapons will be used, and therefore they increase the possibilities that they will become victims. There are few examples similar to Costa Rica, where money has been saved for decades by the absence of a military, but it should be noted that Costa Rica has apparently not become vulnerable to aggression from other countries despite the absence of a military capability.

LONG-TERM EFFECTS. The world is currently reliving the era of World War II as the 50th anniversary of specific events is remembered. We are not surprised by many of the long-term effects as we learn about the disruption of lives and the suicide rates of those who suffered in the Holocaust. We have learned of the ongoing risks resulting from placing of millions of land mines. We understand the long-term effects of prisoner-of-war (POW) camps and the continuing discomfort of those who lived through countless bombing attacks, and we even understand the anger expressed by those who now speak from Dresden or a hundred other cities as they express their helplessness and the resentment they feel toward both sides in the conflict.

What came as a surprise was the price paid even by the victors, beyond the long-term effects of wounds and amputations. We have found that post-traumatic stress disorder was a price paid by Americans who successfully stormed Normandy or Iwo Jima, and some realized that to be the case only 50 years later as they tried to describe on television what had happened on that day. For some, the quality of life has been forever dimmed.

For others, the psychological effects are minimal, but they have lost a period of their life. Gaps in education are never recovered, property losses are never fully recovered, momentum is lost during a crucial period of development, tobacco or alcohol habits, acquired under the stress of combat, shorten the number and quality of remaining years. Even our best efforts fall short of assigning realistic Disability Adjusted Life Year equivalents.

Arms continue to be deadly, despite the improvements in communications that allow a transparency not possible in the past. We do not have adequate surveillance systems to fully measure the direct effects of arms, the famines and infectious diseases that result, or the psychological trauma inflicted on military and civilians alike. The surprise is that the world is not deterred by the horrific tally that is kept, even though that tally is only partial.

Arms Are Costly

Speaking before the American Society of Newspaper Editors on April 16, 1953, President Eisenhower gave his famous "Cross of Iron" speech, saying, "Every gun that is fired . . . is in the final sense, a theft from those who hunger and are not fed, those who are cold and not clothed. This world in arms is not spending money alone. It is spending the sweat of its laborers, the genius of its scientists, the hopes of its children."[5]

That has not changed. But it is not just a gun fired. It is every gun purchased that competes for basic resources because it already reflects other money being invested in military transport, housing, training, and dozens of other competitive activities not available for crucial development of health, education, and nation building. For every sophisticated weapon made, especially those involving chemicals, biological agents, and nuclear materials, additional costs and public health risks must be incurred during both the development and production of those weapons, and also for the eventual disposal of those weapons. While health improvements are increasingly knowledge-based—so that, for example, improvements in health are observed in developing countries at an earlier stage than expected given the per-capita income level—the diversion of financial, human, and natural resources for military purposes means that fewer resources are potentially available for health or other improvements in development.

Table 1-2.   Public expenditures per capita, 1990,
selected countries

Country	For Military	For Health
Ethiopia	$16	$1
Chad	10	1
Sudan	25	1
Mozambique	9	2
Angola	114	8

Every minute 20 children under the age of five die because they have not been immunized, because of malnutrition, or as the result of respiratory infections, diarrheal disease, or other correctable conditions. During the same minute, the world's military machine absorbs in excess of $1,100,000 not available for other purposes.[6] In 1990, the developing world had almost seven soldiers for every doctor. In some countries, public military expenditures may exceed health expenditures tenfold or more. (Table 1-2.) (See Chapter 11.)

Arms Destroy Infrastructure

When the presence of arms leads to the use of those arms, a cascade of events is likely. The morbidity and mortality of both military and civilians due to wounds is the most obvious. In addition, priority is then given to the treatment of trauma, which results in a decrease in time and resources available for other health care delivery or public health programs. As conflict escalates, the problem goes from the shifting of priorities to the halting of public health activities in general. The toll of this diversion has been seen most recently in Liberia, Sudan, Rwanda, and Chechnya.

Sudan has recorded a marked reduction in services, making it difficult for it to keep pace with health improvements seen in other areas. For example, Guinea worm rates have declined so quickly in other African countries that Sudan now leads all other countries in the number of cases. This is not surprising in light of the reports of Cole P. Dodge that thousands of people have become internally displaced persons and that health providers have migrated to cities as health service delivery systems have broken down, leaving the physical facilities useless. Immunizations, the provision of safe water, and even the most basic health services were discontinued for large segments of the population.[7] Surveillance programs are not easily possible; in effect, the world's accumulated public health information and experience is of no use. This is the price of arms.

Rwanda has given vivid testimony to the role of conflict leading to the cessation of public health activities. It was bad enough when basic services were unavailable but worse was in store as a rapid increase in health problems occurred due to dislocation, crowding, inadequate food and water, and the almost inevitable outbreaks of infectious diseases.[8] Mortality rates during the first month of conflict, while the world attempted a response, were between eight and nine percent, a rate that exceeds by two or three times the mortality in Leningrad in January, 1942.[9] No political objectives are worth this price, yet the priority of arms continues to cloud judgment, even in those who have just experienced these conditions of unbelievable depravity. Following the extreme suffering in Rwanda, hopes were raised that the world would conclude that it cannot stand by as a spectator when infrastructure collapses in times of violence. Such hopes were dashed in April and May of 1996, as the world watched ever-younger combatants in Monrovia intimidate peacekeepers from other countries, and, in weeks of killing, looting, and destruction, demonstrate the speed with which a society can travel backwards in time by destroying the commercial and governmental infrastructures.

Does History Predict the Future?

It is easy to read history as an unending attempt at conquest matched by an inevitable investment in defense. This could blind us to evidence of improvements in the human condition, even when history would have suggested otherwise.

The world has never been as healthy as it is today, a condition not predicted by the historical record of unending epidemics. Life expectancy has increased more in the last 40 years than in all previous recorded history.[3] Infant mortality rates have dropped dramatically and specific disease problems have disappeared or are disappearing. This is not an accident. It is the product of global cooperation that has melded the leadership of United Nations agencies, the agreement of donor countries, and the identification of problems by nations in a collective way. This degree of global cooperation and these health outcomes could not have been anticipated even 60 years ago.

The percentage of people held in bondage of various types continues to decrease. Slavery is still a fact of life for some, but the decline in rates is a product of the last two centuries, a remarkably small part of history. The right of women to vote, even in the United States, is recorded in the history of our parents. The slavery of illiteracy is yielding only in recent decades. The empowerment of women is coming to fruition only as we now read about it. Such rapid changes would not have been predicted only a few years before the changes began if one used history as the guide. Famine as the result of crop failure has not occurred in recent decades. Only person-made obstacles now cause scarcity of food. Yet until mid-century famine was a fact of life, every few years, some place in the world, for all of recorded history. And even optimists did not envision a world free of poliomyelitis at mid-century.

The point to be learned is that history, even if consistent for thousands of years, is of limited value in determining what will happen in the immediate future. Just as individuals often develop in an atmosphere of total dependency only to suddenly realize they can have some, even if not total, control over their future, so is the world coming to the realization that it is possible, collectively, to plan a rational future. Norman Cousins once wrote that this was the single most important lesson the history of the United States has taught the world: "It is possible to plan a rational future."[10] It took many attempts by countries in many parts of the world before this experiment worked; it is suddenly becoming the norm for larger and larger parts of the world. It may still require more experience before the same approach is successful on a global basis. But it will happen.

What Can Public Health Do?

It is not enough to deplore the impact of arms on health and the reduction of public health activities. We must ask if there is a role for public health in the promotion of peace.

Until a few years ago, many felt that the single biggest risk in the world was the presence of nuclear weapons. It was theoretically possible for a small number of people to inflict unbelievable suffering on large numbers of people, but also to alter the future quality of the world. The threat has not disappeared, but it has changed in character because the fear of the possible drove leaders to cooperative planning. Will Durant once declared his belief that world leaders would cooperate for the good of the world only if they feared an alien invasion. Nuclear weapons became a surrogate for such an invasion. Having observed this result, could we exploit it? On a small scale the global cooperation that developed to achieve smallpox eradication is a glimpse of the possibilities. All countries worked toward a common objective that would benefit the descendants of each country forever. Smallpox was a common enemy, as are poliomyelitis, Guinea worm, measles, AIDS, tuberculosis, and a hundred other disease conditions. Likewise, we are seeing a global coalition develop around the common enemy of environmental degradation, and even, as the world has worked toward the Social Summit, poverty itself.

Demonstrating what is possible on a national level, in April, 1995, President Jimmy Carter met with both government and rebel leaders in Sudan, to explore the possibility of a cease-fire in order to achieve specific health objectives for the benefit of Guinea worm eradication, the treatment of onchocerciasis with Mectizan, immunization for polio eradication, the provision of other childhood immunizations, and the distribution of oral rehydration salts for the treatment of diarrheal diseases.

For over four months, relative calm prevailed making it possible to establish disease surveillance systems and to arrange health intervention strategies. What was achieved? At the very minimum, a period of reduced morbidity and mortality due to conflict. In addition, real health improvements were implemented, with lasting implications, since the health programs will continue even in the midst of conflict. Perhaps of most significance was the demonstration that it is possible for public health to go beyond days of tranquillity, to months of tranquillity. The question is how to use such experiences to extend peace indefinitely and, finally, permanently.

Public health can help in the redefinition of security and demonstrate the global benefits to be gained if there is a sense of comfort concerning health, housing, and nutrition. If this is to be realized, public health officers must deliberately plan a course of action. This would include global approaches to all public health actions so that local decisions are seen in a global context with a clear vision of the total impact of local activities. It would include an understanding of the long-term impact of current decisions, and it would demand an understanding of how public health decisions affect poverty, literacy, the environment, housing, employment—in short, all aspects of life. Public health officials could then optimize their activities to highlight the benefits of collaborative activities, which would promote security for all, advance the cause of peace, and make explicit the global self-interest in public health activities.

But it would require more than simply declaring that this is important. It would require that we systematically study conflict in the same way that we now study violence. A useful body of knowledge is already accumulating.[11–14] Such study should include a surveillance system that characterizes each conflict, determining the risk factors that led to the conflict, and developing an understanding of the factors that can be altered. Such a study would be expected to present the evidence on what works in preventing conflict and the most effective ways of intervening once conflict has started. It would seek to understand the role of education in preventing conflict as part of a comprehensive approach to security.

Such an approach could start with a global plan developed by a coalition of UN agencies using the ingenuity and suggestions of countries. Global public health security monitoring would be matched to long-term plans that would clearly spell out the rewards for countries taking part in the system and pursuing actions that benefit the entire world in terms of security, health, and development. This, in turn, could be matched with transparent monitoring that makes it clear to the citizens of each country when their leaders are making decisions that do not serve the cause of peace in the world. Countries agreeing to such positive actions would sign a convention that would provide for extra global support in development and would also provide for global interventions if they fail to keep such commitments.

Public health is based on the assumption that this is not a fatalistic world. Risks are decreased by identifying them, developing interventions that lower the risk, and implementing those interventions. The risk of arms, violence, and conflict can be measured and reduced by conscious and deliberative acts. The crucial step is to recognize this risk as a public health problem.

REFERENCES

1. Durant, W. *The story of civilization. Part 1: Our Oriental heritage.* New York: Simon and Schuster, 1954, p. 516.

2. United Nations Children's Fund (UNICEF). *The state of the world's children 1995.* New York: Oxford University Press, 1995.

3. *World development report 1993.* New York: Oxford University Press (for The World Bank), 1993.

4. Kellermann, A.L. and Reay, D.T. Protection or peril? An analysis of firearm-related deaths in the home. *New England Journal of Medicine.* 314(24):1557–1560, 1986.

5. Eisenhower, D.D. "The Chance for Peace." Speech to the American Society of Newspaper Editors, April 16, 1953, Washington, D.C.

6. Sivard, R.L. *World military and social expenditures 1991* (Fourteenth edition). Washington, D.C.: World Priorities, 1991.

7. Dodge, C.P. Health implications of war in Uganda and Sudan, *Soc. Sci. Med.* 31(6):691–698. 1990.

8. Foege, W.H. Famine, infections, and epidemics. Symposia of the Swedish Nutrition Foundation IX. Saltsjobaden, Sweden, August 1970.

9. Michael Toole. Personal communication. October 1994.

10. Cousins, N. Reflections on a "birthday" (Editorial). *Saturday Review,* December 13, 1975, pp, 4–5.

11. Zwi, A. and Ugalde, A. Towards an epidemiology of political violence in the Third World. *Soc. Sci. Med.* 28(7):633–642. 1989.

12. Rosh, R.M. Third World militarization, security webs and the states they ensnare. *Journal of Conflict Resolution.* 32(4):671–698, 1988.

13. Zwi, A.B. Militarism, militarization, health and the Third World. *Medicine and War.* 7: 262–268, 1991.

14. Evans, G. Health and security in the global village. *World Health Forum.* 14(2):133–135, 1993.

2

War, Children, and the Responsibility of the International Community

JAMES P. GRANT

Someone once said that the trouble with modern war is that it does not kill the right people. I am not certain who the *right people* might be, but there is no question that children are the *wrong people*. If anyone should be spared the violence and terror of war, it is children. Their innocence and vulnerability should place them above politics and its continuation in the form of armed conflict. Under the Geneva Conventions and the Convention on the Rights of the Child, children are supposed to receive special protection during armed conflicts.

Nevertheless, in the past decade some two million children have been killed in wars, and dozens of armed conflicts, large and small, continue to claim children's lives around the world. In some cases, children even seem to have become primary targets, accounting for up to half of all casualties. This is a moral abomination, an obscenity that casts a shadow over all human progress on the threshold of the twenty-first century.

Up until the First World War, the vast majority of casualties of armed conflicts were combatants. But modern warfare and weaponry have made armed conflict increasingly deadly to civilians. Since 1945, more than 20 million people have been killed and 60 million wounded in armed strife, and over 80 percent of these casualties have been civilians—mainly women and children (see Chapter 3). Since the end of the Cold War there has been a proliferation of civil wars and inter-ethnic conflicts whose primary battlefields are densely populated neighborhoods where almost all casualties are civilian.

Because monitoring systems are generally weak in developing countries and records are poorly kept or hidden in wartime, we lack accurate global statistics on child casualties. However, rough estimates compiled by the United Nations Children's Fund

(UNICEF) and nongovernmental organizations (NGOs) offer a sense of the magnitude of the direct impact of war on children over the past decade:

- Two million children killed.
- Four to five million handicapped or disabled.
- Twelve million left homeless.
- More than one million orphaned or separated from parents.
- Ten million psychologically traumatized, or one child in every 200 worldwide.

Reports from a number of recent conflicts cite acts of unspeakable brutality, including cases where women and children are deliberate targets of mass slaughter, torture, rape, and violent assaults. ''To destroy the big rats, you must kill the little rats,'' was a message repeated over and over again by an extremist radio station during the ethnic genocide in Rwanda in 1994.

Shocking as casualty rates are, they do not reflect the full magnitude of the problem. The massive uprooting and displacement of people—as refugees in other countries or internally displaced within their own—is a tragedy not to be underestimated (see Chapter 14). Forced emigration, the breakup of families and communities, hostile new environments, and the lack of security and provisions for survival continue to take a devastating toll on people affected by war.

Children constitute between one-third and one-half of the world's 20 million refugees and 24 million internally displaced people. The lack of health care, food, water, and shelter that results from armed conflict is often just as lethal as bullets and bombs. Many millions more have had their education interrupted or ended. For six years, at least 20,000 Sudanese children and youth have trekked long distances, back and forth over national borders, to escape fighting. About 7,000 children live on their own on the streets of Angola's capital, Luanda, surviving as best they can. Generations of children are growing up without knowing anything but the hatred and cruelty of war, thus diminishing the chance for sustained peace.

The effects of war on surviving children are not limited to physical injury or hardship (see Chapter 12). As resilient as children are, war can leave them with psychological and emotional wounds that never heal. The phenomenon of post-traumatic stress syndrome, first studied in depth during the Vietnam War, has been found to affect children every bit as much as adults (Figure 2-1).

- A 1991 study of Iraqi children revealed that 62 percent worried that they may not live to become adults.
- A study of 50 displaced children in Mozambique found that 42 had lost a father or mother by violence, 29 had witnessed a murder, 16 had been kidnapped, and all had been threatened, beaten, or starved.
- A study conducted in September 1994 by UNICEF found that 50 percent of the Rwandan children interviewed had witnessed the killing of family members, and

Figure 2-1. A child stands beside a soldier, holding a rifle, on a street in Sarajevo (Source/ Photographer: UNICEF/93-1149/Senad Gubelic).

more than 75 percent had seen people murdered. More than 50 percent had witnessed mass killings in churches and schools; 75 percent had had their own lives threatened. UNICEF is helping to bury those killed in massacres in Rwanda because of the effect of the profusion of human remains on young children. The decision was reached after a Rwandan child pointed to a skull and said, ''This is my mother.''

These children display symptoms and behaviors typically associated with great stress and trauma, ranging from withdrawal and silence to aggression, anxiety, obsessive replaying of violent memories, and guilt. Therapeutic services for traumatized children have not been part of traditional relief efforts until recently, first because the problem was not widely recognized, and second because there was little experience in methods other than slow-moving, expensive counseling of individuals. Over the past few years, however, several techniques have proven highly effective in relieving stress and trauma in large groups of children, and UNICEF has now built such actions into all emergency programs. Simple methods such as encouraging children to talk, draw or write, or act out or otherwise express their feelings about their experiences— together with even small steps toward regaining a safe and nurturing environment— can help heal the psychological damage of even severe trauma.

Perhaps the most alarming development in children's experiences of armed conflicts has been their inclusion in actually fighting wars. More than 200,000 children have been recruited into armies over the past decade, according to some estimates. Children as young as seven or eight are often used as soldiers, equipped with fully-automatic assault weapons. These children are sometimes forcibly recruited, but more often join warring factions for survival. Many have seen their own parents cruelly murdered. Terrible things have been done to these children, and the children themselves have done terrible things, taking part in the atrocities of war. Reintegrating these children into their communities presents immense problems. All of this lends urgency to the efforts of a number of governments and NGOs to attach an Optional Protocol to the Convention on the Rights of the Child setting the minimum age for recruitment into armed forces at age 18 rather than at age 15, as stipulated in the Convention on the Rights of the Child today.

Related to this is the issue of antipersonnel land mines (see Chapter 10). Momentum is growing for an international moratorium on the export of these cruel weapons that have killed over a million people since 1975 and that take a disproportionate toll among children, who often constitute more than half of all mine victims. The Secretary-General of the United Nations has urged the international community to go one critical step further and adopt a total ban on production, use, stockpiling, sale, and export of antipersonnel land mines. For UNICEF, this cause has a very particular force, inasmuch as the presence of land mines violates the most fundamental rights guaranteed by the Convention on the Rights of the Child. Far greater support needs to be given to mine awareness campaigns, along with deactivation and removal of the over 100 million unexploded mines (one for every 20 children) that continue to wage war against civilians long after the fighting has ended. And certainly the savage use of young boys to clear mine fields must be ended once and for all (Figure 2-2).

The international community must find ways to provide children with greater protection and assistance during and following the wars that victimize and traumatize them. That is why UNICEF welcomes the decision by the General Assembly to implement the proposal from the Committee on the Rights of the Child to undertake a comprehensive study of the impact of armed conflict on children. Ms. Graca Machel, the expert chosen to prepare this important study in consultation with the Centre for Human Rights and other relevant organs and agencies of the UN system, will submit her report in late 1996. The study should be seized by the international community as an opportunity for soul-searching and identifying practical steps to ease the plight of the children of war.

Notwithstanding the seriousness of the situation of children and other civilians caught in contemporary warfare, a longer view indicates that progress has been made in recent decades in the way the world responds to humanitarian emergencies. Today we are seeing the deployment of international aid and relief on a scale and of a nature that would have been unthinkable only a few years ago (see Chapters 19 and 20).

Figure 2-2. A disabled boy maimed by a landmine stands in a courtyard of a UNICEF-assisted rehabilitation center located in the Wat Tan Temple in Phnom Penh (Source/Photographer: UNICEF/5907/Roger Lemoyne).

We sometimes forget that the international community's capacity and will to act to prevent massive suffering in human-made or natural emergencies is, historically speaking, a new phenomenon.

A personal recollection may help to illustrate the point. I was in Calcutta at the end of the 1943–1944 Bengal famine when well over two million people starved to death, including more than a million on the streets of Calcutta. It was my first encounter with a purchasing-power famine, and I shall never forget the images of families slowly starving to death a few feet away from overflowing grain stores protected by troops of the British Raj. The problem was that landless laborers who had lost a season's wages due to floods simply could not pay the war-inflated prices for food. The authorities did little to help, and people dropped like flies. And the world stood by and did nothing.

This was, in fact, the situation that prevailed throughout human history. Just so long as it was not possible to easily provide large-scale relief, and far-away victims of disaster and war remained faceless, it was possible for the rest of the world to turn its back on them.

But much has happened along the road from Calcutta in the 1940s to the present. The technological and communications revolution has gradually transformed the world into an increasingly interdependent global village in which it is no longer possible to conceal or ignore either large-scale famine and violence or the new capacity to respond.

The "loud emergencies" that are now brought live into our homes through TV satellite links create an increasing pressure on governments to act, at a time when there is a vastly increased capacity to act. This is most welcome. Morality does march with perceived changes in capacity.

Just one aspect of UNICEF's emergency effort following the genocide in and massive exodus from Rwanda in mid-1994 illustrates the qualitative change. Together with the International Committee of the Red Cross, and thanks to Kodak's donation of thousands of rolls of film, photographs were made of tens of thousands of Rwandan children who were either orphaned or separated from their families. These photographs, and a central computerized registry, are greatly facilitating efforts to identify and reunite these children with their parents or extended families in their communities of origin. In the meantime, they are receiving food and basic health care, and even some basic education with anti-trauma and peace education components.

The point I want to stress is that, with this new capacity, children can be treated as the individuals they are, individuals with names that can be recorded and faces that can be photographed and rights that can begin to be protected.

In the past, repressive, authoritarian governments have slaughtered millions and conducted pogroms against minorities, religious and ethnic groups, and political opponents behind an impenetrable shield of state sovereignty. Until recently, sovereignty and Cold War rivalries tended to provide ideological cover for atrocities and systematic violations of human rights. Basically, the attitude toward the victims of civil conflict was that it was just too bad, these were internal matters of a sovereign state and therefore not the responsibility of the international community. The world's hands were largely tied so long as the victims did not acquire refugee status by crossing international borders—until 1989, that is.

It was in Sudan in that year that the international community was empowered for the first time, through the UN-sponsored agreement of the two principal parties to the conflict, to come to the aid of internally displaced people on a massive scale. The world invested $400 million in Operation Lifeline Sudan, a pioneering humanitarian intervention in the midst of civil war that saved hundreds of thousands of lives. UNICEF was lead agency during the first phase of the massive interagency effort.

From Sudan, the concept of "corridors of peace" was soon extended, with the blessing of the Organization of African Unity, to Ethiopia, Angola, and Liberia.

UNICEF also helped to develop an earlier modality of reaching vulnerable populations caught in civil strife, which contributed to the "corridors of peace." Since the mid-1980s, UNICEF has worked with governments, armed guerrilla movements, the International Committee of the Red Cross, and churches to develop the concept of children as a "zone of peace." In several civil conflicts—most notably those in El Salvador, Lebanon, and Bosnia-Herzegovina—agreements were hammered out among the parties in conflict to stop fighting for certain periods of time, known as "days of tranquillity,'' to permit the delivery of food and medical supplies, in particular for immunization of children, in predefined areas.

These ''days of tranquillity'' and ''corridors of peace'' are now regularly carved out of war to benefit children. In fact, the concept was formally endorsed at the 1990 World Summit for Children and is embodied in the Convention on the Rights of the Child, which entered into force as international law that same year. Among its provisions relating to the rights of children trapped in wars, the Convention in Article 38 states:

In accordance with their obligations under international humanitarian law to protect the civilian population in armed conflicts, States Parties shall take all feasible measures to ensure protection and care of children who are affected by armed conflict . . .

The World Summit for Children Plan of Action is more explicit, stating:

Recent examples in which countries and opposing factions have agreed to suspend hostilities and adopt special measures such as ''corridors of peace'' to allow relief supplies to reach women and children and ''days of tranquillity'' to vaccinate and to provide other health services for children and their families in areas of conflict need to be applied in all such situations. Resolution of a conflict need not be a prerequisite for measures explicitly to protect children and their families to ensure their continuing access to food, medical care and basic services, to deal with trauma resulting from violence and to exempt them from other direct consequences of violence and hostilities.

These expressions of concern for children caught in armed conflict reflect a new ethos that is struggling to take hold in the last decade of the twentieth century—one that gives children a much higher priority on the world's agenda and places the human being at the center of development efforts. These developments make it possible, in many cases, to obtain the agreement of political and military adversaries to cease fire to permit limited forms of humanitarian assistance for displaced civilians, particularly for women and children, instead of having to wait for them to cross international borders and become refugees entitled, under international law, to protection and assistance.

But things have evolved even further in the past few years, to the point where humanitarian action is possible, in certain circumstances, even when a government does not agree—or when there is no government to agree with. The critical step was taken in early 1991, when the UN Security Council ordered assistance and protection to the displaced and persecuted Kurdish population in Northern Iraq in the wake of the Persian Gulf War. UNICEF became lead agency, under the Department for Humanitarian Affairs mandate, for helping the displaced population in the North, working under international protection, even as it continued to carry out its country program to assist all Iraqi children, and even as it worked to modify an international sanctions regime that, through direct and indirect effects, has contributed to increasing the country's child mortality rate.

A further ethical bridge was crossed when the UN Security Council authorized armed international intervention in Somalia to protect an entire people's right to food and survival. Future historians will judge the wisdom of attempts to pick up all the pieces of a failed state in the absence of a political settlement among contending armed factions, but there is no question that international intervention in Somalia saved the lives of hundreds of thousands of children and adults who certainly would have perished from starvation and disease, if not from bullets, had the intervention not taken place.

The prolonged agony of the peoples of former Yugoslavia may illustrate the limitations of what the United Nations can do in certain complex emergencies, but it must be acknowledged that some measure of international protection and assistance is being provided to many of the innocent victims of this intractable conflict, while the decision to establish an International War Crimes Tribunal (extended, subsequently, to cover war crimes in Rwanda) reflects a lowering of the world's threshold of tolerance toward massive violations of human rights.

As of the end of 1994, an estimated 40 to 50 countries were experiencing manmade or natural disasters, of which the United Nations classified 12 as "complex," or involving multiple causes with more than one political entity directly engaged. There are currently 17 UN peacekeeping operations underway (see Chapter 24). Responding to this proliferation of complex emergencies stretches limited UN capacities to the breaking point. It also challenges the ability of relief and development agencies to fulfill their humanitarian mandate of strict neutrality and impartiality while functioning under the protection of UN forces with a military mandate or under sanctions regimes that often inadvertently hurt innocent civilians along with—or even more than—their intended targets.

Because UNICEF's sphere of development action is children, and because its assistance has been provided in a strictly nonpolitical way, it has enjoyed considerably more "space" than other organizations cooperating with governments. The international community has told UNICEF that it must not restrict itself to providing life-saving supplies, but has given it also a life-saving advocacy role as a defender of children and their rights. UNICEF has sought to exercise this special role seriously and responsibly, but it is not difficult to see what tensions can crop up between cooperation with governments and advocacy for the poor and oppressed. As an illustration, in March 1993 UNICEF denounced the systematic rapes and other atrocities against children in former Yugoslavia before the Commission on Human Rights— even as the agency continued to work impartially with Muslims, Serbs, and Croats throughout the Balkans to gain access to children and their families.

The work of UNICEF has become easier overall as leaders and politicians have understood that helping children can be "good politics" and as the tide of democracy has risen around the globe in recent years. The Convention and the World Summit for Children formalized and further raised the new ethical priority on meeting children's basic needs and respecting their rights.

But the new ethical compulsion to respond to "loud emergencies" threatens our even more urgent response to the "silent emergencies" of massive malnutrition, disease, and illiteracy, affecting mainly the world's one billion poor, who vastly outnumber the refugees and displaced combined. Of the 35,000 children who die each day in developing countries, some 2,000 to 3,000 are victims of the "loud emergencies" of violence and famine; the rest succumb, quietly but just as terribly, to largely preventable hunger and illness. No earthquake, no flood, no war has taken the lives of a quarter million children in a single week; but that is the weekly child death toll of the "silent emergency" associated with poverty and underdevelopment. In 1993, the number of deaths of children under five years of age brought about by "loud emergencies," which horrified and shocked the world, was about 500,000, a small proportion of the 13 million children who died last year and who will die this year. The tragic deaths of 1,000 children per day in Somalia in 1992 captured much more public attention than the 5,000 children who died worldwide every day from dehydration caused by diarrhea, which can be prevented and treated easily and at almost no cost.

UNICEF emergency program expenditures, which mainly assist children affected by armed conflicts, increased more than fourfold in the five years from 1989 (when they totalled US$48 million and made up 10 percent of program expenditures) to 1993 (when they reached US$223 million and accounted for 28 percent of program expenditures). Emergency relief is now UNICEF's single largest program expenditure sector—a sad indicator of the growing toll of armed conflicts. Because funds for emergency relief are raised through special appeals, however, funds are not drawn from regular country development programs.

In emergencies, UNICEF coordinates its actions with other UN agencies and NGOs and provides assistance in health care, supplementary feeding for children, nutrition and household food security, water supply and sanitation services, basic education, assistance for unaccompanied children, land mine awareness and rehabilitation from land mine injuries, and psychosocial treatment for traumatized children. UNICEF has always striven to maintain basic services for children, even in the most difficult conflict situations, and every attempt is made to provide relief in such a way as to speed post-conflict rehabilitation and development.

Unless alternatives to revenge, hatred, and intolerance are taught and effectively opened, cycles of violence will never be broken. UNICEF is developing educational strategies and activities that enable children and parents to explore issues of peace, to sensitize themselves against prejudice and the stereotyping of other cultures and ethnic groups, and to learn conflict resolution skills.

This is an urgent need worldwide, for we have witnessed in recent years an alarming resurgence of prejudice and intolerance, along with the spread of violence and antisocial behavior, among young people in industrialized as well as developing countries. In fact, many of the problems associated with children caught in armed conflict can be found, to one degree or another, in violence-ridden communities of wealthy nations (see Chapter 11).

In the context of evolving international responsibility toward alleviating people's suffering—be they refugees, internally displaced, or simply poor—the world must rapidly come to terms with the reality of increasing demands being placed on ever more severely limited resources. How many operations can the international community afford to mount to rescue the victims of failed states, as in Somalia, or of civil war, as in Rwanda? Surely it is worth spending $2 billion to $3 billion or more to save two or three million people—after all, even a single life is priceless—and we should be able to carve a progressively larger peace dividend out of the post–Cold War era to cover such eventualities. But it would be naive to expect taxpayers to foot the bill for endlessly proliferating emergencies and conflicts.

The terrible costs of war are paid by countries that are, for the most part, among the world's poorest and least able to afford the toll in lives and the costs of reconstruction and rehabilitation. The per-capita gross national products (GNPs) of war-torn countries in 1992 are revealing: Afghanistan, $280; Angola, $610 (in 1991); Liberia, $450; Mozambique, $60; Somalia, $150; and Sudan, $420.

The effects of poverty in many countries are compounded by the impact of budget priorities. Developing countries as a whole spent an estimated $118 billion on the military in 1994. Developed countries, as major arms producers, promote and profit from the arms trade. Military spending worldwide in 1994 was estimated to total $770 billion. I believe that such spending legitimizes tools of destruction, giving them value and importance, while devaluing human life by draining scarce resources needed by all countries for social priorities, particularly the needs of children (see Chapter 11).

This is neither a plea to use the bottom line as an exclusive means of deciding where to put our resources nor a call to turn our backs on the victims of "loud emergencies." What I am saying is that humankind must invest far more than it is today in prevention of emergencies and conflicts, even as we go about the world putting out fires (see box). The UN Secretary-General's *Agenda for Peace* also stresses prevention and makes the critical link to development and democracy. This investment in prevention will prove far less costly—and produce far greater results—than reliance on expensive and not-always-effective rescue operations.

A final word on the relief workers on the front line of emergency operations: As the nature of conflict changes and civilians are increasingly targeted, emergency personnel and peacekeepers themselves face increasing risks. In 1992, seven UNICEF staff members were killed during relief operations in Somalia and Sudan, and one staff member in Sudan has been missing since that year. Three UNICEF staff members perished in Somalia and Uganda in 1993, and in April, 1994, at least seven UNICEF staff members and a larger number of their family members were reported killed in the conflict in Rwanda. Many more in the larger UN family and the NGO community have given their lives. The targeting of relief workers and peacekeepers is absolutely

---

Anti-War Agenda of UNICEF

This chapter was completed just before Mr. Grant's death in January, 1995. His successor as Executive Director of UNICEF, Carol Bellamy, dedicated a major portion of the UNICEF report, *State of the World's Children 1996,* to the plight of children in war. The ten-point Anti-War Agenda of UNICEF included in the report follows.

1. Prevention

The world must no longer wait for the outbreak of hostilities before it pays heed. Much more deliberate effort should be made to address the underlying causes of violence and to invest more resources in mediation and conflict resolution.

2. Girls and Women

In the midst of conflict, specific community-based measures are necessary to monitor the situations and needs of girls and women and especially to ensure their security because of the terrible threat they face of sexual violence and rape. Traumatized girls and women urgently need education and counselling. Because in times of conflict women's economic burdens are greater, access to skills training, credit and other resources must be secured. Education, women's rights legislation and actions to strengthen women's decision-making roles in their families and communities are all needed, both before and after conflicts.

3. Child Soldiers

UNICEF believes that the minimum age of recruitment into the military should be 18 years. At present, under the Convention on the Rights of the Child, it is 15 years. The change could be achieved through the adoption of an Optional Protocol to the Convention. Beyond that, there is a great need to concentrate on rehabilitating child soldiers to prevent them from drifting into a life of further violence, crime, and hopelessness.

4. Land Mines

No international law specifically bans the production, use, stockpiling, or sale and export of anti-personnel mines. It is now time for such a law. UNICEF joins many other organizations in concluding that this is the only way to stop the endless suffering inflicted by these weapons on children and other civilians. UNICEF will not deal with companies manufacturing or selling land mines.

---

unacceptable, and a special convention that will bolster their protection is urgently needed.

The world is now challenged to create a permanent zone of peace around children to ensure their safety, to defuse destructive conflicts, and to assist fragile societies in efforts to move toward stability and sustainable development.

BIBLIOGRAPHY

Anti-personnel land-mines: A scourge on children. New York: UNICEF, 1994.
Arms and the child. A SIPRI Report for UNICEF on the Impact of Military Expenditure in

5. War Crimes

Recent years have seen the most barbaric acts of violence against children and other civilians. These must be denounced as they are revealed. International war crimes tribunals must have both the support and the resources to bring perpetrators to justice.

6. Children as Zones of Peace

This idea should be pursued more vigorously. The gains from establishing such zones may be fragile and temporary. Nevertheless, zones of peace have become an important part of international diplomacy—capable of prising open vital areas of humanitarian space in even the darkest conflicts. As such, UNICEF intends to pursue the possibility that zones of peace be raised to a tenet of international humanitarian law.

7. Sanctions

Economic sanctions are imposed on the assumption that the long-term benefits of pressure on errant regimes outweigh the immediate cost to children. This may not be the case. There should be a 'child impact assessment' at the point at which any set of sanctions is applied, and constant monitoring thereafter to gauge impact.

8. Emergency Relief

In situations of long-term conflict, aid should be seen as part of a process to help rebuild a society's capacity and promote development.

9. Rehabilitation

A much more deliberate effort needs to be made to demobilize both adult and child soldiers and rebuild communities so as to offer not just respite but also reconciliation. An important part of rehabilitation must be to address the psychosocial damage that children suffer.

10. Education for Peace

Disputes may be inevitable, but violence is not. To prevent continued cycles of conflict, education must seek to promote peace and tolerance, not fuel hatred and suspicion.

Sub-Saharan Africa on the Survival, Protection and Development of Children. New York: UNICEF, 1991.

Children and development in the 1990s: A UNICEF sourcebook. New York: UNICEF, 1990.

Children in armed conflict, *Convention on the Rights of the Child briefing kit.* New York: UNICEF and the United Nations Centre for Human Rights, 1993.

Children's rights and squandered opportunities. UNICEF position paper for the World Conference on Human Rights, Vienna, June 1993.

Children: Innocent Victims of War—Update, UNICEF fundraising documentation package, February 1993.

Children need peace. New York: UNICEF, 1994.

I dream of peace: Images of war by children in former Yugoslavia. New York: HarperCollins, 1994.

Refugees, internally displaced and the poor: An evolving ethos of responsibility. Address by James P. Grant, Executive Director of UNICEF, at the Round Table on the Papal Document ''Refugees: A Challenge to Solidarity,'' United Nations, March 9, 1993.

Somalia: Restoring hope. Africa Recovery Briefing Paper No. 7, Jan. 15, 1993, United Nations Department of Information.

The state of the world's children. New York: UNICEF, annual.

The state of the world's refugees: The challenge of protection. Geneva: United Nations High Commissioner for Refugees, 1993.

UNICEF's response to children in emergency situations: 1992/3. UNICEF Office of Emergency Programmes, New York, September 1993.

The arms project of Human Rights Watch and Physicians for Human Rights. *Landmines: A deadly legacy.* New York: Human Rights Watch, 1993.

Ressler, E.M., Tortorici, J.M. and Marcelino, A. *Children in war, a guide to the provision of services.* New York: UNICEF, 1993.

Vittachi, V.T. *Between the guns: Children as a zone of peace.* London: Hodder and Stoughton, 1993.

II

The Impact of War
on Public Health

3

The Human
Consequences of War

RICHARD M. GARFIELD and ALFRED I. NEUGUT

Although warfare is thought to be responsible for high and increasing levels of morbidity and mortality in the modern era, little epidemiologic research is available on the subject. Most research on past wars has been done for purposes of military planning. This chapter analyzes the direct health impacts of various wars on military and civilian populations during the past 200 years as well as risk factors for injury and death. Changes in weaponry, military strategy, and medical services are found to modify morbidity and mortality associated with warfare.

Since the 1960s, the expression ''War is not healthy for children and other living things'' has been popular. The phrase is so understated that one hesitates to ask how unhealthy war might be. Effective warfare should, by definition, have a devastating effect on the health of some part of an opponent population. Broader and long-range effects on morbidity and mortality may be more important than the acute destruction of armed conflict. It is difficult to assess this possibility, as most of the research on this subject is speculative and has recently focused on the potential effects of nuclear war.[1,2] Analysis of casualty data from past wars has been carried out mainly by the armed services in order to prepare for similar future conflicts.[3-5] Given the enormous and growing productive, financial, political, and human effort expended on war in recent centuries, epidemiologic analysis appears to be indicated. A large body of data on casualties in modern wars also offers a heuristic focus for research on this phenomenon. Uncontrolled bias no doubt exists in much of the secondary data presented below, as the data were generated by parties to the hostilities; the reader is cautioned about the limited reliability of the data.

Military and other historians provide fertile impressions on the health effects of

Parts of this chapter were excerpted and adapted from Garfield, R.M., and Neugut, A.I. Epidemiologic analysis of warfare: A historical review. *JAMA* 226: 688–692, 1991. Copyright 1991, American Medical Association.

the ancient wars.[6–9] During the nineteenth century, doctors began to count and analyze the nature of battlefield casualties.[10] Early nursing studies provided the first experimental and statistical analyses of the management of mass casualties.[11] Official and semi-official statistical reports based on data collected by national armies of combatant nations have improved as casualties have become more massive in wars of the twentieth century.[12–18] More precise data and quasi-experimental designs have been employed since World War II for studies on the direct and indirect effects of wars on combatants, prisoners of war, and civilians.[19–32]

Definitions

Soldiers killed before receiving medical assistance for injuries suffered in combat are killed in action (KIA). This is the military equivalent of "dead on arrival." Those who are wounded in battle and survive at least to the point of medical registration by an authorized health worker are wounded in action (WIA). Soldiers who are WIA, but later die from wounds incurred in battle, are classified as died of wounds (DOW). Those who are killed in action, died of wounds, or died of non-battle injuries, diseases, or accidents compose the total military dead. Those wounded in action or otherwise injured or diseased without death constitute the total nonfatal military casualties. Those who suffer fatal injuries, nonfatal injuries, and diseases constitute total military casualties.

In reporting civilian casualties generated by warfare, only those injuries and fatalities that result from wounds caused by military equipment are normally included. A broader definition, including morbidity and mortality caused by the disruption of food and medical systems, is occasionally used. Injuries and deaths to prisoners of war and captive civilian populations are usually counted as military casualties.

Although these definitions appear fairly straightforward, actually applying them for comparative analysis can be problematic. Operational definitions of KIAs and DOWs depend upon the rapidity with which evacuation and medical assistance are implemented. Sources of data on DOWs depend on the availability of curative medical facilities and the average duration of hospitalization. Differing models for surgical evacuation and treatment and the functional definition of "fit for combat" have influenced the distribution of KIAs, WIAs, and DOWs.[32,33]

As in most medical registration systems, data on the wounded, injured, or ill are collected through the clinic and hospital systems. Minor injuries and diseases are usually not included in military morbidity statistics; such cases are "carded," but seldom treated, at field army medical stations. Knowledge about cases that are not treated in these systems is often excluded from accumulated data on casualties in war. For this reason, prisoners of war, troops missing in action, and untreated civilian casualties are often excluded from wartime medical statistics, yielding biased estimates.

Table 3-1.   Estimated average annual military deaths in wars, worldwide, by century[36,65]

Century	Average Annual Military Deaths	World Mid-Century Population in Millions	Average Annual Military Deaths per Million Population
17th	9,500	500	19.0
18th	15,000	800	18.8
19th	13,000	1,200	10.8
20th	458,000	2,500	183.2

War-Related Mortality

Rapidly increasing firepower and a trend toward increasing numbers of large-scale conflicts has resulted in greatly increased absolute average annual military mortality (Table 3-1). Mortality rates from war among the total population rose only in the twentieth century. This increase occurred because military mortality by year of fighting increased most during World Wars I and II (Table 3-2).

Until World War II, more deaths occurred among U.S. troops from disease than on the battlefield.[34] The ratio of deaths from disease to deaths from battle-related causes was estimated at 9.33 in the Crimean War, 5.25 in the Spanish American War, and 1.02 in World War I.[35,36] Many deaths among troops in World War I were due to the influenza pandemic of 1918; among the troops of the American Expeditionary Force before the pandemic, the ratio of disease deaths per battlefield death was only 0.34. Among U.S. troops in Europe in World War II, this rate declined further to 0.01. Even in World War II, however, the natural environment exerted a greater influence than the military environment in some theaters of war. Australian troops who fought in tropical Asian environs experienced mortality rates from infectious diseases that were 16 times higher than those from battle wounds. A dramatic decline in deaths from non-battle diseases appears to have occurred primarily as a result of public health measures.

In the Mexican, Spanish, and Philippine wars, the ratio of non-battle to battle deaths was at least 6 to 1. Since World War I, combat-related deaths among troops have been close to or greater than those caused by non-battle injuries and diseases (Table 3-3).

Although deaths from infectious diseases have dropped, deaths from non-combat accidents have risen. The increasingly technologic environment of the battlefield raised the proportion of deaths from noncombat accidents among all deaths to U.S. troops from 3 percent during the Civil War to 16 percent during World War II[13] to 45 percent in the Persian Gulf War.[37]

A major decline in the death rate from combat wounds attests to the importance of improvements in curative medicine. The Civil War was the only major war fought by the United States in which firepower rose prior to the development of improved

Table 3-2.   Number of military deaths per year of warfare, by war, in thousands[15,30]

War	Duration	Military Deaths per Year in Thousands
Thirty Years War	1618–1648	6
War of Spanish Succession	1701–1713	18
Seven Years War	1756–1763	20
Revolutionary Wars in Europe	1792–1801	38
Napoleonic Wars	1805–1815	51
U.S. Civil War	1861–1865	125
World War I	1914–1918	2,520
World War II	1939–1945	5,561
Korean War	1950–1953	666
Vietnam War	1965–1975	106

medical and surgical techniques. The relatively high rate of KIAs in that war attests to the importance of medical interventions in reducing mortality during subsequent conflicts. Greatly improved firepower since the Civil War would likely have killed troops at rapidly rising rate were it not for medical measures.

In the U.S. Civil War, approximately 75 percent of all deaths were caused by bullet wounds, while nine percent were caused by explosives. The development of powerful explosives has since inverted this relationship. Among U.S. deaths in the Korean War, 28 percent died of bullet wounds, while 64 percent died of wounds caused by explosives. In that war, 51 percent of all deaths were caused by projectile explosives, three percent were caused by land mines, and 10 percent were caused by grenades.[38]

Because most engagements in guerrilla wars are ambushes, a higher percentage of all deaths are caused by bullets and land mines than by projectiles or other kinds of explosives. In a guerrilla war in Thailand in the 1970s, 40 percent of deaths were reportedly caused by bullets,[39] while 33 percent of deaths were attributed to bullets in Croatia in 1991–1992.[40] In 1984 in El Salvador, 43 percent of deaths among government troops were reportedly caused by land mines.[41]

The percentage of deaths occurring among civilians has varied according to the combat strategy employed and the site of fighting. Prior to the development of the bomber in World War II, countries whose wars were fought on foreign territory were largely spared from civilian casualties. Most wars during the eighteenth and nineteenth centuries are believed to have caused relatively few civilian casualties.

Civil wars and wars of national liberation, when compared to conflicts between nations, tend to involve higher rates of deaths among civilians. In the Spanish Civil War, 50 percent of the dead were civilians; in the Korean War, 34 percent; and in the Vietnam war, 48 percent (Table 3-4). In Croatia during 1991–1992, 64 percent of registered deaths were estimated to occur among civilians.[40] The only major exception to this trend occurred in World War II, in which most or all of the casualties in some countries occurred among noncombatants.

Table 3-3. Deaths per 1,000 U.S. soldiers per year of warfare and cause of death[13]

	Battle Deaths		Non-battle Deaths		
	Killed in Action	Died of Wounds	Disease	Injury	Total Deaths
Mexican War	9.9	4.8	103.9	3.7	122.3
Civil War (North)	21.3	13.6	71.9	3.4	110.2
Spanish War	1.9	0.8	34.0	2.0	38.7
Philippine Insurrection	2.2	0.6	12.9	2.8	18.5
World War I	12.0	4.4	16.5	1.4	34.3
World War II	9.0	1.1	0.6	2.2	12.9

The United Nations Children's Fund (UNICEF), counting deaths both directly and indirectly resulting from wars, has estimated that in the 1990s civilian deaths constituted 90 percent of all deaths in war[42] (Figure 3-1).

The mortality rate among prisoners of war can approach 100 percent where policies designed to eliminate prisoners are employed. As soldiers are drawn from the population sectors with the lowest peacetime mortality risk, the expected mortality rate among prisoners is otherwise very low. During the twentieth century, the mortality rate has varied from a low of four percent among Germans in Allied camps in World War I to a high of 26 percent among allies in German camps in World War II.[4] Cause of death among prisoners is concentrated overwhelmingly in the categories of non-battle injuries and diseases.

Despite rapid population growth in recent centuries, deaths in wars have grown faster. This has resulted in rising rates of mortality which are attributable to war, especially in the twentieth century. World War II was the cause of death of approximately 3.0 percent of the world's 1938 population. The Soviet Union, which suffered 40 percent of all deaths in that war, lost 10.1 percent of its population. Almost 20 percent of the Polish people but only 0.7 percent of the British and 0.3 percent of the U.S. population lost their lives.[35] Although wars since World War II have killed fewer people, most deaths have occurred in small countries: Korea lost 10 percent of its people, and Vietnam, 13 percent in their respective wars[36] (see Chapter 15).

Morbidity

The rate of wounding per troop-year has tended to decline. There were 97 wounds per 1,000 U.S. troops in the Civil War, 81 per 1,000 in World War I, and 27 per 1,000 in World War II. The risk of injuries or death used to be largely confined to enlisted men and junior officers prior to the popularization of the repeating rifle. Since World War I, the reach and accuracy of weapons has subjected senior officers to risks that previously had been reserved for those on the front lines.[3] Risk of death is also

Table 3-4. Percentages of war-related deaths estimated to occur among civilians, by war and country[36]

War and country	Percentage
World War I (total)	19
India	50
Russia	50
United Kingdom	2
United States	0
Spanish Civil War	50
World War II (total)	48
Czechoslovakia	100
Poland	93
USSR	50
Japan	50
China	39
Italy	32
Belgium	26
United Kingdom	22
Germany	14
United States	0
Korean War	34
Vietnam War	48

related to the position held by a soldier. Among U.S. Army troops in World War II, 56 of every 1,000 officers and 72 of every 1,000 enlisted men were wounded. The rate of wounding was highest for the infantry at 265 and lowest for the air corps at 10 per 1,000.[12]

Among ground troops in the U.S. Army during World War II, lethality of all weapons was about 20 per 100 wounds. Bullets caused rates as high as 40 per 100 hits in some theaters, while fragments and blasts generally were associated with rates of lethality of 10 to 22 percent.[12,18] The percentage of all WIA who later became DOW has declined markedly in the last 100 years (Table 3-5).

The distribution of wounds by area of the body has changed little during the last 100 years (Table 3-6). The lethality of wounds to the extremities has declined, leaving a greater proportion of all fatal wounds to be located in the head or torso.[38]

Indirect Effects

Many social disruptions caused by war have a potential to raise the mortality rate among civilians. Prime among these are war-induced material deprivations (especially malnutrition), crowding, the breakdown of normal sanitary systems, and shortages of medical care. Taken together, these factors are estimated to have resulted in 800,000

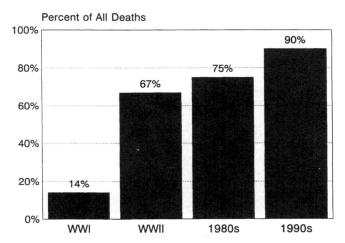

Figure 3-1. Civilian deaths as a percentage of all deaths in selected twentieth-century wars (Source: Adapted from Ahlstram, C. *Casualties of conflict: Report for the protection of victims of war.* Uppsala, Sweden: Department of Peace and Conflict Research, Uppsala University, 1991. Cited in C. Bellamy. *The state of the world's children 1996.* New York: Oxford University Press, 1996.).

non-battle civilian deaths in Germany during the final two years of World War I. In addition, survivors of war-caused deprivations experience elevated mortality rates in later years.[27]

More casualties may be caused following wars than during wars. The influenza pandemic following World War I is the best known, albeit still debated, case of delayed war effects through nutritional deprivation, crowding, and social disruption. In spite of the massive rise in firepower in that conflict, the war was arguably the attributable cause of more deaths after the end of hostilities than during them. Such experiences are common and, because they are not registered as war casualties, are seriously underestimated. As many as 14 deaths due to indirect effects for each death from combat-related activity occurred in low-intensity wars in Angola and Mozambique during the 1980s.[43] Twice as many civilians were registered as killed in the 1980s in the Contra war in Nicaragua, but indirect effects could account for a ratio as high as seven civilian deaths per military death[44] (see Chapter 16). While initial counts suggested two civilian deaths for every three military deaths in the Panama invasion of 1990, a more careful count shows that there were three civilian deaths for every two military deaths. In Iraq, where "smart bombs" minimized battle-related mortality among civilians (approximately 10 percent of all Iraqi deaths during the war), embargo-related shortages of food, postwar civil strife, and the destruction of water and electric infrastructure resulted in a tripling in the mortality rate for children under the age of 5 during the first post-war year.[45] The number of war-related, post-war deaths approached the 100,000 killed during the war[46,47] (see Chapter 17).

So-called "low-intensity conflicts" of the post–Vietnam era have used higher-

Table 3-5. Percentages of wounded combatants who died of wounds, by war[12,17,32]

War	Years	Percentage
Crimean War	1854–1856	20.0
U.S. Civil War (North)	1861–1865	14.1
Franco-Prussian War	1870–1871	13.6
Spanish-American War	1898	6.7
Boer War	1899–1901	8.8
World War I[a]	1914–1918	6.1
World War II[a]	1941–1945	4.5
Korea[a]	1950–1953	2.5
Vietnam[a]	1965–1973	3.6

[a]U.S. troops only

velocity projectiles, more sophisticated weapons, and newly elaborated military strategies that have more pervasive effects on the noncombatant population (see Chapter 16). Such effects have been noted to include extensive social disruption, widespread physical handicapping, and mass psychological disturbances.[48,49] Most notable are the creation of large refugee populations, long-term weakening of the economic infrastructure, and the continuing impact of unexploded mines. Especially when wars occur in underdeveloped countries, as have most conflicts since World War II,[50] such effects go unreported.

Studies during World War II began to estimate the contribution of warfare to individual and collective psychological disturbances.[51–56] More recently, posttraumatic stress syndrome has been recognized as a common problem among combat troops. A 12-year follow-up study of U.S. veterans of combat in Vietnam attributed a 65 percent elevation in the death rate from suicide and a 49 percent elevation in the death rate from motor vehicle accidents to the psychological sequelae of combat.[57–59] Even more difficult to measure, yet possibly more pervasive in its impact on health, is destruction of the environment (see Chapter 5).

Discussion

This review suggests that changes in weaponry and military tactics have been associated with dramatic alterations in the quantity and nature of war-related casualties. The popularization of projectile weapons (arrows) in the Battle of Agincourt in 1415 resulted in an increase in the number of penetrating wounds of the chest and abdomen, with a concomitant rise in mortality.[7] The development of machine guns, tanks, high-power explosives, and computer-guided missiles have each subsequently had a unique impact on the morbidity and mortality profile of military conflict.

Improvements in curative and preventive health care have profoundly reduced the potential impact of modern nonnuclear warfare on some combatants. New techniques

Table 3-6. Percentages of major wounds and fatal wounds among combatants, by war and site of wound[13,20,38,40]

Site of wound	Civil War	Spanish American War	World War I	World War II	Korea	Croatia[c]
Head, face, and neck	11 (41)[a]	12	15	23 (42)	24	(32)
Thorax	18 (51)[b]	10	9	12 (30)	11	(37)[b]
Abdomen		11	5	10 (12)	9	
Upper extremities	36 (3)	30	33	20 (5)	23	(1)
Lower extremities	35 (5)	37	38	32 (8)	31	(2)

[a]Figures in parentheses indicate the percentage of fatal wounds.
[b]These data combine numbers of thoracic and abdominal wounds.
[c]Wounds of multiple sites and unknown sites are not accounted for in this column.

for rehabilitation medicine, circulatory volume replacement, rapid evacuation, and epidemic prevention have resulted from war-related research.[60–64]

Although the modern battlefield may seem relatively empty, the impact of changes in warfare appears to be increasingly devastating for noncombatants, particularly civilian women and children. Just as the repeating rifle extended mortality to the entire battlefield, including officers, modern weaponry and tactics extend the battlefield to the entire society, including civilians.

The tools of conventional epidemiologic investigation, including observational studies and analysis of secular trends over time, are suitable for research on this topic. Long-term and chronic effects of warfare can be studied more effectively with methods that are common in chronic disease epidemiology. Disaster research and occupational health studies appear particularly relevant for research into warfare and those affected by war. There is much research into questionable causes and preventive therapies for other major scourges, such as cancer and heart disease. While the physical causes of morbidity and mortality in wars are well-documented by defense ministries around the world, and despite some agreement on ways to ''civilize'' warfare through international law, little research and public policy discussion has been oriented toward reducing the impact of war on noncombatant populations. While prohibitions on the use of certain weapons were established in the Geneva Conventions, monitoring and enforcement capacity to prevent the deployment of such weapons remains weak. The so-called ''surgical strikes'' in Libya in 1989, which fell instead on foreign embassies, the destruction of an entire neighborhood in the U.S. invasion of Panama in 1990, and civilian deaths in a Baghdad bomb shelter in 1991 suggest a need for new policies to update the rules of engagement.

Opportunities for prevention in this area are striking. New weapons require the calculation of the impact of future engagements on civilian survivors and the environment. New roles for the World Court and the United Nations in monitoring compliance and reducing morbidity and mortality following wars must be explored. Excepting the reduction of acute gastroenteritis and respiratory infections in young children, these actions may contribute more to a worldwide reduction in the number of years of productive life lost than any other prevention strategy. More research is needed in order to predict probable morbidity and mortality profiles to emerge from a particular conflict. Preparations for international emergency interventions are likely to be more effective in reducing the impact of some wars, just as disaster preparedness can reduce the impact of natural disasters.

By contrast, inaction and a lack of new research and policy development in this area would be an important opportunity wasted. With the end of the Cold War and the regional conflicts by proxy it generated, a devolution to rising numbers of small and large conflicts with potentially devastating effects on civilians and the environment is likely. The Persian Gulf War will likely be only the first of these wars. The recommended research and action could reduce the impact of war on noncombatant populations and could lead to changes to make war less unhealthy ''for children and other living things.''

REFERENCES

1. Stockholm International Peace Research Institute. *Warfare in a fragile world: military impact on the human environment.* London: Taylor and Francis Ltd., 1980.
2. Dyer, G. *War.* New York: Crown Publishers, 1985.
3. Arnold, A. and Cuttine, R.T. Causes of death in United States military personnel hospitalized in Vietnam. *Mil. Med.* 143:161–164, 1978.
4. Gordon, C.V. and Bisgard, J.C. Medical readiness planning: identifying critical elements and aggregate requirements. *Mil. Med.* 148:103–107, 1983.
5. Hoeber, F.P. *Military applications of modeling.* New York: Gordon and Breach, 1981.
6. Cash, P. The Canadian military campaign of 1775–1776: medical problems and effects of disease. *JAMA* 236:52–56, 1976.
7. Keegan, J. *The face of battle.* Penguin: New York, 1976.
8. McNeil, W. *The pursuit of power.* Chicago: University of Chicago Press, 1982.
9. McNeil, W. *Plagues and people.* Garden City: Anchor Press, 1976.
10. Addinton, L.H. *Patterns of war since the eighteenth century.* Bloomington: Indiana University Press, 1984.
11. Nightingale, F. *Notes on matters affecting the health of the British army.* In F. Nightingale, *Selected Writings, 1820–1910.* New York: Macmillan, 1954.
12. Howard, J.M. and deBakey, M.F. The cost of delayed medical care. *Mil. Med.* 118:343–357, 1956.
13. Beebe, G.W. and deBakey, M.E. *Battle casualties: incidence, mortality, and logistic considerations.* Springfield: Charles Thomas, 1952.
14. Melsom, M.A., Farrar, M.D. and Volkers, R.C. Battle casualties. *Ann. Royal Col. Surgeons of England* 56:291–303, 1975.
15. Singer, J.D. and Small, M. *The wages of war 1816–1965, a statistical handbook.* New York: John Wiley, 1972.

16. Urlanis B. *War and population.* Moscow: Progressive Pubs., 1971.

17. U.S. Navy Bureau of Medicine and Surgery. The history of the medical department of the U.S. Navy in WWII. *The statistics of disease and injuries.* Vol. 3, NAVMED P-1318 USGPO, Washington, 1950.

18. Wolfe, L.H., Childs, S.B. and Giddings, W.P. Distribution of injuries and other statistical data, General Surgery, Vol. 2. In *Surgery in World War II.* Washington, D.C., Office of the Surgeon General, Dept of the Army, 1955.

19. Bellamy, R.F. Contrasts in combat casualty care. *Mil. Med.* 150:405–410, 1985.

20. Bellamy, R.F. Causes of death in conventional land warfare: indications for combat casualty care research. *Mil. Med.* 149:55–62, 1984.

21. Berg, S.W. and Richlin, M. Injuries and illnesses of Vietnam War POWs. 1. Navy POWs. *Mil. Med.* 142:514–518, 1977.

22. Berg, S.W. and Richlin, M. Injuries and illnesses of Vietnam War POWs. 2. Army POWs. *Mil. Med.* 142:598–602, 1977.

23. Berg, S.W. and Richlin, M. Injuries and illnesses of Vietnam War POWs. 4: Comparison of captivity effects in North and South Vietnam. *Mil. Med.* 142:757–634, 1977.

24. Dudley, H.A.F., Knight, R.J., Mcneur, J.C. and Rosengarten, D.S. Civilian battle casualties in Vietnam. *Brit. J. Surg.* 55:332, 1968.

25. Hartigan, R.S. *The forgotten victim: a history of the civilian.* Chicago: Precedent Publishing, Inc., 1982.

26. Hill J. *Silent enemies: the story of the diseases of war and their control.* New York: G.P. Putnam and Sons, 1942.

27. Horiuchi Shiro. The long-term impact of war on mortality: old-age mortality of the First World War survivors in the Federal Republic of Germany. *Pop. Bul. UN* #15, pp. 80–92, 1983.

28. Lawrence, J.A. The effects of war on the control of diseases of livestock in Rhodesia (Zimbabwe). *Vet. Rec.* 107:82–85.

29. Richardson, L.M. *Statistics in deadly quarrels.* Pittsburgh: Boxwood Press, 1960.

30. Stockholm International Peace Research Institute. *Weapons of mass destruction and the environment.* New York: Crane, Russak and Co., 1977.

31. Vastyan, E.A. Civilian war casualties and medical care in South Vietnam. *Ann. Inter. Med.* 74:611–624, 1971.

32. Carey, M.E. Learning from traditional combat mortality and morbidity data used in the evaluation of combat casualty information systems. *Mil. Med.* 152:6–13, 1987.

33. Henderson, J.V. The importance of operational definitions in design of a combat casualty information system. *J. Med. Systems.* 7:413–426, 1983.

34. Heggers, J.P. Microbial invasion—the major natural ally of war (natural biological warfare). *Mil. Med.* 143:390–394, 1978.

35. Coates J.B., ed. *Preventive medicine in WW II.* Washington, D.C.: Medical Department, U.S. Army, 1958.

36. Sivard, R.L. *World military and social expenditures 1985.* Washington: Worldwatch Institute, 1985.

37. Slater, P.E. The Gulf War and mortality. *Lancet* 338:1336, 1991. See also Helmkamp, J.C. Epidemiologic characteristics of U.S. fatalities during Desert Storm. *Mil. Med.* 157(3):A7, 1992.

38. Reister, F.A. *Battle casualties and medical statistics: U.S. Army experiences in the Korean War.* Washington, DC: Surgeon General, Department of the Army, 1973.

39. Johnson, D.E., Panijayanond, P., Lumjiak, S., Crum, J.W. and Boonkrapu, P. Epidemiology of combat casualties in Thailand. *J. Trauma* 21:486–488, 1981.

40. Kuzman, M., Tomic, B., Stevanovic, R., et al. Fatalities in the War in Croatia, 1991 and 1992. *JAMA* 270(5):626–628, 1993.

41. Miller, M. Salvador mines taking higher army toll. *Los Angeles Times,* Dec. 22, 1985, p. 5.

42. Ahlstrom, C. *Casualties of conflict: Report for the world campaign for the protection of victims of war.* Uppsala, Sweden: Department of Peace and Conflict Research, Uppsala University, 1991. Cited in C. Bellamy. *The state of the world's children 1996.* New York: Oxford University Press, 1996.

43. *Children on the Frontline.* New York: UNICEF, 1988.

44. Garfield, R.M. and Williams, G. *Health care in Nicaragua: The development of primary care under changing regimes.* New York: Oxford University Press, 1992.

45. Asherio, A., Chase, R., Cote, T., et al. Effect of the Gulf War on infant and child mortality in Iraq. *New England Journal of Medicine* 327(13):931–936, 1992.

46. Daponte, B.O. Iraqi casualties from the Persian Gulf War and its aftermath. Unpublished.

47. Lee, I. and Haines, A. Health costs of the Gulf war. *Brit. Med. J.* 303(3):303–306, 1991.

48. Burnet, F.M. and Clark, E. *Influenza.* Melbourne, Australia: MacMillan, 1942.

49. Pyle, G.F. *The diffusion of influenza.* Totowa, NJ: Rowman & Allanheld, 1986.

50. Brogan, P. *World conflicts: Why and where they are happening.* London: Bloombury, 1989.

51. Dahl, B.B., McCubbin, H.I. and Ross, K.L. Second generational effects of war-induced separations comparing the adjustment of children in reunited and non-reunited families. *Mil. Med.* 142:146–151, 1977.

52. Bobob-Schrod, H. and Dethienne, F. Donnees socioeconomiques de 447 anciens prisonniers de guerre hospitalises. *Acta Psychiatr. Belf.* 76:56–71, 1976.

53. Beebe, G.W. *A follow-up study of war neuroses.* Washington, D.C.: Veterans Administration, 1956.

54. Miller, E. *The neuroses in war.* New York: MacMillan, 1940, pp. 1–32.

55. Murphy, J.M. Psychological responses to war stress. *Acta Psychiatr. Scand.* 263(suppl): 16–21, 1975.

56. Zarcone, V.P., Scott, N.R. and Kauvar, K.B. Psychiatric problems of Vietnam veterans: Clinical study of hospital patients. *Compr. Psychiatry* 18:41–53, 1977.

57. Boyle, C.A., Decoufle, P. and O'Brien, T.R. Long-term health consequences of military service in Vietnam. *Epidemiol. Rev.* 11:1–27, 1989.

58. Bullman, T.A., Kang, H.K. and Watanabe, K.K. Proportionate mortality among U.S. Army Vietnam veterans who survived in military region I. *Am. J. Epidemiol.* 132:670–674, 1990.

59. Hearst, N., Newman, T.B. and Hulley, S.B. Delayed effects of the military draft on mortality. *N. Engl. J. Med.* 314:620–624, 1986.

60. Gordon, N.A. Casualty evacuation in the Rhodesian terrorist war. *S. Afr. Med. J.* 52:856–860, 1977.

61. Hauben, D.J. and Sonneveld, G.J. The influence of war on the development of plastic surgery. *Ann. Plast. Surg.* 10:65–69, 1983.

62. Pfeffermann, R., Rozin, R.R., Durst, A.L. and Marin, G. Modern war surgery: Operations in an evacuation hospital during the October 1973 Arab-Israeli War. *J. Trauma* 16:694–703, 1976.

63. Bullough, B. The lasting impact of World War II on nursing. *Am. J. Nursing* 76:118–120, 1976.

64. Simon, R.R. and Hyman, M.H. Establishing underground medical clinics in rural Afghanistan: The International Medical Corps experience. *Ann. Intern. Med.* 108:477–480, 1988.

65. Coale, A.J. History of the human population. *Sci. Am.* 231:40–52, Jan. 1974.

4

The Impact of War
on Human Rights

H. JACK GEIGER

There is a bloody paradox in the political and social history of the twentieth century. Never before, on one hand, has there been such universal recognition of the claim that everyone, regardless of race, nationality, religion, gender, or political belief is entitled to rights—in particular, what have been aptly called "life integrity rights."[1] These include the right to life; the right to personal inviolability—not to be hurt; the right to be free of arbitrary seizure, detention, and punishment; the freedom to own one's body and labor; the right to free movement without discrimination; and the right to create and cohabit with family.

These rights include but transcend the conventional classes of human rights—political and civil rights, aspects of freedom or democracy, and social and economic rights, aspects of equity or just distribution—and they are embodied in a remarkable variety of international human rights and humanitarian laws, conventions, and declarations. No prior period in human history has produced human rights documents of such sweeping scope and rigorous specificity.

They include the Charter of the United Nations; the Universal Declaration of Human Rights; the International Covenant on Civil and Political Rights; the Convention on the Prevention and Punishment of the Crime of Genocide; the Convention against Torture and Other Cruel, Inhuman or Degrading Treatment; the Convention Concerning the Abolition of Forced Labor; the International Convention on the Elimination of All Forms of Racial Discrimination; and the Convention on the Rights of the Child. And these, in turn, are supplemented by specific agreements governing the conduct of armed conflict: The Geneva Conventions of 1949 and the Additional Protocols of 1977.

Yet (with the exception of institutionalized slavery) never before have human rights been violated on so massive a scale, nor with such efficacy and savagery, as in this same century—and the chief instrument of violation has been war. The evolution and varieties of warfare over the last hundred years, aided by the technological sophistication, destructive power, and accessibility of new weapons, has all but obliterated the distinction between warfare and mass terrorism. In the waning years of the century, with this paradox unresolved, the commitment to effective and vigorous protection of human rights is under siege.

"War," of course, is no longer the phenomenon simplistically defined as "a contest between armed forces carried on in a campaign or series of campaigns."[2] The diverse forms of armed conflict now include declared and undeclared wars between nations; full-scale civil wars, including many with genocidal motivations; so-called low-intensity conflicts between competing national political groups; and a wide variety of "dirty wars" of repression mounted by governments against their own citizens. The defining characteristic of most of these types of war is a calculated and deliberate assault on civilians, in contravention of international humanitarian law and the Geneva Conventions, but almost all wars put civilian populations at risk of trauma, illness, or death, threaten to create humanitarian crises, and are marked by the commission of war crimes and crimes against humanity.[3]

In the last six decades alone, at least 80 percent of the approximately 20 million killed and 60 million wounded in declared wars, civil wars, and other major conflicts have been civilians; of these, three of every five have been children.[4] The global total of dependent refugees is 19 million, plus another 25 million "internally displaced" civilians, refugees within their own national borders.[5] These 1994 statistics are already obsolete; they do not include the several millions affected by conflicts in Rwanda and Chechnya (Figures 4-1 and 4-2) (see Chapter 14).

Each of these staggering totals reflects violations of human rights and international law. Many of the chapters in this book describe in detail the morbidity and mortality and the means by which they were produced. From a human rights perspective, the war-related violations will here be grouped broadly into five categories and illustrated briefly.

Direct Assaults on Civilians by "Conventional" Means

In the 1930s, the bombing of Ethiopian civilians by Italian planes, and of Spanish civilians at Guernica by German planes, drew international condemnation as frightening examples of the inappropriate use of powerful military technology to harm innocent noncombatants, as did Japanese assaults on cities in China. (The wanton killing of civilians in war had been affirmed as a crime by the Hague Convention of 1907.) World War II saw the abandonment of such scruples on all sides: Examples of assaults on essentially nonmilitary and civilian targets include (to name only the best-remembered) rocket and bomb attacks on London and Coventry, and the fire-bombings of Dresden, Hamburg, and Tokyo. Death totals ranged from 30,000 to more than 100,000—mostly the elderly, women, and children.

The wanton killing of civilians was reaffirmed as a war crime by the Geneva

Figure 4-1. Bosnian refugees uprooted from their homes by civil war (Source: United Nations/ DPI/186225).

Conventions of 1949—with little effect. While the regional and surrogate conflicts of the Cold War replaced massive international confrontations, they were almost uniformly characterized by the indiscriminate bombing and fire-bombing of cities and villages, typified by the conflicts in Vietnam and Afghanistan. But the almost automatic assumption that civilians were in fact legitimate and inevitable targets of war was reinforced most of all, during the decades of the Cold War, by the targeting of cities by intercontinental ballistic missiles and the elaboration of absurd (but massive) "civil defense" plans in both the United States and the Soviet Union.

The end of the Cold War has done nothing to change this pattern except, perhaps, to emphasize artillery shelling over bombing as the instrument of choice for attacks on noncombatants and the outright destruction of urban life. The conflict in former Yugoslavia was marked by the sustained and systematic shelling of Vukovar, Dubrovnik, Zvornik, Srebenica, Mostar, Bihac, and, above all, Sarajevo.[6,7] Even these,

Figure 4-2. A family of Rwandan refugees, their bicycle loaded, make their way along the road to the Benaco Camp in the remote Ngara District, a day's walk from the river where they crossed from Rwanda (Source/Photographer: UNICEF/94-0065/Howard Davies).

however, are exceeded by the current Russian assault on Grozny in Chechnya. One experienced observer of both sites noted that the highest level of firing recorded in Sarajevo was 3,500 shells per day; in Grozny, shelling reached 4,000 detonations per hour. The first three months of conflict produced an estimated 15,000 civilian dead and hundreds of thousands of refugees.[8,9]

Ethnic Cleansing and Extrajudicial Killings

During the 1980s and 1990s, an old and ugly variant of human rights abuse re-appeared: conflicts in which the central purpose of military action has been the forced removal of civilian populations from their homes and land on the basis of religion, nationality, or ethnic identity—under international law, a crime against humanity. Many of these episodes have involved mass killing; while they do not approach the methodical slaughter of the Holocaust—the planned industrialization of mass mur-der—and have not approached the total extermination of victimized populations, it is fair to label them genocidal in spirit. (The same is true of the systematic mass murders, forced deportations, detention camps, and enslavement carried out by the Khmer Rouge regime of Pol Pot in Cambodia—a bizarre variant in which the victims were characterized not by ethnicity but by urban residence and education.)

The most notorious recent examples are the wars in former Yugoslavia and Rwanda. In both conflicts, the instruments of ethnic cleansing have been massive assaults on noncombatants; the torture and murder of men, women, and children; the widespread and systematic use of rape to terrorize whole communities; the destruction, by explosives and arson, of residences, farms, industries, and basic infrastructures that provide water, electric power, food, fuel, sanitation, and other necessities; denial of medical care and other violations of medical neutrality; and siege, blockade, and interference with humanitarian relief. Soldiers and noncombatants alike have been starved, tortured, or killed in prison camps, to many of which the International Committee of the Red Cross have been denied access.[10] Thousands were victims of arbitrary and extrajudicial execution and were buried in mass graves. Refugees and displaced persons have been denied protection and made victims of deliberate attack; subjected to beatings, rape, and extortion; forced to walk through minefields; or slaughtered in churches, hospitals, and other sanctuaries.

In sum, the implementation of campaigns of ethnic cleansing in Yugoslavia and Rwanda has involved, as a matter of deliberate policy, virtually every variety of human rights violation. But these are only the best-known cases, and attention focused on them has tended to obscure many others: for example, in Sri Lanka, East Timor, Armenia and Azerbaijan, Ossetia and Georgia, China and Tibet, and Iraq and Kurdistan.

The 1988 Anfal campaign by Iraq typifies these less-known campaigns of ethnic cleansing. It involved the destruction of thousands of Kurdish villages across all of Iraqi Kurdistan. A report on the fate of one such village[11] described murder, forcible disappearance, involuntary relocation, the refusal to provide minimal conditions of life to detainees, and in some well-documented cases, chemical weapons attacks against civilians.[3] A report by Middle East Watch and Physicians for Human Rights notes:

A village was often first shelled or bombed . . . the inhabitants, attempting to flee, were trapped by troops enveloping the village. In two instances . . . men and boys among the captured villagers were executed on the spot . . . virtually all the remaining men and older boys [taken to a detention center] disappeared at the hands of security agents; the whereabouts of many tens of thousands of Kurdish males . . . is unknown. Several eyewitness survivors of mass executions testified that the forcibly disappeared Kurds were taken south by truck and later killed and buried in pits in various locations . . .

The Kurdish villages, empty of inhabitants, were then destroyed in their entirety . . . razed to the ground, down to the stone foundations of the schools and mosques . . . the mud brick houses were demolished with bulldozers and backhoes . . .

Anfal was not intended to deter. Anfal was a "final solution" . . . intended to make the Kurds of Iraqi Kurdistan and their rural way of life disappear forever.[11]

There seems every prospect that the blatant human rights violation represented by ethnic cleansing will continue into the next century, for dozens of national states have minorities at risk of such onslaughts.[12]

The history of twentieth-century warfare is replete with smaller-scale, more singular examples of civilian massacres and the punitive destruction of ''enemy'' villages, from Lidice to My Lai to Mozotle; the cumulative suffering and loss of life has been enormous. In the same way, incidents on the ''smallest'' scale, the one-by-one murders by death squads in the so-called ''dirty wars'' of repression in El Salvador,[13,14] Nicaragua, Guatemala,[15] Chile,[16] Argentina, Brazil,[17] Haiti,[18] Colombia, Ethiopia, the Philippines, Kashmir,[19] and (until recently) South Africa have, over the past four decades, reached totals of dead and ''disappeared'' in the hundreds of thousands (see Chapter 16).

Direct Assaults on Civilians Caused by Indiscriminate Weapons

Indiscriminate weapons are those which, by their effects and defining characteristics, are almost certain (and are usually intended) to harm military combatants and civilians alike, and therefore by definition violate the human rights prohibition of wanton killing. They include, but are not limited to, the conventionally defined weapons of mass destruction: nuclear weapons of every type, chemical weapons, and biological weapons.

The transforming events of twentieth-century warfare, the nuclear bombings of Hiroshima and Nagasaki, are described in detail in Chapter 6. The more than a quarter million civilian deaths from blast, incineration, and radiation (in the latter case, still occurring) are widely recognized; the fact that such mass killings are a violation of human rights is not as widely agreed upon, despite the multiple specific provisions in international law prohibiting attacks that cause unnecessary suffering, requiring a principle of proportionality, and affirming the basic immunity of civilian populations and civilians from being objects of attack during armed conflict.

Recent attempts to have the use or threat of use of nuclear weapons explicitly defined as a violation of international law have failed; in general, the approach to containment or prohibition has been technical and diplomatic—in arms control treaties and chemical warfare conventions—rather than in human rights terms.

Though both the United States and the Soviet Union acquired huge stocks of chemical weapons, particularly nerve gases, there is no documented case of their use by the superpowers or their surrogates during the Cold War (Chapter 7). The same is true of biological weapons, though accidents in both the United States and Russia revealed their active development by the military (Chapter 8). The use of nerve and mustard gases during the war between Iran and Iraq is widely acknowledged, however, and recent evidence has confirmed the use of poison gas against Kurdish villages by Iraq during the Anfal.[11,20]

But nerve and mustard gases are not the only poisons that have been used indiscriminately against civilians. Soviet troops used chloropicrin, a World War II gas, against Georgian dissidents in 1989.[21] And in what is surely the most widespread and ongoing use of a chemical weapon against civilians, tear gas—euphemistically labeled a relatively harmless crowd-control agent—has in fact caused deaths in civil conflicts in South Korea,[22] Panama,[23] the West Bank and Gaza Strip,[24] Thailand, and other nations. When CS gas (o-chlorobenzylidene malononitrile) and other forms of tear gas are used in high concentrations or thrown into confined spaces, they can cause skin burns, eye injuries, exacerbation of underlying heart and lung disease, and respiratory arrest, particularly among infants and the elderly.

A recent report[25] has confirmed the use by Japan of biological agents (plague, cholera, and typhoid) against China and the western United States during World War II (see Chapter 8).

By far the greatest current instrument of indiscriminate civilian death, and thus of human rights violation, is the land mine (Chapter 10). More than 250 million land mines have been produced by some 48 nations over the last quarter century; more than 100 million remain uncleared, scattered wantonly across the fields, roads, pasturelands, and village pathways of more than 60 nations, and turning vast areas of the earth into wastelands of death, economic ruin, and social disintegration.[26] In Cambodia, almost half the land area is unsafe for farming or any other human use, and one in every 236 people is a land mine amputee; in former Yugoslavia, an estimated three million mines have been sown, without markers or maps, and the total there is growing by some 50,000 per week. After 18 years of civil war and two million land mines, almost no major road in Mozambique is usable. Angola, Afghanistan, Vietnam, Somalia and Somaliland, Iraq and Kuwait, El Salvador, and Nicaragua are among the most-ravaged countries.

A recent report by Physicians for Human Rights and Human Rights Watch/Arms Project[27] defined the land mine as "a weapon of mass destruction in slow motion." Worldwide, most of the estimated 15,000 land mine victims per year are civilians; the weapon does not distinguish between the boot of a soldier and the footfall of a child, and in the agrarian and subsistence-farming societies that are most affected, women and children are the most common casualties. Often this is by intent. In Afghanistan, thousands of tiny, brightly colored mines designed to look like toys were dropped by helicopter (Figure 10-3).

In 1992 a joint campaign for an international ban on the production, stockpiling, transfer, and use of land mines began with the support of almost every human rights and humanitarian relief organization, the American Public Health Association, and the World Federation of Public Health Associations. The United States, France, the Netherlands, and the European Parliament have moratoriums in place on the export, sale, or transfer of these weapons, but their production (especially by China, Italy, and Russia) continues.

Indirect Assault on Civilian Populations

Modern military technology, especially the use of high-precision bombs, rockets, and missile warheads, has now made it possible to attack civilian populations in industrialized societies indirectly—but with devastating results—by targeting the facilities on which life depends, while avoiding the stigma of direct attack on the bodies and habitats of noncombatants. The technique has been called "bomb now, die later."[28]

U.S. military action against Iraq in the Persian Gulf War included the specific and selective destruction of key aspects of the infrastructure necessary to maintain civilian life and health. During the bombing phase of the war, preceding ground action, this deliberate effort accomplished the virtually total destruction of Iraq's electrical power generation and transmission capacity, as well as almost complete destruction of civilian communications networks. In combination with the prolonged application of economic sanctions and the conventional bombing disruption of highways, bridges, and fuel-refining and distribution facilities, these actions had severe and damaging effects on the health and survival of the civilian population, especially infants and children.

Without electric power, water purification and pumping ceased immediately in all major urban areas, as did sewage pumping and treatment. The appearance and epidemic spread of infectious diarrhea in infants and of waterborne diseases such as typhoid fever and cholera was rapid. At the same time, medical care and public health measures were totally disrupted. Modern multi-story hospitals were left without clean water, sewage disposal, or any electricity beyond what could be supplied by emergency generators designed to operate only a few hours per day. Operating rooms, X-ray equipment and other vital services were crippled. Supplies of anesthetics, antibiotics, and essential medications such as insulin, digitalis, and anticonvulsants were rapidly depleted. Vaccines and medications requiring refrigeration were destroyed, and all immunization programs ceased. Since almost no civilian telephones, computers, or transmission lines were operable, the Ministry of Health was effectively immobilized. Fuel shortages and the disruption of transportation further disrupted civilian access to medical care.[29–31]

It is rare, in warfare, to have a precise and relatively rapid measure of the consequences to civilians. After the Persian Gulf War, however, an international team of public health experts from the United States, the United Kingdom, New Guinea, and Jordan conducted a population-based survey of infant and child mortality in a nationwide sample of Iraqi households.[32] In comparison with pre-war figures, they found a threefold increase in mortality among Iraqi children under five years of age; among children from one to less than 12 months old, deaths increased fourfold, and overall the group estimated that the total of excess deaths of young children was more than 46,900. Trade sanctions, which raised the price of basic foods and infant formula, contributed to the effects (Chapter 17).

This and similar reports provide clear and quantitative evidence of violations of the requirements of immunity for civilian populations, proportionality, and the prevention of unnecessary suffering. They mock the concept of "life integrity rights." In contrast to the chaos and social disruption that routinely accompany armed conflicts, these deaths were the consequence of an explicit military policy, with clearly foreseeable consequences to the human rights of civilians. The U.S. military has never conceded that the policy was a human rights violation under the Geneva Conventions or the guidelines issued to U.S. Air Force, Army and Navy personnel. Yet the ongoing development of military technology, in my view, suggests that—absent the use of weapons of mass destruction—this is a preferred method of warfare in the future.

Violations of Medical Neutrality

The Geneva Conventions, customary international law, and medical ethics all mandate medical neutrality: the protection of medical facilities, personnel, and patients from military attack or interference; the humane treatment of civilians; the right of access to care; and the nondiscriminatory treatment of the ill and wounded in time of war. In the wide range of human rights concerns, medical neutrality is of particular concern to medical and public health workers. This is more than a matter of narrow self-interest on their part. Concern for the rights of individual patients and the health of populations is at the core of health professional mandates.

Yet in almost every current armed conflict, violations of medical neutrality are widespread, systematic, and almost routine. All seven major hospitals in Grozny have been destroyed.[8] In Sarajevo, Vukovar, Srebenica, Gorazde, and Mostar, hospitals were routinely shelled—in some cases, reduced to rubble—and physicians were the special targets of sniper attacks. In Haiti, Kuwait, the West Bank and Gaza Strip, Somalia, and Sudan, hospitals, clinics, and first-aid stations have been invaded and patients, medical personnel, and relief workers have been assaulted, abducted, tortured, or murdered. In El Salvador, where civil conflict was marked by almost every conceivable violation of medical neutrality, health and relief workers were beaten, imprisoned, or murdered for activities as innocent as the vaccination of children. In many conflicts, ambulances are routinely attacked, seized, or blocked; in some civil wars and so-called low-intensity conflicts, the destruction of civilian health services has been defended as a legitimate tactic to punish populations suspected of supporting dissident armed forces. One Contra physician said, ''The [Nicaraguan health] brigadistas are working with the enemy. They are a legitimate target.''[33] In others, physicians have been arrested, tortured, or executed for fulfilling their ethical obligation to provide medical care regardless of the patient's political or military affiliation; in other cases, physicians have actively participated in the torture of dissidents.[34]

In sum, contemporary warfare, focused increasingly on assaulting civilian populations and their support structures, is replacing medical neutrality (in practice, if not in law) with strategies in which no civilian systems—and no rights—are immune.

War and Intellectual Corruption: Justifying Violations

Underlying all these—and many other—violations is the corruption of the principles of the Geneva Conventions and other embodiments of human rights protection by the belief that war, and the goal of victory in conflict, is its own justification, and thus that virtually any abuse or atrocity can be rationalized. It is a position most frequently articulated as a self-evident necessity by the military—the very institution that is supposed to be constrained by human rights law in wartime—and it is strikingly uniform in its expression by soldiers from nations with widely varied political systems.

One recent example is the fierce controversy that erupted in the United States in early 1995 over a proposed Smithsonian Institution exhibit to mark the 50th anniversary of the bombing of Hiroshima. The initial version of the exhibit amply demonstrated the suffering and death of Japanese civilians. This was taken by many U.S. veterans, some of the American public, and many in the Congress as an implicit and unjustified criticism. Their central argument was that the atomic bombings, which killed hundreds of thousands, saved the lives of at least as many American soldiers by averting the need for an invasion. The ensuing debate focused on the magnitude of this "life-saving" effect and whether or not a Japanese surrender was already imminent. No voice was raised to point out that it is not only immoral but illegal, under international law, to equate and substitute civilian for military casualties—in more specific terms, to substitute the deaths of noncombatants, the elderly, women, and children for the deaths of soldiers. The underlying military belief was most succinctly expressed by a general in the U.S. Marines:

> In ideological war the enemy is completely hateful. His unconditional surrender and the total destruction of his society are the only satisfactory objectives. In bringing this just retribution to him, one cannot show compassion for noncombatants.[35]

Asked about the morality of the fire-bombing of Tokyo that caused an estimated 100,000 civilian deaths in 1945, a U.S. bombardier said, "No war is fun. People get hurt, civilians get hurt, children get hurt. The United States was in this war to win it, and if that's what it took to win, that's what should have been done."[36]

That answer is almost identical to the recently quoted response of a participant in the Japanese army's Unit 731, a biological warfare group responsible for more than 3,000 deaths and multiple atrocities during World War II. Asked to explain his own activities, which included literally dissecting Chinese prisoners alive, without anesthetics, experimenting on three-day-old babies, and attempting to poison rivers and wells with dysentery, typhoid, and cholera bacteria, he said, "Because in a war, you have to win." And he added: "There's a possibility this could happen again."[25,36]

REFERENCES

1. Fein, H. "Lives at risk." A Working Paper of the Institute for the Study of Genocide. New York: John Jay College of Criminal Justice, City University of New York, 1990.
2. *The Shorter Oxford English Dictionary,* Third Edition. London: Oxford University Press, 1964.

3. Geiger, H.J. and Cook-Deegan, R.M. The role of physicians in conflicts and humanitarian crises. *JAMA* 270:616–620, 1993.

4. Sivard, R.L. *World military and social expenditures 1991,* (14th ed.). Washington, D.C.: World Priorities, Inc., 1991.

5. Toole, M. and Waldman, R.J. Refugees and displaced persons: war, hunger and public health. *JAMA* 270:600–605, 1993.

6. Rieff, D. On your knees with the dying. In Rabia, A. and Lifswchultz, L. (eds.) *Why Bosnia? Writings on the Balkan War.* Stony Creek, Conn.: The Pamphleteer's Press, 1993.

7. Magas, B. *The Destruction of Yugoslavia.* London: Verso Press, 1993.

8. Cuny, F. Killing Chechnya. *New York Review of Books,* April 6, 1995, pp. 15–17.

9. Human Rights Watch/Helsinki. Russia: Three months of war in Chechnya. New York: *Human Rights Watch,* Vol. 7, No. 6, Feb. 1995.

10. Gutman, R. *A witness to genocide.* New York: MacMillan, 1993.

11. *The Anfal campaign in Iraqi Kurdistan: The destruction of Koreme.* New York and Boston: Middle East Watch and Physicians for Human Rights, 1993.

12. Gurr, T.R. and Scaritt, J.R. Minorities' rights at risk: A global survey. *Human Rights Quarterly* 11:379–405, 1989.

13. *El Salvador: Health Care Under Siege.* Boston: Physicians for Human Rights, 1990.

14. Geiger, H.J., Eisenberg, C., Gloyd, S., Quiroga, J., Schlenker, T., Scrimshaw, N. and Devin, J. Special report: A new medical mission to El Salvador. *New England Journal of Medicine* 321:1136–1140, 1989.

15. *Getting away with murder.* Boston: Physicians for Human Rights, 1991.

16. *Sowing fear: The uses of torture and psychological abuse in Chile.* Somerville, Mass.: Physicians for Human Rights, 1988.

17. *The search for Brazil's disappeared: The mass grave at Dom Bosco Cemetery.* Washington, D.C. and Somerville, Mass.: Amnesty International, Physicians for Human Rights, and American Association for the Advancement of Science, 1991.

18. *Return to the darkest days: Human rights in Haiti since the coup.* Boston: Physicians for Human Rights, 1992.

19. *The crackdown in Kashmir: Torture of detainees and assaults on the medical community.* Boston and New York: Physicians for Human Rights and Asia Watch, 1993.

20. Winds of death: Iraq's use of poison gas against its Kurdish population. Somerville, Mass.: Physicians for Human Rights, 1989.

21. Bloody Sunday: Trauma in Tbilisi. Boston: Physicians for Human Rights, 1990.

22. *The use of tear gas in the Republic of Korea: A report by health professionals.* Somerville, Mass.: Physicians for Human Rights, 1987.

23. *Panama 1987: Health consequences of police and military actions.* Somerville, Mass.: Physicians for Human Rights, 1988.

24. *Human rights on hold: A report on emergency measures and access to health care in the occupied territories, 1990–1992.* Boston: Physicians for Human Rights, 1993.

25. "Japan confronting gruesome war atrocity." *The New York Times,* March 17, 1995, p. 1.

26. Cahill, K.M., ed. *Clearing the fields: Solutions to the global land mines crisis.* New York: Basic Books and the Council on Foreign Relations, 1995.

27. *Landmines: A deadly legacy.* Boston and New York: Physicians for Human Rights and Human Rights Watch/Arms Project, 1993.

28. Geiger H.J., quoted in Kandela, P. Iraq: Bomb now, die later. *The Lancet* 337:967, 1991.

29. Report to the Secretary-General on humanitarian needs in Kuwait and Iraq in the immediate post-crisis environment by a mission to the area led by Mr. Martti Ahtisaari, Under-Secretary for Administration and Management. United Nations, March 10, 1991. S/22366.

30. Report of the WHO/UNICEF Special Mission to Iraq. February, 1991. New York: UNICEF.
31. Iraq's food and agricultural situation during the embargo and the war: Congressional Research Service Report for Congress. February 26, 1991. Washington: The Library of Congress.
32. Ascherio, A., Chase, R., Cote, T., et al. Effect of the Gulf War on infant and child mortality in Iraq. *New England Journal of Medicine* 327:931–936, 1992.
33. Meyer, H. ''Physician's war in Nicaragua.'' *American Medical News,* November 13, 1987, quoting Dr. Manuel Alzugarey.
34. *Medicine betrayed: The participation of doctors in human rights abuses.* London: Zed Books and the British Medical Association, 1992.
35. Henderson General F.P., cited in Stonier, T. *Nuclear disaster.* Harmondsworth: Penguin Books, 1964, p. 19.
36. *The New York Times,* March 9, 1995, p. A4.

5

The Environmental Consequences of War

BARRY S. LEVY, GURINDER S. SHAHI,
and CHEN LEE

War is the antithesis of human health, environmental protection, and development. It can completely disrupt the fabric of society and its organization and lead to distortion of human values and concerns. During times of war, priorities change; people become far more focused on survival and self-preservation than on, for example, maintaining biodiversity or environmental protection. Environmental and ecological integrity, already under stress as a result of humankind's peacetime activities, are at particular risk of degradation, contamination, and destruction during times of aggression and hostility.

This chapter will address the consequences of war on the environment and what can be done to prevent these consequences. Chapter 9 focuses largely on the impact of the preparation for war (peacetime military activities) on the environment in terms of energy use, pollution, nonrenewable resource consumption, and other impacts. Chapter 11 focuses, in part, on the peacetime diversion of resources to military purposes from more socially useful activities, such as environmental protection.

Not only is the environment impacted by war, but environmental issues and circumstances—for example, irrigation and water rights disputes between neighboring countries, such as those in the Middle East—can lead to war.[1,2]

Types of Environments

The environment can be viewed, from the perspective of the individual, as consisting of the internal environment (Claude Bernard called it the *milieu interieur*) and the external environment. This paper will focus chiefly on the interactions between war and the external environment.

The external environment might broadly be defined in terms of the human-altered environment and the natural environment. Both of these aspects of the external environment have been adversely affected by war as well as peacetime military activities. Few locations on the planet are truly unaltered by either direct or indirect impacts of human military activities.

Another way to categorize the environment is in terms of:

1. The physical environment, including the structures in which we live and work, the weather and climate, the soil and type of vegetation, water sources, water supply and sanitation networks, and transportation and communications infrastructure.
2. The chemical environment, including, for example, oxygen and carbon dioxide in the air we breathe and carcinogens and other toxic substances in the water we use. Components of our environment can interact chemically with the physiological systems that make up the *milieu interieur* of life forms and can affect growth, development, health, and well-being.
3. The biological environment, including microorganisms, plants, and animals and the systems that support them. Biological life forms provide much of the food we eat, the clothes we wear, and the energy that drives our modern lives (petroleum and coal, for example, are derived from ancient biological life forms). Our interactions with other organisms can affect our health and well-being.
4. The human or social environment. We live in groups. We have created societies that determine the languages we speak, the norms of our behavior, the nature of our interaction with each other, and the rules by which we live our lives. Hence, all aspects of human intercourse—including the social, cultural, political, legal, ethical, and economic environments—can be considered as constituting elements of the human or social environment.[3]

Any subclassifications of the environment that we make are simply tools for understanding. Clearly, environmental interactions are complex and multifaceted. Hence, forests and the trees in forests, for example, cannot be simply placed in any one definitional compartment but are of significance in several different contexts, constituting important interactors of our physical, chemical, biological, and social environments.

Direct Impact of War on the Environment

The nature of war has changed considerably in the last century:

- Wars had occurred mainly between nation states; now they occur mainly within nations.
- The vast majority of countries that now experience major armed conflict or political violence are developing countries.

- Most people adversely affected by war are civilians. In the past, 90 percent of wartime casualties were military personnel; now, 90 percent of wartime casualties are civilians[4] (Figure 3-1).
- The intensity of warfare is increasing, especially in wars between nations. The air war in the Persian Gulf War lasted for about 6 weeks, with 250,000 weapons dropped by aircraft. The ground war was over in 100 hours. In this short time, more weapons were reportedly used than during the protracted Vietnam War.

As the nature of war has changed, its impact on the physical, social, cultural, and economic environments has increased.

Direct war damage to the environment can be caused by the planned use of fragmentation (high-explosive) and blast munitions, incendiary weapons and other causes of fires, defoliants and other toxic substances, and other factors. Damage can also occur during wartime as a result of accidental detonation of weapons, accidental development of fires or release of toxic substances, and pollution of the ambient air, water, and land with hazardous materials. Damage during wartime can also occur by the release of hazards from nuclear power plants, factories that manufacture toxic chemicals, and dams and other hydrological facilities.[5] Unexploded ordinance, including land mines (see Chapter 10), represent ongoing risks after a war has ended.

Resultant environmental damage, which can persist for decades, includes: destruction of the human habitat; destruction of agricultural land and vegetation; adverse effects on wildlife, even possible elimination of species; cratering of land; and disruption of entire ecosystems.

Destruction of the Human Habitat

War wreaks obvious havoc on the physical, chemical, and biological environments and can severely disrupt the human or social environment, destroying housing, commercial centers, transportation and communications infrastructure, and the very fabric of society and social life. Extreme examples include:

- The devastation of Hiroshima and Nagasaki by the use of nuclear weapons, as described in Chapter 6.
- The destruction of Hamburg, Dresden, and Tokyo during World War II by the use of incendiary weapons that created huge fires (Figure 5-1). (If such weapons were used today, an additional health and environmental concern would be the release during these fires of combustion products that are highly toxic.)

However, all wars have had catastrophic effects on the human habitat. The effects of the Vietnam War, the war in Central America, and the Persian Gulf War are described in Chapters 15–17.

There has been a marked temporal trend of increasing disruption of the human habitat by explosive munitions in war. Munitions expenditures—along with environ-

Figure 5-1. Damage to Osaka in 1945 as a result of a series of attacks by American B-29 bombers. Their bombloads included a high percentage of incendiaries, which destroyed the city's largely wooden houses by fire (Source: Library of Congress, Negative LC-USZ 62-104726).

mental disruption—increased from World War II to the Korean War to the Vietnam War, as illustrated by the following data: U.S. munitions expenditures per enemy soldier killed during these three wars also rose from one to the next in the startling ratio of 1 to 6 to 18.[5]

Physical Damage to "Strategic" Facilities

A strategy that seems increasingly to be used in warfare and that tends to have much greater impact on civilians than on military personnel is the practice of targeted destruction of the environment and the lines of communication and transport in the hope of making modern life impossible. For example, dams, power stations, water supply pipes, hospitals, roads, and airports may be damaged. The scale of devastation has increased, and nations have often used war as an excuse for seeking to destroy social and physical environments in "enemy" societies.[5]

In addition, damage to dams, factories that manufacture chemicals, and one or more of the hundreds of nuclear power plants in operation in the world can lead to widespread death, injury, and illness among the affected population and may cause widespread environmental destruction. So can the setting on fire of combustible forests. An example of damage to a dam—perhaps the most devastating single act in all human history in terms of lives claimed—occurred in 1938 during the Second Sino-Japanese War. In an attempt to stop the advance of the Japanese military, the Chinese dynamited a dike of the Yellow River, drowning several thousand Japanese soldiers and at least several hundred thousand Chinese civilians. This act inundated 11 cities, over 4,000 villages, and several million hectares of farmland, destroying crops and topsoil.[5]

Besides the many cities that were left in ruins during World War II, there was much damage to agricultural areas and forests that served as battlefields. In addition, there were a number of instances of rural devastation in occupied areas, including 200,000 hectares of Dutch farmland destroyed by inundation with saltwater, 1,200,000 hectares in northern Norway systematically laid waste, and the forest resources of Poland systematically pillaged.[5]

Destruction from High Explosives

The United States used about 14 million tons of high explosives in Vietnam, creating more than 20 million bomb craters, covering about 200,000 hectares. Transport, agriculture, and forestry were disrupted. Many craters filled with stagnant water, forming breeding sites for malaria-carrying mosquitoes.[4] (Figure 5-2).

Impacts of Herbicides and Defoliants

The deliberate destruction of crops and natural forest in order to deny the enemy food and cover has long been considered to be "sound" military policy. Perpetrators know no boundaries of time or ethnicity, ranging from Israelites fighting the Philistines in the 12th century B.C., to Genghis Khan conquering China, to the practices of modern-day armed forces.

In Vietnam, an estimated 2.2 billion hectares of forest and farmland were denuded as a direct result of bombing, mechanized land clearing, napalming, and defoliation by the United States and South Vietnam. Some 72 million liters, with almost 55 million kilograms of herbicide ingredients, were used primarily on the forests of South Vietnam, to deny forest cover to Vietcong forces, and also to destroy food crops. One herbicide, Agent Orange, which represented 61 percent of herbicide volume used by the U.S. military, was sprayed one or more times over 35 percent of southern Vietnam between 1961 and 1971. Damage included:

- Destruction of millions of trees and often their replacement with grasses; an estimated 20 million square meters of commercial timber were destroyed;
- 135,000 hectares of rubber plantations;

Figure 5-2. Bomb-destroyed mangrove forest, Bien Hoa Province, South Vietnam, 1971 (Photograph by Arthur H. Westing).

- 124,000 hectares of mangroves (Figure 5-3);
- Widespread debilitation of land via soil erosion and loss of nutrients in the ground;
- Decimation of terrestrial wildlife, primarily by destruction of habitat;
- Losses in freshwater fish, mainly because of reduced availability of food species; and
- Possible contribution to the decline in the offshore fishery.[6]

Dioxin contained in the Agent Orange that was sprayed persists, with elevated levels still being found in soil, food, wildlife, human breast milk, and adipose tissue. Restoration and regeneration from this massive environmental damage is still not complete more than 20 years after the end of the Vietnam War; it may take decades for something approaching full restoration and regeneration to occur.[6–8]

Pollution

The Persian Gulf War provides a number of illustrative examples of pollution during wartime. Ecologic damage was caused by bombing and by oil-related pollution (see Chapter 17). In February 1991, Iraq ignited 752 oilwell fires in Kuwait (Figure 5-4).

Figure 5-3. Herbicide-destroyed mangrove forest, Gia Dinh Province, South Vietnam, 1970 (Photograph by Arthur H. Westing).

These were extinguished more rapidly than had been expected, but the health and environmental impact of the smoke produced is still largely unknown. Carbon soot concentrations were estimated to reach as high as 100 $\mu g/m^3$ at 1.5 meters above the ground (respiratory level) near the fires. Black rains fell in Iran. And major rainstorms and cyclones as far away as Bangladesh have been linked to these fires.[9] In addition, huge pools of oil caused by leakage from sabotaged wells that did not ignite still cover large parts of Kuwait. Oil penetrates the soil and kills plants, birds, and insects.[10,11]

Indirect Impact of War on the Environment

War can be devastating to a country, with thousands of soldiers ransacking farms and taking the produce of farmers, their primary source of livelihood. The laying of land mines, presence of curfews, and destruction of roads, bridges, and other components of infrastructure often leave farmers no way to get what is left of their produce to market, resulting in its spoilage. Lack of access to fertilizers and seed often mean that farmers tend to overburden the soil, depleting its nutrients. With crop yields declining

Figure 5-4. Burning oilwells at the Al Burgan oilfield in Kuwait (Photograph by Jim Hodson; Source: Environmental Picture Library, Ltd., London).

and few opportunities to earn a decent living, rural families often have little choice but to migrate away from their fields in search of alternative means of livelihood.[12]

When they get to the cities, breakdown of infrastructure—with damaged communications and transportation systems, lack of access to safe drinking water, and inadequate food—means that people in the city often starve. The haves can take their possessions and wealth and escape to a country that will take them. The have-nots end up as starving refugees (see Chapter 14), such as those we have seen coming out of Somalia and Ethiopia, where civil war combined with natural drought to devastate the lives of those affected.[12]

The generation of many refugees can have very significant ecological and environmental impacts (see box). In Somalia, for example, war was thought to have accelerated the desertification of the already fragile ecosystems there.

The existence of national boundaries and their enforcement by the military—in contrast to people freely moving from one location to another, as the nomads of North Africa do—has meant that movement is now restricted and people are often forced to stay on fragile lands that cannot adequately hold many people for long. Thus, in many cases, acceleration of soil degradation and desertification occur.

At times of aggression, even small concerns for preserving the environment or

Displaced Persons and Their Impact on the Environment

War is among the most potent disrupters of quality of life and displacers of human beings. It is estimated that there are about 17 million refugees and 25 million internally displaced persons in the world today.[13] The bloodshed in Rwanda alone is thought to have accounted for a million refugees in Zaire and other neighboring countries, and about two million internally displaced persons (see Chapter 17).

The large-scale entry of displaced persons into receiving territories that lack adequate infrastructure or resources can exacerbate existing environmental problems and lead to previously unexpected concerns. Deforestation can be accelerated because of many factors: Land needs to be cleared for refugee camp sites; trees are cut down to provide wood for construction of dwelling places and to provide firewood for cooking or heating purposes; trees and shrubs may provide sources of fodder and foraging for livestock.[1] These same factors can also lead to desertification in arid and semi-arid regions. Population encroachment also causes the destruction and loss of forest ecosystems and biodiversity. Depletion of wood for firewood means that crop residues and animal dung are used for fuel with increasing frequency. Such fuels, because of their poor cooking efficiency and high smoke output, increase the risk of acute respiratory infections and such diseases as tuberculosis.

Land degradation can occur because of overgrazing or the use of poor or inappropriate farming techniques. This can greatly accelerate soil erosion and silting of rivers and streams, and it may so badly denature the soils that many years may be needed for soil to recover. Over time, food availability is reduced, which can lead to famine and widespread malnutrition and hunger.

Water and sanitation problems are major concerns. Poor sanitary conditions and high concentrations of population are likely to result in fecal contamination of water supply in neighboring rivers, wells, or oases. This increases the incidence of water-borne diseases such as cholera and other diarrheal disease. It is not unusual for epidemics to occur under such circumstances.

Waste disposal becomes a major concern. There tends to be an accumulation of solid wastes including garbage and human wastes. If proper disposal mechanisms are not found, these sites can also become public health hazards associated with high populations of flies, rodents, and other pests.

1. Jacobsen, K. The Impact of Refugees on the Environment: A Review of the Evidence. Washington D.C.: Refugee Policy Group, Center for Policy Analysis and Research on Refugee Issues, 1994.

maintaining a semblance of the social environment or environmental integrity are often lost.

What Needs to Be Done

As Arthur H. Westing has written, ''The genocidal and ecocidal possibilities of a future nuclear war are now very widely recognized. But less widely recognized is the potential for human and environmental catastrophe as the result of a nonnuclear war, due to growing potency of conventional weapons and release of dangerous forces from nuclear power plants, chemical factories, and hydrological facilities.''[5]

The release of dangerous forces can be prevented by technical, legal, and cultural approaches.

Technical approaches include rebuilding the facility so that its basic design is safer, adding physical and procedural safety features to it, surrounding it with a buffer zone free of permanent habitation by humans, and eliminating the facility.[5]

Legal approaches include a number of aspects. The use in war of chemical and biological weapons has long been banned (see Chapters 7 and 8). Bans on the use of nuclear weapons are dealt with in accordance with prohibitions on their deployment in certain geographic areas or with the prevention of their proliferation (see Chapters 6 and 22). Given international law, the legality of the use of nuclear weapons is open to question (see Chapter 22). Existing international law is also flawed in that existing treaties have weaknesses. In addition, international law does not include a widely accepted form of unconditional compulsory arbitration or adjudication for nonviolent conflict resolution among nations. Furthermore, the idea of national sovereignty remains sacrosanct.[5]

Two important treaties that are in force, the Bern Protocols I and II of 1977 additional to the Geneva Conventions of 1949, are relevant to the environment during war, but they have not yet received the widespread formal acceptance that they deserve. Only half of the world's nations have become party to them. However, what is needed is a multilateral treaty that enshrines that concept, best enunciated in the Declaration of 1972 on the Human Environment, that nations have a responsibility to ensure that their activities do not cause damage to the human environment in areas beyond their jurisdiction. The Protocols prohibit belligerents from attacking dams or dikes and nuclear power plants if such actions could cause release of dangerous forces that would cause severe losses among civilians. They also prohibit belligerents from rendering unavailable any objects that are indispensable to the survival of the civilian population, including foodstuffs, agricultural areas, livestock, and drinking water installations.[5]

The most important new cultural norm for humans to embrace will have to be a deep recognition that true human security can flow only from a combination of social and environmental security. There are signs that this ethos is now beginning to take hold.

The World Charter for Nature (1982) proclaims that ''nature shall be secured against degradation by warfare or other hostile activities'' and that ''special precautions shall be taken to prevent discharge into natural systems of radioactive or toxic wastes.'' These admonitions need to be taken to heart by all of the world's peoples. These admonitions need to be recognized as obligate prerequisites for the survival and well-being of civilization.

Finally, steps must be taken to eliminate wars between and within nations (see Chapters 21–26).

The only sustainable long-term course would be a lessening of tensions and the establishment of peaceful, human-development-oriented societies. The end of the animosity and mutual suspicion attributed to the Cold War has created a window of opportunity for the global community to take on the challenges of bringing peace through a constructive use of the United Nations and other forums. The UN has seized the opportunity created to restructure and reorient some of its programs to facilitate preventive development. Still, international attention needs to be focused on the concerns of warring factions and disenchanted populations, and efforts should be made to work toward peaceful resolution of differences. The work of international NGOs, including, among many others, the International Physicians for the Prevention of Nuclear War and Physicians for Human Rights, have done much to raise international public consciousness of the impact of war on environment, development, and health.

Governments must guarantee fundamental freedoms and basic human rights to their people, and the UN system needs to play a major role in monitoring, or conducting surveillance, for peace. Any diversion of national resources beyond the minimum required to secure defense should raise an alert, leading to an assessment of the situation by the international community.

Civil society needs to be strengthened and efforts made to resolve tensions amicably through sustainable peaceful solutions. The agreement reached with Haiti's former military rulers by U.S. negotiators in September 1994 to guarantee a peaceful transition to democracy is an excellent example of how a potentially devastating war can sometimes be avoided in the best interests of all concerned.

We hope that humankind is close to reaching a stage in evolution where we will recognize that it is in our long-term interest and that of the generations to come that we avoid war and militarization of our societies.

The impact of war on the environment is totally preventable.

REFERENCES

1. Myers, N. Environment and security. *Foreign Policy* 74:23–41, 1989.
2. Postel, S. The politics of water. *Worldwatch Magazine,* July–August, 1993: 10–18.
3. Dubos, R. Environment. In Wiener P.P. (ed.), *Dictionary of the history of ideas—Studies of selected pivotal ideas, Volume II.* New York: Charles Scribner's Sons, 1973, pp. 120–127.
4. United Nations Development Program. *Human Development Report 1994.* New York: Oxford University Press, 1994.
5. Westing, A.H. (ed.). *Environmental Hazards of War: Releasing Dangerous Forces in an Industrialized World.* Oslo: International Peace Research Institute; Nairobi: United Nations Environmental Program; and London: Sage Publications, 1990.
6. Westing, A.H. Herbicides in warfare: The case of Indochina. In P. Bourdeau, J.A. Haines, W. Klein, et al. (eds.), *Ecotoxicology and Climate.* Chichester, England: John Wiley & Sons, 1989, pp. 337–357.
7. Westing, A.H. Crop destruction as a means of war. *Bull. Atom. Scientists* 37(2): 38–42, 1981.

8. Westing A.H. (ed.). *Environmental warfare: Technical, legal and policy appraisal.* Stockholm International Peace Research Institute/United Nations Environmental Program Series. London: Taylor and Francis, 1984.

9. Sullivan, T.J. The downwind impacts of the oil fires. In S. Bloom, J.M. Miller, J. Warner, P. Winkler, (eds.), *Hidden casualties: Environmental, health and political consequences of the Persian Gulf War.* San Francisco: ARC/Arms Control Research Center; and Berkeley: North Atlantic Books, 1992, pp. 105–106.

10. Ibrahim, Y.M. Kuwait battling huge pools of oil. *New York Times,* April 21, 1992, A1.

11. Arkin, W.M., Durrant, D. and Cherni, M. *On the impact of modern warfare on the environment: A case study of the Gulf War.* Washington: Greenpeace, 1991.

12. Sidel, V.W. and Shahi, G.S. Military activities, environment, development and health. In G. Shahi, B.S. Levy, A. Binger, et al. (eds.), *International perspectives in environment, development, and health: Toward a sustainable world.* New York: Springer, 1996.

III

Effects of
Weapons Systems
on Public Health

6

The Public Health Effects
of the Use of Nuclear Weapons

KENJIRO YOKORO and NANAO KAMADA

The first explosive test of a bomb based on nuclear fission (''Trinity'') was conducted at Alamagordo (White Sands), New Mexico, in July 1945. Nuclear weapons have been used in war only twice, both within a month of the Trinity test: on Hiroshima on August 6, 1945, and on Nagasaki three days later. The bombs produced death and injury by a combined effect of the blast, heat, and ionizing radiation. Exposure to the bombs also resulted in long-term consequences, due largely to radiation and to psychological trauma, to survivors (called *Hibakusha* in Japan) who even 50 years after the bombings are still haunted by fear of becoming ill or dying as a result of the bombs.

The casualties have been studied by the Atomic Bomb Casualty Commission (ABCC); the Radiation Effects Research Foundation (RERF), the successor to the ABCC; Hiroshima and Nagasaki universities; and other institutions. The studies have greatly contributed to health care for the survivors and to the understanding of the biological effects of ionizing radiation on humans. Studies of the survivors have also promoted experimental radiobiological investigations, both *in vivo* and *in vitro*, to explore the mechanism of radiation-induced damage. The findings of biomedical studies on the effects of the nuclear bombs are described in the following sections.

The Power of Nuclear Weapons

The power of the Hiroshima bomb was estimated to be equivalent to the explosive power of 15 kilotons of TNT, and that of the Nagasaki bomb, 21 kilotons.[1] But these data do not reflect the destructive power of the atomic bomb accurately since they do not include the ionizing radiation emitted from the bomb.

The first bomb exploded at an altitude of about 580 meters over the heart of Hiroshima, and the second bomb at an altitude of about 500 meters over the northeast part of Nagasaki. The energy distribution of the Hiroshima bomb was estimated to be: blast, 50 percent; radiant heat, 35 percent; and ionizing radiation, 15 percent. That of the Nagasaki bomb was similar. The Hiroshima bomb used uranium-235 and the Nagasaki bomb plutonium-239 as fissile material. Although the power of the latter was slightly stronger than that of the former, because of the topographical configuration of the city and the detonation of the bomb over its northern outskirts, both the human and material damage was less in Nagasaki than in Hiroshima.

The ionizing radiation released by the detonation may be divided into two categories: initial and residual. The initial radiation, accounting for about five percent of the total energy, consists of alpha and beta particles, gamma rays, and neutrons; only gamma rays and neutrons reach the ground from an air burst since the range of alpha and beta particles is short. Consequently, the effects on humans from the initial radiation are caused by gamma rays and neutrons.

The residual radiation, accounting for about 10 percent of the total energy, emanates from (a) fission products (producing mainly gamma rays and beta particles); (b) uranium or plutonium escaping fission (mainly alpha particles and gamma rays); and (c) radioactive isotopes induced by the interaction of neutrons with bomb fragments and with substances in the air or on the ground (beta particles and gamma rays). Exposure to residual radiation includes external exposure to gamma rays and internal exposure to beta and alpha particles taken into the body by ingestion, inhalation, or through wounded skin.

So-called "black rain," to which many people in Hiroshima and Nagasaki were exposed, should also be included as a source of residual radiation. In Hiroshima, black rain containing radioactive fallout poured down over a large area from north of the hypocenter (the point on the ground below the center of an air burst) to the west for about seven hours, starting about 45 minutes after explosion. In Nagasaki, black rain poured down intermittently in the Nishiyama District, 2.0 to 2.5 km southeast of the hypocenter and shielded by a mountain (and thus not directly exposed), starting about 20 minutes after explosion until night. The black rain in this district may have contained more radioactive substances than the black rain in Hiroshima.[2]

Physical Effects

Blast

The explosion produced atmospheric pressures several hundred thousand times normal atmospheric pressure that caused an intensive blast by an enormous expansion of the surrounding air. The wind velocity was estimated at 280 meters per second (630 miles per hour) at the hypocenter, and 28 meters per second (63 miles per hour) at 3.2 km (about two miles) away. A vertical cloud, which was caused by a reversed centripetal blast, followed. A huge mushroom cloud gradually formed, reaching up to about 4,000 meters (13,000 feet) above the hypocenter one minute after the explosion, 6,000 meters (20,000 feet) at two to three minutes after, and 12,000 meters (40,000 feet) at 20 to 30 minutes after. The pressure directly below the point of explosion, assumed to be 4.5 to 6.7 tons per square meter in Hiroshima and 6.7 to 10.0 tons in Nagasaki, lasted for about 0.4 second.[3,4]

Radiant Heat

The maximum instantaneous temperature of the fireball produced in the air simultaneously with the explosion reached up to 1 million°C 0.3 seconds later; the surface temperature on the earth beneath the hypocenter was about 7,000°C. The quantity of heat absorbed was estimated to be 99.6 cal/cm^2 on the ground of the hypocenter area and 1.8 cal/cm^2 on the ground 3.5 km (2.2 miles) away. Wooden materials were charred (burned black) up to 3.0 km (1.9 miles) from the hypocenter, and naked skin suffered radiant burns up to 3.5 km (2.2 miles) away. Humans had never before experienced such a degree of heat in an open situation.[4]

The enormous radiant heat caused fires and conflagrations that, combined with intense blast pressure, resulted in extensive destruction of structures by which about 13 km^2 (8.1 miles^2) in Hiroshima and 6.7 km^2 (4.2 miles^2) in Nagasaki were reduced to ashes.

Ionizing Radiation

The total quantity of the initial ionizing radiation was estimated to consist of 35 Gy of gamma rays and 6.04 Gy of neutrons at 500 meters (1,640 feet) from the hypocenter, and 0.07 Gy of gamma rays at 2.5 km (1.6 miles).[4]

In order to estimate the biological effect of ionizing radiation, preciseness of dosimetry is a prerequisite for an accurate assessment of dose-effect relationship. A dosimetry system, the "tentative dosimetry system 1965" (T65D),[5] had previously been used for risk assessment. However, doubts about the accuracy of T65D were raised by some U.S. scientists in the late 1970s.[6] These doubts led to reassessment of the system by a U.S.-Japan joint study. A more comprehensive and sophisticated dosimetry system, the "dosimetry system 1986" (DS86), was established in 1987.[1] The DS86 consists of computer programs and databases that can be used to compute kerma in air (with adjustment for external shielding), and organ dose estimates for individual survivors, with adequate shielding information.

Estimated Human Casualties in Hiroshima

According to an official report published in 1971 by the Hiroshima City Authority,[7] the total number of people who died within one year after the bombing was 118,661.

The number of deaths during the ''acute phase'' (from August 6 to December 31, 1945) was estimated to be about 114,000, and about 4,000 people exposed died between January and August, 1946, due to severe injuries. Ninety-five percent of these 114,000 people who died had been exposed within 2.0 km (1.3 miles) of the hypocenter. These data, however, do not include the casualties among military personnel and Korean people in Hiroshima because official information on these populations has not been available; these populations reportedly totalled about 40,000, and about one-half of them died.

The number of people seriously wounded was about 30,000, and nearly all of them were exposed in a range of 1.0 to 2.5 km (0.63 to 1.6 miles). The number of slightly wounded was estimated to be about 48,000, most of whom were exposed in a range of 1.0 to 3.0 km (0.63 to 1.9 miles) (Figure 6-1).

Human casualties caused by the nuclear bombs were much greater than the sum of injuries caused by each of the three components (blast, heat, and ionizing radiation) since the three components acted simultaneously and in combination with each other.[4]

In general, the severity of acute injuries was in inverse relationship to the distance between the site of exposure and the hypocenter.

Bodily Injury in the Acute Stage

TRAUMA. Physical injuries by the blast were divided into primary injuries caused directly by the blast and secondary injuries caused by destruction of dwellings and other structures (Figure 6-2). Some of the proximally exposed victims were blown far away by the blast, with resultant damage to their viscera. These injuries caused instant or early deaths among those proximally exposed.

THERMAL BURNS. Severe thermal burns were frequent among those exposed. Flash burns, the most severe thermal burns caused by the direct action of heat, of over Grade 5 occurred within 1.0 to 1.5 km (0.63 to 0.95 miles) of the hypocenters in both cities; those proximally exposed succumbed to instant death with carbonization of the body. Burns of Grades 1 to 4 occurred among those exposed up to 3.5 to 4.0 km (2.2 to 2.5 miles). Some people with primary thermal burns and trauma were trapped in the flames of fire and conflagration, causing scorched, contact, or flame burns.[8]

RADIATION ILLNESS. As a consequence of the exposure to single total-body irradiation, the prodromal symptoms of radiation sickness (nausea, vomiting, polydipsia, anorexia, general malaise, fever, and diarrhea) appeared on the same day of the explosion. Then, the typical syndrome started to appear from the second week, showing hair loss, fever, hemorrhagic diathesis, stomatitis, vomiting, fatigue, anorexia, vertigo, headache, diarrhea, and other symptoms. The severity of the syndrome was dependent on the distance of the point of exposure to the hypocenter and on any shielding. Victims with earlier onset of the syndrome had a poorer prognosis.[9]

Figure 6-1. Hiroshima, August 6, 1945, about 3 hours after the bombing, in front of a police box, west end of Miyuki Bridge, 2.2 km southeast of the hypocenter (Photograph by Matushige Yoshito; used with his permission).

The $LD_{50/60}$ is defined as a radiation dose that results in a 50 percent death rate within 60 days after a single total-body irradiation. In Hiroshima and Nagasaki, it is estimated that about one-half of those exposed at about 1.0 km (0.63 miles) from the hypocenter died within 60 days. It seems appropriate to consider that the bone-marrow dose of these people was about 3.0 Gy.[10] This value was derived from surveys on the casualties, but it may be modified by various factors such as age, gender, nutritional status, presence of other injuries, and life situation at and after exposure.

Staging of Casualties in the Acute Phase

According to a report prepared by Hiroshima and Nagasaki city officials and sent to the Secretary-General of the United Nations in 1976,[11] the total deaths by the end of 1945 were 140,000 ($\pm$ 10,000) in Hiroshima and 70,000 ($\pm$ 10,000) in Nagasaki. In Hiroshima, about 40,000 victims were presumed to have been killed instantly or later on the day of the explosion.

The exact number of instant deaths, day-1 deaths, or other "early" deaths is unknown. But nearly 90 to 100 percent of those suffering severe thermal injuries from exposure with no shielding within 1.0 km (0.63 miles) of the hypocenter died within a week of exposure. The mortality rates at an early stage among those exposed at 1.5

Figure 6-2. Nagasaki, August 10, 1945 (the day after the bombing), near the Matsuyan-Machi intersection close to the hypocenter (Photograph by Yosuke Yamahata; used with the permission of Shogo Yamahata).

to 2.0 km (0.95 to 1.3 miles) from the hypocenter were about 14 percent for the shielded and about 83 percent for the unshielded.

From the biomedical point of view, the acute phase of nuclear bomb injury can be divided into four stages.[8]

STAGE 1—EARLY OR INITIAL STAGE. Approximately 90 percent of the fatalities occurred during the period from immediately after explosion to the end of the second week, the vast majority due to severe thermal injury. Numerous victims were instantly killed as a result of collapse of buildings on them, heavy trauma, and fires or extensive burns. Those who escaped from instant death but suffered intense trauma or heavy burns involving more than 20 percent of the body surface complained of fever, vomiting, or polydipsia immediately after injury, then fell into shock and died in one week. The vast majority of heavily irradiated victims, regardless of their having burns or trauma, suffered general malaise, nausea, and vomiting immediately after exposure, followed by a severe radiation syndrome with such symptoms as high fever, hematemesis, hemoptysis, bloody diarrhea, and hematuria; they died within 10 days after exposure with severe emaciation.

STAGE 2—INTERMEDIATE STAGE. Symptoms of moderate injury, caused by total-body exposure to ionizing radiation, became evident from week 2 through week 8, and many people died.

STAGE 3—LATE STAGE. During months 3 and 4, various symptoms began to be mitigated, and the physical condition of survivors improved somewhat.

STAGE 4—LATER STAGE. Various delayed effects, such as distortion, contracture, and keloid following recovery from thermal injury or trauma, as well as anemia and sterility due to radiation injury, developed from month 5 onward.

Development of Keloids Following Exposure to Thermal Radiation

Keloids developed between 1946 and 1949 among survivors exposed to thermal radiation at about 1.0 to 2.5 km (0.63 to 1.6 miles) from the hypocenter, as a consequence of thermal burns of Grades 2 and 3. There were no preferential areas of the body for these lesions. The keloids developed somewhat more frequently than those following ordinary burns. Ugly upheavals gradually declined and transformed to the usual scars. In some cases, however, skin cancers, for which survivors seem to be at increased risk, originated from the lesions after a long latency period. The mechanism of nuclear-bomb keloids is unknown, although the roles of both thermal radiation and nuclear radiation have been considered.[12,13]

Induction of Microcephaly with Mental Retardation Among Those Exposed *In Utero* to Nuclear Radiation

Induction of microcephaly was one of the most significant and tragic effects of exposure *in utero* to nuclear radiation both in Hiroshima and Nagasaki. According to the ABCC survey following the National Census in 1960, there were 2,310 survivors who had been exposed *in utero* in Hiroshima and 1,562 in Nagasaki. The incidence of microcephaly is well correlated with both exposure dose and gestational stage at the time of exposure. Most frequently affected were those exposed between weeks 8 and 15. Those receiving higher doses often also had mental retardation, which lowered their social adaptability. The threshold in inducing this condition is estimated to be around 0.2 Gy.[14,15]

Induction of Cataracts

The cataracts induced among survivors is a direct effect of nuclear radiation and is characterized by the development of lenticular opacity in the posterior pole. The first case of the lesion was found in a Hiroshima bomb survivor in 1948, followed by many cases among survivors in both Hiroshima and Nagasaki. The induction rate is dependent on the quantity and quality of radiation. Since the Hiroshima bomb emitted more neutrons, the frequency of the lesion was slightly higher among the Hiroshima survivors than among Nagasaki survivors, even if they were exposed to a similar total dose of nuclear radiation. In recent years, however, the picture of the lesion is becoming rather complicated as aging of survivors progresses.[16,17]

Genetic Effects

Genetic effects of the nuclear bombings have carefully been examined at RERF. Studies included the occurrence of mutations and alterations in the electrophoretic mobility or activity of a series of 30 proteins of children whose parents had been proximally and distally exposed. There have been no radiation-induced mutations among children of proximally exposed parents.[18] Furthermore, on the strength of their long-standing study of the genetic effects using eight different indicators, it was concluded that there were no statistically significant increases in genetic anomalies as a result of the nuclear bombings.[19]

Delayed Effects Due Mainly to Radiation Exposure

Delayed effects caused mainly by radiation began to appear in 1946. Although each case was closely observed, there were no symptoms found to be unique to radiation exposure. Therefore, it was impossible to discern whether or not they were caused by radiation. However, since the radiation-exposed population had a high incidence of certain diseases, there was a good reason to ascribe these diseases to radiation. Existence of the late radiation effects was clarified by advanced statistical analyses.

Many studies were carried out to investigate the delayed effects of the nuclear bomb, such as keloids and hypertrophic scars, blood disorders, ocular lesions, abnormal spermatogenesis, growth and developmental disorders, abnormal aging, reduced life span, psychoneurological disorders, abnormal immune responses, malignant tumors, and chromosomal abnormalities in directly exposed people and in children exposed *in utero*. Genetic effects of nuclear-bomb radiation on the children of survivors were also investigated, including abnormal pregnancy outcomes, abnormal sex ratio, abnormal growth and development, chromosomal aberrations, malignant tumors, and increased gene mutation frequency.

The late effects of nuclear bomb radiation were divided into three categories:

1. Effects with a confirmed relationship to nuclear-bomb exposure: Radiation caused an enormous increase in the incidence of malignancies, including leukemia, thyroid cancer, breast cancer, and lung cancer, and in the incidence of chromosomal abnormalities and microcephaly with mental retardation.
2. Effects with a possible relationship to nuclear-bomb radiation exposure: Radiation seemed to have influenced the incidence of other malignant tumors like esophageal cancers, salivary gland tumors, urinary tract cancers, skin cancers, and malignant lymphomas, and abnormalities in humoral and cell-mediated immunity.
3. Effects with no known correlation with nuclear-bomb radiation exposure: There was no increase in the incidence of chronic lymphocytic leukemia and osteosarcoma in exposed people, no change in the infertility rate, no increases in birth defects, and no increased mortality in the second generation.

The onset time for the development of several tumors in the exposed population after exposure is illustrated in Figure 6-3. A high incidence of leukemia appears six years after exposure (1951), followed by thyroid cancer in the 1960s, breast and lung cancer in the 1970s, and stomach cancer, colon cancer, and multiple myeloma in the late 1970s.[20]

Leukemia

There was an increase in both acute and chronic leukemia starting in 1948, with a higher incidence in 1951 and 1953. After that, the number of leukemia cases gradually decreased. Even now, however, a slightly higher incidence of acute leukemia continues. The characteristic features of nuclear-bomb-radiation-induced leukemia are:

1. The higher the exposed dose, the greater the risk of leukemia.
2. The younger the age at the time of exposure, the greater the risk of leukemia.
3. The peak of leukemia development occurred six years after exposure.
4. The incidence of chronic myelocytic leukemia (CML) in Hiroshima was higher than that in Nagasaki, probably due to a greater release of neutrons from the Hiroshima bomb.

Estimated relative risks for the exposed population for various malignant tumors are shown in Figure 6-4 in comparison with the non-exposed population.[21] The incidence of leukemia was the highest, followed by colon cancer and breast cancer. In

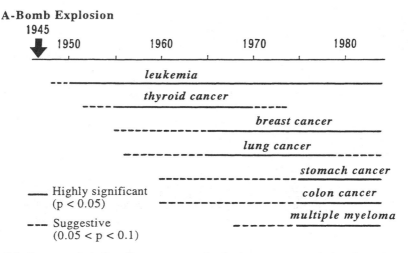

Figure 6-3. Latent period of malignant tumors developing among atomic-bomb survivors.

most diseases, the incidence of neoplasia was well correlated with dose of radiation exposure.

Solid Tumors

The characteristic features of nuclear-bomb-radiation-induced solid tumors are:

1. The higher the exposed dose, the greater the risk of development of solid tumors.
2. The latent period does not correlate with the exposed dose, but does correlate with age at the time of exposure.
3. Solid tumors develop when the exposed survivors have reached an age where cancer incidence is frequent.

Thyroid Cancer

Thyroid cancer began to increase approximately 10 years after exposure, with an increased incidence continuing until about 1970. Many of those affected were survivors under age 20 at the time of bombing (ATB), and many had been exposed to over 0.5 Gy.[22]

Breast Cancer

Breast cancer began to increase approximately 10 years after exposure and showed a significant increase 20 years after the bombing, with a linear correlation with the dose received by breast tissue. Also, an excess incidence of radiation-related breast cancer

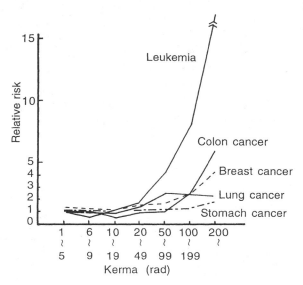

Figure 6-4. Relative risks, by estimated radiation dose (in rads), for leukemia and four other malignancies, based on studies of atomic-bomb survivors in Japan.

was observed among women under age 10 ATB, with the breast cancer risk tending to increase with a decrease in age ATB.[23]

Stomach Cancer

Stomach cancer began to exhibit a significant increase from around 1975, with the incidence significantly high among the high-dose population and among the population under age 30 ATB. Classification according to histologic type reveals a tendency for a high incidence of well-differentiated adenocarcinoma among the low-dose population and a high incidence of poorly differentiated adenocarcinoma among the high-dose population.[24]

Lung Cancer

Lung cancer began to increase around 1955, with a significantly high increase after 1965. Lung cancer risk increased with increase in smoking, and it is believed that radiation adds to the effect of smoking; lung cancer risk also increased with increased exposure to radiation. In the same manner as leukemia and stomach cancer, the lung cancer risk tends to rise with a decrease in age ATB, but for those who were young at the time (aged 10 years or less) a final conclusion cannot be made since those survivors are still only in their fifties.

Other Malignancies

Multiple myeloma began to increase around 1975, along with the aging of the exposed population. The relative risk among the nuclear-bomb survivors exposed to over 1 Gy of radiation was 5.3 times greater than among those not exposed.

Recent studies have revealed an increase in skin cancer among nuclear-bomb survivors since the late 1970s, with a clear relationship between dose of radiation exposure and incidence of the disease.[25]

Non-cancerous Disease

The most prominent disease in this category is hyperparathyroidism. Hyperparathyroidism is clinically characterized by a continuously elevated hypercalcemia and high serum parathyroid gland hormone levels. The prevalence of hyperthyroidism increases significantly with doses in excess of 0.5 Gy.[26] Also, this tendency increases with a decrease in age ATB.

Cytogenetic Effects

Chromosome Aberration in Healthy Survivors

Chromosome aberrations are direct, residual effects of radiation. There have been reports on T and B lymphocytes in the peripheral blood, and on bone-marrow cells and skin fibroblasts.[27,28]

In short, the characteristics of chromosomal aberrations in healthy nuclear-bomb survivors are as follows:

1. The aberrations were of the most stable types in the order of translocation, deletion, and inversion.
2. There was little variation in the aberration frequency in different tissues.
3. A dose-related aberration rate was clearly demonstrated.
4. Most of the aberrations were random, but some were clonal with clustering at some important chromosome sites related to proto-oncogenes.

Most importantly, there is evidence that chromosome aberrations exist in bone-marrow stem cells, which are the origin of all blood cell components. This finding is believed to be the reason for the increase in leukemia incidence and also for persistence of chromosomal aberrations found even 50 years after exposure.

Chromosome Aberrations in Leukemia Patients

In a span of 30 years, from 1962 to 1991, we examined the chromosomes of 75 acute leukemia patients who had a history of nuclear-bomb exposure, including 16 patients

Table 6-1. Chromosome aberrations in acute non-lymphocytic leukemia found among nuclear-bomb survivors

	Controls[a]	0 rad[b]	0.01-0.99 Gy	≥1.0 Gy
No. of cases examined	261	25	34	16
Percent of cases with chr. abers.	60.9	56.0	52.9	100[c]
Percent of cases with more than 3 chr. abers.	26.4	24.0	41.8	75[d]
Percent of cases with abnormalities in chrs. 5 or 7	21.6	22.2	9.5	75[e]

[a]Leukemia patients born before August 5, 1945.

[b]Bone marrow dose by means of DS86 dosimetry system given by RERF.

[c]Statistically significant ($p < .001$), compared with the controls.

[d]Statistically significant ($p < .05$), compared with other groups.

[e]Statistically significant ($p < .01$), compared with other groups.

exposed to more than 1 Gy. All of the patients who had been exposed to more than 1 Gy had clonal abnormalities in their leukemic cells, while only 52 to 60 percent of the cells of patients exposed to less than 1 Gy and the control group had abnormalities (Table 6-1).

Seventy-five percent of the patients in the heavily exposed group showed more than three chromosome abnormalities in the stem lines, representing more complex types of aberrations. A statistically significant difference was observed between the heavily exposed group and the other groups.

Molecular genetic studies revealed no increased or consistent point mutations in N- or K-RAS genes in patients with radiation-induced acute or chronic leukemias. They also involved the presence of BCR gene rearrangement in patients with CML, irrespective of radiation exposure.[28]

Immunologic Effects

The late effects of nuclear-bomb radiation on the immune system of survivors had been speculated.[29] A number of immunological studies have since been conducted. Table 6-2 is a list of the results of studies on the late effects related to immunocompetence.

T lymphocyte response to PHA (phytohemagglutinin) showed a marked age-related decrease in nuclear-bomb survivors exposed to T65D doses of 2 Gy, compared to the control population.[30]

A high cancer mortality rate among nuclear-bomb survivors is well known, but it

Table 6-2.   Studies on late effects related to immune responses[29]

Types of Cell/Antibodies	Study Period	Radiation Effect
Bone marrow cells		
Number of cells	1947–59	absent
Bacteriolysis	1959	absent
Phagocytosis	1962	absent
Chemotaxis	1977	absent
Lymphocytes		
Number of lymphocytes	1958–72	absent
T-lymphocytes		
PHA response	1974–77	decreased in aging survivors
MLC response	1984–85	decreased in aging survivors
IL-2 production	1983–86	absent
Number of cells	1983–86	decreased in aging survivors
B-lymphocytes		
Number of cells	1983–86	absent
Natural killer cells		
NK activity	1983–86	absent
Interferon production	1983–86	absent
Number of cells	1983–86	absent
Humoral factors		
Immunoglobulin levels	1968–69	absent
	1970–71	absent
	1987–89	increased IgA in females
	1987–89	increased IgM in aging survivors
Auto-antibodies		
Anti-parietal antibody	1971–72	absent
Anti-nuclear antibody	1987–89	absent
Thyroid microsome antibody	1987–89	absent
Rheumatoid factor	1987–89	increased
Immune complex		
Anti-influenza virus antibody production	1961	decreased
Anti-EB virus antibody	1983	increased
	1988–89	increased
Interferon	1983–86	absent

has not been adequately clarified as to whether the immune system in some way affects the development and progression of cancer.

Nuclear-Bomb Orphans

A tragedy brought about by the nuclear bombings was the creation of many so-called ''atomic-bomb orphans'' in both cities. By order of the government, a large-scale group evacuation of school children began in early 1945 in order to protect the children from continuous air raids. More than 20,000 children from Hiroshima and many from Nagasaki were reportedly sent to the countryside. It is estimated that in Hiroshima there were 4,000 to 5,000 orphans and vagrant waifs after the bombing because of the instant loss of their parents, siblings, and relatives. One of the authors of this chapter (K.Y.) occasionally saw roving orphans around the Hiroshima railroad station one or two years after the bombing. The vast majority of these orphans have never received any support from the government as nuclear-bomb victims since government services are restricted to irradiated victims.[31]

The Impact on the Socioeconomic Status of the Survivors

The nuclear bombings indiscriminately destroyed major aspects of traditional society in both cities. Community life and the social system were seriously devastated. Facing such an unprecedented situation, most of the survivors did not know what to do and were gloomily transfixed. Furthermore, they may not have been conscious of the distressful future to come.

Emergency preparedness for conventional attacks was complete in both cities. However, the damage of the nuclear attacks far exceeded this preparedness and rendered it virtually useless. During the war, hospitals and physicians working in other medical facilities were forced to remain where they were by order of the government. Nearly 300 physicians died in Hiroshima, and 60 in Nagasaki either instantly or after giving first aid to injured survivors despite their own injuries. In addition to thermal and blast injuries, massive doses of total-body irradiation caused a variety of disorders and hindered the physical recovery of the survivors. Furthermore, due to the impoverished state of the country resulting from the long-lasting war, the government was unable to give the victims any special help, and the general public did not have time to give attention to the difficulties of the survivors. Thus, their oppressed socioeconomic status was largely ignored for a long period of time after the war was over, and their recovery was delayed in many ways.

Psychological Effects

The following is adapted from "Psychological Trends among A-Bomb Victims in Hiroshima and Nagasaki: The Physical, Medical and Social Effects of the Atomic Bombings,"[32] which describes their painful experiences.

The exposed victims, starting from the moment of the explosion, suffered hitherto unknown kinds of psychological effects. The survivors experienced physically evoked ghastly phenomena: an intense flash, blast, thermal rays, complete demolition of buildings, outbreaks of conflagration, and observation of heavily burned and heavily injured victims everywhere. As a result, the victims felt overwhelmed and confused; some lost their presence of mind. Wild rumors among maimed survivors, like ''another air raid is coming,'' renewed and intensified the sense of panic. Many people lost all ability to cope with the overwhelming array of stimuli and simply followed along aimlessly with the fleeing crowds. People eventually reached some place they felt to be safe, where they rested, slept, and may have received food and treatment. At last, they began gradually to recover rational psychological function.[33]

The ideation of the nuclear-bomb victims that has been described is not merely an expression of ''restored'' and ''recovered'' psychological function. In the view of the victims, this ideation represents a higher level of consciousness attained through the strenuous processes of recovering these functions. For the victims, the forging of this ideation has changed the vague and remote concept of ''humankind'' into a real and close feeling for actual people. The view of human life held by most people is constricted. Life in the nuclear-bomb victims' ideation has expanded spatially to embrace all the living, and chronologically to include all yet to be born. Furthermore, each victim is felt to be a ''very important member'' of the whole human community and to have something unique to contribute to it and to our common future. Rarely have a few people been challenged to fulfill so crucial a role in human history. But the nuclear-bomb victims, though they may lack superior intelligence or stamina, can fulfill their vision as they strive to overcome hardships and opposition. And these lessons, the nuclear-bomb victims believe, can and should be learned by all people who wish to live on into the twenty-first century.

Conclusion

These bombs were dropped at the terminal stage of World War II. Although the two bombings and resulting nuclear holocaust might have brought the war to an earlier end and may have saved the lives of some U.S. military personnel and possibly caused a net savings of the lives of some Japanese military personnel and civilians, in our view the use of nuclear weapons can never be justified.

The controversy continues. One view is: ''It is clear that from the outset this new weapon was not intended for use in war theaters where opposing armies were locked in battle; rather, it was to be dropped on densely populated centers that contained military facilities and industries as well as a high concentration of houses and other buildings. Moreover, the A-bomb attacks were needed not so much against Japan— already on the brink of surrender and no longer capable of mounting an effective counteroffensive—as to establish clearly America's postwar international position and strategic supremacy in the anticipated cold war setting. One tragedy of Hiroshima and Nagasaki is that this historically unprecedented devastation of human society stemmed from essentially experimental and political aims.''[32]

It has been estimated that the numbers of inhabitants at the time of the bombings were approximately 350,000 in Hiroshima and 250,000 in Nagasaki, respectively, and they were variously affected according to the condition of exposure. In 1995, 50 years after the disaster, about half of the survivors are still living not only in Japan but also abroad. As their aging progresses, quality health care for them is essential. For that, the Atomic Bomb Victims Medical Care Law, enacted in 1957, has been applied to survivors of Japanese nationality, but not to exposed foreigners.

Many Koreans were exposed to the bombing, and many are said to be living in the Republic of Korea and the Democratic People's Republic of Korea. The authors believe that these foreign survivors should have a right to get the same benefits as Japanese survivors.

Albert Einstein noted, "The explosive force of nuclear fission has changed everything except our modes of thinking, and thus we drift toward the unparalleled catas-

---

Health Risks of Current Nuclear Weapons

Victor W. Sidel and Barry S. Levy

This chapter describes the health consequences of the bombing of cities by single nuclear weapons in the 15-megaton range. In addition to these health effects of their use, the development, production, testing, stockpiling, and even dismantling of nuclear weapons have health consequences, as described in Chapter 9.

Furthermore, if nuclear weapons are again used in the destruction of population centers, the health effects are likely to be far more severe than those in Hiroshima and Nagasaki. During the 1950s the United States and the Soviet Union developed nuclear bombs based on the principle of nuclear fusion rather than nuclear fission. These new weapons, called "hydrogen" or "thermonuclear" bombs, have an explosive force 1,000-fold greater than those detonated over Japan. In 1995, some 48,000 nuclear and thermonuclear weapons existed in the stockpiles of the eight self-declared nuclear states and of at least three other states widely believed to possess nuclear weapons. The total destructive capacity of these stockpiles is estimated to be equivalent to the explosive force of 11 billion tons of TNT, over 2 tons of TNT for every human being on our planet.

If more than a small number of these were used in war, the possibility of outside aid being available to the attacked populations, as occurred in Hiroshima and Nagasaki, is small. Furthermore, the possibility exists of adverse health consequences to populations far removed from the population centers directly bombed. These health effects include radiation injury from fallout of radionuclides at distant sites around the globe and the consequences of what has been termed "nuclear winter," the cooling of the earth's surface because of absorption and reflection of the sun's rays by clouds of soot and debris collecting in the atmosphere from the fires and explosions caused by nuclear bombs. That such clouds would reduce surface temperatures on the ground beneath them is well accepted; even relatively small forest fires cause such cooling. Controversy remains, however, about the size and density of the clouds that would be caused by any specific number of bombs, their types and targets, and the climatic conditions existing at the time of their detonation.

Further discussion of the health risks of the use of current nuclear weapons may be found in Chapter 22.

trophe. We shall require an entirely new pattern of thinking if mankind is to survive.'' Although there has been much progress in the field of biomedical science for the last 50 years, we have no breakthrough to cope with radiation injury. It is indisputable that the only way to avoid catastrophe, such as occurred in Hiroshima and Nagasaki, is to prevent nuclear war and to work for nonviolent resolution of conflicts (see Chapters 22 and 25).

REFERENCES

1. Malik, J., Tajima, E., Binninger, E., Kaul, D.C. and Kerr, G.D. Yields of the bombs, the U.S.-Japan Joint Reassessment of Atomic Bomb Radiation Dosimetry in Hiroshima and Nagasaki. Final Report, Vol. 1, pp. 26–36, Roesch, W.C. (ed.), Radiation Effects Research Foundation, Hiroshima, 1987.
2. Okajima, S., Takeshita, K., Antoku, S., et al. Radioactive fallout effects of the Nagasaki atomic bomb. *Health Physics* 34:621, 1978.
3. Brode, H.L. Numerical solution of spherical blast waves. *J. Appl. Phys.* 26:766, 1955.
4. Hirschfelder, J.O., et al. (eds.). *The effects of atomic weapons.* Washington: U.S. Government Printing Office, 1950.
5. Auxier, J.A., Cheka, J.S., Haywood, F.F., et al. Freefield radiation dose distribution from Hiroshima and Nagasaki bombings. *Health Physics* 12:425, 1966.
6. Sinclair, W.K. and Failla, P. Dosimetry of the atomic bomb survivors. *Radiation Res.* 88:437–447, 1981.
7. *Record of the Hiroshima A-bomb war disaster (RHAWD).* Published by Hiroshima Shi-yakusho, 1971.
8. The course of the atomic bomb injury. In *Atomic Bomb Casualty Investigation Report, Summary Report,* Publication Committee of the Atomic Bomb Casualty Investigation (ed.), pp. 9–18. Tokyo: The Japan Society for the Promotion of Science, 1951.
9. White, D.D. *An atlas of radiation histopathology.* Tech. Inform. Center Office of Public Affairs, U.S. Energy Research Development Administration, 1975.
10. Fujita, S., Kato, H., and Schull, W.J. The LD50 associated with exposure to the atomic bombing of Hiroshima and Nagasaki. *J. Radiat. Res.,* Supp., 154–161, 1991.
11. *To the United Nations, Hiroshima-shi and Nagasaki-shi,* Expert Committee for the Compilation of Materials to Appeal to the United Nations (ed.), p. 31, 1976.
12. Lielow, A.A., Warren, S. and Decoursey, E. Pathology of atomic bomb casualties. *Amer. J. Pathol.* 25:853, 1949.
13. Tsuzuki, M. Keloid problem as a late effect of the atomic bomb injury. Research in the Effects and Influences of the Nuclear Bomb Test Explosions, II. *Japan Society for the Promotion of Science,* p. 1459, 1956.
14. Wood, J.W., Johnson, K.G., Omori, Y., Kawamoto, S. and Keehn, R.J. In-utero exposure to the Hiroshima atomic bomb. An evaluation of head size and mental retardation—20 years later. *Pediatrics* 39:355, 1967.
15. Otake, M. and Schull, W.J. Radiation-related small head sizes among the prenatally exposed survivors in Hiroshima and Nagasaki. Radiation Effects Research Foundation, TR 6–92, 1992.
16. Cogan, D.G., Martin, S.F. and Kimura, S.J. Atomic bomb cataracts. *Science* 110:654, 1949.
17. *Ocular lesions in Hiroshima and Nagasaki: The physical, medical and social effects of the atomic bombings.* Committee for the Compilation of Materials on Damage caused by the

Atomic Bombs in Hiroshima and Nagasaki (eds.). Tokyo: Iwanami Shoten, Publishers, 1981, pp. 203–210. (Translated by E. Ishikawa and D.L. Swain.)

18. Neel, J.V., Satoh, C., Goriki, K., Asakawa, J., Fujita, M., Takahashi, N., Kageoka, T. and Hazama, R. Search for mutations altering protein charge and/or function in children of atomic bomb survivors: Final report. *Am. J. Hum. Genet.* 42:663–676, 1988.

19. Neel, J.V., Schull, W.J., Awa, A.A., Satoh, C., Kato, H., Otake, M. and Yoshimoto, Y. The children of parents exposed to atomic bombs: Estimates of the genetic doubling dose of radiation for humans. *Am. J. Hum. Genet.* 46:1053–1072, 1990.

20. Shigematsu, I., Ito, C. and Kamada, N. Review of "Effects of A-bomb radiation to human body 1992," ed. by Hiroshima International Council for Health Care of the Radiation-Exposed (in Japanese), Tokyo: Bunko-do, 1992, pp. 3–19.

21. Shimizu, Y., Kato, H. and Shull, W.J. Studies of the mortality of A-bomb survivors, Mortality, 1950–1985: Part 2. Cancer mortality based on the recently revised doses (DS86). *Radiat. Res.* 121:120–141, 1990.

22. Parker, L.N., Belsky, J.L., Yamamoto, T., et al. Thyroid carcinoma after exposure to atomic radiation. *Ann. Intern. Med.* 80:600–604, 1974.

23. Tokunaga, M., Land, C.E. and Tokuoka, S. Follow-up studies of breast cancer incidence among atomic bomb survivors. *J. Radiat. Res.,* 32 (Suppl.):201–211, 1991.

24. Ito, C., Kato, M., Yamamoto, T., et al. Study of stomach cancer in atomic bomb survivors. Report 1. Histological findings and prognosis. *J. Radiat. Res.* 30:164–175, 1989.

25. Sadamori, N., Mine, M., Ichimaru, M., et al. Incidence of skin cancer among Nagasaki atomic bomb survivors (Preliminary Report). *J. Radiat. Res.* 31:280–287, 1990.

26. Fujiwara S. Hyperparathyroidism. A review of forty-five years study of Hiroshima and Nagasaki atomic bomb survivors. *J. Radiat. Res.* 32 (Suppl.):245–248, 1991.

27. Kamada, N., Tanaka, K. and Hasegawa, A. Cytogenetic studies of hematological disorders in atomic bomb survivors. In *Radiation induced chromosome damage in man,* Ishihara, T. and Sasaki, M.S. (eds.). New York: Alan R. Liss, 1983, pp. 455–474.

28. Kamada, N. Cytogenetic and molecular changes in leukemia found among atomic bomb survivors. *J. Radiat. Res.* 32 (Suppl):172–179, 1991.

29. Akiyama, M. Immune function. In *Effects of A-bomb radiation to human body 1992.* Hiroshima International Council for Health Care of the Radiation-Exposed (eds.) (in Japanese). Tokyo: Bunkodo, 1992, pp. 258–273.

30. Akiyama, M., Yamakido, M., Kobuke, K., et al. Peripheral lymphocyte response to PHA and T cell population among atomic bomb survivors. *Radiat. Res.* 93:572–580, 1983.

31. Moritaki, I. Atomic bomb orphans. In *The atomic bomb and Hiroshima.* Hiroshima: Hiroshima Kyoshokuin Jigyobu, 1954, pp. 40–51.

32. *Hiroshima and Nagasaki: The physical, medical and social effects of the atomic bombings.* Committee for the Compilation of Materials on Damage Caused by the Atomic Bombs in Hiroshima and Nagasaki, (eds). Tokyo: Iwanami Shoten, Publishers, 1981, pp. 484–500. (Translated by E. Ishikawa and D.L. Swain.)

33. Kubo, Y. Study of human behavior immediately after the atomic bombing of Hiroshima. Socio-psychological study pertaining to the atomic bomb and atomic energy, 1, *Shinrigaku Kenkyu* (Japanese Journal of Psychology) with English Abstract, 22:103, 1952.

7

The Public Health Effects of the Use of Chemical Weapons

ALAN H. LOCKWOOD

Chemical weapons are poisonous or toxic compounds that have been developed to kill or disable combatants by direct effects on body organs or systems. Although the alleged intent is for their use against combatants, like virtually every other weapon that has been developed, noncombatants and civilian populations are also vulnerable and likely to be affected if they are used. In the case of chemical weapons, there are convincing data to demonstrate that some civilian populations, for example children and people with chronic medical problems, are more susceptible to the effects of chemical weapons than the generally healthy military population. This fact, coupled with many examples of deliberate or inadvertent use of chemical weapons against civilians, makes it important to understand these weapons from a civilian perspective. Indeed, the mere existence and plans for the destruction of stockpiles of these weapons poses a threat to civilian populations that has important medical and public policy implications.

Although naturally occurring poisons and toxic chemical compounds, such as curare and physostigmine, have been used for centuries because of their biological effects on humans, widespread, deliberate production and use of chemical weapons did not occur until World War I, when mustard gas, chlorine, and phosgene were all used in combat (Figure 7-1). The horror of chemical warfare led to adoption of the Geneva Protocol of 1925, which outlawed the first use of chemical and biological warfare agents. The accords did not prohibit the development, testing, and stockpiling of chemical agents. Indeed, thousands of tons of chemicals for use in warfare have been synthesized, along with an enormous expenditure of resources to deliver and defend against attacks by chemical warfare agents.

Chemical warfare agents are predominantly of three general types: (1) nerve agents that act by the inhibition of acetylcholinesterase, (2) vesicants that produce chemical burns of the skin and respiratory tract, and (3) "harassing agents" (or tear gas) that cause disability that is usually, and is intended to be, temporary. Although the exact

Figure 7-1. U.S. troops learning to correctly use gas masks in France during World War I (Source: Library of Congress, Negative LC-USZ 62-92733).

amount of chemical agents in military stockpiles is not known, the U.S. stockpile of nerve agents alone is likely between 22,000 and 27,000 metric tons. Republics of the former Soviet Union have declared that they possess less than 50,000 metric tons of chemical agents. Although the United States is committed by law to dispose of its stockpile of chemical weapons, there have been delays in the timetable because of safety issues that have arisen. These issues have centered on possible threats to populations that may be exposed to these agents during the course of disposal.

Properties of Chemical Weapons

To better understand the public health threats that are posed by chemical weapons, it is necessary to understand the mechanisms of action and properties of these agents (see Table 7-1).

Table 7-1.   Chemical warfare agents and their properties

Agent	Properties	Toxicity
GA (tabun)	Anticholinesterase, less volatile and more persistent than GB	Long-term toxicity unknown
GB (sarin)	Anticholinesterase, volatile and therefore less persistent than GA, with lower threat of absorption through skin compared to inhalation	Potential for producing delayed neuropathy, not teratogenic, long-term changes of unknown significance on electroencephalogram
VX	Anticholinesterase, less volatile than G agents, therefore more persistent and more likely to be absorbed through skin	No delayed neuropathy, not teratogenic or mutagenic
H/HD mustard gas, sulfur mustard Bis(2-chloro-ethyl)-sulfide	Vesicant, low volatility therefore very persistent, delayed toxic effects	Carcinogenic, predisposes to bronchitis, permanent injury to eyes and skin are possible
HT Bis[2(2-chlor-ethylthio)ethyl]-ether	Vesicant, less volatile and more persistent than HD, more toxicologically active than HD on skin and lungs	Carcinogenic, mutagenic
L (lewisite)	Vesicant, more volatile than HD therefore less persistent, skin burns more corrosive than with HD, but similar inhalation toxicity	Probably teratogenic and mutagenic

Source: Adapted from Carnes, S.A. and Watson, A.P. Disposing of the U.S. chemical weapons stockpile: An approaching reality. *JAMA* 262:653–659, 1989.

Nerve Agents

Nerve agents are compounds that bind irreversibly to molecules of acetylcholinesterase (AChE), the enzyme that terminates the action of the neurotransmitter acetylcholine (ACh), leading to the accumulation of ACh and persistence of the cholinergic effect.[1] In addition, some nerve agents have a direct effect on the postsynaptic ACh receptor that mimics the effect of ACh. In skeletal muscle, the accumulation of ACh causes a desynchronization of transmitted neural impulses, continuous uncoordinated muscle fiber contractions (fibrillations), and weakness. The massive increase of ACh causes the glands of the tracheobronchial tree to produce an enormous volume of secretions that, along with bronchospasm, obstructs the airway. The combined effects of respiratory muscle paralysis and obstruction of the airways causes death by asphyxiation. In the heart, excessive ACh causes severe bradycardia. The ensuing reduction in cardiac output and circulatory collapse contributes to the cause of death. Cholinergic neurotransmission is also disrupted in the central nervous system and convulsions may occur. This, along with the effects of hypoxia, causes epileptic seizures that may progress to status epilepticus and death. Thus, multiple effects of excessive amounts of ACh combine to cause death.

Long after immediate life-threatening effects of anti-AChE agents clear, residual effects may be observed. Persistent miosis (contraction of the pupil) is common and may last for weeks or longer.[2] More importantly, low doses of nerve agents cause abnormalities of the electroencephalogram in animals that may last a year or more.[3] This finding may be related to observations of persistent disturbances of mentation, seen as altered behavior and depression in exposed humans. Peripheral neuropathy may occur after exposure to sarin.[4] Soman and sarin both produce lesions in the cortex, hippocampus, amygdala, and thalamus in animals.[5] Cardiomyopathy may follow exposure to some of these agents.

Low-dose exposure to nerve gas produces a variety of symptoms.[6] Up to one-third of all exposed subjects report one or more of the following symptoms: irritability, impaired memory, impaired concentration, depression, visual difficulties, or fatigue. Schizophrenic reactions were seen in 25 percent of a group of exposed individuals, although this diagnosis may be erroneous, because auditory hallucinations, paranoid ideation, or severe depression occurred in more than 10 percent of this exposed population. Impaired consciousness, increased sexual desire, nightmares, and a variety of other symptoms were also reported. It is difficult to determine whether these complaints are of pure psychic origin due to the stress associated with exposure or whether they are the consequence of disturbed cholinergic neurotransmission, an unmasking of one or more preexisting conditions, or some combination of these mechanisms. Regardless of what mechanism is responsible for the production of the symptoms, disabling symptoms occur with a high frequency. It is likely, therefore, that chronic or repeated exposures to nonlethal amounts of nerve agents are likely to produce a variety of symptoms and disability in the exposed population, whether it be military or civilian.

Since relatively few people have been exposed to sublethal doses of nerve agents, it is possible that additional effects could occur. This is a difficult problem to approach experimentally because there appears to be much species-specific variation in the effects of the various anticholinergic agents in spite of an apparently common mechanism of action. Thus, it is impossible to predict the effects of sublethal exposures of large populations that might be due to organic lesions in the nervous system.

Vesicants

Vesicants were used widely in World War I, and there is convincing evidence for their use—largely ignored by the world community—in conflicts between Iraq and Iran. These agents all act by producing chemical burns, typically affecting epithelial membranes of the skin and respiratory tract.[7] Severe exposure, particularly by inhalation, impairs gas exchange in the lungs, and victims die of hypoxia. Nonfatal inhalations may be followed by pneumonia. Severe skin burns may also be fatal due to loss of body fluids or secondary infections. Nonfatal exposures produce permanent disability due to damage to the epithelial surfaces of the lung, cornea, and other tissues.

Many of these vesicants are mutagenic and carcinogenic. This property of these compounds has received less attention than the properties that cause death or long-term disability.

Tear Gas

In addition to widespread use of tear gas by civil authorities to control crowds and disable criminals, military forces have used these compounds for similar reasons (see reference 8 for review). Correct use is purported to be safe because the effects are believed to be transient and free of long-term effects. Use of these compounds is alleged to be more humane than alternative more violent measures. However, deaths due to direct toxic effects of tear gas have been documented. Explosions of tear gas bombs or impacts by delivery vehicles may also cause injury or death. Because of these considerations, 80 countries voted that tear gas should be included among the chemical weapons banned by the Geneva Protocol.

About 15 compounds have been used as tear gas. Of these, four have been used most extensively (omega-chloroacetophenone or CN, *o*-chlorobenzyl-idenemalonitrile or CS, 10-chloro-5,10-dihydrophenarasazine, and α-bromo-α-tolunitril). These chemicals are potent lacrimators and irritants. Fatal pulmonary edema may follow brief exposure. Other populations, such as children and patients with asthma or obstructive or restrictive pulmonary disease, are likely to be more susceptible to these agents and are at greater risk. Studies in animals have shown that ingestion can cause gastroenteritis with perforation. CS is metabolized to form cyanide in peripheral tissues. It is not clear whether the amounts of cyanide formed under these circumstances are likely to have important biological effects. Long-term human studies are nearly impossible to perform because of the circumstances that surround use of these agents.

Psychological Effects of Chemical Weapons

The gaps in our knowledge of the psychological effects of chemical warfare agents are even larger than the gaps in our knowledge of the immediate and delayed physical effects of these agents. From a public health perspective, psychological effects may be divided into those associated with actual use of these agents, effects associated with impending or threatened use, and effects produced by presence of these agents and plans for their destruction.

The impact of impending use of chemical agents has been studied fairly extensively in a military setting.[6] The substantial nature of the effects and their impact on expected behavior of troops trained to deal with a chemical warfare environment suggests that substantial effects are also likely to be observed in civilian populations. Evidence for this was seen at the time of the Persian Gulf War, when threatened nerve gas attacks led to casualties among Israelis who feared use of these compounds.[9]

Symptoms described during chemical-warfare training exercises provide some insight into the nature of the symptoms that might be observed in civilian populations.[6,10] Complaints, such as shortness of breath, anxiety, irritability, disturbed vision, loss of the sense of time, the urge to micturate, poor concentration, nausea, auditory hallucinations, tremor, disorientation, impaired judgment, and confusion, have been described. Some of these were undoubtedly attributable to the trainees' wearing protective clothing—Mission Oriented Protective Posture (MOPP) gear—which consists of a gas mask and dual-thickness rubberized cloth surrounding a layer of activated charcoal. This clothing restricts vision and movement and elevates temperature, creating special hazards in desert climates where dehydration is a concern. However, not all of these symptoms are likely to be caused by the gear; the experience itself is almost certainly critically important in causing symptoms. The occurrence of severe and disabling psychological symptoms in an elite, highly trained cohort of healthy subjects (military personnel) suggests strongly that similar disabling symptoms would be prevalent in civil populations.

Even under conditions where nerve agent exposure is possible, and therefore training of emergency response personnel should be optimal, published accounts of incidents suggest that elements of confusion and erroneous interpretation of signs and symptoms leads to iatrogenic complications. Treatment administered by care-givers who are less well trained is likely to be associated with a higher incidence of complications.[11] If, as has been advocated by some, civilian populations were provided with drugs used to treat people exposed to nerve agents (atropine or diazepam self-injectors), it is likely that these drugs would be used inappropriately and would produce illness and possibly death. There is a substantial overlap of symptoms caused by the real effects of nerve agent exposure and the symptoms reported during chemical-warfare training exercises. Thus, it is likely that at least some individuals provided with anti–nerve agent drugs would mistake symptoms of psychic origin for symptoms of nerve agents and would use the drugs inappropriately.

Post-traumatic stress disorder (PTSD) is relatively common in combat veterans and may also be seen in civilians. It may occur as a sequel to any situation associated with extreme stress. Even the anticipation of combat may be sufficiently stressful to precipitate the disorder. In the event of an attack by nerve gas, it is likely that the associated stress would be sufficient to produce PTSD in both civilian and military personnel.

Personal experience with Persian Gulf War veterans suggests that at least some victims of so-called "Gulf War syndrome" suffer from PTSD. These men and women were uprooted—abruptly, in many cases—from relatively tranquil circumstances as reserve units were activated and sent to a pre-war environment where chemical warfare was expected. Although chemical weapons were not used, many of these veterans describe terror associated with a sense of helplessness in anticipation of attack or combat in the presence of unknown compounds, such as chemicals coming from storage areas. Fear of the unknown and helplessness would also commonly occur in civilian populations, and did occur in Israel during scud missile attacks during the Gulf War.

Domestic Chemical Exposure

Although nerve agents and other chemical warfare weapons are stored in guarded arsenals in a small number of locations, similar chemicals are used in the home and in agriculture. The most common of these are the organophosphate insecticides. These chemicals and nerve agents have identical mechanisms of action and cause identical signs and symptoms. They vary substantially in potency and affinity for the active site on the acetylcholinesterase molecule. Because of these similarities, emergency medical care providers see patients, including children, with physical findings that may be identical to those associated with nerve gas exposure. In addition, these exposed populations may develop signs and symptoms associated with chronic exposures.

Recent reports from the National Academy of Sciences on pesticide residues in the diet and the exposure of the public to neurotoxic agents emphasize the pervasive nature of these exposures, the virtual absence of reliable data about long- and short-term neurotoxic effects of chemicals in the home and workplace, and the special vulnerability of children.[12,13] Since many people in the United States at risk for exposure to this class of chemicals may be undocumented agricultural workers, there are additional formidable problems that need to be considered.

Disposal of Chemical-Warfare Agents

As a part of the Department of Defense Authorization Act of 1986, Congress mandated the destruction of the U.S. stockpile of chemical weapons. The Act stipulated that the disposal should maximize the protection of the environment, the general public, and the workers involved with the destruction (see reference 7 for review). In addition, the Act provided for the construction of facilities designed for this purpose and the cleanup and disposal of facilities at the conclusion of the program. The original target date for completion was September 30, 1994.

As long as there was little or no public attention drawn to the existence of chemical warfare agents, shown by location in Table 7-2, there was little overt public concern. The "out of sight, out of mind" maxim applied. As initial plans for the destruction of the aging U.S. stockpile of weapons began to take shape, predictable public reactions occurred. The "out of sight, out of mind" approach was replaced by "not in

Table 7-2.   Chemical weapons stockpiles in the United States

Site	Percent of Total	Agent[a]	Form
Tooele Army Depot, Utah	42	H	projectiles
		HD	cartridges, projectiles, ton containers
		HT	cartridges, projectiles
		GB	cartridges, projectiles, rockets, bombs, ton containers
Umatilla Depot, Oregon	12	HD	ton containers
		GB	projectiles, rockets, bombs
		VX	projectiles, rockets, mines, spray tanks
Pine Bluff Arsenal, Arkansas	12	HD	cartridges, ton containers
		HT	ton containers
		GB	rockets
		VX	rockets, mines
Pueblo Depot, Colorado	10	HD	cartridges, projectiles
		HT	cartridges
Anniston Army Depot, Alabama	7	HD	cartridges, projectiles, ton containers
		HT	cartridges
		GB	cartridges, projectiles, rockets
		VX	projectiles, rockets, mines
Lexington Blue Grass Army Depot, Kentucky	2	H	projectiles
		GB	projectiles, rockets, ton containers
		VX	projectiles, rockets
Newport Army Ammunition Plant, Indiana	4	VX	ton containers
Aberdeen Proving Ground, Maryland	2	HD	ton containers

Source: Carnes, S.A. and Watson, A.P. Disposing of the U.S. chemical weapons stockpile: An approaching reality. *JAMA* 262:653–659, 1989.

[a]For abbreviations, see Table 7-1.

my backyard.'' The systematic analysis of the hazards of disposal attempted to quantify the risks of disposal and compare them with risks associated with doing nothing.

The analysis of the risks associated with various alternatives at various sites produced results, in terms of expected fatalities, that ranged from a zero or negligible risk to predictions of a catastrophic event with more than 1,000 deaths. These estimates were based on 1980 population data, varied meteorological conditions, and varied releases of different agents. Specifically, a release of 1 to 10 kg of a nerve agent near Tooele Army Depot (the repository for 42 percent of all chemical agents) could cause as many as five deaths. The release of 100 to 1,000 kg of an agent near a moderately populated area, such as the Aberdeen Proving Ground or the Lexington-Bluegrass Army Depot (repositories for mustard gas, sarin, and VX), could cause more than

Figure 7-2. Rockets loaded with sarin being destroyed by detonation in Iraq in 1992, under the supervision of the United Nations Special Commission (UNSCOM) (Source/Photographer: United Naitons/DPI/159092/H. Arvidssor).

1,000 deaths. The probability of an accident was estimated to vary from one chance in 10,000 to less than one chance in 10 billion during the duration of the disposal process or the lifetime of storage of the entire stockpile.

Formal procedures were developed to compare various options and to determine which alternative was associated with the smallest risk to public health and the environment. There is risk associated with any course of action. Disposal carries risks associated with manipulation of the agents and failures in the disposal or incineration process (Figure 7-2). Continued storage risks inadvertent release of an agent due to failure of the storage vessel (Figure 7-3). The risks associated with disposal were judged to be smaller in the long run than the risks associated with continued storage. As a result of this process, on-site incineration or chemical inactivation were recommended as the lowest risk options.

However, the analysis conducted concluded that emergency planning in communities potentially at risk was inadequate and that improvement was needed. In addition, it was determined that there was much confusion and misunderstanding about these processes and serious deficiencies in the strategies used to communicate risk information to the public. As a result of these findings, recommendations were made to continue plans for eventual disposal. Again, at each step of this process the "not in

Figure 7-3. Chemical weapons, prior to their destruction, stockpiled in Iraq. (Source: United Nations/DPI/158434).

my backyard'' advocates will become vocal and further delays are almost certain to occur. The educational programs required are likely to focus attention on the presence of the agents and the risks associated with their presence and disposal. As a result, further delays could occur, even though this may pose greater overall risks, since the risk of accidental release of stored agents increases as the containers age. There is no easy solution to this complex problem. Clearly, more effort and funding are required to find a solution.

Terrorist Use of Chemical Weapons

Although use of chemical weapons against civilian populations in the Iran–Iraq War is well documented,[14] more recent use of nerve gas in two separate terrorist attacks in Japan reawakened public concerns.[15-17] Two separate attacks are alleged to have been planned and executed by the Aum Shinrikyo sect. Since these attacks occurred in densely populated areas where excellent medical care and high media exposure were instantly available, they are particularly well documented and publicized.

The first attack occurred in June 1994 in Matsumoto (population 200,000) in the central highlands of Honshu. The initial ambulance call was made by a man whose wife had become unconscious and whose dog had died outside their home. Within the next three hours, three people were found dead, four died on their way to hospitals, 56 were admitted to hospitals, and 253 consulted physicians. Ten days later, police and governmental officials announced that they had found traces of sarin, which was identified by gas chromatography and mass spectrometry in samples taken from a pond.

The second attack occurred in the Tokyo subway system in March 1995. There were several deaths, and approximately 5,000 people were injured. Many of those hospitalized—39 at one hospital alone—were emergency medical technicians who were exposed to sarin while conducting rescue operations.

These two attacks received extensive media coverage. Details of the clinical presentation, treatment, and long-term observation of exposed victims have been published in prominent medical journals. A number of points have emerged from this experience.

The first attack occurred at night with release of sarin in an open environment, with relatively calm winds (0.5 m/s). There have been speculations that this attack was conducted as an exercise to prepare for the subsequent attack. Even under these conditions, which were suboptimal for maximizing casualties from sarin, there were many casualties. The second attack, conducted in the Tokyo subway system, targeted highly vulnerable civilians and was seemingly designed to maximize casualties. Subways in Tokyo are densely populated, particularly during rush hour, and air exchange rates are low, confining the gas to a small volume with many people.

In the wake of these attacks, questions were again raised concerning control of chemical weapons. Since many of the raw materials are common reagents, such as pyrophosphate and phosphoric acid, complete control of all of them is neither practical nor desirable in a free economy. However, an editorial in *Nature* noted that "the treaty on chemical weapons signed last year is weaker than it should be because of the reluctance of legitimate chemical manufacturers to volunteer full disclosure of their use of raw materials."[15] Predictably, there were also suggestions that monitoring systems should be considered to detect the release of chemical agents so that corrective action might be taken sooner.

Proliferation and Control of Chemical Weapons

Chemical weapons are inexpensive to manufacture and therefore may be attractive to certain governments or terrorist groups. Since many of the production facilities needed to make chemical weapons are similar to those required for the synthesis of other chemicals, such as insecticides and other agrochemicals, chemical weapons can be produced much more easily than nuclear weapons. Nuclear weapons require massive reprocessing plants, other highly technical facilities, and sophisticated components. Chemical weapons production facilities are far less complex, making it difficult to monitor conventions that regulate production and proliferation of nuclear weapons.

In spite of these problems, there are reasons to be optimistic that the impetus to control and dispose of chemical weapons will proceed toward elimination. Chemical companies have shown unusual restraint, and on occasion, have refused to provide precursor chemicals required to produce chemical warfare agents to military contractors, in spite of strong profit motivations. International monitoring of trade in precursor chemicals adds to the continued assurance that proliferation will not occur. It is necessary that there be continued development and fostering of the will, coupled with the necessary resources and treaties, to control these agents.

Nations throughout the world have recognized that existing treaties do not provide adequate protection or safeguards to prevent proliferation of chemical weapons. Consequently, the United States and 129 other countries signed a new treaty in January 1993. This treaty, the Chemical Weapons Convention (CWC), bans production, possession, or transfer of chemical weapons and requires destruction of existing weapons within 10 years of going into effect. An intrusive inspection system that requires chemical companies to open plants to inspection is included. The treaty will go into effect six months after ratification by 65 nations. In anticipation of ratification by the United States, a step that is predicted to lead to rapid ratification by many other nations, President Clinton sent the treaty to the Senate in November 1993 for advice, consent, and ratification. In May 1994, implementing legislation, required to make provisions of the treaty binding on U.S. companies and citizens, was sent to Congress. Additional steps toward ratification have been made by reorganizations within the Bureau of Export Administration's Office of Chemical and Biological Controls and Treaty Compliance. The 1996 fiscal year budget submitted by President Clinton contains a request for $3.5 million to fund 30 new staff positions required for implementation and compliance. As of November 3, 1995, 159 states had signed the new convention and 42 had deposited instruments of ratification with the Secretary General of the United Nations.

Information on Chemical Weapons

The rapid proliferation of the World Wide Web and internet connectivity allows users to gain access to current information about chemical weapons and treaties banning their use.

The following sources of electronic information can be consulted: The Organization for the Prohibition of Chemical Weapons provides data on the treaty and steps to ratification (http://www.opcw.nl/guide.html). Other sites provide information about the agents themselves (http://www.opcw.nl/chemhaz/cwagents.htm). Search tools, such as Lycos (http://www.lycos.cmu.edu) and Yahoo (http://www/yahoo.com), will also yield much information.

Chemical and Engineering News publishes information about chemical warfare agents and treaties.

Medical Professionals

Medical professionals occupy unique positions in the realm of chemical warfare agents. The principles and mechanisms of action that underlie the development of these compounds are all based on medical knowledge. Unlike nuclear weapons, developed by physicists and theoreticians, we, as health professionals, have developed these agents. Therefore, we have a special responsibility to continue efforts that will lead to their elimination. The fundamental principle of medicine—first, do no harm—must guide our actions. We must be aware of what may often be a fine line that separates legitimate research, particularly in the realm of neurotransmitters and drugs that affect neurotransmitter actions, from research that is oriented toward the development of a chemical-weapons capacity. We must also distinguish between drug development and development of chemical warfare capacities. Funding for legitimate research in these areas should be consolidated in the budgets of the National Institutes of Health, the National Science Foundation, and other agencies that fund peer-reviewed research.

Health professionals must continue their efforts to implement the Chemical Weapons Convention and to help guarantee that there is no offensive research on chemical weapons; that there is no production, testing, stockpiling, transfer or use of these weapons; and that existing stockpiles are destroyed promptly and with appropriate safeguards.

REFERENCES

1. Lockwood, A.H. Nerve gases. *PSR Quarterly* 1:69–76, 1991.
2. Rengstroff, R.H. Accidental exposure to sarin: vision effects. *Arch. Tox.* 56:201–203, 1985.
3. Duffy, F.H. and Burchfiel, J.L. Long-term effects of the organophosphate sarin on EEGs in monkey and humans. *Neurotoxicology* 1:667–690, 1980.
4. Abou-Donia, M.B. Organophosphate ester-induced delayed neurotoxicity. *Annual Rev. Pharmacol. Toxicol.* 21:511–548, 1981.
5. McLeod, C.G., Jr. Pathology of nerve agents: Perspectives on medical management. *Fund. Appl. Toxicol.* 5:S10–S16, 1985.
6. Fullerton, C.S. and Ursano, R.J. Behavioral and psychological responses to chemical and biological warfare. *Military Med.* 155:54–59, 1990.
7. Carnes, S.A. and Watson, A.P. Disposing of the U.S. chemical weapons stockpile: an approaching reality. *JAMA* 262:653–659, 1989.
8. Hu H., Fine, J., Epstein, P., et al. Tear gas: Harassing agent or toxic chemical weapon? *JAMA* 262:660–663, 1989.
9. Chartrand, S. I was sure it was chemical weapons and that I was dead. *New York Times,* January 19, 1991, A7.
10. Dunn, M.A. and Sidell, F.R. Progress in medical defense against nerve agents. *JAMA* 262:649–652, 1989.
11. Sidell, F.R. Soman and sarin: Clinical manifestations and treatment of accidental poisoning by organophosphates. *Clin. Tox.* 7:1–17, 1974.

12. National Research Council. *Pesticides in the diets of infants and children.* Washington, D.C.: National Academy Press, 1993.

13. National Research Council. *Environmental Neurotoxicology.* Washington, D.C.: National Academy Press, 1992.

14. Hu, H., Cook-Deegan, R. and Shukri, A. The use of chemical weapons: Conducting an investigation using survey epidemiology. *JAMA* 262:640–643, 1989.

15. Murder on the metro. *Nature* 374:392, 1995.

16. Morita, H., Yanagisawa, N., Nakajima, T., et. al. Sarin poisoning in Matsumoto, Japan. *Lancet* 346:290–293, 1995.

17. Suzuki, T., Morita, H. and Ono, K. Sarin poisoning in Tokyo subway (letter). *Lancet* 345: 980, 1995.

8

The Public Health Effects
of Biological Weapons

ROBERT GOULD and NANCY D. CONNELL

Biological weapons, which are agents of disease designed for use against humans, animals, and plants, are antithetical to public health. The World Health Organization (WHO) defines biological weapons as those "that depend for their effects on multiplication within the target organism, and are intended for use in war to cause disease or death in man, animals, or plants." In addition, weapons that involve toxins produced by biological organisms outside the target, such as botulinum toxin which causes botulism, can also be considered biological weapons. However, if toxins are synthetically made, they may be categorized as chemical weapons.

Biological weapons span the range of potential infection-causing organisms, promoted through various vectors and modes of dispersal. Table 8-1 provides illustrative examples of these organisms and the diseases they cause.[1,2]

Possession of biological weapons is strictly prohibited by the Biological Weapons Convention (BWC) of 1972, the first treaty to outlaw an entire class of weapon. As of August, 1994, 134 nations had become States Parties to the Convention. Article I of the convention requires signatory nations "never to develop, produce, stockpile or otherwise acquire or retain . . . microbial or other biological agents, or toxins whatever their methods of production, of types or in quantities that have no justification for prophylactic, protective, or other peaceful purposes."

The treaty is interpreted to allow biological weapons research and possession in any quantities deemed necessary for defensive research. Biomedical defense primarily takes the forms of vaccination and prophylactic drugs, which are useful against attack only if the exact agent to be used is identified well in advance. With the advent of recombinant DNA technology and hybrid strain construction, these forms of defense become a virtual impossibility. Antibiotics, antivirals, and other treatments rely on rapid detection devices. Purely defensive methodologies—"material" defenses against biological weapons (that is, respirator filters and clothing)—may be necessary

Table 8-1. Illustrative biological weapons

Disease/ Organism	Clinical Features of Disease	Outcome
Brucellosis/ *Brucella* sp.	Febrile illness; 5% recurrence from relapse or reinfection	Complications (skeletal, CNS, genitourinary, cardiovascular) 1–30%
Dengue/Arbovirus (Flavivirus)	Rash, hemorrhagic fever; rare myocarditis and encephalopathy	Case-fatality rate 1–3% with good medical care; untreated as high as 50%
Epidemic Typhus/ *Rickettsia prowazekii*	Unremitting fever; vasculitis most marked in skin, heart, CNS, skeletal muscle, kidneys	Variable case-fatality, as high as 40% under adverse conditions
Plague/*Yersinia pestis*	Bubonic plague with fever, buboes, bacteremia, vasculitis/purpura ("Black Death"); highly contagious pneumonic plague	Overall untreated plague case-fatality 50% (pneumonic 100%); 5% overall with early and appropriate antibiotics
Rift Valley Fever/ Arbovirus	Retinitis, encephalitis, fulminant hemorrhagic hepatitis (up to 1%)	Most with fulminant hepatitis die
Rocky Mountain Spotted Fever/ *Rickettsia rickettsii*	Rash, fever, vasculitis, renal failure in severe disease	Case-fatality rate 3–7% with early and appropriate antibiotics; otherwise 20%
Salmonellosis/ *Salmonella* sp.	Gastroenteritis, bacteremia; enteric (typhoid) fever with high rate of complications	Case-fatality rate for enteric fever 12–16% before antibiotics; now probably less than 1%
Tularemia/ *Francisella tularensis*	Febrile illness; some with pleuropulmonary complications	Case-fatality rate 5–15% before antibiotics, now 1–3%
Venezuelan Equine Encephalitis/ Arbovirus (Alphavirus)	Febrile illness, 4% with severe encephalitis, most often in children	Case-fatality rate less than 1%; 20% with encephalitis
Yellow Fever/ Arbovirus (Flavivirus)	Damage to liver, kidney, heart, GI tract ("black vomit"), CNS	Overall case-fatality rate 5%; 20–50% with patients developing jaundice

components in the event of biological weapons use; these constitute a defensive capability within the guidelines of the BWC.

The development and use of biological weapons to target large populations has become technologically feasible. The successful strategic use of biological weapons is, however, limited by a number of difficulties, such as the successful delivery of agents while sparing one's own soldiers or civilians, or, worse, the possibility of unleashing a global epidemic. Nevertheless, for some powers biological weapons may provide a potential key ingredient in the type of warfare euphemistically called "low-intensity conflict (LIC)" (see Chapter 16). Such warfare, spanning economic destabilization through "unconventional" warfare, has increased during the past two decades. Although use of biological weapons in such contexts has never been unequivocally documented, reports alleging such use have provoked serious international concern.

History of Biological Warfare

The history of the ancient world yields examples of biological warfare. Diseased corpses of humans and animals were used by Roman armies to contaminate sources of drinking water for military purposes. In the fourteenth century, Genoans defending the Black Sea port city of Caffa from a Tartar siege prevailed until the Tartars catapulted corpses infected with bubonic plague. The city fell after the epidemic of plague spread among the defenders, and the few escaping Genoans carried the Black Death westward through Europe. In the 1750s, during the French and Indian War, the British delivered blankets with scales from smallpox victims to American Indians, causing a case-fatality rate as high as 30 percent.[3]

However, it was in the twentieth century that biological warfare took on its most life-threatening manifestation. Although World War I evokes visions of the horrors of mass gas attacks, there were also allegations of German use of biological weapons, as made by George Merck in a report to the U.S. War Secretary in 1946. According to Merck, there was firm evidence that cattle and horses departing U.S. ports for overseas allies were inoculated by German agents in 1915 with disease-producing bacteria. The Germans were also implicated by other sources with infecting cattle with anthrax and horses with glanders at Bucharest in 1916. Other reports accuse the Germans of similar actions at the French front in 1917, as well as attempting to spread cholera in Italy.[4]

The international public horror at the effects of the use of chemical weapons during World War I led to the establishment of the Geneva Protocol of 1925. The Protocol forbade the "first-use" of chemical weapons and "bacteriological methods of warfare." However, the Protocol placed no limits on the development, production, testing, or stockpiling of either chemical or biological weapons. By 1986, a total of 108 countries were parties to the agreement, with the United States becoming the last major power to ratify it in 1975.[3,5,6]

The loopholes in the 1925 Geneva Protocol were exploited by the Japanese in the interwar period to establish a viable biological warfare program. By 1939, the Japanese had established Pingfan, a biological warfare research and production center near Harbin in northeastern China. Pingfan produced a number of biological weapons including the agents of anthrax, typhoid, cholera, and bacillary dysentery.

The Japanese germ warfare unit Detachment 731, commanded by Lieutenant-General Shiro Ishii, conducted ghastly experiments that killed at least 3,000 Chinese, Soviet, Korean, American, British, and Australian prisoners of war. Some of the experiments included tying prisoners to stakes and exposing their buttocks to shrapnel caused by the detonation of remotely activated anthrax and gas gangrene bombs. Other prisoners were infected with cholera and plague so as to monitor the degeneration of their visceral organs, through post-mortem—or sometimes ante-mortem—dissection. Any prisoners who survived the experiments at Pingfan were killed when the germ warfare center was hurriedly destroyed in August 1945 when the Soviet Union entered the war against Japan.[3,7–9]

According to the record of the 1949 Soviet war crimes trial investigating the activities at Pingfan, the Soviets estimated that, at its peak, Pingfan was capable of producing more than 500 pounds of bacteria per day. Detachment 731 and its branches reportedly possessed 4,500 incubators for breeding fleas on rats and mice, allowing the breeding of 500 million plague-carrying fleas a year.[3,7]

During its invasion of China, the Japanese reportedly put their biological warfare experiments to practical "field use." Official archives of China, as well as several other sources, report that at least 11 Chinese cities were attacked by biological weapons through 1944. In one incident, Japanese planes in 1941 reportedly dropped grains of rice and wheat and pieces of cotton and paper infected with plague bacillus over the city of Changteh. Chinese authorities estimate 700 deaths from plague attacks between 1940 and 1944. In addition, the Japanese are accused of poisoning more than 1,000 Manchurian wells with typhoid, cholera, and dysentery.[3–4]

While the Japanese biological warfare program has been well documented, the existence of a parallel Nazi program has never been proven, despite accusations by the Soviet Union that the Germans took deliberate steps to spread typhus among the Soviet population and the Red Army, and testimony from the Nuremberg trials that the Germans conducted biological warfare experiments on prisoners at Buchenwald and other concentration camps.[4–5]

The Allies Plan for Biological Warfare

Citing the potential of Axis biological warfare capabilities, the United States, in cooperation with Great Britain, initiated its own program in 1941. The program, which cost under $60 million and involved about 4,000 workers and scientists, originally focused on the development of botulism and anthrax weapons, with about 28 universities receiving government contracts to do secret research.[10]

During the early 1940s, the British conducted experiments with anthrax on Gruinard Island, off the coast of Scotland, that left this island uninhabitable for 45 years.[9] Winston Churchill, in response to German V-1 bombing raids over London, reportedly considered bombing six German cities, including Berlin, with anthrax bombs in mid-1944. An extensive air raid requiring 40,000 bombs was planned, which would have likely resulted in the deaths of half the population of these cities through inhalation and skin absorption of the organisms. In addition, each city would have likely been rendered uninhabitable for decades.[11–12]

The U.S. Chemical Warfare Service (CWS), with British technical assistance, developed anthrax bombs for such raids, and a bomb plant was constructed in Indiana. The CWS also produced botulism toxin and Brucella cultures in large volume. In 1944, it received $2.5 million to manufacture anthrax and botulinum toxin bombs, permitting the CWS to produce either 275,000 botulinum toxin bombs or 1 million anthrax bombs per month. Although a prototype weapon was built and tested, the deadly bombs were never deployed: U.S. efforts in biological warfare were eclipsed by the nuclear detonations at Hiroshima and Nagasaki.[7,10]

After World War II, the U.S. military harvested the fruits of the Japanese research for its own biological war program, offering Shiro Ishii and thousands of Japanese scientists and researchers immunity from war crimes prosecution and the protection of ongoing secrecy in exchange for information on the experiments. This contrasted with the attitude of the Soviets, who publicized the Japanese experiments while prosecuting those responsible people who were in Soviet custody for war crimes. The U.S. government also suppressed information about the biological warfare experiments performed on American prisoners of war who survived their ordeal at another Japanese facility in Mukden, Manchuria, although these veterans, by the early 1980s, had developed ailments that they attributed to the Japanese experiments.[3,8–9,11,13–14]

The U.S. incorporation of the Japanese biological warfare program in the immediate post-war period was an important factor in the analysis of the 1952 North Korean allegations that captured U.S. bomber pilots had confessed to dropping "germ bombs" during the Korean War. After official U.S. government denials, the Chinese formed a commission of international experts that issued a report that the people of Korea and China had served as targets for bacteriological warfare. The report accused the United States of utilizing a range of vector techniques, including feathers infected with anthrax, and plague- and yellow-fever-infected fleas, lice, mosquitoes, rabbits, and rodents, which were assessed as being "a continuation of methods used by the Japanese army in the Second World War."

The United States denied all charges, calling for a follow-up study to be conducted by the United Nations. However, the Chinese and North Korean governments blocked this from happening. A 1966 assessment of the international commission's report by

Robin Clarke, editor of the *British Science Journal,* described it as "such a curious mixture of blatant propaganda and what appears to be accurate observation that it is difficult to know how much credence should be attached to it."[3,4,7]

The Cold War: U.S. Preparations for Biological War

Ties between the chemical and biological weapons program and the American pharmaceutical industry were firmly in place by the end of World War II and remained so during the post-war years. In 1946 George Merck, who directed the War Research Service, issued a report through the War Department that described the activities at Fort Detrick and urged the U.S. government to retain a strong biowarfare program.[15]

In 1948, the Committee on Biological Warfare was founded at the request of the Research and Development Board of the Secretary of Defense. The Committee's report stated that "the current biological warfare research and development program is not now authorized to meet the requirements necessary to prepare defensive measures against special biological weapons operations."[16] This rationalization and accompanying proposals for detection devices, dissemination, susceptibility, and protection are echoed in today's Pentagon proposals.[17]

Immediately after World War II, the Department of Defense's chemical and biological weapons expenditures, under the auspices of the Chemical Corps, dropped to as low as $16 million. But during the late 1950s, the budget began to rise again. Invoking the threat posed by alleged Soviet advances in biological weaponry, the United States redoubled its efforts to develop a competent biological arsenal, stimulated by the promise of more "humane" weapons, which introduced flexibility into the heavily atomic strategic arsenal. In addition, the Chemical Corps began to disseminate alarming reports of Soviet advances in biological weapons build-up. By 1964, chemical and biological weapons appropriations had increased 10-fold to $158 million.[18] These expenditures supported largely classified research projects and even some human experimentation. During this period, over $700 million was spent to develop biological weapons that included organisms causing plague, Rocky Mountain spotted fever, Rift Valley fever, Q fever, and various forms of encephalomyelitis. Accompanying this surge in financing were policy modifications that abandoned constraints calling for "no first-use" of weapons; the new policies called for the preparedness for use of biological weapons at the discretion of the President. The U.S government initiated the "Operation Blue Skies" public relations campaign to create public support for biological weapons as a "humane" prerogative of warfare.

Fort Detrick, Maryland, opened in a top-secret manner in 1943, was central to U.S. biological warfare capabilities. This facility had control over the procurement, testing, research, and development of all biological weapons and products, including vaccines. Since the end of World War II, personnel at Fort Detrick had used human volunteers to test vaccines, but in the mid-1960s volunteers were tested to determine the virulence of airborne disease. Conscientious-objector volunteers from the Seventh Day Adventist Church reportedly were exposed to organisms causing diseases such as tularemia and Q fever.[7,11,19]

In the early 1950s, the United States also built a factory to manufacture biological weapons at Pine Bluff, Arkansas. After the end of the Korean War, this plant was producing supplies of brucellosis and tularemia organisms, and by the late 1950s researchers had developed pilot plants for the mass production of anthrax and a number of other biological warfare agents. Laboratories were built at Fort Detrick to breed millions of mosquitoes and fleas per month, and by the end of the decade there were stocks of mosquitoes infected with yellow fever, malaria, and dengue; fleas infected with plague; ticks infected with tularemia; and flies infected with cholera, anthrax, and dysentery. In 1956, in order to test the utility of insect vectors, uninfected female mosquitoes were released first into a residential neighborhood of Savannah, Georgia, and then dropped from an aircraft over a Florida bombing range, with the spread of bitten civilians being duly documented by authorities.

During this time, a plan was drawn up to package the mosquitoes with yellow fever in cluster bombs for dropping from aircraft or placing in missile warheads. By 1967, researchers at Fort Detrick had developed a biological warhead for the Sergeant missile that was capable of delivering disease up to 100 miles behind enemy lines.[7,11] Simultaneously, the U.S. Army, through a contractual relationship with the University of Utah, conducted secret experiments at the Dugway Proving Ground, with large-scale field-testing agents that cause tularemia, Rocky Mountain spotted fever, plague, and Q fever.[5]

The CIA operation named MKNAOMI, based at Fort Detrick, involved collaboration with the Army's Special Operations Division (SOD) in the development, testing, and maintenance of biological agents and delivery systems. According to the final report of the 1975 Senate Select Committee to Study Governmental Operations with Respect to Intelligence (the Church Committee), the SOD was interested in assessing "the vulnerability of sensitive installations, such as the Pentagon, air bases, and subway systems, to biological sabotage by the enemy." A 1951 study by the Joint Chiefs of Staff indicated that the Army regarded such tests as providing useful information for offensive purposes, an aim also subscribed to by the CIA.

Consistent with these aims and the 1948 recommendations of a high-level biological warfare committee, the United States conducted 239 top-secret open-air dispersals of simulant organisms, with some of the sites including the Washington National Airport and the subway system of New York City. The 1950 release of large quantities of aerosolized "nonpathogenic" *Serratia marcesans* and *Bacillus subtilis var. niger* by the U.S. Navy into the San Francisco Bay Area led to a number of infections and at least one death.[11,19-22]

These U.S. experiments were contemporaneous with those carried out by the British, who had established a biological warfare research station next to their chemical warfare center at Porton Downs. In the 1950s, the British also aerosolized simulant organisms and conducted a number of exercises in the Caribbean, as well as off the coast of Scotland, allegedly using animals to test lethal agents that cause anthrax, brucellosis, and tularemia. Both the United States and Great Britain attempted to mimic germ warfare attacks by dispersing clouds of zinc cadmium sulfide over populated areas. A 1953 dispersal of this substance by the U.S. Army over Minneapolis included spraying a public elementary school where former students have reported an unusual number of stillbirths and miscarriages.[11,23]

By the end of the 1960s, the U.S. government had built a large infrastructure of laboratories, test facilities, and production plants committed to biological warfare, spread through contractors in approximately 300 universities, research institutes, and corporations. Along with the adoption of eight anti-personnel and five anti-crop agents, at least 10 different biological and toxin weapons were available for military use.[19]

The Biological Weapons Convention (BWC) of 1972

There was considerable domestic and international pressure for biological and chemical disarmament dating from the 1960s as a result of the extensive use of herbicides during the Vietnam War and a number of accidents at military test sites in the United States. In addition, by the late 1960s, most military planners realized that biological weapons have intrinsic limitations that make it difficult to substitute them for conventional weapons. Defensively, their high specificity precludes rapid detection and protection. Offensively, their relatively slow mode of action is impractical for most battlefield situations. There is also the possibility of accidental release and of mutation to a more virulent strain that evades immunity.

The Nixon administration and many Pentagon advisors were well aware of the political liabilities of pursuing a biological weapons program. Proliferation of such weapons of mass destruction could considerably upset the balance of power, with biological weapons posing a threat to U.S. security in view of the ease and low expense with which such weapons could be developed.[19] As a result, the Nixon administration in 1969 unconditionally renounced the development, production, stockpiling, and use of its biological arsenal. The United States announced that it would unilaterally dismantle the biological weapons program, and stockpiled agents were reportedly destroyed, with the exception of a cache of weapons retained by the CIA. However, on the same day that President Nixon renounced biological weapons, National Security Decision Memorandum 35 was issued. Signed by National Security Adviser Henry Kissinger, the memo contained a significant loophole, holding that the Nixon renunciation did ''not preclude research into those offensive aspects of . . . biological agents necessary to determine what defensive measures are required.''[19,24]

In 1972, the Convention on the Prohibition of the Development, Prevention, and Stockpiling of Bacteriological (Biological) and Toxin Weapons and on Their Destruction was negotiated. This so-called Biological Weapons Convention (BWC) prohibits the development or acquisition of biological agents or toxins, as well as weapons carrying them and means of their production, stockpiling, transfer, or delivery, except for "prophylactic, protective, and other peaceful purposes."[25]

After the agreement was signed in 1972 by the United States, the Soviet Union, and Great Britain, all known stockpiles of biological and toxin weapons were reportedly destroyed by the end of the decade. However, by the end of the 1970s, new developments in genetic engineering and greater abilities to mass-produce viruses led to increased military attention.[26,27]

Resurgence of Interest in Biological Weapons

During the 1980s the Reagan administration made a series of allegations about Soviet violations of the 1925 Geneva Protocol and the 1972 Biological Weapons Convention. Major purported violations were that an illegal biological weapons facility exploded in Sverdlovsk in 1979, and that the Soviets or their surrogates used "yellow rain" toxins as weapons in Afghanistan and Southeast Asia in the late 1970s and early 1980s.

Although there was a long dispute between Soviet and U.S. authorities as to whether an anthrax outbreak in Sverdlovsk in 1979 was due to contaminated meat or related to work at a secret biological warfare facility, U.S. allegations were finally supported. A study released in late 1994, conducted by U.S. and Russian scientists and led by Harvard biologist Matthew Meselson, concluded that the anthrax outbreak was caused by a leak from the Sverdlovsk facility.[28]

Throughout the early 1980s, the United States asserted that "yellow rain," consisting of trichothecene toxin derived from fungi, was dropped on civilians in Afghanistan, Cambodia, and Laos. However, subsequent expert examination of the "evidence" cited by U.S. authorities led to the conclusion that yellow rain was nothing more than showers of bee feces, not uncommon in the region.[29]

The U.S. government successfully capitalized on its charges, as well as unproved allegations of aggressive biological weapons programs in other countries, to initiate intensive efforts to conduct "defensive" research within the loophole provided by the Convention. The budget for the U.S. Army Biological Defense Research Program (BDRP) grew by 400 percent from 1980 to 1988, with $558 million in funding during this time allocated to 132 colleges, universities, Army bases, agencies, and private businesses nationwide.[30]

The Pentagon also spurred its activities by invoking the threat of biotechnology, including accusations that the Soviets were developing novel biological weapons through recombinant DNA techniques. As a May 1986 report to Congress asserting that biotechnology made biological warfare easier, cheaper, and more effective claimed, biological warfare is not new, but it has a new face. By 1987, the Defense

Department was spending about \$119 million annually for all its uses of biotechnology, a sum second only to the National Institutes of Health.[26]

Recent Biological Weapons Research:
Fort Detrick and Dugway Proving Ground

The stated goals of the BDRP are the production of defenses against biological weapons and basic research on threat agents for peaceful purposes, in accordance with the guidelines of the 1972 BWC. The program is headquartered at Fort Detrick, where its lead facility is the U.S. Army Medical Research Institute of Infectious Diseases (USAMRIID). In turn, USAMRIID is part of the larger U.S. Army Medical Research and Development Command.[31]

Dugway Proving Grounds in Utah is the Department of Defense's premiere defensive research center and is now a multimillion dollar state-of-the-art research facility, where the U.S. Army has continued its open-air testing program with simulants. The Army announced in May 1991 that it would test simulants outdoors and pathogens indoors at Dugway, to evaluate the performance of biological detector systems, with much of the work being done without a safety monitoring system.

The Army's plans to upgrade its Dugway facilities by building a high-level containment facility to conduct aerosolization experiments have been vigorously challenged by a number of scientists and citizen groups, who have been concerned about the potential danger posed by accidental release of highly lethal organisms, as well as the implications for offensive biological warfare capabilities.[32,33]

Concerns about safety at Dugway also need to be viewed in light of findings uncovered by a review of biological warfare programs performed by a U.S. Senate subcommittee in 1989. These findings included: violations of federal and state hazardous waste management regulations in 89 different areas of the Aberdeen Proving Ground, a major biological warfare testing site; the lack of formal risk assessment and safeguard management procedures for the BDRP; and safety problems uncovered at USAMRIID, which included the loss of about 2,500 milliliters of the highly infectious Chikungunya virus.[19]

Efforts to obtain comprehensive listings of the projects funded by the BDRP have been met with significant resistance. The persistence of a number of researchers has yielded some insight into the nature of the BDRP's research. In particular, Susan Wright, Charles Piller, Keith Yamamoto, and the Center for Public Integrity's Seth Shulman have been able to piece together a picture of the BDRP, but not without great difficulty and perseverance. The reader is referred to these excellent analyses for details.[3,6,34] Many of the BDRP projects focus on exotic agents, with little attention paid to medical defense against known threats. Some projects are directly offensive in nature. There is an obvious lack of peer review in the grant-awarding system within the BDRP, and an analysis of publication histories indicates low rates of productivity, with publication in obscure journals. All three reports conclude that the workings of the BDRP are inconsistent with its stated goals, namely, to maintain an accountable program of first-tier scientists conducting open research on defensive projects, within the guidelines of the 1972 BWC.[3,34,35]

In addition, while individual BDRP projects may not appear offensive, when examined in the aggregate they foreshadow a vigorous offensive weapons capability.[3] Most disturbing are the number of research programs devoted to increasing the lethality of organisms, such as anthrax, which are hardy enough for dispersal through bombs and other munitions.[9] Because of the offensive potential of the BDRP work, more than 2,000 biomedical researchers had by late 1993 signed a pledge circulated by the Council for Responsible Genetics against the military use of biological research. The signers included 29 Nobel Laureates and 180 members of the National Academy of Sciences.

By the end of the 1980s biological warfare research programs had expanded globally in tandem with U.S. activities. In 1987 and 1988, the U.S. Disarmament Agency registered biological defense activities in Bulgaria, Canada, China, Czechoslovakia, France, Germany, the Netherlands, Norway, Poland, Sweden, the United Kingdom, the Soviet Union, and the United States.[26] A number of military projects using genetic engineering were located in countries such as Britain, Israel, and Sweden.[19]

International Proliferation

Throughout the 1980s, the U.S. government voiced concerns about global proliferation of both chemical and biological weapons—the ''poor man's nuclear weapons''—focusing on alleged threats from terrorists and various Middle Eastern nations. A study issued by a panel of the House Armed Services Committee in 1993 asserted that 11 nations either possess or could develop biological weapons.[36] A separate inquiry conducted by the British newspaper the *Independent* determined that the likely countries include: China, Cuba, India, Iran, Iraq, Israel, Libya, North Korea, Russia, and Syria.[37] Many of these countries are believed to possess ballistic missiles, such as SCUDs, that would be capable of delivering biological warheads over long range.[38]

In September 1992, Russia, announcing that it had violated the 1972 BWC by producing biological weapons until March 1992, promised that American and British specialists could conduct visits to any nonmilitary biological site at any time in order to remove ambiguities; the permission involved unrestricted access, sampling, interviews, and audio- and videotaping. On-site visits were conducted through 1993 to investigate allegations regarding work on tularemia and bubonic plague, including an antibiotic-resistant strain of bacteria packed into weapons shells that could produce a ''super-plague'' capable of wiping out tens of thousands of people within a week. Visits to various facilities in St. Peterburg, Berdsk, and Pokrov were inconclusive.[39–41] However, unconfirmed reports continue to surface of secret work by the Russian military on biological weapons. Based on evidence three Russian defectors gave to British and U.S. intelligence services, *The London Sunday Times* reported in March 1994 that work on a superplague is being carried out in defiance of President Yeltsin, who has supposedly been misled into believing the research has been halted. The plague that Russia is allegedly developing is reportedly so powerful that just 440 pounds sprayed from planes or using airburst bombs could kill 500,000 people. Secret work allegedly persists in factories that U.S. and British inspectors never visited, with a new facility reportedly being built at Lakhta near St. Petersburg.[42]

Prior to the Gulf War, Iraqi scientists ordered and received lab samples of biological warfare agents from the U.S. Centers for Disease Control, apparently including anthrax and at least four viruses. UN inspections soon after the Gulf War revealed that Iraq was conducting research that would lead to a biological weapons capability, with the Salman Park laboratory near Baghdad having the capacity to produce a little more that 200 quarts of anthrax each week, an amount capable of contaminating more than 600 square miles.[43] In 1995, Iraq admitted to making and storing nearly 5,300 gallons of *Clostridium botulinum,* estimated to have the potential to kill millions of people. In addition, Iraq admitted creating and storing about 158 gallons of concentrated anthrax bacteria, an amount estimated by UN officials to be enough to be packed inside 40 to 50 bombs that could each kill tens of thousands of people.[44] According to UN investigators, the Iraqi program included work on viral agents that cause hemorrhagic conjunctivitis and chronic diarrhea, as well as novel ways to deliver agents over wide areas, including spraying agents from aircraft.[45] According to a report issued by the Russian Foreign Intelligence Service, North Korea is studying the development of anthrax, cholera, bubonic plague, and smallpox, with tests being carried out on offshore islands. Egypt also allegedly has research centers focusing on "pathogenic microorganisms and dangerous disease-bearing agents."[46]

Possible Biological Warfare Scenarios

The degree of international proliferation of biological weapons has raised questions as to how they might be used, and with what effects, in warfare. The 1970 WHO report on CBW made a number of quantitative estimates of the primary effects of possible small-scale airborne attacks on cities containing from 500,000 to 5 million people in industrially developed and developing countries. Some of the conclusions were:

- If a biological agent such as anthrax were used, an attack on a city by even a single bomber disseminating 50 kg of the dried agent in a suitable aerosol form would affect an area far in excess of 20 square kilometers, with tens to hundreds of thousands of deaths.
- Limited sabotage of a communal water supply with the typhoid fever bacillus or

a stable botulinum toxin could cause considerable disruption and deaths in a large city, affecting tens of thousands of people.

- Sabotage-induced or open attacks, causing the secondary spread of epidemics of yellow fever, pneumonic plague, smallpox, or influenza, might under certain conditions ultimately result in many million ill and dead people.
- With technologically advanced weapons and a larger scale of attack, the magnitude of destructiveness from the use of biological weapons would be considerably increased.[1]

Low-Intensity Conflict

While the preceding estimates have relied on theoretical models of biological warfare, other possible scenarios derive from the recent historical practice of "low-intensity conflict (LIC)," military strategies that include counterinsurgency or the economic and political destabilization of governments alleged to be inimicable to the dominant political order.

Over the years, there have been a number of allegations of possible covert use of organisms as antipersonnel and anti-crop agents as an adjunct to the practice of LIC. According to *New York Times* journalist Seymour Hersh, the United States has conducted anti-crop research at Fort Detrick since the early 1940s, with renewed emphasis during the 1960s, on various forms of bacteriological, viral, and fungal diseases, with special attention given to rice blast and stem rust.[7] In 1951, the first anti-crop bombs were placed in production for the U.S. Air Force. As reported by the *Washington Post*, CIA documents released in 1977 disclosed that the CIA maintained a clandestine "anti-crop warfare" research program targeted during the 1960s at a number of countries throughout the world.[11,47]

The U.S. Army directly advised the CIA on using biological weapons in covert operations. Scientists from the Army's Special Operations Division (SOD), based at Fort Detrick, prepared reports for the CIA listing pathogens endemic in various parts of the world. The CIA also studied using biological weapons against plants, with a 1962 memo noting that the agency had developed "three methods and systems for carrying out a covert attack against crops and causing severe crop loss."[19]

There has been much evidence, albeit incompletely confirmed, relating to possible U.S. covert biological warfare against Cuba, including allegations of dispersal of the agent that in 1971 caused the first serious outbreak of swine flu in the Western Hemisphere, leading to the slaughter of 500,000 pigs to prevent a more far-reaching epidemic.[3,48] This represented a devastating blow to the economy of Cuba, which had plowed surpluses from its sugar industry into a promising program of animal husbandry to become more economically self-sufficient in the face of intense economic and political pressure from the United States. A decade later, the Cubans accused the United States of conducting biological warfare against the Cubans in the wake of a widespread epidemic of dengue-2 fever that swept the island. Over 300,000 cases were reported between May and October 1981, with 158 deaths, 101 of which were of children under 15 years.[49] The charges against the United States certainly need to be seriously considered given the enmity of the United States against the accusers, as well as the record of advanced U.S. research on dengue fever and its transmission by mosquitoes.[50,51] However, deniability of the charges by the United States remains plausible, given the fact that diseases such as dengue are endemic in the Caribbean and Central American region.[50,51]

A more compelling case for biological warfare—as part of counterinsurgency strategy—centers around the example of the outbreak of anthrax in Southern Rhodesia (now Zimbabwe) in the late 1970s, toward the end of its civil war. This largest recorded outbreak of anthrax among humans, and possibly the largest among animals, causing over 10,000 human cases and 182 human deaths, was reviewed by Dr. Meryl Nass in articles that attempted to differentiate between a natural outbreak and possible biological warfare. Supported by testimony of veterans of the white government's counterinsurgency campaign, Nass postulated a likely scenario of the Rhodesian military's having introduced anthrax spores into the guerrilla zones, possibly by airdropping. This would have exposed cattle to anthrax through ingestion and/or inhalation, with human acquisition of the disease occurring through the ingestion of meat or meat products. The impoverishment of the affected rural populations that was the net result of the epidemic fit in with the counterinsurgency tasks of the white minority government, which included escalating the military conflict and limiting food supplies to the black population, while blaming guerrillas infiltrating from Mozambique in the process.[52–54]

Biological War and Public Health Effects: Summary and Future Prospects

The preceding examples lend cogency to the 1970 conclusions of the WHO regarding the public health effects of biological (and chemical) warfare agents:

- Biological weapons pose a special threat to civilians both because of the often indiscriminate nature of such weapons and because the high concentrations in which they would be used in military operations could lead to significant unintended involvement of the civilian population within the target area and for considerable distances downwind.
- The large-scale or, with some agents, even limited use of biological weapons could cause illness to a degree that would overwhelm existing health care resources and facilities.
- Large-scale use of biological weapons could also cause lasting changes of an unpredictable nature in the environment.

- Although advanced weapons systems would be required for the employment of biological agents on a militarily significant scale against large civilian targets, isolated and sabotage attacks not requiring highly sophisticated weapons systems could be effective against such targets in certain circumstances with some of these agents.[1]
- Use of biological weapons can cause long-term health effects such as chronic illness; delayed effects including mutagenesis, teratogenesis, and carcinogenesis from viral infections; creation of new foci of infective disease; and effects mediated by ecological change. In addition, the use of anti-plant agents could also produce new foci of disease by creating conditions favoring the establishment of new vectors or reservoirs of disease infective to humans. The use of anti-crop agents or other biological warfare agents could result in a major reduction in the quality or quantity of the food supply, with significant long-term adverse impact on human health.[1]

The WHO concluded that any nation undertaking elaborate measures to defend against specific agents would be engaging in an essentially large and wasteful effort. In addition, taking such measures would likely add credibility to projected fears of annihilation in other countries. The consequent reciprocal fears between nations might lead to a proliferation of biological weapons that could result in a vastly increased danger of deliberate or accidental release of biological weapons.

Although WHO believes that developing certain relatively low-cost detection, diagnostic, and decontamination capabilities could be of value in providing a deterrence to terrorist attacks and potentially reducing casualties from a small-scale attack, major protection from a determined attack could not be guaranteed. Ultimately, if biological research on such items remains organized within a military paradigm, the research could lead to the development of more destructive agents. Thus, WHO concludes that the best interests of humankind would be served by the rapid implementation of steps that would ensure the outlawing of the development and use of biological weapons.[1]

The WHO conclusions serve as a sobering reminder of the weaknesses of a BWC that has permitted a number of nations, including the United States, to pursue the illusory goal of competent defense against the many possible warfare agents. According to a recent report issued by the Center for Public Integrity, the U.S. military has spent over $1 billion since World War II in an unsuccessful effort to defend against potential biological warfare threats. In the 1991 Gulf War, the Army failed to provide adequate vaccination for troops against potential biological threats such as anthrax.[55,56]

According to a U.S. Government Accounting Office (GAO) Report from 1993, numerous U.S. and coalition troops would have died if Iraq had used biological weapons during the Gulf War. Before the war began in January 1991, troops were given anthrax vaccine, which after three doses over a month is effective only if the disease is contracted through the skin, but of no value if spores are inhaled. Troops had also been given kits designed to manually detect anthrax and botulism, meant to be helpful in diagnosing and treating troops following an Iraqi germ attack. However, postwar analysis conducted by the military concluded that "there could have been enormous fatalities and the Army's medical treatment system could have been overtaxed" if such an attack had occurred.[57]

The "close call" in the Gulf War, occurring under relatively controlled and perhaps optimal conditions of warfare, serves to underscore the potential devastation of biological war taking place within a world progressively armed to the teeth with lethal agents of all sorts. Unfortunately, while the U.S. government has moved to strengthen the biological weapons regime through steps such as engaging the Russians in a mutually verifiable inspection process, it has maintained its own vigorous "defense" programs and ultimately relied on its own superior arsenal of weapons of mass destruction to impose its concept of global stability.

For example, in December 1993, the Clinton administration launched a new counterproliferation program against what it sees as the increasing danger of weapons of mass destruction—nuclear, chemical, and biological—in the hands of terrorists or nations such as North Korea and Iraq. Counterproliferation calls for new weapons and equipment for U.S. and allied troops to use when nonproliferation efforts fail. The Pentagon has proposed for development by the end of the decade weapons that can destroy underground command bunkers, sensors that can detect the presence of nerve gas, new ways to deploy aircraft, and interceptors that can knock down enemy missiles.

The Department of Defense budgeted about $400 million for the counterproliferation initiative for fiscal 1995. Critics of the program believe the program represents a diversion from important diplomatic initiatives, such as the renewal of the Nuclear Non-Proliferation Treaty, or the strengthening of the biological and chemical weapons regimes, while expanding the role of nuclear weapons in antiproliferation efforts.[58–60] In addition, if measured by the history of weapons proliferation and counterproliferation in this century, the new U.S. doctrine will most likely open a new era of instability, with various nations attempting to counter U.S. military hegemony by redoubling their own weapons programs. What is needed is a bolstering of all disarmament regimes, including the BWC, by steps that center on building a global stake in the process.

As science historian Susan Wright has argued, the BWC should be strengthened by formulating a strict interpretation of the treaty while initiating steps toward oversight and confidence-building verification. Certain "defensive" activities should be prohibited, such as the creation of novel pathogens or toxins in volumes or concentrations greater than those used for public health purposes, and the open-air release of pathogens and toxins. In addition, because biochemical substances other than toxins have provoked military interest, prohibition of the use of such agents needs to be strictly incorporated into the BWC.[26]

A new approach toward adjudicating global conflict, particularly in areas of persistent tension, could bolster the BWC, which as of December 31, 1987, had only been ratified by 110 nations, and signed but not yet ratified by an additional 25 nations[61]; as of 1991, 10 nations in or near the Middle East were not parties to the BWC.[26]

Ultimately, the successful banning of biological weapons must flow from new strategies of dealing with international conflict that recognize the central importance of redressing the political and economic inequities that lead nations to resort to militarization and armed conflict in the first place. As such, the United States and other wealthy members of the developed ''North'' need to provide a more visionary leadership that demonstrates, by example, the counterproductiveness and futility of basing security on the possession of military power in general, and weapons of mass destruction in particular.

REFERENCES

1. World Health Organization. *Health aspects of chemical and biological weapons: Report of a WHO group of consultants.* Geneva, Switzerland: World Health Organization, 1970.
2. Mandell, G.D., Douglas, R.G. Jr. and Bennett, J.E. (eds.) *Principles and practice of infectious diseases,* 3rd ed. New York: Churchill Livingstone, 1990.
3. Piller, C. and Yamamoto, K.R. *Gene wars: Military control over the new genetic technologies.* New York: Beech Tree Books, 1988.
4. Cookson, J. and Nottingham, J. *A survey of chemical and biological warfare.* New York: Monthly Review Press, 1969.
5. Sidel, V.W. Biological weapons research and physicians: historical and ethical analysis. *PSR Quarterly* 1:31–42, 1991.
6. Wright, S. (ed.) *Preventing a biological arms race.* Cambridge, Mass.: MIT Press, 1990.
7. Hersh, S.M. *Chemical and biological warfare: America's hidden arsenal.* Indianapolis: The Bobbs-Merrill Company, 1968.
8. Williams, P. and Wallace, D. *Unit 731: Japan's secret biological warfare in World War II.* New York: The Free Press, 1989.
9. Nass, M. The labyrinth of biological defense. *PSR Quarterly* 1:24–30, 1991.
10. Bernstein, B.J. Origins of the U.S. biological warfare program. In: Wright, S. *Preventing a biological arms race, op. cit.,* pp. 9–25.
11. Harris, R. and Paxman, J. *A higher form of killing.* New York: Hill and Wang, 1982.
12. Nakaso, D. Historian says Churchill weighed biological warfare. *San Jose Mercury News.* January 6, 1987.
13. Epstein, A. Japanese experiments on POWs alleged. U.S. made hasty decision not to prosecute, ex-MacArthur aide says. *San Jose Mercury News.* Dec. 7, 1985.
14. Furgurson, E.B. Germ warfare victims. Americans seek justice for WWII suffering. *San Jose Mercury News.* February 7, 1989.
15. Merck, G.W. Special Consultant for Biological Warfare. Report to the Secretary of War in Senate Hearings, Biological Testing, Jan 3, 1946.
16. Baldwin, I.L. Chairman, Committee on Biological Warfare, ''Report on Special BW Operations''. Memorandum of the Research and Development Board of the National Military Establishment, Washington, D.C., Oct. 5, 1948.
17. U.S. General Accounting Office. Report to the Chairman, Committee on Governmental Affairs, U.S. Senate: Chemical and Biological Defense: U.S. Forces Are Not Adequately Equipped to Detect All Threats. January 1993.

18. Stockholm International Peace Research Institute. *The problem of chemical and biological warfare,* Vol. II. *CB Weapons Today.* Oxford: Oxford University Press, 1973.

19. Wright, S. Evolution of biological warfare policy, 1945–1990. In: Wright, S. *Preventing a biological arms race, op. cit.,* pp. 26–68.

20. Cole, L.A. *Clouds of secrecy: The army's germ warfare tests over populated areas.* Totowa, New Jersey: Rowman and Littlefield, 1988.

21. Office, Chief of Legislative Liaison, Department of the Army. Information for Members of Congress: U.S. Army in the U.S. Biological Warfare Program. Washington, D.C.: Office of the Secretary of the Army, March 8, 1977.

22. Trial Transcript, Mabel Nevin et al., Plaintiffs, vs United States of America, Defendant, before Judge Samuel Conti, United States District Court, Northern District of California, No. C-78-1713 SC, March 16–31, 1981.

23. Minneapolis called toxic test site in '53. *The New York Times.* June 11, 1994.

24. Select Committee to Study Government Operations with Respect to Intelligence Activities. Unauthorized storage of toxic agents. Hearings, U.S. Senate, 94th Congress, 1st session. Washington, D.C.: U.S. Government Printing Office, 1975.

25. Text of the 1972 biological weapons convention. In: Wright, S. *Preventing a biological arms race, op. cit.,* pp. 370–376.

26. Wright, S. Biowar treaty in danger. *Bulletin of the Atomic Scientists.* 47(7):36–37, 1991.

27. Novick, R. and Shulman, S. New forms of biological warfare? In Wright, S. *Preventing a biological arms race, op. cit.,* pp. 103–119.

28. Kirchhoff, S. Russian anthrax linked to military site's leak. *Philadelphia Inquirer,* Nov. 18, 1994.

29. Cole, L.A. Sverdlovsk, Yellow Rain, and Novel Soviet Bioweapons: Allegations and Responses. In: Wright, S. *Preventing a biological arms race, op. cit.,* pp. 199–219.

30. Foreman, J. Army funding spurs germ warfare fears. *Boston Globe.* Oct. 21, 1990.

31. Testimony by Col. David Huxsoll, U.S. Senate Governmental Affairs Committee and its Permanent Subcommittee on Investigations. May 17, 1989.

32. Sullivan, L. Work resumes at Dugway on chemical-test plant. *The Salt Lake Tribune,* Feb. 9, 1994.

33. Siegel, L. Dugway is adding deadly bacteria to tests. *The Salt Lake Tribune.* Feb. 18, 1994.

34. Shulman, S. Biohazard: How the pentagon's biological warfare research program defeats its own goals. The Center for Public Integrity, 1993.

35. Wright, S.P. and Ketcham, S. The problem of interpreting the U.S. biological defense research program, In Wright, S. *Preventing a biological arms race, op. cit.,* pp. 169–196.

36. Report cites greater global threat from biological, chemical weapons. *Houston Chronicle.* February 26, 1993.

37. Wilkie, T. Students in germ weapons alert. *The Independent.* March 16, 1993.

38. Orient, J.M. Chemical and biological warfare. Should defenses be researched and deployed? *JAMA* 262:644–648, 1989.

39. Report of RIA, Moscow-based news agency, February 15, 1993, summarized in transcript from Summary of World Broadcasts, British Broadcasting Corporation, February 17, 1993.

40. Gordon, M.R. Moscow is making little progress in disposal of chemical weapons. *The New York Times.* Dec. 1, 1993.

41. Gertz, B. Russia has biological weapons, defector says. *Washington Times.* Jan. 22, 1993.

42. Russia military reported working on plague bomb. *San Francisco Chronicle.* Mar. 28, 1994.

43. Iraq's germ warfare capacity 'substantial,' new U.N. report says. *San Jose Mercury News.* Aug. 15, 1991.

44. Smith, R.J. Iraq admits to U.N. it made deadly bacteria before Gulf War. *San Jose Mercury News.* July 6, 1995.
45. Wright, R. Iraqis admit wide study in germ war. U.N. probers surprised by the scope of research. *Philadelphia Inquirer.* Sept. 6, 1995.
46. Cockburn, P. KGB lifts lid on the world's dirty weapons. *The Independent.* February 28, 1993.
47. *Washington Post.* Sept. 16, 1977. In: Blum, W. *The CIA: A forgotten history.* London and New Jersey: Zed Books, Ltd.
48. *San Francisco Chronicle.* Jan. 10, 1977, from *Newsday* (Long Island, New York). In: Blum *op. cit.,* p. 211.
49. Schaap, B. The 1981 Cuba dengue epidemic. *Covert Action Information Bulletin* 17:28–31, Summer 1982
50. *San Francisco Chronicle.* Oct. 30, 1980, In: Blum *op. cit.,* p. 211.
51. Langer, E. Chemical and biological warfare. I. The research program. *Science* 155:174–179, 1967.
52. Nass, M. Anthrax epizootic in Zimbabwe, 1978–1980: due to deliberate spread?, *PSR Quarterly.* 2:198–209, 1992.
53. Nass, M. Zimbabwe's anthrax epizootic. *Covert Action* 43:12–18, Winter, 1992–93.
54. Rhodesian forces used anthrax, cholera in guerrilla warfare: report. *Agence France Presse.* July 8, 1993.
55. Yost, P. $1 billion-plus for meager results on germ warfare defense. *Associated Press.* April 1, 1993.
56. Lapin, L. Germ warfare vaccines: too little, too late? *San Jose Mercury News.* Jan. 6, 1991.
57. Sinai, R. GAO report: germ warfare would have killed many in Saudi Arabia. *Associated Press.* March 12, 1993.
58. Pine, A. Nuclear world: U.S. has plans to counter war threat. *Los Angeles Times.* May 12, 1994.
59. Lippman, T.W. Nonproliferation may yield to 'counterproliferation.' *Washington Post.* May 16, 1994.
60. Quinn-Judge, P. U.S. plans to combat spread of weapons. *Boston Globe.* Dec. 8, 1993.
61. States parties to the 1925 Geneva protocol and the 1972 biological weapons convention. In: Wright, S. *Preventing a biological arms race, op. cit.,* pp. 379–383.

9

Environmental and Health Effects of Weapons Production, Testing, and Maintenance

MICHAEL RENNER

More than three decades ago, U.S. President Dwight D. Eisenhower warned that ''the problem in defense is how far you can go without destroying from within what you are trying to defend from without.'' Meant as a warning against creating an all-powerful military-industrial complex, Eisenhower's statement is equally applicable to a problem the world is just beginning to grapple with: the military's war on the environment.

Modern warfare entails large-scale environmental devastation, as conflicts in Vietnam, Afghanistan, Central America, and the Persian Gulf amply demonstrate (Chapters 5 and 15–17). In some cases, environmental modification has consciously been employed as a weapon. And it is generally agreed that nuclear war is the ultimate threat to the global environment (Chapter 6).

But even in ''peacetime''—preparing for war—the military contributes to resource depletion and environmental degradation, in some instances heavily. The production, testing, and maintenance of conventional, chemical, biological, and nuclear arms generates enormous quantities of toxic and radioactive substances, and contaminates the earth's soil, air, and water (see also Chapters 7 and 8). Keeping troops in a state of readiness imposes a heavy toll on large tracts of often fragile land.

As a series of pathbreaking arms control and disarmament treaties comes into effect in the aftermath of the Cold War, a substantial volume of military equipment that far surpasses any routine scrapping of obsolete stocks now awaits disposal. The array of weapons and materials that need to be destroyed or dismantled includes nuclear and chemical warheads, conventional explosives and propellants, solid and liquid rocket fuel, and reactor cores from nuclear-powered submarines. Although today's methods of getting rid of surplus weaponry are less crude than the ocean dumping, land burial, or open-air burning employed up to the late 1960s, there is still no well-developed, environmentally fully acceptable way to dispose of unwanted weapons; arms treaties have usually skirted the issue.

Data that would permit a truly comprehensive picture of the military's resource use and its health and environmental effects are largely unavailable. This chapter is based on both statistical and anecdotal evidence.

Land and Air: The Battlefields at Home

Modern armed forces require large expanses of land and airspace. Not only have the arsenals of many nations grown to simply phenomenal proportions, but the amount of space needed to maneuver jet fighters, tanks, and warships has risen an astonishing amount—over 50,000 times per soldier since ancient times.[1] A 1982 UN study noted that "military requirements for land have risen steadily over the course of this century owing to the increase in the size of standing armed forces and, more particularly, the rapid pace of technological advances in weaponry."[2] During World War II, a U.S. mechanized infantry battalion with about 600 soldiers needed fewer than 16 square kilometers to maneuver; a similar unit today has to have more than 20 times as much space. A World War II fighter plane required a maneuvering radius of about nine kilometers, compared with 75 kilometers today and a projected 150 to 185 kilometers for the next generation of jets.[3]

Global estimates of direct military land use outside of wartime are sketchy at best. In 1981, it was estimated at one percent of total territory for 13 industrial nations, but is believed to be in the range of 0.5 to 1.0 percent worldwide (approximately 750,000 to 1.5 million square kilometers). This may sound small, but it represents an area sized between Turkey and Indonesia. To arrive at a truly comprehensive measure, however, the space occupied by arms-producing enterprises would need to be added to the land controlled by the armed forces themselves—information that is not readily available.

The best information on military land use exists for the United States. The Department of Defense directly holds 100,000 square kilometers,[4] about the size of Virginia. The armed services also lease about 80,000 square kilometers from other federal agencies. The nuclear weapons complex of the U.S. Department of Energy, meanwhile, spreads over 10,000 square kilometers. Altogether, at least 200,000 square kilometers—two percent of total U.S. territory—is devoted to military purposes. In the former Soviet Union, the Defense Ministry controlled about 420,000 square kilometers, roughly two percent of the total territory. When Kazakhstan was a Soviet republic, more land was devoted to military purposes than to growing wheat. The now closed Semipalatinsk nuclear test ground in eastern Kazakhstan, for example, occupies approximately 2,000 square kilometers. Direct military land use in Western Europe is estimated at one to three percent of the total land mass. Yet indirect or nonexclusive use tends to be much higher.

With its choreographed violence, the military destroys large tracts of the land it is supposed to protect. Land used for war games often suffers severe degradation. Maneuvers demolish the natural vegetation, disturb wildlife habitat, erode and compact soil, silt up streams, and cause flooding. NATO maneuvers in West Germany, for example, caused at least $100 million in assessed, quantifiable damages to crops, forests, and private property in a typical year during the 1980s.[1] Bombing ranges transform the land into a moon-like wasteland, pockmarked with craters. Shooting ranges for tanks and artillery contaminate soil and ground water with lead and other toxic residues. Some anti-tank shells, for example, contain uranium rods. One of the most enduring and perilous legacies of war preparation is large tracts of land strewn with unexploded bombs which, in effect, will be off limits to civilian use permanently because even an intensive effort can fail to locate all unexploded bombs. Preparing for war resembles a scorched-earth policy against an imaginary foe.

In fragile desert environments, the recovery of natural systems may take thousands of years. The Southern California desert still bears the scars of tank maneuvers conducted by General George Patton in the early 1940s. And the damage is far heavier in Libya, where British and German armies fought major battles during World War II.

The armed forces have far broader access to airspace than they have to land. This has been the case in the former West Germany, perhaps the country most intensively used by the military. Almost all of the country's airspace was open to military jets, and two-thirds of it to low-level flights. Each year, between 700,000 to 1 million military sorties took place, accounting for approximately 15 percent of all of air traffic.[5]

Much of the military flying in the United States is done in the relatively open spaces of the West. Some 90,000 training sorties a year, one-fifth of them at very low levels, are flown in a 47,000-square-kilometer expanse above California's Mojave Desert, for example.[6] According to Citizen Alert, a Nevada grassroots group, 180,000 square kilometers of airspace, about 70 percent of the state's total, is either designated "special use" or is used for training purposes.[7] For the United States as a whole, at least 30 percent and perhaps as much as 50 percent of airspace is used militarily in one way or another.[8]

Canada may have the world's most extensive military-purpose airspace. The zone assigned to Goose Bay Air Base at the northeastern coast of Labrador extends over 100,000 square kilometers, an area larger than the entire neighboring New Brunswick province.[9]

Low-level and supersonic flights constitute the aspect of military aviation that is the most dangerous and most detrimental to health. They impose an underdocumented health and psychological toll, impairing the habitability of affected areas. A plane flying at an altitude of 75 meters generates noise levels up to 140 decibels, at which acute hearing damage may occur. An F-18 jet flying at supersonic speed for 10 minutes, for example, can "boom" an area of more than 5,000 square kilometers.

Table 9-1.   United States: Energy consumption of selected military equipment

Equipment	Operating Distance or Times	Fuel Consumption (liters)
M-1 Abrams tank, average use	1 kilometer	47
F-15 jet, at peak thrust	1 minute	908
M-1 Abrams tank, peak rate	1 hour	1,113
F-4 Phantom fighter/bomber	1 hour	6,359
Battleship	1 hour	10,810
B-52 bomber	1 hour	13,671
Non-nuclear aircraft carrier	1 hour	21,300
Carrier battle group	1 day	1,589,700
Armored division, 348 tanks	1 day	2,271,000

Sources: "Defending the Environment? The Record of the U.S. Military," *The Defense Monitor,* Vol. 18, No. 6, 1989; Tom Cutler, "Myths of Military Oil Supply Vulnerability," *Armed Forces Journal International,* July 1989; Greg Williams, "The Army's M-1 Tank: Has It Lived up to Expectations?" Project on Government Procurement, Washington, D.C., June 12, 1990; Center for Disarmament, *Economic and Social Consequences of the Arms Race and Military Expenditures,* Disarmament Study Series No. 11. New York: United Nations, 1983.

Startled by a sudden sonic boom, the human body releases adrenalin, raising blood pressure, increasing heart rate, and disturbing the intestinal tract and other organs.

In response to growing political opposition to low-level flights, West Germany's air force relocated its aerial maneuvers to Canada and Turkey. Canada continues to ignore protests not only by the peace and environmental movements but also by the Innu, the native people of Ntesinan (Labrador), about the illegal use of their land. Their livelihoods are imperiled because the exercises disturb the migration and feeding behavior of caribou herds. Such unwelcome intrusions also occur in the United States, where flight training is conducted on the territories of 14 Native American nations.

The Drain on Energy and Materials

Whether it is jets roaring through the skies, tanks rumbling across the land, or warships navigating the high seas, the armed forces clearly use large amounts of energy (see Table 9-1). An F-16 jet taking off for a regular training mission is likely to consume as much as 3,400 liters of fuel before returning to its base. In less than an hour, the plane thus uses almost twice as much gas as the average U.S. motorist during one year. Afterburners will triple a jet's speed to supersonic levels, but will also increase consumption 20-fold. And a modern battle tank's fuel consumption is so voracious that it is better measured in gallons per mile than in miles per gallon.

Unfortunately, however, few aggregate statistics are available. Petroleum products account for roughly three-quarters of all energy use by the armed forces worldwide, but by far the most important is jet fuel. Worldwide, nearly one-quarter of all jet fuel—42 million tons per year—was used for military purposes in the late 1980s.

The U.S. Department of Defense consumes an amount equivalent to about 37 million tons of oil a year. This equals two to three percent of total U.S. energy demand and three to four percent of oil demand, but would be somewhat higher if military-related activities of the Department of Energy and the National Aeronautics and Space Administration were included. The Pentagon is the single largest consumer domestically, and very likely worldwide. It uses enough energy in one year to run the entire U.S. urban mass transit system for almost 14 years. During World War II, the Pentagon's share of national energy use jumped from one percent in 1940 to 29 percent in 1945.

Military-related energy consumption would be considerably higher if energy used in manufacturing weapons were included. Up-to-date data, however, are virtually unavailable. In 1971, arms production in the United States used about 47 million tons of oil equivalent. Leaving the issue of energy intensity aside, an estimate for 1989 based on 1971 and 1989 expenditures for U.S. arms procurement and revenues from arms exports yields a usage of about 68 million tons of oil equivalent, almost twice the armed forces' direct use of energy.[10]

Worldwide, energy use for weapons production is probably relatively lower because most countries do not have a significant arms industry. Still, the military sector's share of total oil and energy use may well be double the armed forces' direct share of three to four percent. If these assumptions are correct, the world uses about as many petroleum products for military purposes as Japan, the world's second largest economy, does for all purposes.

Because military equipment is designed for superior combat performance, not for energy efficiency, it seems reasonable to assume that the military's share of pollution surpasses its share of energy consumed. According to a 1983 estimate by Gunar Seitz, a German environmental writer, emissions from the operations of the armed forces alone account for at least 6 to 10 percent of global air pollution. Others have calculated the contribution of the West German armed forces to air pollution as having been 6.5 percent of carbon monoxide, 5.4 percent of oxides of nitrogen, 3.9 percent of hydrocarbons, and 1.3 percent of sulfur dioxide emissions. Since warplanes consume the bulk of the military's petroleum use, tallying their emissions of air pollutants tells a large part of the story (Table 9-2).

Little work has been done to date on the military's contribution to global warming. In 1988, the Pentagon's activities resulted in carbon emissions of about 46 million tons, or roughly 3.5 percent of the U.S. total. If approximations of energy use in arms production are correct, the total military-related carbon release could be as high as 10 percent.

Estimating a global figure for carbon emissions from the military is fraught with uncertainty. A back-of-the-envelope calculation for the late 1980s yields an estimate of about 150 million tons: almost three percent of the global total, or nearly equal to the annual carbon emissions of the United Kingdom. If the energy consumption of arms-producing industries were included, these numbers could well double.

The military has a larger impact on certain non-fuel minerals and other materials.

Table 9-2.   Fuel consumption and estimated air pollutant emissions of military aircraft, selected countries and world, late 1980s

Area	Fuel Consumption Total (million tons)	Share (percent)	Emissions (thousand tons)[a] CO	Hydrocarbons	NO$_x$	SO$_2$
United States	18.6	44.1	381	78	157	17.9
Soviet Union	11.8	28.1	244	50	100	11.4
West Germany[b]	1.5	3.5	31	6	13	1.4
World	42.2	100.0	865	178	357	40.6

Source: Worldwatch Institute, based on Olaf Achilles, "Militär, Rüstung und Klima," MÖP Studie VII, Arbeits- und Forschungsstelle Militär, Ökologie und Planung, Bonn, West Germany, June 1990, and on Tom Cutler, "Myths of Military Oil Supply Vulnerability," *Armed Forces Journal International,* July 1989.

[a]Global, U.S., and Soviet emissions data calculated on basis of West German data, assuming, similar aircraft engine characteristics and flight patterns. Emissions are given for carbon monoxide, hydrocarbons, nitrogen oxides, and sulfur dioxide.

[b]Jets of the German Air Force and those of NATO contingents stationed in former West Germany, including U.S. planes whose fuel consumption is included in the U.S. total.

Iron and steel are the traditional backbones of any military machine. Some nine percent of global iron consumption, approximately 60 million tons, is used for military purposes. However, as the emphasis of the arms race has shifted to qualitative advances, the relative importance of iron and steel had declined, while that of more "exotic" materials has increased. Many of these are essential ingredients for high-temperature alloys desired for their strength and extreme resistance to heat, wear, and corrosion.

Titanium, for example, accounts for 20 to 30 percent of the weight of a sophisticated combat aircraft today, compared with 8 to 10 percent in the 1950s. Titanium is also an important component of submarine hulls. Manufacturing a single F-16 jet engine requires almost 5,000 kilograms of materials, including 2,044 kilograms of titanium, 1,715 of nickel, 573 of chromium, 330 of cobalt, and 267 of aluminum. The construction and deployment of a single land-based mobile intercontinental missile requires 4,450 tons of steel, 1,200 tons of cement, 50 tons of aluminum, 12.5 tons of chromium, 750 kilograms of titanium, and 120 kilograms of beryllium.

Global figures, in the absence of reliable data, are rough estimates. It appears, though, that the estimated worldwide use of aluminum, copper, nickel, and platinum for military purposes surpasses the entire Third World's demand for these materials.[2]

Leading the way in high-tech weaponry, the United States accounts for, by far, the largest share of military consumption of such valuable raw materials. The Pentagon's portion of total U.S. use of non-fuel minerals ranges generally from 5 to 15 percent, but rises to 25 to 40 percent for beryllium, cobalt, germanium, thorium, thallium, and titanium. For China and all the nations of Europe, the share is estimated to be three to seven percent.

The end of the Cold War suggests that the armed forces may begin at last to make

Figure 9-1. At ''Pit Nine,'' a radioactive-waste burial ground in Idaho, approximately 150,000 cubic feet of plutonium-contaminated and low-level radioactive waste was buried between 1967 and 1969 (Photograph by Robert Del Tredici).

less of a claim on the world's scarce resources. This is certainly true to the extent that the number of weapons declines. At the same time, however, there are no indications that the quest for technological sophistication will slow, let alone come to a halt. This trend will offset at least part of any lower demand for materials that results from smaller quantities of arms.

Toxic Effects

In their incessant pursuit of prowess and preparedness, the armed forces are poisoning the land and people they are supposed to protect (Figure 9-1). Military toxic materials are contaminating water used for drinking or irrigation, killing fish, befouling the air, and rendering vast tracts of land unusable for generations to come. Having been dumping grounds for a lethal soup of hazardous materials for decades, military bases have become health time-bombs, detonating in slow motion (Table 9-3).

The production, maintenance, and storage of ''conventional,'' chemical, and nuclear weapons and other pieces of military equipment generate vast amounts of materials inimical to human health and environmental quality. These wastes include fuels, paints, solvents, heavy metals, pesticides, polychlorinated biphenyls (PCBs),

Table 9-3.   United States: Selected military hazardous waste sites

Location	Observations
Otis Air Force Base, Massachusetts	Groundwater contaminated with trichloroethylene (TCE), classified as a probable carcinogen, and other toxins. In adjacent towns, lung cancer and leukemia rates 80 percent above state average.
Picatinny Arsenal, New Jersey	Groundwater at the site shows TCE levels at 5,000 times (EPA) standards; polluted with lead, cadmium, polychlorinated biphenyls (used in radar installations and to insulate electrical equipment), phenols, furans, chromium, selenium, toluene, and cyanide. Region's major aquifer contaminated.
Rocky Mountain Arsenal, Colorado	125 chemicals dumped over 30 years of nerve gas and pesticide production. The largest of all seriously contaminated sites, called ''the most contaminated square mile on earth'' by the Army Corps of Engineers.
Hill Air Force Base, Utah	Heavy on-base groundwater contamination, including volatile organic compounds up to 27,000 parts per billion (ppb); TCE up to 1.7 million ppb; chromium up to 1,900 ppb; lead up to 3,000 ppb.
McChord Air Force Base, Washington	Benzene, a carcinogen, found on-base in concentrations as high as 503 ppb, nearly 1,000 times the state's limit of 0.6 ppb.

Source: Michael Renner. Assessing the military's war on the environment. In Lester R. Brown et al., *State of the world 1991.* New York and London: W.W. Norton and Co., 1991.

cyanides, phenols, acids, alkalies, propellants, and explosives. Knowledge about the health effects of these substances remains limited, but it is suspected that human exposure through drinking, skin absorption, or inhalation may cause cancer, birth defects, and chromosome damage, or may seriously impair the function of the liver, kidneys, blood, and central nervous system.[11]

The military is quite likely the largest generator of hazardous wastes in the United States and the world. In the late 1980s, the Pentagon generated between 400,000 and 500,000 tons of toxic materials annually, more than the top five U.S. chemical companies combined.[12] Its contractors produced tens, if not hundreds, of thousands of tons more.

Assessing the extent of toxic contamination is akin to opening Pandora's box: The number of U.S. sites on which problems have been spotted mushroomed from 3,526 on 529 military bases in 1986 to 14,401 on 1,579 installations in 1989. In addition, more than 7,000 former military properties are being investigated. Some 96 bases are so badly polluted that they are already on the Superfund National Priorities List (NPL). But Gordon Davidson, deputy director of the Federal Facilities Compliance Task Force of the Environmental Protection Agency (EPA), believes as many as 1,000 military sites may eventually be added to the NPL. ''Clean-up'' is proceeding at a snail's pace and appears designed primarily to preclude any further deterioration. Meanwhile, new wastes are generated each day, though the Pentagon apparently cut the volume in half by 1992 and has initiated programs to handle its wastes more responsibly than in the past.

U.S. military installations abroad have been exempt from the U.S. National Environmental Policy Act and, under basing agreements, from pertinent host-nation laws as well. But with the end of the Cold War, host governments began to demand compliance with their environmental rules. As the U.S. forces withdrew from bases in Europe, the Philippines, and Panama, the question of who is responsible for cleanup costs became an important, though not easily resolved, issue. Available evidence suggests that contamination at these bases and others in Japan, South Korea, and elsewhere is likely to be extensive.[13]

As Soviet forces withdrew from Eastern Europe, it became clear that the bases they occupied are in desperate need of cleanup. In addition, fuel, wastes, and unexploded ammunition were dumped in many unmarked off-base locations. The groundwater beneath Frenstat in Northern Moravia in the Czech Republic is so contaminated, says Deputy Environment Minister Jaroslav Vlcek, that "you could practically drill for diesel there." In Vysoke Myto in central Bohemia, groundwater tests reveal toxic materials in concentrations 30 to 50 times allowable levels. Up to 8,000 square kilometers—six percent of the territory of the Czech and Slovak Republics—have been polluted or despoiled.[14-16]

In Hungary, parts of Kiskunsag National Park have been used as firing ranges and ammunition dumping grounds. In the former East Germany, at least 90 Soviet installations are severely polluted. At Lärz Air Base in Mecklenburg, for example, more than 50,000 tons of fuel leaked into the soil. An estimated 10 percent of East German territory has been despoiled by Soviet military operations. Even less is known about the toxic materials used in the arms industry and about workers' exposure to them. Military secrecy has hampered efforts to monitor and enforce safety at aerospace and other factories. It is indisputable, however, that the manufacture of explosives, composite materials, and electronic components can endanger human health. The production of explosives and propulsion systems, for example, entails potential exposure to such hazardous emissions as chlorine gas, dibenzodioxins, and dibenzofurans.

Composite materials like carbon fiber and glass fiber that make military aircraft lighter, stronger, and less visible on radar screens are suspected of poisoning workers who handle them. Chemicals used to bond these materials, including phenol formaldehyde and methylene dianiline, are thought to cause cancer when inhaled or absorbed through the skin, while fiber fragments can damage the lungs and also cause cancer. Workers at plants involved in top-secret projects, such as the F-117 Stealth jet fighter, were not permitted to explain fully even to their own doctors the circumstances that may cause their illnesses. Inspectors of the Occupational Safety and Health Administration (OSHA) need special security clearances to visit some arms production facilities. Between 1985 and 1989, Lockheed workers in California who had fallen ill filed 352 claims against the company, charging that they were never informed of the hazards involved. In 1989, management agreed to pay $1.4 million in penalties for 440 violations of workplace safety rules.[17]

The production of semiconductors and other electronic components involves many highly toxic materials. In the United States, roughly 20 percent of that industry's output was purchased by the Pentagon during the 1980s. Workers may be exposed to solvents, alkalies, and metals used in electroplating, etching, stripping, soldering, and degreasing; to vapors from phosphine, arsine, and phosgene gases; and to ionizing and non-ionizing forms of radiation. Hazards derive mostly from long-term exposure to a multitude of substances that are suspected carcinogens, teratogens, or mutagens. But knowledge about the full range of effects is still in its infancy.

Nuclear Wasteland

Of all the different ways in which military operations have an impact on human health and the environment, nuclear weapons production and testing is the most severe and enduring. While the effect of toxic wastes is relatively localized, the spread of nuclear debris is global, and while hazardous substances will be with us for generations, plutonium has a half-life of 24,000 years. Even if nuclear arsenals were abolished tomorrow, their waste products could not be.

In 1955, Thomas E. Murray, a member of the Atomic Energy Commission (AEC), the government body in charge of the U.S. nuclear weapons program, asserted: "We must not let anything interfere with this series of [nuclear] tests—nothing." Made in closed session, it was a statement emblematic of the priorities of the time in both East and West: the brisk build-up of nuclear arsenals—from uranium mining, to warhead design and manufacture, to testing and deployment—won unambiguous precedence over the health and safety of workers, soldiers, and residents.[18] For decades, officials knowingly subjected their own unsuspecting citizens to the dangers of radioactivity in the name of national security.

Only at the end of the Cold War did the U.S. government acknowledge that radiation doses emanating from its plutonium production facility in Hanford, Washington, in the 1940s and 1950s were sufficient to cause cancer.[19] Similarly, only in 1989 did Soviet authorities finally confirm a fatal accident had occurred at a plutonium processing plant 32 years before.[20]

Like a nuclear reactor reaching critical mass, the late 1980s and early 1990s saw a flood of front-page newspaper articles, official investigations, and hearings in the United States, showering the public with shocking new revelations about the nuclear weapons complex. What emerged was a story ranging from gross negligence and excessive secrecy to pervasive deceit and outright criminal conduct. Despite all ideological differences, these are attributes shared by bomb makers in West and East. While the worst practices seem to belong to the past—a number of nuclear weapons plants in the United States and the former Soviet Union are closed at least temporarily for safety or political reasons—the peril of highly radioactive wastes will exist for many centuries.[21]

Worldwide, there are an estimated 257 tons of weapons-grade plutonium either stored or assembled in warheads; in addition, there are 1,300 to 1,800 tons of highly

Figure 9-2. Barrels of transuranic waste sit on a concrete pad in temporary storage at Savannah River Site, South Carolina (Photograph by Robert Del Tredici).

enriched uranium.[22] Every step in the bomb-making process involves severe environmental threats. At the Purex plant at the Hanford Reservation in Washington, which is now closed, the production of a single kilogram of plutonium generated about 1,300 liters of liquid high-level radioactive waste laced with hazardous chemicals, more than 200,000 kilograms of low- to intermediate-level waste, and almost 10 million liters of contaminated cooling water[23] (Figure 9-2). Military nuclear reactors are responsible for, by volume, an estimated 97 percent of all high-level nuclear waste and 78 percent of all low-level nuclear waste in the United States. Measured in curies, the military portion is six percent of high-level nuclear waste and 74 percent of low-level nuclear waste. The military-related high-level waste inventory has been estimated at about 1.4 billion curies. (A curie measures the intensity of radiation and is equal to 3.7×10^8 disintegrations per second; by comparison, about 50 million curies were released during the accident at Chernobyl.)

By 1989, more than 3,200 sites in about 100 locations owned by the U.S. Department of Energy (which took over the work of the Atomic Energy Commission) had been identified as having tainted soil, groundwater, or both. Five years later, the number of identified contaminated sites had climbed to about 4,500. Decades of deliberate and accidental releases of radioactive material and toxic substances make for a modern-day horror story (Table 9-4). More than 50 Nagasaki-size bombs could be manufactured from the waste that has leaked just from Hanford's underground tanks.

Table 9-4.   Radioactive and toxic contamination at major nuclear weapons production facilities, U.S., 1990

Facility (Task)	Observations
Feed Materials Production Center, Fernald, Ohio (converts uranium into metal ingots)	Since plant's opening, at least 250 tons of uranium oxide (and perhaps six times as much as that) released into the air. Off-site surface and groundwater contaminated with uranium, cesium, thorium. High levels of radon gas emitted.
Hanford Reservation, Washington (recycles uranium and extracts plutonium)	Since 1944, 760 billion liters of contaminated water (enough to create a 12-meter-deep lake the size of Manhattan) have entered groundwater and Columbia River; 4.5 million liters of high-level radioactive waste leaked from underground tanks. Officials knowingly and sometimes deliberately exposed the public to large amounts of airborne radiation in 1943–1956.
Savannah River, South Carolina (produces plutonium and tritium)	Radioactive substances and chemicals found in the Tuscaloosa aquifer at levels 400 times greater than government considers safe. Released millions of curies of tritium gas into atmosphere since 1954.
Rocky Flats, Colorado (assembles plutonium triggers)	Since 1952, 200 fires have contaminated the Denver region with unknown amount of plutonium. Strontium, cesium, and cancer-causing chemicals leaked into underground water.
Oak Ridge Reservation, Tennessee (produces lithium-deuteride and highly enriched uranium)	Since 1943, thousands of pounds of uranium emitted into atmosphere. Radioactive and hazardous wastes have severely polluted local streams flowing into the Clinch River. Watts Bar Reservoir, a recreational lake, is contaminated with at least 175,000 tons of mercury and cesium.

Sources: "Status of Major Nuclear Weapons Production Facilities: 1990," *PSR Monitor,* September 1990; Robert Alvarez and Arjun Makhijani, "Hidden Legacy of the Arms Race: Radioactive Waste," *Technology Review,* August/September 1989; and other sources.

At Rocky Flats, enough plutonium has accumulated in ventilation ducts to make seven nuclear bombs. After a large 1969 fire there, investigators found the highest concentrations of plutonium ever measured near an urban area, including around Nagasaki.[24]

Additional danger looms from wastes that have not yet escaped into the environment. Some storage tanks at Savannah River and Hanford holding plutonium by-products, such as cesium, strontium, and iodine, are apparently in danger of exploding, according to a U.S. government advisory panel (Figure 9-3). Should such a detonation occur at Savannah River, nearby residents could develop up to 20,000 additional cases of cancer. In other locations, radioactive waste was buried underground (Figure 9-4).

Radiation is known to cause leukemia, multiple myeloma, brain tumors, thyroid disorders, sterility, miscarriages, and birth defects. Damage to the human body depends on the size and type of the radiation dose and on how fast it is absorbed. It is difficult to establish a causal link between a specific radiation exposure and adverse health effects. However, recent studies conclude that the risks of ionizing radiation are three times higher than previously thought, and many scientists believe there is no "safe" level of radiation exposure.[25]

Some 300,000 people, or half of those who ever worked in the U.S. nuclear weap-

Figure 9-3. Million-gallon, double-walled, carbon-steel tanks under construction at Hanford in 1984. These tanks are designed to contain high-level radioactive waste from plutonium-production operations (Photograph by Robert Del Tredici).

ons complex, are believed to have been affected by exposure to radiation. A study of almost 4,000 Rocky Flats workers found elevated incidence of brain tumors, malignant melanoma, respiratory cancer, and chromosome aberrations, even though they had been exposed to only billionths of a curie of radioactivity. Hundreds of workers at Hanford were absorbing every six months a quantity of plutonium equal to the current lifetime limit.[26]

People living near the Hanford Reservation in the Pacific Northwest have received some of the largest amounts of radiation in the world over a long period. More than 400,000 curies of radioactive iodine—26,000 times the amount released at Three Mile Island in 1979—were emitted between 1944 and 1947 alone, exposing over 250,000 unsuspecting people. Close to 14,000 residents, about five percent, received doses of 33 rads ("radiation absorbed dose," which measures the amount of radiation absorbed by the human body but not the biological damage). This is 1,200 times the level currently considered safe by the U.S. government. Some residents were even exposed to doses of up to 2,900 rads. People living near Hanford have an unusually high number of various cancers, miscarriages, and other disorders.[27]

Mikhail Gorbachev's *glasnost* gave the world its first insights into the consequences of the Soviet nuclear weapons program. The picture that has emerged is one of enor-

Figure 9-4. ''Good news—we've reduced the nuclear threat from abroad''—Copyright 1993 by Herblock in the Washington Post

mous contamination. At Kyshtym in the eastern Urals (the Soviet counterpart to Hanford), perhaps over 6,000 workers were exposed to radiation doses of more than 100 rem.[28] (This measure recognizes that different types of radiation have different biological effects. One rem is roughly equivalent to seven or eight X-rays. A 500-rem dose is usually fatal, while 100 to 200 rem could produce cancer after a number of years.) Cesium, strontium, and other liquid radioactive wastes were dumped from the late 1940s into the Techa River. The river became so polluted that traces of radioactivity showed up in the Arctic Ocean, nearly 1,000 miles away. Those living along the Techa had to be evacuated[29] (Figures 9-5 and 9-6).

From 1952 on, nuclear waste was dumped into nearby Lake Karachay; the heat of the radionuclides began to dry out the 10-square-kilometer body of water. By 1988,

Figure 9-5. Demonstration of radiation at 28 times background level on bridge 14 feet above the River Techa in Russia, not far from the Chelyabinsk nuclear weapons facility (Photograph by Robert Del Tredici).

it contained 120 million curies of strontium-90, cesium-137, residual plutonium, and other long-lived isotopes, two-and-a-half times more than was released at Chernobyl. The lake is now covered by a thick layer of concrete.[30]

In September 1957, high-level nuclear waste stored at Kyshtym in the southern Urals region underwent a chemical explosion. The accident severely contaminated 15,000 square kilometers of land that was home to more than 250,000 people, forcing the evacuation of 10,000 of them. The explosion released about one-third as much overall radiation as at Chernobyl.[31]

In late 1994, Russian scientists disclosed that the Soviet Union had pumped billions of gallons of civilian- and military-generated nuclear waste directly into the earth. About half of all the nuclear waste ever generated by the Soviet Union was "disposed of" in that manner at three different sites: Dimitrovgrad, Tomsk, and Krasnoyarsk. The waste originally comprised about 3 billion curies, but radioactive decay over the years has reduced this to about 1.5 billion curies now. These injections were apparently resorted to in order to avoid aboveground storage disasters like the one at Kyshtym. But the wastes at one of the three sites have already spread over a great, though undisclosed, distance.

Warhead testing is the final phase in the development of nuclear arms, but it was

Figure 9-6. The Church at Metlino, 7 km. from the point of dumping extremely hazardous liquid high-level radioactive waste in the Techa River, was abandoned because of radioactive contamination (Photograph by Robert Del Tredici).

the activity that elicited the earliest health concerns. Since 1945, more than 2,000 bombs have been exploded at more than 35 sites around the world.[32] Roughly one-fifth of all tests, most of them before 1963, were conducted in the atmosphere, injecting far more radioactive debris into the atmosphere than the Chernobyl accident. The fallout may have caused as many as 86,000 birth defects worldwide and, according to a 1977 UN estimate, some 150,000 premature deaths.

Hundreds of thousands of people, including soldiers ordered to observe atmospheric testing (Figure 9-7), test-site workers, and residents of "downwind" communities, were directly exposed to radioactive fallout, with deadly consequences. Bikini atoll in the Pacific was rendered uninhabitable (Figure 9-8), and many residents of neighboring Rongelap have developed thyroid tumors. Many millions of people around the globe are thought to bear trace amounts of plutonium in their tissues and organs.[33]

The Soviet Academy of Medical Sciences determined in 1989 that residents of Semipalatinsk, near the main test site in Kazakhstan, had experienced excess cancers, genetic diseases, and child deaths because of radiation exposure from pre-1963 atmospheric tests. In 1988, the incidence of cancer was 70 percent above the national average. Kazakh activists claim that life expectancy in the republic has declined by four years over the past two decades, and that the number of people suffering from blood diseases has doubled since 1970.[34]

Figure 9-7. American troops exposed to nuclear weapons test in Nevada in 1951 (Source: Library of Congress, Negative LC-USZ 62-47325).

Making Peace with the Environment

As the East-West confrontation has faded, the environmental legacy of the Cold War is slowly being put on the agenda. The cost of repairing the damage wrought by permanent war preparation will be staggering, as experience in the United States shows. The U.S. Department of Energy currently projects the costs of nuclear waste management and decontamination at $200 to $350 billion, or roughly $3 to $5 million for every nuclear warhead the nation has produced. Estimates for required outlays to deal with toxic wastes at U.S. military bases have skyrocketed from $500 million in 1983 to $20 to $40 billion today, and are likely to escalate further as cleanup work progresses.

Funding has risen dramatically. The budget for environmental restoration programs at U.S. military installations, for example, has risen from virtually nothing in the early 1980s to about $600 million in 1990 and close to $2 billion in 1994—still a small share of the total military budget. The budget for coping with contamination of the

Figure 9-8. U.S. atomic-bomb test at Bikini atoll in the Pacific in 1946 (Source: Library of Congress, Negative LC-USZ 62-66049).

nuclear weapons complex has grown more than five-fold since the mid-1980s, to $5 to $6 billion annually in recent years.

There are no reliable estimates of military cleanup funds available in Russia, which has inherited most of the Soviet military legacy. Alexey Yablokov, head of the Interagency Commission on Ecological Security of the Russian Federation National Security Council, has indicated that actual spending is minuscule. Cleanup funds have been growing in other countries, however. Germany, for example, now spends the equivalent of about $700 million a year on military-related environmental cleanup and protection.[35]

Even with adequate funding, the time required for decontaminating sites polluted by toxic and radioactive wastes will have to be measured in decades and generations. The most severely poisoned areas will be impossible to "clean up" or otherwise rehabilitate. Fenced-off and unsuitable for any use, they may become "national sacrifice zones," ghastly monuments to the Cold War. Environmental destruction is certain to be the most lasting legacy of the East-West rivalry.

The military sector has long considered itself beyond the purview of existing environmental laws and regulations, and that has been slow to change. In the United States, then-Secretary of Defense Cheney launched a "Defense and the Environment Initiative" in 1989. Military cleanup budgets began to grow, and environmental issues started to be taken much more seriously in the armed forces. In fact, Pentagon officials maintain that their institution is undergoing a "major culture change" with regard to environmental protection.

Although growing environmental awareness without doubt plays an important role, the 1992 Federal Facilities Compliance Act has been a key factor. The Act requires military facilities to comply with existing environmental laws; the EPA and state regulators are now able to levy fines against military violators. In addition, the courts have affirmed that base commanders can be held personally liable and potentially face the prospect of going to jail in cases of severe violations. Strong public pressure played an important role in changing the military's attitude toward the environment. Whereas the military used to adopt a confrontational attitude toward grassroots groups concerned with military pollution, there is now greater openness and some willingness to cooperate.

Still, the essence of all military operations is achieving a margin of superiority over real or perceived adversaries, at whatever environmental or other cost. A world that wants to make peace with the environment cannot continue to fight wars or to sacrifice human health and the earth's ecosystems preparing for them. It needs to move away from the sentiment expressed by a U.S. military base commander at a community hearing in Virginia in the late 1980s: ''We are in the business of protecting the nation, not the environment.''[36]

Environmental quality joins a long list of solid reasons for moving toward disarmament.

REFERENCES

1. Vertegaal, P.J.M. Environmental impact of Dutch military activities. *Environmental Conservation,* Spring 1989.
2. Center for Disarmament. *The Relationship between disarmament and development.* Disarmament Study Series No. 5. New York: United Nations, 1982.
3. Moore, M. Land squeeze hampers U.S. military. *Washington Post,* December 31, 1988.
4. U.S. Department of Defense. *Our nation's defense and the environment: A Department of Defense initiative.* Washington, D.C.: U.S. Government Printing Office, 1990.
5. Achilles, O. and Lange, J. *Tiefflieger: Vom Täglichen Angriff auf die Bürger.* Reinbek bei Hamburg: Rowohlt Verlag, 1989.
6. Reinhold, R. Military and conservationists clash over Mojave's future. *New York Times,* June 25, 1988.
7. Bukowski, G. The militarization of Nevada. *Earth Island Journal,* Spring 1990.
8. Stuebner, S. Homing in on the range. *Earth Island Journal,* Spring 1990.
9. Robinson, B. Games air forces play. *Ploughshares Monitor,* December 1989.
10. Stockholm International Peace Research Institute (SIPRI). *SIPRI Yearbook 1990: World Armaments and Disarmament.* Oxford: Oxford University Press, 1990.
11. Cancer deaths high among aircraft workers. *Federal Times,* November 23, 1987.
12. Holusha, J. Ed Woodward walks DuPont's tightrope. *New York Times,* October 14, 1990.
13. Broder, J.M. U.S. military leaves toxic trail overseas. *Los Angeles Times,* June 18, 1990.
14. Kamm, H. Americans help Czechs clean up after the Soviets. *New York Times,* July 24, 1990.
15. Green, P.S. Cleaning up after the Soviet Army. *U.S. News & World Report,* May 28, 1990.
16. Rich, V. Departing Red Army leaves its rubbish behind. *New Scientist,* June 2, 1990.
17. Noble, K.B. Health troubles at military plant add mystery to top-secret project. *New York Times,* September 18, 1988.
18. Ball, H. Downwind from the bomb. *New York Times Magazine,* February 9, 1986.

19. Schneider, K. U.S. admits peril of '40s emissions at A-bomb plant. *New York Times,* July 12, 1990.

20. Clines, F.X. Soviets now admit '57 nuclear blast. *New York Times,* June 18, 1989.

21. Alvarez, R. and Makhijani, A. The hidden legacy of the arms race. *Technology Review,* August/September 1988.

22. Cochran, et al. Status of major nuclear weapons production facilities. In *Nuclear Weapons Databook.* Vols. II and IV. Cambridge, MA: Ballinger, 1990.

23. Steele, K.D. Hanford: America's nuclear graveyard. *Bulletin of Atomic Scientists,* October 1989.

24. Butterfield, F. Dispute on wastes poses threat to weapons plant. *New York Times,* October 21, 1988.

25. Thompson, L. Scientists reassess the long-term impact of radiation. *Washington Post,* August 15, 1990.

26. Schneider, K. U.S. releases radiation records of 44,000 nuclear workers. *New York Times,* July 18, 1990.

27. Schneider, K. Radiation peril at Hanford is detailed. *New York Times,* July 13, 1990.

28. Wald, M.L. High radiation doses seen for Soviet arms workers. *New York Times,* August 16, 1990.

29. Keller, B. Soviet city, home of the A-bomb, is haunted by its past and future. *New York Times,* July 10, 1989.

30. Medvedev, Z.A. The environmental destruction of the Soviet Union. *The Ecologist,* January/February 1990.

31. Rich, V. Thirty-year secret revealed. *Nature,* June 22, 1989.

32. Norris, R.S. and Arkin, W.M. Nuclear notebook: Known nuclear tests worldwide, 1945–1993. *Bulletin of Atomic Scientists,* May/June 1994.

33. Schneider, K. Senate panel describes data on nuclear risks. *New York Times,* August 3, 1989.

34. Lysenkov, V. Campaign to close Semipalatinsk. *Nature,* September 7, 1989.

35. Yablokov, A. Interagency Commission on Ecological Security, Russian Federation National Security Council, Moscow, private communication, August 1, 1994.

36. Shulman, S. Toxic travels: Inside the military's environmental nightmare. *Nuclear Times,* Autumn 1990.

10

The Public Health Effects
of Land Mines: Long-Term
Consequences for Civilians

ERIC STOVER, JAMES C. COBEY,
and JONATHAN FINE

Every year, in numerous war-torn countries, thousands of men, women, and children are victims of antipersonnel mines (Figure 10-1). While the Stockholm International Peace Research Institute published landmark studies in 1978[1] and 1985,[2] this man-made epidemic went largely unreported until early 1988, when relief workers drew attention to the thousands of limbless victims of mines in Afghanistan and Cambodia. Now there are over 100,000,000 mines strewn across 64 countries, including Angola, Ethiopia, Iraq, Kuwait, Laos, Mozambique, Myanmar (formerly Burma), Somalia, Sudan, Vietnam, Uganda, and the former Yugoslavia.[3]

Mines not only maim and kill, they also render large tracts of land uninhabitable with a loss of livelihood for millions. Those most likely to encounter antipersonnel mines are the rural poor. Peasants foraging for wood and food or tilling their fields are particularly at risk. Children herding livestock are vulnerable as they often traverse wide tracts of land in search of fresh pastures.

Once the fighting ends, refugees and internally displaced people often fear returning to their farms or villages because of mines. Many returning refugees therefore gather in cities and large towns where they often find little work and poor housing. In the meantime, mine-clearing operations, particularly in hilly terrain, may take years and even decades to complete. In Afghanistan, the United Nations has deployed 112 de-mining teams and estimates that it will take 15 years to clear priority zones and a further 4,285 years to clear mines manually from only 20 percent of Afghan territory.[3]

The authors wish to thank Barbara Ayotte of Physicians for Human Rights for her assistance in the preparation of this chapter.

Figure 10-1. United Nations medical soldiers attend to a child wounded by a landmine, outside the Central Hospital in Kigali, Rwanda. Many houses in the capital were planted with mines (Source/Photographer: UNICEF/94-0454/Betty Press).

Mines strewn over huge areas of Cambodia—four million mines is the estimate—constitute ''one of the worst man-made environmental disasters of the century,''[4] according to a United Nations observer.

The first use of antipersonnel mines dates back to World War II, when German and Allied troops used them to prevent enemy soldiers from removing larger anti-tank mines. In the early 1960s, the United States introduced the use of a new and sophisticated class of antipersonnel mines, known as remotely delivered mines or ''scatterables,'' to stop the flow of men and material from North to South Vietnam through Laos and Cambodia.[5] American pilots dropped so many of these mines they referred to them as ''garbage.'' Weighing only 20 grams, they could flutter to the ground without detonating but still contain enough explosive to tear off a man's foot.

Since the increase in internal wars and conflicts beginning in the 1970s, the antipersonnel mine, like the automatic rifle, has become a weapon of choice for many government and guerrilla armies around the world. Cambodian soldiers and guerrillas were so enamored of mines that they referred to them as their ''eternal sentinels,'' never sleeping, always ready to attack. Cambodia now has the highest percentage of inhabitants disabled by land mines of any country in the world.[6]

Mines are cheap, easy to carry, extremely durable, and highly effective. They are also readily available from the vast global network of government and private arms

Figure 10-2. The Valmara 69 is an Italian-made antipersonnel bounding mine that has a plastic case with a removable fuse mounted on the top. The mine is fitted with a tripwire but its fuse can also be activated by direct pressure on one or more of the five fuse prongs. To obtain a more effective fragmentation pattern, the main charge surrounded by more than 1,000 metal splinters, is projected about half a meter into the air, by a propelling charge before detonation. The mine has a lethal radius of at least 25 meters (Drawing by Pamela Blotner. Copyright: Physicians for Human Rights and Human Rights Watch Arms Project).

suppliers. The 1989 edition of *Jane's Military Vehicles and Logistics* lists 76 pages of different kinds of mines in use, and the list is not comprehensive[7] (Figures 10-2, 10-3, and 10-4).

What makes mines especially abhorrent is the indiscriminate destruction they cause. Unlike bombs or artillery shells, which are designed to explode when they approach or hit their target, mines lie dormant until a person, a vehicle, or an animal triggers the mechanism. Modern mines often have nonmetallic casings that render most mine-detection gear all but useless. Many models have camouflaged casings that make visual identification extremely difficult. Some antipersonnel mines are about the size of a thermos-bottle top, so a soldier can easily strew scores of them during a single patrol.

Mines cannot distinguish between the footfall of a soldier and that of a child. Mines recognize no cease-fire; long after the fighting has stopped, they can maim or kill the children or grandchildren of the soldiers who laid them.

Figure 10-3. The Soviet-made PFM-1 is a small air-delivered plastic antipersonnel mine. When large numbers of these green, wing-shaped mines were dropped in Afghanistan, Afghan tribesmen named it the ''Green Parrot.'' It is also called the ''Butterfly'' mine. The PFM-1 is also made of white or sand-colored, low-metallic signature plastic and is usually sown by Mi-8 Hip or similar helicopters. The mine drifts to the ground, where it becomes activated. From then on, any distortion of the plastic body will cause the mine to detonate. This distortion may be produced by stepping on or kicking the mine or by the accumulation of light pressures such as those produced by handling. Afghan children, mistaking the mine for a toy, have been killed or maimed (Drawing by Pamela Blotner. Copyright: Physicians for Human Rights and Human Rights Watch Arms Project).

Mines, unlike chemical and biological weapons, have never been banned. On the contrary, international law specifically permits the use of mines to achieve military objectives. In 1981, the United Nations adopted a convention and protocol restricting the use of ''mines'' (any munitions placed under, or near the ground or other surface area and designed to be detonated or exploded by the presence, proximity, or contact of a person).[8] It calls on military commanders to warn civilians of the presence of minefields, maintain maps of where they place mines, and remove the mines when they are no longer required. Remotely delivered mines are banned entirely unless they include a mechanism that renders them harmless after a specific period of time.

Figure 10-4. The Italian-made Valsella VS-50 is a plastic antipersonnel mine that is fitted with a pressure fuse and can be laid conveniently or scattered from ground vehicles, helicopters, or low-flying aircraft. The VS-50 is non-magnetic, waterproof, and has a long storage and field life (Drawing by Pamela Blotner. Copyright: Physicians for Human Rights and Human Rights Watch Arms Project).

The convention, however, has had little effect. As of September 1995, only 52 countries had signed and ratified it, including two of the world's major mine suppliers, the former Soviet Union and China. The Soviet Union used mines in Afghanistan in ways that clearly violated the convention's provisions. According to Afghan refugees, Soviet troops left mines in abandoned houses, mosques, on roads, and in grazing areas.[9] China supplied most of the mines used by the Khmer Rouge in Cambodia.[10] The Khmer Rouge, one of three guerrilla groups fighting against the Cambodian government, used mines intentionally against the civilian population. It mined rice paddies and country paths to prevent peasants from cultivating food crops and so to cause privation.

A major weakness of the land-mine protocol is that it applies only to international conflicts. Most of today's conflicts are internal or a mixture of internal and international. The International Committee of the Red Cross (ICRC) has rightly suggested that the protocol be modified to apply to internal conflicts as well, and although this was proposed to government representatives at the 1995 Review Conference of the protocol, they were unable to reach a consensus.

Medical Aspects of Mine Casualties

Mines commonly kill or inflict ravaging wounds, usually resulting in traumatic or surgical amputation. Mines produce damage by either blast or by driving dirt, bacteria, clothing, and metal and plastic fragments into the tissue and bone, often causing severe secondary infections.[11] Damage is rarely confined to one leg; lesser but still severe damage is frequently caused to the other leg, the genitals, arms, chest, and face. The force of the exploding mine can destroy blood vessels well up the leg, forcing surgeons to amputate much higher than the site of the primary wound.[12] In many cases, amputation is required because those helping the victim fail to loosen tourniquets on the wounded limbs at regular intervals.

Medical studies of combatants injured by mines indicate that early evacuation from the battlefield and prompt surgical care is crucial to saving lives and reducing disabilities. In Vietnam (1965–1973)[13] and Lebanon (1982),[14] medical facilities operated by the United States and Israeli military, respectively, achieved treatment results previously unsurpassed in war surgery. This was due to the short transportation distances, the availability of helicopters, and well-equipped medical facilities. In most conflicts, however, battlefield first aid, evacuation, and treatment facilities are far from ideal, with resultant high morbidity and mortality.

Military personnel injured by antipersonnel mines stand a better chance of receiving prompt and appropriate medical care than civilians. Foot soldiers usually travel in groups and carry first-aid equipment. They can also radio to military bases or camps for transport and further medical assistance. In contrast, few, if any, civilians living in or near war zones have access to rapid transport.

Many mine blast victims die in the fields or on the way to a hospital from loss of blood. In a 1991 study of civilian mine casualties in Cambodia, Physicians for Human Rights (PHR) and Asia Watch (now Human Rights Watch/Asia) found that mine blast victims from rural areas spent an average of 12 hours from the moment of injury until they reached a hospital with surgical facilities.[4] An ICRC study of 757 patients being treated for mine injuries in two hospitals in an unspecified developing country found that most patients were admitted 6 to 24 hours after injury.[8] This delay of care can result in sepsis and severe shock.

Even when civilians injured by mines reach medical facilities, they often fail to receive proper care because blood and medical supplies, such as surgical instruments, X-ray film, anesthesia, or antibiotics, are in short supply or unavailable. Victims of mine blasts are also more likely to require amputation[15,16] and remain in hospital longer than those wounded by other munitions. Hospitals in or near war zones, however, are usually understaffed and have few, if any, orthopedic surgeons, let alone general surgeons with extensive experience treating blast-related injuries.[4,17] In northern Somalia, the principal hospital has only a part-time volunteer staff of doctors and nurses, few antibiotics, and, according to its only orthopedic surgeon, an 80 percent wound infection rate. Until recently, mine-blast patients in government-run hospitals in Cambodia had to pay doctors and nurses for their services, medicines, and intravenous fluids. If blood was needed, the patient's family had to find donors and pay them.

In many developing countries, mine amputees leave the hospital without artificial limbs and return to their villages with little hope for the future. In agrarian or pastoral societies where muscle power means survival, amputees are often viewed by themselves and their families and communities as unproductive and simply another mouth to feed. Most developing countries have no laws to protect amputees against discrimination or exploitation. In Thailand, Cambodia, Somalia, and other developing nations, land-mine amputees are stigmatized because of their handicap and as a rule are unemployable. Male amputees may drift to the larger towns where they become beggars or petty criminals. In some countries, such as Cambodia, many employers refuse to hire amputees under the assumption that they are thieves.[18] For young female amputees, marriage may be impossible. However, there have been few if any adequate studies to provide insight into the psychological consequences of mine injuries in the affected countries. Acute and especially long-term psychological trauma must be studied in the context of the life-style and culture of the handicapped person. The experience with wounded veterans in the United States and other developed countries may not be highly relevant. The consequences may vary and be specific to each community.[19]

There are few, if any, state-run rehabilitation facilities, and those that do exist usually fit soldiers with artificial limbs before civilians are fitted. Even in those cases where prosthetic workshops exist, civilians often elect to return to their villages rather than incur the financial burden of these services and the inconvenience and expense of being away from home. Many are not even aware of the advantages of prosthetic devices. Back home, a few will fashion limbs out of scraps of wood and metal, but most amputees will grow accustomed to their crutches and, as time passes, simply keep postponing the trip to the workshop for financial or other reasons.

Several international humanitarian agencies, including the ICRC and Handicap International, are trying to produce prostheses for those injured by mines around the world. The ICRC now maintains orthopedic workshops in over 14 countries. In 1991, ICRC workshops made artificial limbs for 7,979 amputees, the majority of whom were mine-blast victims.[20] Despite the network of ICRC and other private organizations that support prosthetic and rehabilitation services, facilities available to civilian amputees are totally inadequate in number, distribution, and capacity to the need.

New techniques for constructing more flexible and easily fitted artificial limbs are being developed in a number of countries. One device called the "Jaipur foot," invented in the mid-1980s in Jaipur, India, is covered entirely in vulcanized rubber and can be fabricated for less than US$30. It requires no imported materials other than sheets of raw aluminum, is impervious to mud and water, and lasts up to 5 years. The ICRC fabricates inexpensive and durable prostheses in Cambodia, using simple polypropylene technology. Another artificial limb called the "Seattle Shapemaker," developed at the Prosthetics Research Foundation in Seattle, Washington, uses a springy, lifelike foot, which may allow amputees to walk with less limp.

Finding and clearing mines, of course, would be far better than the best prosthesis or system of medical care for victims. But it is a difficult and dangerous job because detection is precisely what mines are designed to avoid. The problem is further compounded because those who are most experienced and best equipped to clear mines are members of military forces, who use techniques that are better suited to breach minefields, rather than to eradicate small mines that are buried or strewn about by the thousands on agricultural and grazing lands and along secondary roads.

A Ban on Antipersonnel Mines

What can the international community do to prevent the use of antipersonnel mines? There appears to be no reasonable hope that technological developments will end the devastation that mine warfare has wreaked on rural communities throughout the world, or to prevent similar horrors elsewhere. The only way forward may be an international prohibition on the use of mines similar to the ban on poison gas that was agreed upon nearly 70 years ago.

In October 1991, Physicians for Human Rights and Human Rights Watch were the first two international organizations to call for an unconditional ban on all mines that detonate on contact. During the same month, Prince Norodom Sihanouk of Cambodia urged the United Nations to prohibit mine warfare. In 1992, the Mines Advisory Group, the Vietnam Veterans of America Foundation, Handicap International, and Medico International—all organizations that provide rehabilitative services to mine-blast victims—joined the campaign to ban mines. As of late 1995, the International Campaign to Ban Land Mines included over 350 human rights, medical, arms control, and religious organizations in over 30 countries.

The campaign advanced in July 1992 when Senator Patrick Leahy, joined by 35 cosponsors, introduced the Landmine Moratorium Act in the United States Senate. Congressman Lane Evans introduced identical legislation in the U.S. House of Representatives and, in conference, it was included in the Fiscal Year 1993 defense authorization bill signed into law by President George Bush in October 1992.[21] The legislation imposed a one-year U.S. moratorium on the sale, export, or transfer of antipersonnel mines. It declared the ''sense of Congress'' that the President should actively seek verifiable international agreements or a modification of the existing international agreements or a modification of the existing international land-mine protocol to prohibit the use of mines. In 1993, the export moratorium was extended for another 3 years.

The United States was one of approximately 35 countries that exported antipersonnel mines, though its exports were quantitatively insignificant compared to other countries. U.S. Congressional leadership, in halting this deadly trade, influenced policies of other supplier countries. In December 1992, the European Parliament drafted a "Motion for a Resolution" on mines. The motion called on all member states "to agree to a five-year moratorium on the sale of, transfer, or export of antipersonnel mines and the military skills to plant them." Two months later, President François Mitterand declared that France would stop exporting antipersonnel mines. In September 1995, France joined Belgium in declaring a complete ban on the production, use, and export of mines. By late 1995, 22 countries had adopted export legislation.

It will not be easy enforcing an international ban on the production of antipersonnel mines. Monitoring the transfer of a weapon that can fit in a vanity case is far more difficult than monitoring missile shipments. On the positive side, mines are inexpensive weapons that do not offer nations export earnings comparable to higher-technology munitions such as anti-aircraft guns and shoulder-fired missiles. Restrictions on their manufacture and export may therefore be easier to achieve.

The medical profession can prevent the use of land mines by helping document the physical and mental suffering exacted from civilians by antipersonnel mines. Individual doctors and medical and relief organizations, such as Médecins Sans Frontières and Médecins du Monde (see boxes in Chapter 20), could begin keeping records on injuries caused by mines and their social and economic consequences on civilian populations. Several medical and public health associations, including the Australian Medical Association, the American Public Health Association, and the American Nurses Association, have already adopted resolutions calling for a ban on mines. More professional associations should follow suit.

For its part, the ICRC with its dozens of expatriate specialists worldwide has begun to gather data on civilian mine injuries. The information that the ICRC collects at its field hospitals includes the patient's hospital number; age; sex; time between injury and admission; activity at time of injury; bodily location of injuries; whether there was traumatic amputation of limbs; whether the patient died; whether the patient underwent surgical amputation; whether there was another disability and, if so, of what nature; the number of times the patient went to the operating room; and the number of units of blood received by the patient. For the purposes of the ICRC studies, noncombatants are defined as women, boys less than 16 years old, and men over 50 years old.[8]

Medical and demographic information on the nature and scope of mine-related deaths and injuries can serve as a powerful and objective weapon in the struggle to make the world's governments recognize the full horror of these weapons. The next step must be an unconditional ban on the production, trade, and use of mines. A ban may not end their use entirely, but it would help stigmatize the users and suppliers and thereby help reduce the injuries and deaths during and after future wars.

REFERENCES

1. Stockholm International Peace Research Institute. *Antipersonnel weapons.* London: Taylor and Francis, Ltd. 1978, pp. 180–189.
2. Martin, E.S. and Hiebert, M. Explosive remnants of the Second Indo-China War in Vietnam

and Laos. In Westing, A.H. (ed.), *Explosive remnants of war: Mitigating the environmental effects.* London: Taylor and Francis, 1985, pp. 39–49.

3. International Committee of the Red Cross. *Mines: A perverse use of technology.* Geneva, Switzerland: International Committee of the Red Cross, 1992, p. 14.
4. Lewis, F. Make a Misstep and You're Dead. *New York Times,* May 4, 1992:A17.
5. Asia Watch and Physicians for Human Rights. *Land mines in Cambodia: The coward's war.* New York: Human Rights Watch and Physicians for Human Rights, 1991, p. 2.
6. Asia Watch and Physicians for Human Rights. *Land mines in Cambodia: The coward's war.* New York: Human Rights Watch and Physicians for Human Rights, 1991, p. 9.
7. United Nations Convention on Prohibitions or Restrictions on the Use of Certain Conventional Weapons Which May Be Deemed To Be Excessively Injurious or To Have Indiscriminate Effects. UN Doc.A/Conf.95/15; 1980.
8. Asia Watch. *Afghanistan: The forgotten war.* New York: Human Rights Watch, February, 1991.
9. Stover, E. and Charles, D. The killing minefields of Cambodia. *New Scientist,* October 19, 1991:27.
10. Coupland, R.M. and Korver, A. Injuries from antipersonnel mines: The experience of the International Committee of the Red Cross. *Brit. Med. J.* 303:1509–1512, 1991.
11. Traverso, L.W., Fleming, A., Johnson, D.E. and Wongrukmitr, B. Combat casualties in northern Thailand: Emphasis on land mine and levels of amputation. *Milit. Med.* 146:682–685, 1981.
12. Hardaway, R.M. Vietnam wound analysis. *J. Trauma* 18:635–643, 1978.
13. Danon, L.D., Nili, E. and Dolev, E. Primary treatment of battle casualties in the Lebanon war. *Israel J. Med. Sci.* 20:300–302, 1982.
14. Rautio, J. and Paavolainen, P. Afghan war wounded: Experience with 200 cases. *J. Trauma* 28:523–525, 1988.
15. Johnson, D.E., Panijayanond, P., Lumjiak, S., Crum, J.W. and Boonkrapu, P. Epidemiology of combat casualties in Thailand. *J. Trauma* 21:486–488, 1981.
16. Physicians for Human Rights. *Hidden enemies: Land mines in northern Somalia.* Boston: Physicians for Human Rights, 1992.
17. Personal communication from the American Friends Service Committee Workshop Staff, Phnom Penh, April 1991.
18. Personal communication with Richard Mollica, M.D., Harvard School of Public Health, March 1993.
19. Russbach, R. Antipersonnel mines: A disgrace for humanity. *ICRC Bull.,* Nov. 1992:202.
20. United States House of Representatives. *National Defense Authorization Act for Fiscal Year 1993.* Oct. 1, 1992; 102nd Congress, 2nd session: 255–257.

IV

Effects of War and Other Military Activities on Populations

11

The Impact of Military Activities on Civilian Populations

BARRY S. LEVY and VICTOR W. SIDEL

Since the end of World War II in 1945, more than 23 million people have been killed in the over 150 major wars that have been fought.[1,2] During this period, the percentage of civilian casualties in war has increased from 10 percent to 90 percent of all casualties[3] (see Chapter 3). Many millions of civilians have died from war-related hunger and disease due to the destruction of agricultural and overall economic systems. Many more have died from injury and disease while being forced to flee their homes. The number of refugees and displaced persons has also grown substantially[4] (see Chapter 14).

In addition to these direct casualties of war, there have been indirect effects due to preparation for war, such as diversion of resources and pollution caused by the productions, testing, stockpiling, and even destruction of arms. Finally, civilian populations are subject to the destructive effects of the social, economic, and psychological atmosphere created by war and preparations for it, often termed ''militarism.''

Impact on Developing Countries

Almost all the wars since 1945 have been fought in developing countries, often as surrogate wars between the United States and the Soviet Union. More recently, civil wars—often based on opposition to oppressive governments, or on historic ethnic

Parts of this chapter were adapted from a presentation by Reed Tuckson at the Annual Meeting of the American Public Health Association in Atlanta in 1991. Other parts were adapted from: Sidel, V.W. Farewell to arms: The impact of the arms race on the human condition *PSR Quarterly* 3:18–26, 1993; and from Sidel, V.W. The international arms trade and its impact on health. *Brit. Med. J.* 311: 1677–1680, 1995.

enmities, or arising from artificial geographic aggregations created by the colonial powers—have produced the greatest number of casualties. UNICEF has estimated that during the decade since 1985, war has taken a terrible toll among children: two million killed; four to five million disabled; 12 million left homeless; more than one million orphaned or separated from their parents; and 10 million psychologically traumatized[2] (see Chapters 2 and 12).

The most direct impact of military activities on health in developing countries is the use of arms to kill and maim. Some military leaders may find it more advantageous to wound rather than to kill enemy personnel—military or civilian—since the opponents must then consume valuable resources to take care of their wounded. The vast majority of the weapons being used today are therefore antipersonnel weapons. Among the most pernicious of these weapons are land mines (see Chapter 10). Another weapon that has received worldwide condemnation is the blinding laser, which can burn out a human retina from a distance of 3,000 feet.[5] Nations believed to have pursued or to be pursuing laser weapon research and development include China, France, Germany, Israel, Russia, Ukraine, the United Kingdom, and the United States.[6]

Military Spending in Developing Countries

From 1960 to 1990, several trends have been observed in military spending and the size of armed forces (Table 11-1):

- Public military expenditures (in constant dollars) increased more than fourfold in developing countries, although, as a percentage of GNP, they remained about the same.
- Per-capita public military expenditures (in constant dollars) in developing countries doubled despite rapid population growth.
- The size of the armed forces doubled in developing countries; despite rapid population growth, the ratio of the number of people in the armed forces to the total population remained about the same in the developing countries.
- Public expenditures (in constant dollars) per soldier more than doubled in developing countries.

The Indirect Health Consequences of Military Activities

The damage to health and human services and to economic development related to the human and economic costs of weapons are also extremely well documented. Developing countries are the most severely affected, suffering delay or reversal of economic development and deprivation of essential nutrition, housing, education, and health services.[4,7–10] (See box on p. 152.)

Overall, although developing countries spend less when measured in equivalent currency on arms (see Figure 11-1), they spend much more when measured in human hours of productivity (see Figure 11-2). The resources spent on arms pose a greater

Table 11-1.   Trends in military expenditures and armed forces, 1960–1990

	1960	1970	1980	1990
Public Expenditures (billion 1987 US $)				
World	322	454	549	676
Developed countries	295	395	447	557
Developing countries	27	59	102	119
Public Expenditures (percent of GNP)				
World	5.7	4.8	4.3	3.8
Developed countries	5.9	4.8	4.2	3.7
Developing countries	3.9	4.6	4.6	3.9
Public Expenditures (1987 US $ per capita)				
World	115	129	126	131
Developed countries	341	391	408	478
Developing countries	14	24	31	30
Armed Forces (in millions)				
World	18.6	21.5	25.1	26.8
Developed countries	10.2	10.4	10.2	10.0
Developing countries	8.4	11.1	14.9	16.8
Armed Forces (soldiers per 1,000,000 population)				
World	6135	5848	5682	5076
Developed countries	11111	10309	9259	8547
Developing countries	3984	4149	4484	4098
Public Expenditures (per soldier, 1987 US $, in thousands)				
World	18.1	22.2	22.9	26.5
Developed countries	29.0	37.9	44.0	56.0
Developing countries	3.6	5.9	7.4	7.7

Source: Sivard, R.L. *World military and social expenditures 1993 (Fifteenth edition).* Washington, DC: World Priorities, 1993, p. 42.

burden to many developing countries than they do for even heavily spending industrialized countries. As summarized in the report of the 1987 United Nations International Conference on the Relationship between Disarmament and Development, ". . . (T)he continuing global arms race and development compete for the same finite resources at both the national and international levels."[11]

Finally, militarism has other impacts on developing countries. Economic embargoes, a form of economic warfare, cause great hardships, particularly to the civilian populations. (See box on pp. 156-158 and Chapter 17.) Militarism is also closely associated with despotic governments that use large military forces to maintain themselves in office.

The International Arms Trade

Most modern weapons of war are manufactured in industrialized countries, and many of these weapons are sold or given to developing countries by industrialized countries. This militarization is, in part, due to the view in many post-colonial countries that

The Human Development Cost of Arms Imports

Many countries continue to import expensive arms, even though they have a long list of more essential items. This is clear from the arms deliveries and orders in the categories covered by the UN arms register. Some of the choices by developing countries in 1992:

- *China*—purchased 26 combat aircraft from Russia in a deal whose total cost could have provided safe water for one year to 140 million of the 200 million people now without safe water.
- *India*—ordered 20 MiG-29 fighter aircraft from Russia at a cost that could have provided basic education to all the 15 million girls out of school.
- *Iran*—bought two submarines from Russia at a cost that could have provided essential medicines to the whole country many times over; 13% of Iran's population has no access to health care.
- *Republic of Korea*—ordered 28 missiles from the United States for an amount that could have immunized all the 120,000 unimmunized children and provided safe water for three years to the 3.5 million people without safe water.
- *Malaysia*—ordered two warships from the United Kingdom at a cost that could have provided safe water for nearly a quarter century to the five million people without safe water.
- *Nigeria*—purchased 80 battle tanks from the United Kingdom at a cost that could have immunized all of the two million unimmunized children and provided family planning services to nearly 17 million of the more than 20 million couples who lack such services.
- *Pakistan*—ordered 40 Mirage 2000E fighters and three Tripartite aircraft from France at a cost that could have provided safe water for two years for all 55 million people who lack safe water, family planning services for the estimated 20 million couples in need of such services, essential medicines for the nearly 13 million people without access to health care, and basic education for the 12 million children out of primary school.

Source: United Nations Development Program, *Human Development Report, 1994.* New York: Oxford University Press, 1994.

possession of large arsenals is essential to being recognized as a "developed" nation. The arms may fall into the hands of those who use them for private vendettas or private gain, or even into the hands of children. In addition, some industrialized countries, including the United States, use their "foreign aid" as a method of transferring funds to their military industries, requiring the recipient governments to use the funds they receive to purchase arms from private industries in the "donor" country.[12]

Estimates of the amount of arms traded depend on the definitions used and on adequacy of reporting, but it is clear that over 90 percent of arms transferred to other countries are supplied by the five permanent members of the UN Security Council (China, France, Russia, United Kingdom, and the United States) and Germany, often termed the "Big Six." A 1988 study by the UN estimated arms transfers between countries at $14 billion annually in the early 1960s.[13] In 1994, the total rose to over

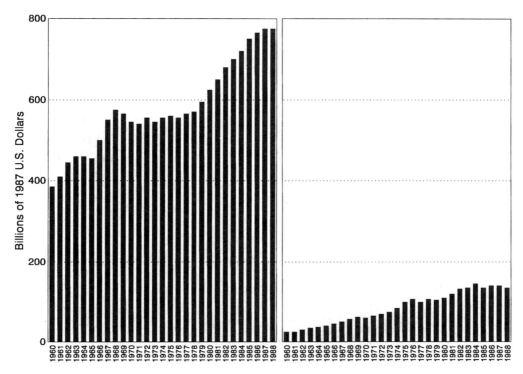

Figure 11-1. Burden of military expenditures in 1987 U.S. dollars in industrialized (developed) countries (left) and developing countries (right). (Source: Ruth Leger Sivard. *World Military and Social Expenditures, 1991 [Fourteenth Edition].* Washington, DC: World Priorities, 1991, p. 11).

$35 billion. The U.S. Arms Control and Disarmament Agency estimated that the United States negotiated 47 percent of the dollar value of all new arms sales agreements in 1993; the U.K., 20 percent; Russia, 12 percent; Germany, 5 percent; France, 4 percent; and China, 4 percent[14] (Figures 11-3 and 11-4).

In the 1980s, the United States sold more than $134 billion in weapons and military services to more than 160 nations and political movements. U.S. sales increased further during the 1990s. In 1993, the United States controlled nearly 73 percent of the weapons trade to the Third World.[15] An estimated 85 percent of U.S. arms exports went to nondemocratic and often brutal regimes; in Panama, Iraq, and Somalia, such arms were turned against American forces. U.S. arms also fuel conflicts and increase regional tensions. The Clinton administration has done little to curb the proliferation of arms sales, and the results of the 1994 congressional elections dampened efforts by some members of Congress to reduce these sales.

The U.K. is a major participant in the international arms trade and, by some esti-

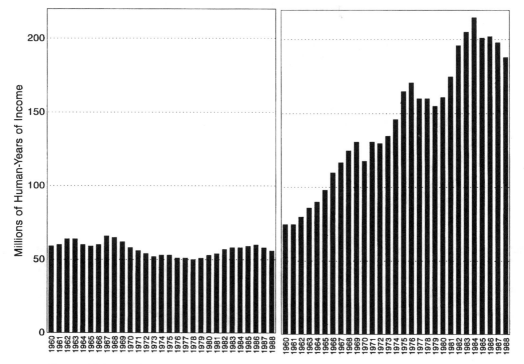

Figure 11-2. Burden of military expenditures in equivalent human-years of income in industrialized (developed) countries (left) and developing countries (right). (Source: Ruth Leger Sivard. *World Military and Social Expenditures, 1991 [Fourteenth Edition].* Washington, DC: World Priorities, 1991, p. 11).

mates, has moved beyond Russia into second place. In 1993, approximately £2000 million ($3 billion) worth of military equipment was shipped overseas, and during that year new orders totalling some £6000 million ($9 billion) were signed. Former colonial countries with enormous problems in development, such as India, are among Britain's largest customers. Britain, like the United States, sells military equipment to countries that use it to violate the human rights of their citizens, such as Indonesia, South Africa in the period before the end of apartheid, Uganda under Idi Amin, and Nigeria under its military government that executes political prisoners.

France also appears to be increasing its involvement in the international arms trade. In 1994, France negotiated $11.4 billion in new arms sales agreements with Third World nations, while the United States negotiated agreements totalling $6.1 billion.[16] This comparison is misleading because the bulk of France's sales came from three exceptional multibillion dollar sales of a kind that are not likely to be repeated, and because the figures fail to reflect a number of deals negotiated directly by U.S. industry with foreign purchasers.

The 1987 Conference on the Relationship between Disarmament and Development summarized the issue for developing countries and for other nations:

> The world can either continue to pursue the arms race with characteristic vigour or move consciously and with deliberate speed towards a more stable and balanced social and economic development within a more sustainable international economic and political order; it cannot do both.[11]

Impact on Industrialized Countries

While war, preparation for war, and militarism have had their most dramatic health impact on developing countries, these forces have also had an enormous impact in a number of industrialized countries. The direct impact of war on industrialized countries includes over 50,000 deaths and over 300,000 wounded among U.S. troops in the Vietnam War (see Chapter 15) and many casualties among Soviet and then Russian troops in areas such as Afghanistan and Chechnya. In addition, refugees have come, sometimes in large numbers, to industrialized countries and often place great strains on public health, education, and other human services (see Chapter 14).

However, in industrialized countries the greater impact on civilian populations has been caused by military activities other than wars:

- Diverting huge amounts of financial and human resources to arms, instead of improving quality of life and the health of people.
- Developing, producing, testing, stockpiling, and dismantling chemical, biological, nuclear, and ''conventional'' weapons and their components (see Chapters 6–9).
- Leading people to believe in resolving conflicts by violent means, thereby contributing to increasing violence in industrialized countries, especially in urban areas.
- Driving individuals in disproportionate numbers from minority communities, particularly in the United States, into the military, with diversion of many of the best and brightest individuals from these communities from positive roles they could play there.

Diversion of Resources to the Arms Race

Many industrialized nations, and even more developing nations, have squandered their financial and human resources on destructiveness (see Figure 11-5). Furthermore, many of them have not paid the bills for the costs of war and preparations for war, leaving an enormous debt to their children. This diversion has had a major adverse effect on the availability of resources for constructive purposes—including health and

The Health Impact
of Economic Sanctions

Richard M. Garfield

Economic sanctions have become more common as a prelude or alternative to warfare in the twentieth century. Multistate sanctions, such as those imposed by the UN, were applied only to Rhodesia prior to the dissolution of the Soviet Union in 1991. Since that date, collective international sanctions have been applied against Iraq, the Yugoslav federation of Serbia and Montenegro, Libya, and Haiti. The United States has also instituted unilateral sanctions against Nicaragua, Cuba, Iran, Sudan, South Africa, and Rwanda. There are likely to be many more countries subject to economic sanctions in the years ahead.

The health impact of embargoes is difficult to specify. Threats to health caused by an embargo are seldom direct and may become apparent only after years of resource shortages. Major impacts occur through the effect of an embargo on the production, importation, and distribution of essential goods. Other threats to a social system that often accompany embargoes, including economic inefficiencies, inequitable distribution of goods, civil conflicts, and population movements, are also threats to a population's health. Thus, the unique impact of an embargo is difficult to specify due to the multicausal and indirect nature of the outcomes. Further, reactions of the populace to an embargo may confound its effects on health. Data for key indicators of health effects in embargoed states are often missing, unavailable, or inaccurate. What is known about the health impact of the embargoes against Vietnam, several Central American countries, and Iraq are described in Chapters 15, 16, and 17.

Embargoes have been described as "foreign policy on the cheap." Not only are cheap sanctions likely to be ineffective, but the costs of sanctions are very real, especially to the poor and powerless in target countries.[1] This review is consistent with a UNICEF analysis, which found: "The heaviest consequences often fall on those who are least culpable and most vulnerable."[2] By contrast, military and political groups, which are the most common targets of embargoes, may hardly be affected. They may even find an embargo profitable.[3] Very often it is because governments are unresponsive to the needs of the population that embargoes are enforced; worsening conditions for the poor are unlikely to have the desired impact of pressuring such groups or governments to reform.

Given the large role for international and charity organizations in the supply of such goods for some developing countries subjected to embargoes, exemptions play a critical role in making basic goods available. Since it is the vulnerable who suffer the most, social services should be maintained to mitigate the effects of embargoes on nontarget populations.[4] Shifting interpretations of definitions for exemptions limit the ability of such organizations to provide humanitarian assistance and inhibit supply firms from trading with the embargoed country, even among exempted goods.

Ironically, when embargoes mobilize local populations and prioritize government action to protect the most vulnerable, health can sometimes be improved, likely the result of the more efficient use of increasingly scarce resources. Examples include promotion of breastfeeding, equitable rationing of food, and the popularization of preventive health campaigns. Infant mortality decline has been noted in several countries where overall mortality rose during an embargo. This is to be expected, as a healthy microenvironment for young children is easier to bring about with limited resources than such an environment for older people. When a society is well organized and an embargo is not complete, living standards can stabilize at lower levels, with only limited impact on

1. Doudi, M.A. and Dajan, M.S. *Economic sanctions: Ideas and experiences.* Boston: Routledge and Kegan, 1983.

2. UNICEF. *UNICEF emergency operations.* New York: UNICEF, E/ICEF/1993/February 1993, p. 15.

3. Macree, J. and Zwi, A. Food as an instrument of war in contemporary African famines: A review of the evidence. *Disasters* 16 (4): 299–321, 1993.

4. Rodley, N. (ed.). *To loose the bands of wickedness: International interventions in defense of human rights.* London: Brassey's, 1992.

morbidity and mortality. Even these effects can be abated or reversed among children, as their health generally responds to simple interventions. Effects on women, older people, and individuals with chronic or multisystem health problems are harder to address when economic activity declines and imports are restricted. When distribution of basic goods is not done efficiently and equitably, the health impact will likely be much worse.

Modern wars have had increasing effect on civilians, stimulating international agreements on shielding civilians from war. To date, civilians are provided none of the war-related protections under the less bellicose expression of warfare created by sanctions.[5]

The embargo against Cuba was imposed by the United States in 1960 and made more stringent to include prohibition of sales on food and medicine in 1964. Not the result of a single act of Congress, this embargo is composed of many actions over more than three decades.[6] From 1975 to 1992, the embargo was partially relaxed as part of the U.S. policy of detente with the Soviet Union.

The current statute supporting this embargo is part of the "Cuban Democracy Act of 1992" signed into law by former President George Bush. This is the most restrictive law since the embargo in the early 1960s. Almost all goods, including food, medicines, and transportation and medical equipment, are restricted, as is the re-export of U.S. products from third countries. Ships docking in Cuba are not permitted to visit U.S. ports for six months. Cuban assets in the United States are frozen; civil and criminal punishments for violations have been increased; and unilateral presidential power has been established to deny aid to any country providing "assistance" to Cuba. This tightening of the embargo coincided with the dissolution of Soviet Community for Mutual Economic Assistance (CMEA) and the loss of markets accounting for 85 percent of Cuba's trade.[7] It was reported that in 1992 the loss of markets, credits, and favorable terms of trade through CMEA dropped the dollar value of this commerce by 93 percent compared to 1988.[7] The ability to import goods dropped to $2.2 billion in 1992, leaving Cuba with a 73 percent decline in productive activity[7] and a 45 percent drop in GNP.[8]

About half of all proteins and calories intended for human consumption were imported in the 1980s; importation of foodstuffs declined by about 50 percent from 1989 to 1993. Reduced imports and a shift toward lower quality proteins are significant health threats. Milk production declined by 55 percent from 1989 to 1992. A daily glass of milk used to be provided to all children in schools and day-care centers through age 13; it is now provided only up to age seven. From 1989 to 1992, per capita protein availability declined by 25 percent, caloric availability by 18 percent.[9] The nutritional deficit falls mainly on adult males, who comprise almost all of the 50,000 victims of a neuropathy epidemic associated with B-vitamin deficits.[10]

Unavailability of supplies and raw materials from U.S. subsidiaries greatly increases the costs of production of essential goods in Cuba. Overall, it is estimated that the embargo creates a "tax" of 30 percent on all imports, which must be purchased from markets that are smaller and more distant than the United States.

Several essential medical products are produced only in the United States. Even when exceptions to the embargo have been granted, serious delays have occurred while foreign firms sought U.S. authorization for sale. Because of this, on several occasions, the product was useless by the time it arrived.

A highly organized public food distribution system, combined with a highly professionalized and universally accessible system of public medical care and nutritional supplementation, has sought

5. Damrosch, L.F. The civilian impact of economic sanctions. In Damrosch, L.F. *Enforcing restraint, collective intervention in internal conflicts.* New York: Council on Foreign Relations Press, 1993.

6. Krinsky, M. and Golove, D. (eds.) *United States economic measures against Cuba: Proceedings in the United Nations and international law issues.* Northhampton, Mass: Aletheia Press, 1993.

7. Some antecedents on the availability of goods in Cuba at the beginning of 1993. Ministry of Foreign Trade, mimeo.

8. American Public Health Association. *The politics of suffering: The impact of the U.S. embargo on the health of the Cuban people.* Washington: APHA. 1993.

9. Programa nacional de accion. *Cuba: segunda informe de seguimiento y evaluacion.* La Habana, 1993.

10. Cotton, P. Cause of Cuban outbreak neuropathologic puzzle. *JAMA* 270(4):421–423, 1993.

to limit the effects of shortages on women and children. Despite these efforts, the percentage of babies born with inadequate weights rose from 7.3 percent in 1989 to 8.7 percent in 1993, wiping out 10 years of progress.[11] The number of women with inadequate weight gains during pregnancy and with anemia also increased rapidly. Infectious diseases, including tuberculosis and diarrheal diseases, have risen rapidly among those age 65 and older. While infant mortality continues at stable low rates, mortality among those 65 and older rose 15 percent from 1989 to 1993. This increase was associated with declining access to food and water, shortages of medicines for chronic diseases, and lack of laboratory reagents to monitor such patients.

In summary, age- and cause-specific health impacts of the embargo on Cuba since 1992 have been well documented. The major impacts include nutrition-related diseases in young children, men, and women, and chronic disease mortality among older adults.

11. MINSAP. *Informe Anual, 1992.* MINSAP: La Habana, 1993.

human services—in the United States and other industrialized countries as well as in developing countries.

MILITARY SPENDING IN INDUSTRIALIZED (DEVELOPED) COUNTRIES. From 1960 to 1990, the following trends were observed (Table 11-1)):

- Public military expenditures (in constant dollars) increased sharply in industrialized countries, almost doubling, although they decreased as a percentage of GNP.
- Per-capita public military expenditures (in constant dollars) in industrialized countries increased by more than one-third.
- Public expenditures per soldier almost doubled in industrialized countries.

U.S. MILITARY SPENDING. During the 1980s, annual military spending in the United States increased dramatically. The total amount of military spending (in current dollars) during the eight years of the Reagan administration was about $2 trillion—equivalent to about $20,000 for each U.S. family. The U.S. share of world military spending increased annually from 1979 (approximately 22 percent) to 1989 (almost 30 percent). Meanwhile, the U.S. federal budget deficit increased fourfold during the Reagan and Bush administrations to $4 trillion.[17]

IMPACT OF MILITARY SPENDING IN THE SOVIET UNION. The impact of military spending in the Soviet Union was even greater than in the United States during the years of the Cold War. Although the two countries spent about the same amounts of money on arms from 1960 to 1981, the Soviet Union, because of its lower GNP, spent a substantially higher percentage of its GNP on arms—an estimated 11.5 percent of GNP by the Soviet Union, as compared with 6.2 percent of GNP by the United States. Such enormous expenditures had major adverse effects on the economy and on health and human services in the Soviet Union.[18]

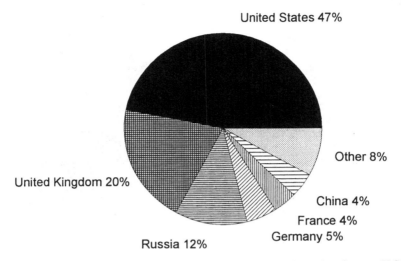

Figure 11-3. Distribution of new arms sales agreements, 1993 dollar value (Source: U.S. Arms Control and Disarmament Agency estimate, reprinted from: *British Medical Journal,* December 23-30, 1995, p. 1679).

MILITARY SPENDING AS COMPARED WITH DEVELOPMENT ASSISTANCE. To the extent that industrialized countries spend money for military purposes, it appears they spend proportionately less money on development assistance to developing countries. The Scandinavian countries allocated in 1994 in the range of 1.0 percent of their GNP for official development assistance, as compared to 0.15 percent by the United States (Figure 11-6). Scandinavian countries and Japan allocated for official development assistance monies that ranged from 30 to 54 percent of their military expenditures, as compared to 4 percent for the United States (Figure 11-7).

EMPHASIS ON MILITARY RESEARCH. Spending of approximately three-fourths of U.S. federal research and development funds on the military has meant that less money is available for research that might have improved the quality of life. In fiscal year 1987, for example, military programs consumed 71 percent of the total federal research and development budget. In three years in the mid-1980s, military research and development increased by 28 percent while health and human services research and development decreased by five percent. This focus on military research has resulted in a "brain drain" that has drawn bright scientists away from performing research in nonmilitary areas that could contribute to the quality of life. World expenditures on weapons research exceed the combined spending on developing new energy technologies, improving human health, raising agricultural productivity, and controlling pollutants.

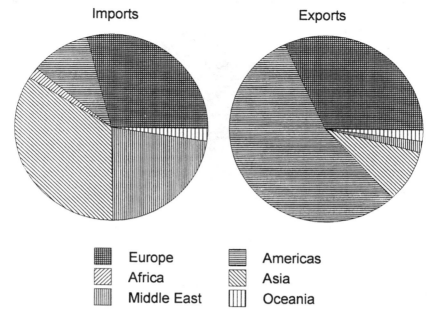

Figure 11-4. Volume of trade in conventional weapons, 1994. Among the imports, 58 percent are into the developing world and 42 percent are into the industrialized world. Among the exports, 93 percent are from the industrialized world and 7 percent are from the developing world. (Source: Table 14, *SIPRI Yearbook 1995,* New York: Oxford University Press, 1995. Reprinted from: *British Medical Journal,* December 23–30, 1995, p. 1679).

INADEQUATE FUNDS FOR SOCIAL DEVELOPMENT AND HUMAN SERVICES. The huge amounts of tax revenues spent on arms divert monies from health and other human services (see Figure 11-8). After correcting for inflation, the United States increased its military spending during the 1980s by 46 percent, while nonmilitary spending decreased by 19 percent for child nutrition, 33 percent for mass transit, 48 percent for employment and training, 70 percent for education, and 77 percent for housing. According to the National League of Cities, direct federal aid to U.S. cities fell from almost $25 billion in 1981 to less than $10 billion in 1991 (in 1982 dollars). And, during this period, an increasing number of people lived below the poverty line in the United States: 29 million people in 1980, 33 million in 1985, and approximately 40 million in 1994. Over 40 million people in the United States lack health insurance and risk being turned away from receiving health care if they are unable to pay. The U.S. emphasis on achieving military supremacy in the world has had costs in its social development, as illustrated in Table 11-2.

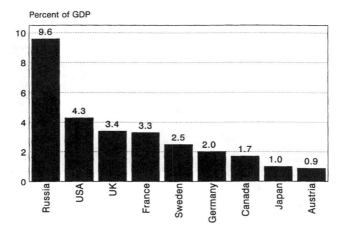

Figure 11-5. Military Expenditures as a Percentage of Gross Domestic Product, 1994 (Source: United Nations Development Program, *Human Development Report 1996*. New York: Oxford University Press, 1996.).

Impacts on the Domestic Economy

Excessive military spending has profound adverse effects on the domestic economy.[19,20]

DIMINISHED PRODUCTIVITY. One result of massive arms investment is the diversion of capital away from productivity expansion in the civilian economy. Industrialized countries that spent far less on arms, such as Japan, the former Federal Republic of Germany (West Germany), Denmark, Italy, and Sweden, surpassed the United States and the former Soviet Union in the rate of growth of manufacturing productivity. Money invested in nonmilitary products, services, and technologies broadens the overall economic base and potential for further expansion. Although short-term deficit spending has benefited the rich, the resultant overwhelming debt will inevitably diminish the scope of future advancement. Adequate public support for health care and other human services depends on an expanding economic pie. The inevitable contraction based on excessive military spending is likely to restrict publicly funded services for middle-income and low-income families.

INFLATION. Military spending exerts inflationary pressure by pumping money into the economy without increasing the supply of purchasable goods and services. Military procurement diminishes resources that would otherwise be used for the production of consumer goods.

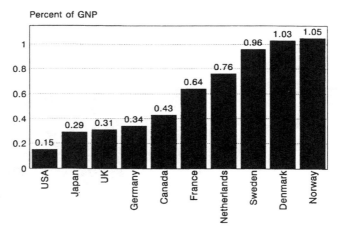

Figure 11-6. Official Development Assistance as a Percent of Gross National Product, 1994 (Source: United Nations Development Program. *Human Development Report, 1996.* New York: Oxford University Press, 1996).

UNEMPLOYMENT. The inflationary pressure of military spending generates anti-inflationary responses; in order to diminish the upward spiral of costs, the government tolerates an unacceptably high level of unemployment. Despite assertions to the contrary, military spending creates far fewer jobs than expenditure for many civilian services. For example, $1 billion spent on military contracts and personnel in 1992 created 24,000 jobs; the same amount of money spent on mass transit created 28,000 jobs; on housing, created 34,000 jobs; on health care, created 38,000 jobs; and on education, created 40,000 jobs.[21]

Maintaining or Increasing Military Spending in the United States

According to the International Institute for Strategic Studies, the United States in 1993, with a military budget of $277.1 billion, outspent the next 10 countries combined ($240.1 billion). Analyses by the Center for Defense Information before the 1994 U.S. Congressional elections, for example, indicated that proposed military spending outlays by the Clinton administration would remain at Cold War levels (in the range of $257 billion per year). Maintaining this level of expenditure, while most other countries of the world reduce their expenditure, would mean that the U.S. share of world military spending would move from its level of 20 to 30 percent in the 1980s to 45 percent by 1997. The driving forces for this maintenance or increase in military spending include not only perceptions of the need for military weapons and personnel for national security but also desire for profits and for jobs. In 1995, the U.S. executive branch maintained expenditures and the leaders of the U.S. Congress

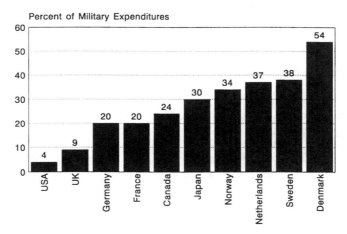

Figure 11-7. Official Development Assistance as a Percent of Military Expenditures, 1994 (Source: United Nations Development Program. *Human Development Report, 1996.* New York: Oxford University Press, 1996).

proposed increased expenditures despite the advice of analysts that the U.S. military budget can be reduced by at least $40 billion annually with no threat to national security[22,23].

The military-industrial complex in the United States and in other arms-producing nations wields considerable power and influence. Major industries involved include aerospace, communications, electronics, computing, and transportation. The incestuous relationship between the Pentagon and military contractors has created the opportunity to generate enormous profits when expressed as a percentage of investment. Such financial outlays produce the political leverage to promote a military agenda that bears little relevance to meeting an external military threat. In such a climate, cost overruns, deception, and fraud become the norm.

Impact on the Physical Environment

The development, production, testing, use, and dismantling of chemical, biological, nuclear, and ''conventional'' weapons and their components adversely affects the human environment and, in turn, human health (see Chapters 5 and 9).

Influence on Community and Domestic Violence

International and civil war—and preparation for war—influences community and domestic violence in a number of ways:

- It promotes the idea that violence is an acceptable method of resolving conflicts.

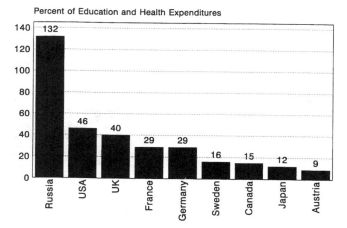

Figure 11-8. Military Expenditures as a Percent of Combined Education and Health Expenditures, 1990-91 (Source: United Nations Development Program. *Human Development Report, 1996.* New York: Oxford University Press, 1996).

- It makes human lives appear cheaper.
- It makes lethal weapons, including military assault weapons, readily available at the community and domestic level.
- It makes local violence a little easier to accept.

Social conditions help to cause both war and violence. In the United States and other industrialized countries, the quality of life is lower and rates of tuberculosis, HIV infection, and murder are higher in low-income areas than in high-income areas.

Disproportionate Impact on Minority Communities in the United States

Individuals from minority communities comprise a disproportionate fraction of those serving in the military; in the process, many of the best and the brightest from these communities are taken away from roles they might otherwise play in improving education, political action, health, and hope in these communities.

In addition, militarism and war glorify violence, a fact that may be especially relevant to minority communities in which living conditions lead to frequent conflict that may escalate into violence (Figure 11-9). Limited possibilities for the future contribute to pessimism in these communities. Young African-Americans perceive from their personal experience that the community is a dangerous place to be, and a place where there are inadequate social supports and limited access to health care and other services. In this context, the military can look like a very attractive environment, especially as it is portrayed in television commercials: Come join the military; get

Table 11-2.   U.S. rank among 140 countries

Area	Rank
Military Power	
Arms exports	1
Military expenditures	1
Military technology	1
Military bases worldwide	1
Military training of foreign forces	1
Military aid to foreign countries	1
Naval fleet	1
Combat aircraft	1
Nuclear reactors	1
Nuclear warheads and bombs	1
Armed forces personnel	3
Social Development	
Population with safe water (percent)	1
Literacy rate	4
Gross National Product per capita	6
Economic-social standing	9
Public education expenditures per capita	9
Life expectancy (years)	10
Public health expenditures per capita	11
Teachers per school-age population	12
Population with family planning (percent)	15
Infant mortality rate	21
Physicians per population	22
Economic aid given as a percent of GNP	24

Source: Sivard, R.L. *World military and social expenditures, 1993 (15th edition).* Washington, DC: World Priorities, 1993, p. 37.

scholarships for school; work in a place where your employer is committed to promoting your health and well-being.

In addition, there is a perception that the military is one of the few meritocracies in our society. It is an educator, a teacher of skills, and a place for positive behavior reinforcement by peers. And for those in the military reserves, including many black health workers, it offers a reasonable income supplement for fairly interesting and career-enhancing work. As a result, African-Americans, who comprise 12 percent of the U.S. population, make up approximately 22 percent of the recent active-duty recruits into the U.S. Army. In the Persian Gulf War, approximately 30 percent of U.S. Army personnel and approximately 25 percent of the combat troops were African-American. Interestingly, the percentage of high school graduates among new African-American recruits exceeded the percentage of high school graduates among new white recruits.

Yet, the primary goals for which many African-Americans joined the military are often unrealized: Almost one-third of recruits leave the military before completing

Figure 11-9. Children play with a machine gun during Armed Forces Day, Washington, DC, April 1983 (Photograph by Robert Del Tredici).

their initial tours. The educational benefits are not nearly as great as the television commercials make them seem, and individuals often have to forego some pay in order to achieve some of these benefits. Little of the on-the-job training in the military is directly applicable to employment in the civilian workforce.[24]

Conclusion

The public health consequences of military activities, in both industrialized and developing countries, go far beyond the direct casualties caused by weapons of war. The consequences of preparation for war and of militarism require the attention of public health professionals, who can play an important role in their prevention.

REFERENCES

1. Sivard, R.L. *World military and social expenditures 1993.* Washington, D.C.: World Priorities, 1993.
2. Bellamy, C. *The state of the world's children 1996.* New York: Oxford University Press, 1996.
3. Ahlstrom, C. *Casualties of conflict: Report for the world campaign for the protection of victims of war.* Uppsala, Sweden: Department of Peace and Conflict Research, Uppsala University, 1991, pp. 8–19. Cited in Bellamy, C., *op. cit.,* p. 13.

4. United Nations Development Program. *Human development report 1994*. New York: Oxford University Press, 1994.
5. U.S. Department of Defense News Release, Reference Number 482–95, September 1, 1995. Cited in Blinding Laser Weapons. *Human Rights Watch Arms Project,* Vol. 7, No. 1, September, 1995.
6. Blinding Laser Weapons. *Human Rights Watch Arms Project,* Vol. 7, No. 1, September, 1995.
7. Brauer, J. and Chatterji, M. (eds.). *Economic issues of disarmament.* London: Macmillan Press Ltd., 1993.
8. Sidel, V.W. The arms race as a threat to health. *Lancet* 2:442–444. 1988.
9. Woolhandler, S. and Himmelstein, D.U. Militarism and mortality. An international analysis of arms spending and infant death rates. *Lancet* 1:1375–1378. 1985.
10. Stott, R. The Third World debt as a symptom of the global crisis. *Medicine and Global Survival* 1:92–98. 1994.
11. Report of the International Conference on the Relationship Between Disarmament Development. (A/Conf. 130/39) New York; United Nations, 1987.
12. Sidel, V.W. The international arms trade and its impact on health. *British Medical Journal* 311:1677–1680.
13. *Disarmament: Responding to new realities in disarmament.* (Sales No.E. 94.IX.8) New York: United Nations, 1994.
14. U.S. Arms Control and Disarmament Agency. *World military expenditures and arms transfers, 1993–1994.* Washington, D.C.: U.S. Government Printing Office, 1995.
15. Hartung, W.D. *And weapons for all.* New York: Harper Collins, 1994.
16. Congressional Research Service. *Conventional arms transfers to developing nations 1987–1994.* Washington, D.C.: Congressional Research Service, 1995.
17. Two trillion dollars in seven years. *The Defense Monitor,* Vol. 16, No. 7, 1987.
18. Sivard, R.L. *World military and social expenditures 1989.* Washington: World Priorities, 1989.
19. Dumas, L.J. *The overburdened economy: Uncovering the causes of chronic unemployment, inflation and national decline.* Berkeley, CA: University of California Press, 1986.
20. Dumas, L.J. Policy dimensions of economic conversion: Separating the wheat from the chaff. In Brauer and Chatterji, *op. cit,* pp. 137–151.
21. Anderson, M., Bischak, G. and Oden, M. *Converting the American economy.* Lansing, MI: Employment Research Associates, 1991.
22. Korb, L.J. Our overstuffed armed forces. *Foreign Affairs* 74(6):22–34, 1995.
23. O'Hanlon, M. *Defense planning for the late 1990s: Beyond the Desert Storm framework.* Washington: Brookings, 1995.
24. Tuckson, R. The impact of war and militarism on minority communities in the U.S. Presentation, American Public Health Association Annual Meeting, 1991, Atlanta.

12

The Psychological Effects
of War on Children

JOANNA SANTA BARBARA

We know that childhood needs to be a protected time. We know it in our hearts and in our lives with our own children. We know it from our research on what promotes and hinders good human development. We have agreed to international standards to protect children. What actually happens to many children in Bosnia, Sudan, Liberia, Guatemala, Burma, Afghanistan, and a score of other countries with zones of violent conflict is very different from the standards we have set ourselves. In addition, parts of the decayed cores of some U.S. cities and other countries resemble zones of violent conflict for the children who live there.

Any modern war must be considered a war on children (see Chapter 2). Based on data about civilian casualties in recent wars and the proportion of children in populations, one can say that for every ten people who die in current wars, nine are civilians and of these six are children. Some soldier-casualties are children, defined here as under 18 years of age. In addition, many children are injured, and many more are displaced and become refugees, some after seeing gross atrocities before they flee. Millions of children are affected by war. As citizens who, willingly or unwillingly, support the war system of our own nations, we must face what it means to wage war on children. And as citizens who are part of a social structure in the United States that results in an extremely unusual level of social violence compared with other nations, it is important to confront the outcome.

Gifted children have done this themselves in accounts of their experiences, especially *The Diary of Anne Frank* and *Empire of the Sun*,[1] an extraordinary account of a boy interned in a Japanese prisoner-of-war camp. Many children have drawn pictures of what they have seen of war. Since World War II, researchers have studied the impact of war on children, and long-term follow-up studies of veterans of that war and of Jewish Holocaust victims have continued to the present decade, together with studies of the effects on the children of these people. Studies of children caught in wars since then have proceeded in Ireland, Israel, Palestinian Occupied Territories,

Mozambique, South Africa, Nicaragua, Iraq, and Lebanon. Research is in progress on U.S. children who have witnessed homicide and rape.

Standards for Care and Protection of Children in Times of War

In 1959, the governments of the world, at the UN General Assembly, adopted unanimously the Declaration on the Rights of the Child. It stated that children had "the right to be among the first to receive relief in times of disaster" and "the right to be brought up in the spirit of universal peace and brotherhood." This declaration was then shaped into a Convention on the Rights of the Child, adopted by the General Assembly in 1989. The majority of countries have signed this Convention; the United States did so in 1995. The Convention states that "no child under 15 years may be recruited into an army" and that "states will do all they can to protect and care for children affected by war."

In 1990 world leaders gathered in New York for the Summit for Children. They signed a document pledging, "We will work carefully to protect children from the scourge of war and to take measures to prevent further armed conflicts, in order to give children everywhere a peaceful and secure future. We will promote the values of peace, understanding, and dialogue in the education of children." UNICEF has been promoting the idea of "children as zones of peace" to emphasize their right to protection from war.[2]

What Happens to Children in War

Exposure to Frightening Information

The most minimal phenomenon is that the child hears adults talking about incipient danger, and lives day to day with fear of adverse events—having a father go to fight, being bombed, having the family attacked, being driven from home. Even children in safe circumstances, such as North America during the Persian Gulf War, experience fear of being bombed when they are too young to assess risks and probabilities.

Children may become aware of appalling events occurring to people they know and create a traumatic visual image of an event they have not witnessed. This is enough to cause post-traumatic stress disorder (PTSD) in some children.[3] The child may experience parents who are immobilized by fear, crying, or screaming with overwhelming emotion.

Children may be prepared and deliberately trained by parents to deal with extreme circumstances, such as their not revealing facts when confronted with parents being tortured.

Separation from One or Both Parents

> I saw my mother assassinated by Obote's people. I saw them come to my house and kill my father. I just ran away. I heard that Museveni's people were collecting boys and girls, so I joined them. (Fourteen-year-old George Kokosi, corporal in the Ugandan army)[4]

Children are separated from their parents in many ways, ranging from distressing to atrociously traumatizing situations. In Mozambique during the 1980s, an estimated 200,000 children were separated from their parents or orphaned. Other large-scale wars have produced many orphans. Cambodia has 200,000 orphans.

Even very young children whose soldier-parents are sent into battle are likely to know that this is more frightening than a business trip. Older children have clearer ideas of possibilities of injury and death to their soldier-father or mother.

Political detention is a common phenomenon in many countries. Many detainees leave children at home. At times, both parents are imprisoned simultaneously. The child may witness the parent's being beaten on arrest or be aware of the parent's being tortured in prison.[5] A parent may go "underground" to escape detention or death. In such a case, one or both parents simply disappear from the child's life. The child cannot be told for fear of revealing their whereabouts under interrogation.

"Disappearance" now refers particularly to secret detention, when the family has no knowledge of the detainee's whereabouts. It commonly ends in extralegal murder, but often children do not know whether their parent is alive or dead for many years after.

Children may be told of a parent's death on a distant battlefield, see the parent murdered in front of them (Figure 19–2), or watch them die of starvation and illness. Young children, of course, do not understand the finality of death and have been observed clinging to the parent's dead body or trying to revive her.

In the extreme emergency situations that give rise to mass exodus from any area before an invading army, children become separated from parents. They may be herded to different refugee camps with no mode of communication available. Years may pass before families reunite.

Children may themselves be abducted into armies. For children who suffer this fate, separation from parents is but the first of many appalling abuses.

War-ravaged countries are the least able to provide substitute parenting for children who are separated from parents. Some children are cared for in huge institutional orphanages; some become street children.

Exposure to Destructive Violence

Children in Iraqi towns, Kurdish villages, Israeli border settlements, Palestinian refugee camps, and Sri Lankan cities, and children in Ireland, Afghanistan, Bosnia, and all the war zones where modern weaponry is used experience the explosion of bombs, shells, mortar fire, sniper rifles, car bombs, and, in the case of the Kurds, chemical bombs on their settlements. In some cases, air raid sirens warn and the children are rushed to basements or bomb shelters. They may spend many nights there. In Eritrea, the children lived in caves during the day. In Gaza, children saw Israeli army bull-dozers demolishing neighborhood homes.

Losing One's Home

> We didn't usually go to the shelter. I think my mother didn't like being underground. But that night, so my dad told me years later, he'd come home from his air-raid patrol duties and insisted we go down. . . . I never went back to that flat. When I next saw the block where we had lived, there was no outside wall where the bedroom had been. . . . Part of the block opposite ours was just a heap of rubble. Several people there were killed. (Heather Laskey, writing of London in World War II, when she was a pre-schooler)[7]

For many children caught in war, destruction of or expulsion from one's home is blotted out by the death of family members or others that occurs at the same time. But having one's secure space destroyed or invaded is in itself a potential trauma for a child. UNICEF estimates that 17 million children currently have lost their homes.[8]

Being Forced to Flee

> One night the bandits [Renamo soldiers] attacked and we fled into the bush. I saw some people shot as I ran but I managed to get away with my family and we gathered together in the bush. We knew that Renamo was burning the village and were scared they'd come after us. We walked into the bush about 30 kilometres from our village. We were afraid to go back and didn't know where to go for help. . . . We lived in the bush for two years. Our life was very hard. (Eleven-year-old Mozambican girl)[6]

Children under such circumstances of rural or urban hiding are subject to extreme physical deprivation, including starvation.

Five million children now dwell in refugee camps, some longing for, some dreading repatriation to their violence-riven countries. Where mass repatriation occurs, as to Vietnam and Guatemala, it is a very uncertain process. Will there be punishment for parents' political leanings? Will there be land to grow food? Will the army, from whom they fled, leave them in peace?

Children may migrate from refugee camps to rich countries in Europe or North America, either with parents, or as unaccompanied minors. The orphaned children may join relatives, families of their own ethnicity, or families of the dominant eth-nicity, or they may be cared for in group homes. Each child will be faced with challenges, including adequacy of physical and emotional care, new language mastery, academic gaps, peer acceptance, and identity formation.

Witnessing Death or Other Atrocities

The following account was reconstructed from a series of interviews with Franisse, an eight-year-old boy in Mozambique:

> Franisse was five or six years old when Renamo attacked his village. The bandits captured him and took him to his family's house, where he lived with his parents and five brothers and sisters. The bandits forced Franisse to set fire to the house while his family was still asleep inside. The bandits made Franisse watch as his father, a local Frelimo official, and his mother ran outside where they were stabbed to death by the bandits. The bandits then chopped off his parents' heads and jammed them on stakes and planted the stakes in front of the burning house. The bandits also killed other people from the village, including his brothers and sisters.
>
> Later, Franisse watched as the bandits hacked his parents' decapitated bodies into small enough pieces to throw into a large pot in which they were cooking a goat. The bandits also threw his little brother's body into the pot and ate and drank from the pot. The village was burned to the ground; a base was established nearby. . . . [7]

The child during war or lesser social violence may see dead bodies in the street or deliberately publicly displayed to terrorize the population. The child in a concentration camp or massively destroyed areas may see many corpses over extended periods.

Children may see family members die of illness or starvation in the privation of war. They are especially likely to be aware of the demise of younger siblings, given the soaring infant mortality that accompanies and follows war.

As in Franisse's account, children may witness the murder of their parents or siblings, or their deaths in bombings. Occasionally, as with Franisse, they are forced to participate in such atrocities. Sometimes children are forced to witness the torture of parents to extract information from them.

Children may witness rapes or be raped.

> I saw the bandits rape older women, and I saw them rape many girls who were just beginning to grow breasts. The bandits raped the girls and left them there. Some girls were used by many different bandits; when one bandit finished with a girl another one took his place. I think some of the girls got sick and died of sickness because they were raped. (Twelve-year-old Mozambican boy)[6]

Being Imprisoned

In countries where the political situation is highly polarized and violent, children are imprisoned and sometimes tortured.

Being Beaten, Injured, or Raped

In war zones with high civilian casualties, it is likely that half of the dead and injured are children. In many war zones, medical services to such injured children may have been at a low level before war, may have been selectively destroyed during fighting, and medical aid from outside may have been specifically blocked by armed forces.

Girls who are raped, as in Bosnia, may be from cultures where an enormous and crippling burden attaches to such an event. In addition to psychological effects, physical injuries, and sexually transmitted disease including AIDS, the girl suffers profound shame, as if she herself were at fault. Although they may describe other terrible experiences, many girls will keep to themselves the shame of rape, perhaps precluding help for resolution of this trauma. In some cultures, a raped girl is considered unmarriageable. In such a situation, the girl knows she has not only lost her virginity and sense of bodily integrity, but she has also lost the only acceptable future her culture offers: marriage and children. If she becomes pregnant as a result of rape, she may be torn between the conflict of giving birth to an unwanted, even hated, child and having an abortion, which is proscribed by religious laws and cultural mores.

Being Permanently Disabled

In the last decade, four million children have been disabled by war.[8] There are many children and teenagers in every war zone who will suffer permanently from war injuries. Many of them are amputees. Some suffer ongoing neurological damage from head injuries. Many of these children have no access to prostheses or wheelchairs or to rehabilitation.

In former war zones throughout the world, millions of land mines are sown in roads and fields. In Cambodia, 700 amputations on adults and children are done each month[9] (see Chapter 10).

Disabled children may be further disabled by social exclusion. Hopes of education, work training, and marriage may be diminished, and childhood play-time is lost.

Child Soldiers and Army Slaves

In the UN Declaration of the Rights of the Child, bearing of arms in battle is proscribed below age 15. Many would agree that 18 years of age would be more appropriate. There are and there have been many child soldiers younger than 15 working in national armies and opposition armed forces.

Some are persuaded to join by partisan propaganda and religious fervor.

Come on, come on, plunge on. Those who step on mines will go to Paradise. (Marching chant of a column of 15,000 Iranian children on their way to the front with Iraq)[10]

It is said that these Iranian children were sent across mine-fields ahead of more valuable trained solders.

Children may join an army to seek vengeance. David Kabanda, aged 11, watched guerilla fighters in Uganda murder his parents.

> I decided to join the army. I want to beat the people who killed my mother. If I find them, I'll kill them.[4]

Children may join an army because it is the only alternative to starvation. Uganda's President Museveni in 1986 defended the practice:

> We don't use them as soldiers. They just come and stay in the camps because we have no orphanages. Then they can eat.

They carried guns, he said, because they asked for them.

> We wouldn't stop them from doing it. They would feel very miserable.

President Museveni said the youngest soldiers were only five.[4]

Renamo in Mozambique, the Contras in Nicaragua, and several sides in Sri Lanka are said to have abducted children and to have used them as soldiers, camp servants, body guards for leaders, porters for provisions, and sexual slaves. Neil Boothby's interviews with Mozambican children delineate a terrible process of breaking down moral prohibitions in such children and socializing them in cruelty.

Franco, a tall 13-year-old abducted by Renamo, described his experience as he moved up the ladder from servant to bodyguard to combatant:

> I was chosen by a bandit chief named Johanes to be his servant. I washed and ironed his clothes and did whatever was necessary. The chief liked my work and made me his bodyguard. He gave me a pistol and a bayonet and told me to guard his belongings while he was away on raids. I also watched his three women to make sure they did not get approached by other bandits or go with them. . . .
>
> The chiefs told us to look at people when they are beaten and to never act like we don't like it. They told us we could not cry or be sad when people were killed. . . .
>
> I had been at the base for five months when Johanes made me kill a man. . . . I took my bayonet and stabbed him in the stomach. . . . They told me that I was now one of them.[6]

The experience of children enslaved as porters has been particularly severe. The children are used as pack animals.

In some cases children may apparently choose to contribute to a war effort without extreme coercion or persuasion and even against parental preference. Children found roles as secret messengers in underground movements in Europe in World War II, as voluntary food carriers in the Somalian uprising against dictator Siad Barre, as guards in the Nicaraguan uprising against Somosa, and in Palestinian Occupied Territories as stone-throwers against Israeli soldiers.

Being a Prostitute

An army on foreign soil, especially when there is massive poverty in war-wrecked economies, will induce large-scale prostitution, including child prostitution. Some young girls are sold by parents or are abducted to fetch high prices as virgins.

Being a Child Born to a Raped or Prostituted Woman

Some of these children are born to women who explicitly express their hatred for the baby. When the child has been fathered by an enemy soldier, it may be difficult to find substitute parents who accept him or her, as in Bosnia today and in Southeast Asia when U.S. troops were there. These children may be accepted and loved, reared with ambivalence, or seriously rejected.

Having Parents Who Are Seriously and Adversely Affected by War Experiences

Reports from former Yugoslavia and elsewhere describe increased domestic violence by men returning from battle. Parents who have been tortured or have witnessed or committed atrocities may be psychologically incapacitated, and their parenting is very likely to be affected. Physical injuries in parents will affect the rearing of children in multiple ways.

Loss of Life-Sustaining Infrastructure of Society and Economic Deprivation

These factors have their most demonstrable effects on mortality and physical morbidity, causing more suffering to children in war zones than direct violence. Being hungry; seeing family members hungry and ill; having inadequate, dirty, crowded, noisy housing in refugee camps; and having schooling interrupted may cause psychological as well as physical suffering to children.

Poverty may be caused by a variety of factors in war. Sometimes poverty is one of the preexisting causes of war. The bread-winner may be lost. The nation's wealth is spent on armaments at the cost of services to people, or the village is impoverished by the demands of guerilla fighters. Economic sanctions imposed on the nation may depress or ruin the livelihoods of many families (see box on p. 156–58 and Chapter

17). Families threatened by war leave their land and thus their food supply. Children are taken from school and sent to work; or, in cities, take to the streets to beg.

Psychological Effects

How these events are processed in each individual to produce "psychological effects" is an interaction between the individual child, these events, and ameliorating factors such as community support.

Short-term changes might arbitrarily refer to those that might be seen in the days or months after adverse events, and long-term, in years or decades after. Children in many countries examined for short-term changes knew of the realistic possibility of further adverse events.

As the child continues to assimilate new information of threat to life and security or of loss, his or her internal map of the world must be extensively revised. Where one had assumed one's home was a given in life, one has to revise to accommodate the fact that it was burned or bulldozed down or bombed to rubble. Where one had assumed that adults were benign, one has now to accommodate the experience of being beaten, verbally humiliated, and raped by an adult. Where one had assumed that one's parents were there every day, now one of them is dead and the other is so grief-stricken as to be unavailable.

Children, much more than adults, are engaged in an active, ongoing process of socialization, adapting their behavior to their immediate social group. This process interacts with their mental constructs of what the world is like. The ability to adapt cooperatively also depends on the modulation of emotions of fear, anger, and the distress of pain, hunger, loneliness, and separation. Under normal circumstances, parents and other care-givers modulate these emotions for children, adjusting the environment so that the child is not overwhelmed. Coping with minor fear, anger, and distress occurs without disrupting socialization.

In war, this may not be the case. Parents attempt to protect their children from fear-provoking information and from dangerous circumstances. But they cannot. Events overwhelm their protective efforts. The child suffers major fear, anger, and distress. In young children, adaptive behavior is temporarily disrupted.

As the child struggles to incorporate terrible new information into his or her internal map of how things are, memories or images of the events may recur mentally and appear in drawings and play. The memories themselves are painful and the child may try to avoid them, such as by avoiding reminders or triggers. The memories, however, also surface in nightmares, which may seriously disrupt sleep or cause the child to resist going to sleep. This cluster of phenomena amounts to what we call post-traumatic stress disorder. It occurs in children, as in adults.[11] When the information to be incorporated is of significant loss, as of a parent or a limb, depression may be prominent.

Short-Term Effects

Children are presented with verbally mediated information that evokes fear, or they directly experience events that threaten them. Depending on their developmental age, children may misinterpret information (North American children frightened of being hurt in the Persian Gulf War). Children may have fear responses to brief acute danger (being shelled) or live in immediate danger for lengthy periods (children abducted into army camps).

Anxiety levels of fifth- and sixth-graders in a Tel Aviv school were measured before the Yom Kippur War and again two months later, while the army was still mobilized. There were notable increases in their anxiety, although they were not directly involved in the war, but had family members who were. The increases in anxiety were related to pre-war anxiety, the least anxious children in peacetime becoming the most anxious soon after war.[12]

Two other studies over the same period, however, found no differences in manifest anxiety between children in Israeli settlements that had recently undergone shelling and those that had not.[12,13] This was not due to habituation to shelling, as the same result appeared when children were shelled after 18- and 24-month periods of calm.[14,15]

Lebanese children aged three to nine living in areas of cities recently subject to heavy fighting and shelling were studied. The results suggest a sensitization process— that is, the effects of trauma are cumulative in their disturbing impact on children's behavior. For some undesirable behaviors, the previously "traumatized" children were twice as likely to begin or increase the behavior after a heavy shelling episode. These behaviors were thumb-sucking, bed-wetting or soiling, physically hurting others, trouble-making, being generally unhappy, being disruptive, being overdependent and submissive with other children, and being submissive, overaggressive, and suspicious with adults. This study showed the special vulnerability of traumatized children.[16]

Similar findings have been reported in Palestinian children living in the occupied West Bank and Gaza Strip: The degree of psychological disorder correlated with the number and level of traumatic events to which the child had been exposed. Aggression, enuresis, phobias, and anxiety were particular problems.[17]

Symptoms in Palestinian children after the onset of the Palestinian uprising (Intifada) were studied.[18] Compared with Palestinian children living in Israel, these children showed considerably higher levels of disobedience to parents and fighting among themselves.

The psychological responses of South African preschoolers whose parents had been detained for political reasons has also been studied.[5] During detention, most children were described as overdependent and clinging, unable to sleep alone, and continually asking about the detainee. They were moody, irritable, and suffered from head and abdominal pains, bed-wetting, and nightmares.

A study of children in the Philippines whose parents had been detained for political reasons showed clinging behavior, other signs of separation anxiety, general anxiety, attention-seeking behavior, oversensitivity in social interaction, and low self-esteem.[19]

There are less frequently occurring severe reactions to circumstances the child interprets as grave. An eight-year-old Kurdish girl tending livestock when Iraqi planes bombed her village with chemical weapons saw her parents and brother die gruesomely of poisoning, along with many other people there. She was mute for four weeks afterwards.[20]

For many war-affected children, there is a long exposure to cumulative adverse events, sometimes over years. Habituation to horrifying sights may occur, and there may be unusual adaptations.

Longer Term Effects

Where traumatic events have not been too intense and numerous, and community support has been good, the outcome for war-affected children may be only a little worse than that for controls, especially when the adverse events do not involve extensive revisions to the child's view of the world as benign and stable.

However, for many children that is not the case. Severe losses lead to long-lasting depression. Severe and multiple psychological trauma lead to post-traumatic stress disorder. Many of these children accumulate further stress and trauma occasioned by the loss of family, home, community integrity, and life sustenance due to the war. Fleeing war by dangerous routes, taken into warehouse orphanages or refugee camps, these children may continue to face deprivation, physical violence, and sexual abuse and exploitation. Even entering an economically better situation as a refugee in a rich country may bring further stresses. In some young people, apparently long-suppressed memories of atrocities break through years later, leading to the onset of post-traumatic stress disorder. Depression may persist for years.

Cambodian young people who had lived through the Pol Pot regime between the ages of 6 to 12 had suffered catastrophically traumatic events. Their depression declined over time, but post-traumatic stress disorder was diagnosed at high rates.[21,22]

That traumatization by war experiences in childhood can cause suffering over decades of adulthood has become clear from studies of survivors of the Holocaust.[23] Chronic anxiety, obsessional rumination, difficulty enjoying life, difficulty trusting and feeling a sense of belonging,[24] hypochondriasis, feelings of shame and aggression are described, as well as continuing to deal with huge and multiple losses.[25]

The long-term psychological effects of war may be visited upon generations succeeding those who were directly traumatized. This has been studied in Jewish Holocaust survivors,[26] U.S. veterans of World War II,[27] and U.S. veterans of Vietnam.[28] Children of Nazi concentration camp survivors are described as suffering from problems with separation and individuation, pathologic identification with their traumatized parents, depression, guilt, and aggressiveness.

There are 19 million war veterans in the United States and millions more in other countries. Among U.S. veterans of Vietnam, the rates of PTSD are 3.5 percent in people exposed to physical combat and not wounded, 20 percent in those who were wounded.[29] The rates of depression in other populations exposed to war trauma seem to be roughly similar;[21,22,30] the two conditions often coexist in the same person. This suggests that many children in the world are growing up in circumstances like those described above.

Moral Development

Researchers on the psychological effects of war on children have questioned how these experiences will affect their moral development and the social institutions that are the projections of our moral attitudes.

War-traumatized children were found to be 1.7 times more likely to show troublesome aggressive behaviors after an episode of shelling than "non-traumatized" children.[16] Aggression was highest after the shelling. After death of their fathers in war, 2- to 10-year-old Israeli children showed marked increases in aggression.[35]

In war zones children "are exposed repeatedly, at an age of high susceptibility, to familiar, real-life aggressive models who are rewarded with recognition, status, and privileges. The risk . . . is that of wholesale acquisition by new generations, of antisocial behaviors which are highly likely to contribute to the perpetuation of those very same catastrophic social circumstances which fostered these behaviors in the first place!"[16]

Children are influenced by the attitudes to war and to "the enemy" of important adults in their lives. When a country has committed its armies to battle, dissent from this choice is poorly tolerated. For children who had lost family members, the idea that this altruistic sacrifice was unnecessary and meaningless would be shattering. Similarly, for children who had themselves experienced the dangers of military violence, it would be unlikely to be seen as other than hardship and danger endured for the necessary good of the whole society. Repeated exposure to dehumanizing reference to "the enemy" will of course be incorporated into children's cognitive maps.

Children's willingness to surrender their own moral values to military authority is interesting. Endorsement of the idea, "In war one should execute every order, even those which I think are wrong," was 87 percent for Israelis, 66 percent for Palestinians, and 24 percent for U.S. children.[32] The lessons embodied in the Nuremberg Principles had evidently not been passed on to these children.

The children whose moral development has been most destructively affected are those who have been trained to kill. When fighting is over and the children have to return to society, it is very difficult to place them in schools or families. Their moral system is ruled by fear of violence from whoever is superior in the hierarchy. How can they learn from unarmed adults? How can they work? How can they marry and rear children?

Thousands of children have been left without the guidance in moral development that caring adults can provide. In Somalia, war has destroyed much of society's institutions, including those of social control. Society is organized around fear of violence. Teenagers acquire guns and enjoy the power they can exert to extort food, money, health care, and sex.

Under some circumstances, especially when a child has not identified with perpetrators of violence, cooperation and altruism may develop, even in conditions of extreme deprivation. In addition, when children from such adverse circumstances grow up, some appear to identify compassionately with the suffering of others and to become particularly altruistic.[24]

Protective Factors and Vulnerability Factors

Some children who suffer severely emerge as happy, functional adults.

Rotenberg, reflecting on his own experiences, believes that the following factors enabled him to develop well despite severe loss and deprivation: having had a warm, nurturing, predictable environment until he was seven years old; believing life was basically good (a belief he astonishingly retained after his parents died of typhus and he was starving); a feeling of being special, of having a purpose to fulfill; being clever and adaptive; and finding someone to care for him in various situations.[40]

A suggestion of the obverse of this relationship is to be found in an epidemiological study of PTSD in a U.S. population.[29] The presence of behaviorial problems before the age of 15 (stealing, lying, truancy, vandalism, running away, fighting, etc.) predicted a greater likelihood of suffering PTSD. This correlation comprised two factors: (1) People with a history of behavior problems were more likely to be beaten or mugged, and if in Vietnam, more likely to be in combat and incur a traumatizing experience. (2) Of all those who suffered beatings, mugging, or combat experience, the prior presence of behavior problems in childhood predicted who would suffer PTSD.

The Cambodian adolescent refugees who were studied over many years were considered to have done well academically and occupationally, despite very high levels of PTSD and depression. Some of these children carried the awareness that their dead parents wanted them to study hard and do well, and they did their best to fulfill these expectations.

The importance of past and present family influences is highlighted by the finding that among Mozambican refugee children, the effects of adverse events were worse if the child's mother had been victimized.[33]

Helping and Healing

Article 39 of Convention on the Rights of the Child states:

States Parties shall take all appropriate measures to promote physical and psychological recovery and social reintegration of a child victim of . . . armed conflicts. Such recovery and reintegration shall take place in an environment which fosters the health, self-respect and dignity of the child.

The major issues are:

- Family reunification.
- Reestablishing order, routine, schooling, and usefulness in children's lives.
- Helping adults understand children's symptoms.
- Letting children tell their story, share, and understand the meaning of their experiences.
- Helping children become peace-builders with training in prejudice reduction, non-violent conflict resolution, and reconciliation.

Community and Large-Scale Approaches

Mental health needs of war-affected people are important, even alongside outstanding basic physical needs. Adaptation to their new situation is at stake.

> Doctors and nurses found many mothers apathetic, unresponsive to their children, and unable to concentrate or to remember simple instructions about feeding or taking medicines. Teachers found some children withdrawn and apathetic while others sought attention through difficult or disruptive behavior or just lived in a "world of their own," unable to concentrate outside it.[33]

Family reunification schemes are fundamental in helping war-affected children from areas of mass chaotic exodus, and these are operating in many African countries, especially under the aegis of UNICEF and the International Committee of the Red Cross/Red Crescent.

It is important to use community institutions that already exist or are being brought into existence to serve war-affected people—religious institutions, schools, clinics, and women's groups. There can be work with teachers to promote understanding of traumatized children and to develop classroom activities to promote more care and support for the children. There must be emphasis on working within the culture, building on the strengths of the community, and letting the affected people participate in decision-making.[34]

Where there are many war-traumatized children and few resources to help, a school-based approach seems best. Such approaches have initially involved input to school personnel to help them understand difficult behavior and to be less punitive. But going further to have the children give an account of recent history by telling of their own experiences, setting them in context with those of others, understanding the meaning of the events that affected them, and experiencing the support of their peers may be a healing process for children. In addition, parents need assistance in understanding and responding helpfully to symptoms of depression, anxiety, and PTSD.

In Mozambique it was found that acute exposure to adverse events may be followed by rapid recovery.[35,36] Long-term and severe stress, such as loss of parents, had a much longer recovery period. A treatment facility dealt with boys who had been trained as soldiers. It was found that it was the length of time spent in the military camp, rather than their direct involvement in violence, that was related to their later abilities to act on traditional concepts of right and wrong. When they had spent less than six months there, boys saw themselves as victims, and their initial aggressive distrustful behavior soon subsided into behavior based on traditional tribal values. Boys who had spent one to two years there saw themselves as members of the army. Only after several months, when they began to establish warm relationships with their new adult caretakers, did remorse for their violence emerge. The center used oral story-telling, dance, drama, and art for therapeutic purposes. Volunteers from the Mozambique Women's Organization took care of the boys, who were eventually returned to their families or communities. Rehabilitation of these children involved both child and society. Society had to understand, forgive, and reintegrate them.

UNICEF is using a school-based approach in Sri Lanka. In this setting of ongoing ethnic conflict, it is also attempting to teach tolerance for difference and nonviolent conflict resolution. UNICEF is also fostering a school-based project in Croatia, involving training seminars for classroom teachers, art teachers, and school psychologists. Professionals are taught to understand war-traumatized children and their art work, classroom management, and relaxation for children.[37] Street Kids International has organized schooling for thousands of Sudanese orphaned and war-displaced children to begin to restore order and normality in their lives.

In Lebanon, UNICEF has promoted peace education in summer camps. Each camp must have children from all ethnic communities and run an active peace program in which children share differences and commonalities and explore ways to resolve differences without violence. Northern Ireland and Israel/Palestine have had a number of inspired organizations of youth coming together across the lines of division to promote a more hopeful future. These may be models for the patient, careful reconstruction of a peaceful, tolerant society in former Yugoslavia.

Children fleeing war zones to settle in other countries are likely to do better if placed with foster families of the same ethnicity.[36] In some situations, for example, when a child lives in or migrates to a country with adequate, affordable health services, individual treatment for war-traumatized children can be provided. Cultural beliefs, child-rearing practices, and norms for child development need to be understood as a context for diagnosis. Expectations of physicians, such as in prescribing medication, must be taken into account in trying to help.

Three stages of recovery from severe psychological trauma have been described: establishing safety, recollection and mourning, and reconnecting with life.[39] Reconstructing a coherent tale and having traumatic memories validated have seemed very important to some traumatized people. These healing tasks can be accomplished in individual therapy, but may be particularly appropriate for groups. In work with sexually abused children, some of the recollection and mourning is seen to occur in play and art, rather than words, but there is reason to think that the tasks are similar to the healing of adults.

The idea that a child who has been through terrible experiences should be encouraged to tell his or her story may run counter to the views of protective adults who want the child to forget the past, to "shut the book" and start anew. Helping professionals and parents to understand the need to replay the story is important.

Peace Building

Representatives at the Summit for Children have collectively vowed to "work carefully to protect children from the scourge of war . . ." and ". . . to promote the values of peace, understanding, and dialogue in the education of children." Whether we live and work in the rich or the poor world, there is much to be done to counter violence and militarism, to delegitimize war as a means of conflict resolution, to teach children principled negotiation, and to convey ways of understanding and respecting each other. This needs to happen in all countries until we no longer inflict war on children.

REFERENCES

1. Ballard, J.G. *Empire of the Sun.* New York: Pocket Books, Simon and Schuster, 1985.
2. UNICEF. *Children in situations of armed conflict.* New York: UNICEF, 1985.
3. Saigh, O.A. The development of post-traumatic stress disorder following four different types of traumatization. *Behav. Res. Ther.* 29(3):213–216, 1991.
4. Gampel, Y. Facing war, murder, torture and death in latency. *Psychoanalytic Review* 75(4): 499–509, 1988.
5. Skinner, D. and Swartz, L. The consequences for preschool children of a parent's detention: A preliminary South African clinical study of care-givers' reports. *J. Child Psychol. Psychiat.* 30(2):243–259, 1989.
6. Boothby, N., Upton, P. and Sultan, A. Children of Mozambique: The cost of survival. Special Issue Paper, U.S. Committee for Refugees, Washington, D.C., 1992.
7. Laskey, H. Surprise! Unspeakable horror is part of any war. *The Medical Post,* April 9, 1991.
8. UNICEF. *The state of the world's children 1992.* New York: United Nations Children's Fund, 1992.
9. Pilger, J. A menace to civilization. *New Internationalist,* April 1993, pp. 23–24.
10. Children and war. *Action for Children* 1(3):7. UNICEF, New York, 1986.
11. Saigh, P. Pre- and post-invasion anxiety in Lebanon. *Behav. Ther.* 15:185–190, 1984.
12. Milgram, R.M. and Milgram, N.A. The effect of the Yom Kippur War on anxiety level in Israeli children. *Journal of Psychology* 94:107–113, 1976.
13. Ziv, A. and Israeli, R. Effects of bombardment on the manifest anxiety level of children living in kibbutzim. *Journal Consult. Clin. Psychol.* 40:287–291, 1972.

14. Milgram, N.A. War-related stress in Israeli children and youth. In Goldberger L. and Breznitz, S. (eds.), *Handbook of stress*. New York: The Free Press, 1982, pp. 656–676.
15. Ziv, A., Kruglanski, A.W. and Shulman, S. Children's psychological reactions to wartime stress. *Journal Pers. Soc. Psychol.* 30:24–30, 1974.
16. Chimienti, G., Nasr, J.A. and Khalifeh, I. Children's reactions to war-related stress: Affective symptoms and behavior problems. *Soc. Psychiatry Psychiatr. Epidemiol.* 24:282–287, 1989.
17. Punamaki, R. Psychological stress responses of Palestinian mothers and their children in conditions of military occupation and political violence. *Quarterly Newsletter of the Laboratory of Comparative Human Cognition* 9(2):76–84, 1987.
18. Baker, A. The psychological impact of the Intifada on Palestinian children in Occupied West Bank and Gaza. *American Journal of Orthopsychiatry* 60(4):496–505, 1990.
19. Protacio-Marcelino. Psychological help to children of political prisoners in the Philippines. Paper presented at the World Psychiatric Association Regional Symposium. Athens, 1985.
20. Hu, H., Cook-Deegan, R. and Shukri, A. *Winds of death: Iraq's use of poison gas against its Kurdish population.* Report of a medical mission to Turkish Kurdistan. Somerville, Mass.: Physicians for Human Rights, 1989.
21. Kinzie, J.D., Sack, W., Angell, R., Clarke, G. and Ben, R. A three-year follow-up of Cambodian young people traumatized as children. *J. American Academy Child Adolescent Psychiatry* 28(4):501–504, 1989.
22. Sack, W.H., et al. A six-year follow-up study of Cambodian refugee adolescents traumatized as children. *J. American Academy Child Adolescent Psychiatry* 32(2):431–437, 1993.
23. Moskovitz, S. Love despite hate: Child survivors of the Holocaust and their adult lives. New York: Schocken, 1982.
24. Kestenberg, J. and Kestenberg, M. The sense of belonging and altruism in children who survived the Holocaust. *Psychoanalytic Review* 75(4):533–560, 1988.
25. Fogelman, E. Intergenerational group therapy: Child survivors of the Holocaust and offspring of survivors. *Psychoanalytic Review* 75(4):619–640, 1988.
26. Freyberg, J.T. Difficulties in separation—individuation as experienced by offspring of Nazi Holocaust survivors. *American Journal Orthopsychiatry* 50:87–95, 1980.
27. Rosenheck, R. Impact of post-traumatic stress disorder of World War II on the next generation. *J. Nervous and Mental Diseases* 174(6):319–327, 1986.
28. Rosenheck, R. Secondary traumatization in children of Vietnam veterans. *Hospital Community Psychiatry* 36(5):538–539, 1985.
29. Helzer, J.E., Robins, L.N. and McEvoy, L. Post-traumatic stress disorder in the general population. *N. Engl. J. Med.* 317:1630–1634, 1987.
30. Ramsay, R., Gorst-Unsworth, C. and Turner, S. Psychiatric morbidity in survivors of organized state violence including torture. *British Journal of Psychiatry* 162:55–59, 1993.
31. Kaffman, M. and Elizur, E. Children's bereavement reactions following death of the father. *Int. J. Family Therapy* 6:259–283, 1984.
32. Punamaki, R.L. Children living under war and threat: Israeli and Palestinian children's attitudes and emotional life. Unpublished manuscript, 1984.
33. McCallin, M. Psychological needs of Mozambican refugees—a community-based approach. *Tropical Doctor,* Supp. 1:67–69, 1991.
34. Kanji, N. War and children in Mozambique: Is international aid strengthening or eroding community-based policies? *Community Development Journal* 25(2):102–112, 1990.
35. Boothby, N. Recovery from war's trauma. *Africa News,* July 15, 1991.
36. Richman, N. Mozambique's beleaguered children. *Southern Africa Report,* May, 1991.

37. Bloch, E. Psychologists in Croatia work to ease trauma among young war victims. *Psychology International* (APA Office of International Affairs) 4(3):1, 3, 1993.
38. Porte, Z. and Torney-Purta, J. Depression and academic achievement among Indochinese refugee unaccompanied minors in ethnic and non-ethnic placements. *American Journal of Orthopsychiatry* 57(4):536–547, 1987.
39. Herman, J.L. *Trauma and recovery*. New York: Basic Books, 1992.
40. Rotenberg, L. A child survivor/psychiatrist's personal adaptation. *Journal of American Academy of Child Psychiatry* 24:385–389.

13

The Impact of War on Women

MARY-WYNNE ASHFORD
and YOLANDA HUET-VAUGHN

As the weapons of war become more brutal and horrifying, armies increasingly disregard the Geneva Conventions that protect civilians. In fact, the strategies of war today target the essential infrastructures needed for survival: water and sewage systems, power stations, and food supplies. The ability to wage war from a distance has meant that indiscriminate attacks on civilian targets kill thousands of noncombatants and throw the survivors into the most primitive struggle to sustain life. Bombs and missiles kill men and women indiscriminately, but other aspects of war affect women and girls disproportionately. In this chapter, we will focus on the consequences of war and militarism on the health of women and girls.

War has always resulted in women dealing with the death or maiming of loved ones, the loss of a husband or father being particularly serious because of women's economic dependence on men. Indeed, in the past, when only a small percent of all war deaths were civilians, most of the war dead were men; today, 90 percent of people who die in war are civilians (see Chapter 3). The world has never seen the scale of population displacement we are seeing today: wars have left some 19 million dependent refugees and 25 million internally displaced persons[1] (see Chapter 14). Women are affected directly as casualties of attacks, and as victims of the upheaval of war, but also indirectly through the economics of militarism. In many war-torn countries, women have no voice in setting policies of war or peace because laws exclude them from decision making, or because illiteracy effectively disenfranchises them.

Effects of New Military Strategies on Women and Girls

The change in military strategies that began in World War II, when civilian populations were targeted and whole cities fire-bombed, became further refined in the Gulf

War and in the war in former Yugoslavia. The new strategy goes further than bombing population centers; its goal appears to be making war on public health.[2] This is a modern refinement of old tactics of blockades, crop burning, and introduction of pestilence to a city under siege. Today the systematic destruction of water purification facilities, sewage treatment plants, power generators, hospitals, food production and distribution systems, and communications lines is a ruthless assault on basic survival needs of the population, both short and long term. This strategy is particularly devastating for women.

In war zones, women continue to be responsible for procuring and preparing food and for caring for children, the elderly, and the ill. Faced with food and fuel shortages, lack of electricity, shortages of medicines, and lack of safe water, women suddenly face issues of survival every day. Women interviewed in Iraq in 1991[3] described the increased burden they suffered as men's roles within the household did not change, but women's duties expanded to include securing water and firewood for their families on a day-to-day basis. Massive unemployment, large price increases, and reduction in real wages most affect the vulnerable sections of the population, which include widows and abandoned and divorced women. Women in Iraq spend most of their time trying to find food for their families. The effects of continued sanctions have caused women to sell their jewelry and other assets and to incur heavy debts. Some have been driven to prostitution and begging. Gold jewelry given to a woman as her dowry is often her only security; its sale represents the desperate attempt of the family to provide for its needs.

In Bosnia, winter brought untold suffering because of lack of fuel, chronic food deprivation, shelling, and illness. Snipers compounded the reign of terror as they targeted women and children seeking food.[2]

Effects of War and Sanctions on Maternal Health

The destruction of health care systems as well as the shortage of food and medical supplies results in poor obstetrical care with increased numbers of spontaneous abortions and miscarriages, and increased maternal and infant mortality. In addition to the lack of prenatal care in war zones, malnutrition, lack of treatment for complications of pregnancy, and psychological stress contribute to the poor outcomes. In both Bosnia and Iraq, doctors have reported having to perform cesarean sections without anesthetic.[2,3]

Famine is frequently a result of war. The effects of famine on women were well documented in World War II. The severe famine in Holland following a Nazi blockade in 1944 to 1945 resulted in marked increases in stillbirths, first-week newborn deaths, and infant deaths in birth cohorts with prenatal exposure to the famine at critical times during gestation.[4]

Women as Refugees

Women and children make up 80 percent of refugees worldwide[5] (see Chapter 14). Amidst chaos, extreme crowding, illness, and starvation, relief workers struggle to provide the essentials of food, water, and sanitation, often with political obstacles both inside and outside the camp. Where tens of thousands of people have fled to escape death, border camps attract not only the best in humanity, the volunteers and workers who have come to help, but also the worst in humanity, the warlords and exploiters.[6] Camps are often sites of corruption and violence, where rape and sexual exploitation are rarely documented or punished. Women often must resort to prostitution in order to gain food for themselves and their children.

In male-dominated societies, women's inferior position may be reflected by lack of property rights, discrimination in education and employment, lack of security outside of marriage, and low status in the family. All of these factors limit women's alternatives in times of war. Low status in the family means that men and boys are fed first, with the result that women and girls often suffer malnutrition.

Testimony by a 68-year-old Kurdish refugee[3] is a searing indictment of this disregard for the human rights of women:

> When we fled to Turkey it was very difficult to get food. All the younger men ran fast and got all the food the Americans were handing out. We only had my husband with us and he can't run, So we ended up as a family without food. This happened to all the women who fled without their men. We were just left out, as if we weren't there. Three of my grandchildren died in those mountains.

The United Nations High Commission on Refugees (UNHCR) has observed in refugee camps in many countries that even when food supplies have been adequate, the men still eat first, resulting in starving women and children alongside well-fed men.[7,8] In a Bangladeshi camp, the death rate among Rohingya girls younger than one year was almost twice that of boys, and for refugees over five years, the death rate among females was 3.5 times that of males.[1] Although most refugees are women and children, reports of mortality and morbidity rates in refugee camps are not usually broken down by sex, which would expose gender bias against women and girls if it exists.

AIDS and Other Sexually Transmitted Diseases

The risk of spread of sexually transmitted diseases (STDs), including HIV infection, is increased in war because of the sexual activities of troops and the lack of prophylaxis. The seriousness of syphilis and gonorrhea in populations with poor access to diagnosis and antibiotics should not be forgotten, even though the common STDs seem to pale in comparison with the spread of AIDS. Prostitutes and victims of rape in war, as well as women whose husbands return from military duty carrying HIV, are obviously at risk for contracting HIV, particularly if the man also has another STD infection. Refugees may carry HIV to a host country or bring it back with them when they return.

Low-intensity warfare has destabilized several countries, including Mozambique, Angola, Zimbabwe, and Nicaragua. Civil strife, roaming bandits, and open military conflicts result in civilians from rural areas shifting to towns or settlements near army barracks. There HIV can spread through a transient population that typically has many heterosexual partners: members of the armed forces, migrant workers, prostitutes, and street children. The psychological impact of war may also alter the way an individual processes information about AIDS prevention. Despair, helplessness, and desire for revenge may result in high-risk behavior.

Rape

Man should be trained for war and woman for the recreation of the warrior (Nietzsche, 1885).

The history of war is replete with stories of rape and sexual atrocities against women and girls, with women regarded as part of the booty claimed by the victor. Until recently, rape has been treated as an expected and even inevitable part of war. The reports of the rape camps in Bosnia and of the forced impregnation of women have finally aroused sufficient outrage that rape is now, for the first time, included within the framework of war crimes. Estimates of the number of women raped in Bosnia range from 10,000 to 60,000 and include the systematic rape of girls as a strategy of war.[9]

Boutros Boutros-Ghali, Secretary-General of the UN, writes:

[T]he practice of so-called ''ethnic cleansing'' and rape and sexual assault, in particular, have been carried out by some of the parties so systematically that they strongly appear to be the product of a policy, which may also be inferred from the consistent failure to prevent the commission of such crimes and to prosecute and punish their perpetrators.[10]

The scale of rape in war is often hidden for many years. It is only recently that the existence of some 100,000 to 200,000 ''comfort women'' abducted by Japanese soldiers as sex slaves during World War II has been revealed.[11] Most of the women were Korean, but the numbers included Chinese, Filipinos, Indonesians, Burmese, and Dutch. Korean women are leading the movement demanding an apology and compensation from the Japanese government. Confronted with historic documents showing government and army orders concerning the comfort women, the Japanese government has expressed its regret, after years of denial of responsibility. In army documents, women were described as war supplies. The women were raped and brutalized, some had their breasts sliced off with swords; some had crude surgery to remove their sexual organs so that they would not menstruate and would therefore be available constantly.

The records of the Japanese abductions of Korean women show that the goal appears to have been to provide their troops with large numbers of virgin women who would not infect the men with sexually transmitted diseases. Testimony of the Global Tribunal on Violations of Women's Human Rights at the UN World Conference on Human Rights in 1993 estimated that less than 10 percent of comfort women survived at the end of the war.

> In some military outfits, the comfort women were ordered to commit suicide along with the Japanese soldiers. In other locations, they were killed in the caves or trenches, or even locked in submarines scheduled to be sunk in a deep sea.[12]

In her study of rape as a crime of war, Shana Swiss[11] lists examples of recent wars in which hundreds of thousands of women were raped. These include wars in Bangladesh, Liberia, and Uganda. The UNHCR reported that in 1985, 39 percent of Vietnamese boat women were abducted and/or raped at sea.

As a strategy, public rape may be used to terrorize a whole community and to force it to flee, or it may be an expression of ethnic group hatred. Rape and sexual brutality are often a part of torture of women in custody.[8,13] During the Holocaust, women were subjected to horrendous sadism and savagery at the hands of the Nazis, some of the torture cloaked as scientific experimentation.

The trauma of rape is greatly multiplied for those women who become pregnant as a result of the assault. Religious convictions and prohibitions may prevent the woman from seeking an abortion, where abortions are available, and even those who have the choice of abortion face the risks and psychological costs of the procedure. Depression, suicidal ideation, and rejection of the infant are some of the effects found in Bosnia, where the impact of sexual violence on Muslim women is deepened by religious and cultural condemnation.

Many women suffer long-term psychological effects as a result of the fear and profound sense of helplessness experienced in rape. These sequellae include flashbacks, difficulty reestablishing intimate relationships, persistent fears, and a blunting of enjoyment in life generally.[11] Many of the Japanese troops' comfort women who survived the war did not marry and were unable for years to disclose what happened to them because of the profound shame associated with sexual violation. The consequences of rape are far-reaching and may reveal themselves as somatic or psychological complaints years after the events.

Land Mines

There are more than 100 million antipersonnel mines scattered throughout the world, mostly in developing countries with few resources to deal with them[14] (see Chapter 10). Called "weapons of mass destruction in slow motion," they pose a particular threat to women. Frequently they are seeded in agricultural land, where they remain long after hostilities are over, to explode when farmers return to till the fields. Women account for 80 percent of the food production in Africa and are thus the most likely victims. In Mozambique, which used to be self-sufficient for food, huge areas of fertile land cannot be farmed because of the vast number of mines left behind. There is speculation that as peace is being restored in Cambodia, the proportion of women and children injured by mines will increase, as they return to traditional work in the fields or venture further from their homes in search of firewood and wild foods. Women who have lost limbs not only lose their ability to work as farmers, but are often abandoned by their husbands.

It will be women who will bear the brunt of the loss of farmland and will suffer the injuries and death as land mines long buried are triggered. Systems for mine removal are slow and dangerous because mechanical systems, such as flails, have an unacceptable failure rate. Effective mine removal requires probing the ground by hand every two centimeters before carefully disabling the mine—a process that requires expertise and will take years and cost many lives to complete.[14]

Militarism and Women

The excessive emphasis on military power affects public health by the diversion of resources needed for health, by the problems of alcoholism and prostitution associated with military bases, by the psychosocial problems specific to military families, and by the limitations imposed on health care by military secrecy.

Militarization of the Economy

Former U.S. President Dwight Eisenhower recognized the dangers inherent in the close linkages between the military and the industries providing weapons systems when he wrote, "We must guard against the acquisition of unwarranted influence, whether sought or unsought, by the military-industrial complex. The potential for the disastrous rise of misplaced power exists and will persist."[15]

Militarization of an economy diverts financial resources from the social needs of a society, leaving little available for education and health care, two areas where gender bias is already significant. Pakistan, for example, devotes 28 percent of its central government expenditures to defense, and only one percent to health and two percent to education.[9] Maternal mortality in Pakistan is 500 per 100,000 compared to five in Canada; female literacy in 1990 in Pakistan was 21 percent compared to 47 percent for males.[9]

The stark contrast in government priorities is illustrated by the comments of a geologist working in Kenya:

> When I was leaving Nairobi one morning in a van, I passed a woman walking barefoot at the side of the road, bent double with a huge load of firewood she was carrying to town to sell for a few cents. She was carrying a baby in a sling and two other children walked alongside. Meanwhile, a military transport truck passed by, filled with well-fed, well-shod young men with the latest weapons in their hands.[16]

Military Bases

Military bases are associated with prostitution and the spread of sexually transmitted diseases, including HIV infection. A report in the Far Eastern Economic Review[17] states that Olongapo City, next to the Subic U.S. naval base in the Philippines, had 6,000 licensed prostitutes, and another 6,000 swarmed into town when a ship docked. Angeles City, next to Clark air base, had 3,000 licensed prostitutes and 6,000 unlicensed prostitutes.

Military Families

In North America, military families move frequently from base to base, with concomitant disruption of friendships and schooling for children. Military wives are alone for long periods of time, often raising their children on their own while their husbands are deployed elsewhere. Marriage breakdown is a significant problem compounded by the hierarchical structure of the military. Women often find that their friendships are constrained by their husbands being of different ranks, and they worry that discussing the stresses on one's marriage could affect one's husband's career.

Military families are at high risk for spousal abuse. A *New York Times* article cites a U.S. Army survey of 55,000 soldiers at 47 bases, indicating that one of every three families has suffered some kind of domestic violence—from slapping to murder—twice the rate found in groups of civilians. The Pentagon has disclosed that an average of one child or spouse dies each week at the hands of a relative in the military.[18]

Military Secrecy

Military secrecy continues to prevent epidemiologists from studying the full records of populations exposed to the effects of nuclear weapons testing by China, France, the former Soviet Union, the United Kingdom, and the United States. Tests have often been carried out without the consent of the population at risk, and often on aboriginal lands. Women in French Polynesia continue to demand studies of the effects of French testing in the Pacific, claiming a high incidence of miscarriages and birth defects. The health data needed for such studies are not available for independent review because of military secrecy. Similarly, in Kazakhstan, people believe that cancers and birth defects are the result of Soviet nuclear tests carried out near Semipalatinsk, but authoritative studies have not been done. Without a comprehensive test ban, testing may be resumed in the future, still without scientific evaluation of the effects on this and future generations.

Secrecy has also surrounded the contamination of large areas around military bases where toxic waste has been dumped or is stored in deteriorating containment vessels. In the United States, military installations include more than two-thirds of the sites classified by the U.S. Environmental Protection Agency as highly toxic and dangerous.[19]

Studies of the effects of Agent Orange on Vietnamese women and infants[20] indicate an increased risk of birth defects, including anencephaly, oral clefts, and a variety of other anomalies; increased spontaneous abortion (miscarriage); and an increase in hydatidiform moles. Further assessment of this research is needed because major methodological problems have been identified, and at present the Vietnamese studies have not been published in a form that permits all the relevant information to be evaluated.

War and Manhood

In her study of the links between masculinity and violence, Myriam Miedzian notes that studies of aggression and warfare generally describe male behavior as representative of all human behavior, and female behavior as inadequate or defective in comparison: "Since male behavior is the norm, warfare and violence are not only accepted as central, normal parts of human experience but they are transformed into heroic, exciting events."[4]

The glorification of war is so pervasive that, generation after generation, young males are drawn into proving their manhood by going into battle. Masculinity is, in effect, measured by violent behavior. The masculine traits of dominance and competition for position and status are expressed in a wide range of behavior, from sports and business to the way males make conversation. When these traits are expressed in violence, they become a public health concern, whether the violence is against women and children in the home or against an enemy in war. We cannot conclude that war is inevitable as a biological imperative, because it is clear that not all males are violent—in fact, most men live out their lives without physical violence. Miedzian concludes that the social reinforcements of violent behavior and particularly the glorification of war must be challenged in order to decrease violence.

Men in power demonstrate their toughness and manhood by their willingness to send young men to war. During the Persian Gulf War, journalists often referred to

President Bush's overcoming the "wimp factor" by the massive bombings of Iraq. Political leaders rise in popularity as they project an image of being hard and ruthless, and fall as they appear to be soft or empathetic.

While the leaders go into war to gain power, economic advantage, and prestige, the enlisted men often do not know why they are fighting. Interviews with Vietnam veterans[21] revealed that living out a John Wayne fantasy—being tough, unemotional, ruthless, and competitive—was foremost in their minds when they signed up. The desire for young men to see themselves as superior to young females is exploited in boot camp training where contempt for women is pervasive.

In a world with nuclear weapons, demonstrating the "right kind of manhood" brings catastrophic risks. The stand-off between two male leaders, John Kennedy and Nikita Khrushchev, in the Cuban missile crisis of 1962 put the world in danger of the use of nuclear missiles.

The development and control of nuclear weapons has been an almost exclusively male domain, the nuclear arms race a manifestation of competition carried to an irrational extreme. Scilla Elworthy, founder of the Oxford Research Group, has identified 650 nuclear decision-makers worldwide, only five of whom are women.[22]

Countless grim cartoons during the Reagan years played on the phallic symbolism of nuclear missiles, but the connections between male sexual fantasies and weaponry are far from humorous. Carol Cohn,[7] in her research into the language used by nuclear weapons strategists, has written of the denial of reality that is necessary for people to think of 40 million dead as "acceptable losses," and of human death as "collateral damage." Cohn was appalled to hear one strategist apologize for "thinking like a woman," when he appeared to respond emotionally to the idea of millions dying. Sexual imagery applied to weapons is shown graphically in advertisements that appear in military magazines, where weapons are described in terms of hardness, penetration, and thrust. In arms bazaars, glamorous young women are often hired to pose beside the latest weapon systems.

Conclusions

Many of the health problems we have addressed in this chapter are basic human rights issues that are exacerbated by war. Peace and development are impossible without equality for women. Male domination is a central factor in the atrocities of war experienced by women, and it is central to the absence of women's voices where decisions are made about war and aggression.

The threat of nuclear war led Albert Einstein to challenge us to find a new way of thinking or drift into unparalleled catastrophe. It is hardly new to think of women as having equal rights, but it is surely revolutionary to guarantee women's rights in every country. Health for all people and health for the planet are impossible without these guarantees.

REFERENCES

1. Toole, M. and Waldman, R.J. Refugees and displaced persons: War, hunger and public health. *JAMA* 270:600–605, 1993.
2. Mann, J., Drucker, E., Tarantola, D. and McCabe, M.P. Bosnia: The war against public health. *Medicine and Global Survival* 1(3):130–146, 1994.
3. Bhatia, B., Kawar, M. and Shahin, M. Women's survey; The impact of the Gulf crisis on the women in Iraq. In *Health and welfare in Iraq after the Gulf crisis; an in-depth assessment.* Cambridge: Harvard International Study Team, 1991.
4. Susser, E.S. and Shang, P.L. Schizophrenia after prenatal exposure to the Dutch Hunger Winter of 1944–1945. *Arch. Gen. Psychiarty* 49.: 983–988, 1992.
5. Martin, S.F. *Refugee women.* London: Zed Books, 1991.
6. Porter, R.C.J. A perspective on the start of the relief operation. In Levy, B.S. and Susott, D.C. (ed.), *Years of horror, days of hope: Responding to the Cambodian refugee crisis.* Millwood, New York: Associated Faculty Press, Inc., 1986, pp. 13–26.
7. Barnaby, F. *The Gaia peace atlas: Survival into the third millenium.* London: Doubleday, 1988.
8. Brock-Utne, B. *Feminist perspectives on peace and peace education.* New York: Pergamon Press, 1989.
9. United Nations Children's Fund. *The state of the world's children 1994.* New York: Oxford University Press, 1994.
10. Gunby, P. Varied health risks confront physicians in former Yugoslavia's embattled areas. *JAMA* 272:337–340, 1994.
11. Swiss, S. and Giller, J.E. Rape as a crime of war; a medical perspective. *JAMA* 270:612–615, 1993.
12. Chung, C.S. Testimonies of the global tribunal on violations of women's human rights. In Reilly, N. (ed.), *United Nations World Conference on Human Rights.* Vienna: Center for Women's Global Leadership, 1993.
13. Matthews, I. Daughtering in war: Two "case studies" from Mexico and Guatemala. In Cooke, M. and Willcott, A. (eds.), *Gendering war talk.* Princeton: Princton University Press, 1993, pp. 148–173.
14. Landmines, A Deadly Legacy. A report to the May 1993 London meeting of nongovernmental organizations promoting a ban on the production, transfer and use of antipersonnel landmines. In *Human Rights Watch/Arms Project.* Boston: Physicians for Human Rights, 1993.
15. Eisenhower, D.D. Farewell Broadcast. *New York Times,* Jan. 18, 1961.
16. Padgham, T. Personal communication, 1986.
17. A view from the bases. *The Economist* 312:28, 1989.
18. Schmitt, E. Domestic abuse rising in military, Pentagon says. *New York Times,* May 23, 1994: A1, 12.
19. Leaning, J. War and the environment: Human health consequences of the environmental damage of war. In Chivian, E., McCally, M., Hu, H., et al. (eds.), *Critical condition: Human health and the environment.* Cambridge MA: MIT Press, 1993.
20. Constable, J.D. and Hatch, M.C. Reproductive effects of herbicide exposure in Vietnam:

Recent studies by the Vietnamese and others. *Teratogenesis Carcinog. Mutagen.* 5(4):231–250, 1985.

21. Miedzian, M. *Boys will be boys: Breaking the link between masculinity and violence.* New York: Doubleday, 1991.

22. Vickers, J. *Women and war.* London: Zed Books, 1993.

23. Cohn, C. "Clean bombs" and clean language. In Elshtain, J.B. and Tobias, S. (eds.), *Women, militarism and war: Essays in history, politics, and social theory.* Savage, MD: Rowman and Littlefield, 1990.

14

Displaced Persons and War

MICHAEL J. TOOLE

The cycle of war, intimidation, hunger, migration, and death that has affected millions of civilians in several continents during recent years poses one of the greatest contemporary public health challenges. By mid-1994, just two conflicts—in the former Yugoslavia and Rwanda—had between them generated four million refugees and internally displaced persons. Refugee camps have become the modern-day international equivalent of the clinician's emergency department. The indirect public health consequences of war have been mediated by mass population displacement, food shortages, hunger, and the destruction of health services, and have been especially severe in developing countries, where basic services and food reserves are already inadequate. In some situations in the Third World, the public health impact of population displacements induced by war has been relatively more severe than the direct impact of the violence.

Refugees who have crossed international borders fleeing war or persecution for reasons of race, religion, nationality, or membership in particular social and political groups are protected by several international conventions.[1] During the two decades following the end of World War II, the most dramatic refugee emergencies took place in South Asia—first when 10 million were displaced following the partition of India and Pakistan, and later when Bangladesh seceded from Pakistan. The number of refugees worldwide has steadily increased from five million in 1980 to an estimated 21 million by August 1994.[2,3] Since 1990 alone, more than nine million refugees have been accorded protection and assistance by the international community (Table 14-1).[2]

While most refugees are still in Africa, the Middle East, and South Asia, there has been a rapid increase in the number of refugees in Europe since 1990. Almost two million refugees have been displaced within or have fled the republics of former Yugoslavia.[3] Wars in the Azerbaijan enclave of Nagorno-Karabakh, ex-Soviet Georgia, and the rebellious Russian province of Chechnya have generated almost one million refugees. During the early 1990s, increasing numbers of refugees took to boats and sought asylum directly in Western, industrialized countries. These included many

Table 14-1. Estimated number of refugees arriving in countries of asylum, 1990–1994.

Country of Origin	Country of Asylum	Year of Arrival	Estimated Population
Liberia	Guinea	1990	300,000
Liberia	Côte d'Ivoire	1990	200,000
Somalia	Djibouti	1990	30,000
Somalia	Ethiopia	1990–1991	200,000
Sudan	Ethiopia	1990	40,000
Kuwait, Iraq	Jordan	1990	750,000
Mozambique	Malawi	1990–1992	250,000
Azerbaijan	Armenia	1990–1992	290,000
Armenia	Azerbaijan	1990–1992	200,000
Iraq	Iran	1991	1,100,000
Iraq	Turkey	1991	450,000
Sierra Leone	Guinea	1991	185,000
Ethiopia	Sudan	1991	51,000
Somalia	Kenya	1991–1992	320,000
Croatia, Bosnia-Herzegovina	Other Former Yugoslav republics	1991–1993	750,000
Croatia, Bosnia	Western Europe	1991–1993	512,000
Georgia	Russia	1991–1993	140,000
Somalia	Yemen	1992	50,000
Ethiopia	Kenya	1992	80,000
Sudan	Kenya	1992	20,000
Mali, Niger	Algeria	1992	40,000
Myanmar	Bangladesh	1992	250,000
Bhutan	Nepal	1992	75,000
Mozambique	Zimbabwe	1992	60,000
Tajikstan	Afghanistan	1993	60,000
Togo	Ghana	1993	120,000
Togo	Benin	1993	120,000
Burundi	Tanzania	1993	350,000
Burundi	Rwanda	1993	370,000
Rwanda	Tanzania	1994	400,000
Rwanda	Burundi	1994	100,000
Rwanda	Zaire	1994	1,000,000

Sources: U.S. Committee for Refugees and UNHCR.

thousands of Haitians and Cubans who sought refuge in the United States, Albanians in Italy, Vietnamese in Hong Kong, and East Timorese in Australia. The reluctance of these wealthy countries to provide asylum may have contributed to a growing worldwide trend to deny refugee status.

Before 1990, most of the world's refugees had fled countries that ranked among the poorest in the world, such as Afghanistan, Cambodia (Figure 14-1), Mozambique, and Ethiopia. However, during this decade, an increasing number of refugees have originated in relatively more affluent countries, such as Kuwait, Iraq, the former Yugoslavia, and Armenia. Nevertheless, the reasons for the flight of refugees generally

Figure 14-1. Huts made of thatch and burlap at Khao-I-Dang camp for Cambodians in Thailand in 1980 (Photograph by Barry S. Levy).

remain the same: war, civil strife, and persecution. Hunger, while sometimes a primary cause of population movements, is all too frequently only a contributing factor. For example, during 1992, although severe drought in southern Africa and the Horn of Africa affected food production in all countries in those regions, only in war-torn Mozambique and Somalia did millions of hungry inhabitants migrate in search of food.

Although many people fled the generalized violence of war, most fled because they were specifically targeted by one or another armed faction. Civilians in Somalia have been targeted by armed militia because of their membership in a patrilineal clan. Muslim Rohingyas of Myanmar were victims of religious persecution by their government. Ethnic Nepalis were harassed by Bhutanese authorities. Liberians were attacked or murdered because of their ethnicity. And Croatians, Serbs, and Bosnian Muslims were victims of ancient ethnic and religious feuds.

The most dramatic recent example of mass population displacement resulted in Rwanda from attempted genocide of the Tutsi minority by extremist elements of the Hutu majority following the deaths in April 1994 of both the Rwandan and Burundian presidents in a plane crash near the capital of Kigali. Initially, more than 500,000 refugees fled into Burundi and Tanzania; later, in July, when the Rwandan Patriotic Front militarily defeated the Rwandan government and took over the country, one

Table 14-2. Estimated numbers of internally displaced persons, by country, December 1994

Country	Displaced Persons
South Africa	4,000,000
Sudan	4,000,000
Angola	2,000,000
Turkey	2,000,000
Bosnia and Herzegovina	1,300,000
Rwanda	1,200,000
Liberia	1,100,000
Afghanistan	1,000,000
Iraq	1,000,000
Sierra Leone	700,000
Azerbaijan	630,000
Colombia	600,000
Lebanon	600,000
Peru	600,000
Zaire	550,000
Sri Lanka	525,000
Mozambique	500,000
Myanmar	500,000
Somalia	500,000
Russian Federation	450,000
Burundi	400,000
Ethiopia	400,000
Croatia	290,000
Cyprus	265,000
Georgia	260,000
India	250,000
Kenya	210,000
Guatemala	200,000
Cambodia	110,000
Yemen	110,000
Togo	100,000

Source: U.S. Committee for Refugees.[3]

million ethnic Hutus abruptly fled to eastern Zaire, provoking an unprecedented refugee crisis (see Figure 4-2).

While the number of refugees has steadily grown worldwide, the number of internally displaced persons has exploded during the past few years. Approximately 27 million people have fled their homes in order to escape war and persecution and to search for food and shelter, often in bleak and remote locations, without crossing international boundaries.[3] Therefore, they do not qualify for the protection and assistance provided by the international community to refugees (Table 14-2). An estimated 18 million of these internally displaced persons live in Africa—more than two million

Figure 14-2. Tent city created by internally displaced Somalis in Baidoa in 1992 (Photograph by Michael J. Toole).

in Rwanda alone. Almost two million people have been displaced within the former Yugoslav republics of Croatia and Bosnia-Herzegovina[3] (see Figure 4-1).

Those who are internally displaced are in a particularly precarious situation because they remain within or close to zones of conflict, and international relief agencies experience extreme difficulty in providing them with relief aid (Figure 14-2). Although the Geneva Conventions guarantee the basic human rights of civilian victims of war, the International Committee of the Red Cross, which is mandated with implementing the conventions, is often denied access to these populations by either the governments or rival political organizations.

Public Health Consequences

While the critical health problems affecting refugees and internally displaced persons are similar in nature, their severity may be greater among internally displaced populations because assistance is often delayed and inadequate in quantity. Internally displaced persons may suffer more injuries because they are usually located close to zones of conflict; for example, thousands of displaced Bosnians have been killed in attacks on the so-called safe havens of Sarajevo, Srebrenica, Zepa, and Gorazde. Both refugees and internally displaced persons are often victims of land mines, particularly as they travel between zones controlled by rival armed factions (see Chapter 10).

Mortality Rates

The most specific indicator of health status among refugee populations is the crude mortality rate (CMR); a community cannot be ''healthy'' if its death rate remains high. CMRs have been estimated from hospital and burial records, community-based surveys, and 24-hour burial site surveillance. Among the many problems in estimating mortality under emergency conditions are (1) inadequate access to information, (2) recall bias in surveys, (3) families' failure to report perinatal deaths, (4) inaccurate estimates of population size, and (5) lack of standard reporting procedures. In general, however, bias tends to underestimate mortality rates, since deaths are usually under-counted, and population size is often exaggerated.[4]

Most reports of mortality related to conflict and food scarcity have come from displaced populations. Comparisons of mortality between displaced and nondisplaced populations that are affected by conflict and famine are problematic because displacement itself may reflect a more serious baseline situation. Nonetheless, comparisons between displaced and nondisplaced populations, and between refugees and local, host-country populations, show that in nearly all cases the displaced and refugee populations experience significantly higher CMRs.[4]

During the early phase of an emergency, it is useful to express the CMR as deaths per 10,000 people per day. In most developing countries, the baseline annual CMR is approximately 20 per 1,000, corresponding to a daily rate of approximately 0.6 per 10,000. In emergencies, a daily rate of 1.0 per 10,000 has been commonly used as a threshold to indicate an elevated CMR.[4] Before 1990, extremely high death rates were documented among refugees during the early phase of an influx; for example, CMRs among refugees in Thailand (1979), Somalia (1980), and Sudan (1985) were up to 30 times higher than baseline rates.[5]

During the early 1990s, there was some improvement. Nevertheless, death rates were between 5 to 12 times the CMR in the country of origin among 30,000 Sudanese refugees in the Ethiopian camp of Itang (July 1990), newly arrived Somali refugees in Ethiopia (June 1991), Somali refugees in Kenya (January 1992), ethnic Nepali refugees from Bhutan (May 1992), and newly arriving Mozambican refugees in Zim-babwe and Malawi (July 1992) (Table 14-3).[6] Between March and May 1991, the average daily CMR among 400,000 Kurdish refugees on the Turkey-Iraq border was 4.2 per 10,000—a death rate 18 times higher than the normal rate in Iraq.[7] However, since Turkey provided asylum to less than 10 percent of these people, most remained internally displaced in northern Iraq.

Following the massive influx of Rwandan refugees into the North Kivu region of eastern Zaire in July 1994, daily CMRs ranged between 25 and 50 per 10,000 per

Table 14-3.   Estimated crude mortality rates[a] (CMRs) in selected refugee populations, 1990–1994

Date	Host Country	Country of Origin	Baseline CMR	Refugee CMR
July 1990	Ethiopia	Sudan	1.7	6.9
June 1991	Ethiopia	Somalia	1.8	14.0
March–May 1991	Turkey/Iraq	Iraq	0.7	12.6
March 1992	Kenya	Somalia	1.8	22.2
March 1992	Nepal	Bhutan	1.3	9.0
June 1992	Bangladesh	Myanmar	0.8	4.8
June 1992	Malawi	Mozambique	1.5	3.5
August 1992	Zimbabwe	Mozambique	1.5	10.5
Dec 1993	Rwanda	Burundi	1.8	9.0
May 1994	Tanzania	Rwanda	1.8	1.8
June 1994	Burundi	Rwanda	1.8	15.0
July 1994	Zaire	Rwanda	1.8	102.0

[a]Deaths per 1,000 per month.

day.[8] Population surveys conducted in the refugee camps estimated that between seven percent and nine percent of the refugees died during the first month after the influx; these death rates are among the highest ever documented among refugees.

The risk of death is usually highest during the period immediately after refugees arrive in the country of asylum, reflecting long periods of inadequate food and medical care. For example, during July and August 1992, the daily CMR among Mozambican refugees who had been in the Zimbabwean camp of Chambuta for less than one month was 8 per 10,000, which was four times the death rate of refugees who had been in the camp between one and three months, and 16 times the death rate normally reported for nondisplaced populations in Mozambique[9] (Figure 14-3).

Demographic Risk Groups

Most deaths in refugee populations have occurred among children under five years of age; for example, 65 percent of deaths among Kurdish refugees on the Turkish border occurred in the 17 percent of the population under five years of age. Among newly arrived Mozambican refugees in Malawi in 1992, the death rate for children under five years of age was four to five times the overall crude death rate. An exception to this trend was documented in the Rwandan refugee camps of eastern Zaire where under-five death rates were no higher than CMRs during the first four weeks after the influx—probably because most deaths in this population were caused by cholera, which is highly lethal in all age groups. The massacres in Rwanda in early 1994 and the high death rate among Rwandan refugees in eastern Zaire led to an unprecedented number of unaccompanied children among the refugee population. By mid-August, more than 12,000 such children, most of whom were probably orphans, had been

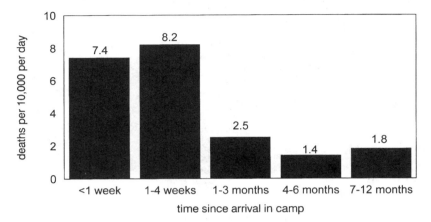

Figure 14-3. Death rate by duration of stay in camp, Chambuta camp, Zimbabwe, July–August 1992 (Source: United Nations High Commissioner for Refugees, Zimbabwe).

registered in North Kivu, and death rates in the sites where they were placed reached as high as 100 per 10,000 per day.[8]

Mortality data disaggregated by gender are frequently not available. However, in the Gundhum II camp for Burmese refugees in Bangladesh, the death rate among Rohingya girl infants (less than one year of age) was almost twice the rate of boy infants; among refugees older than five years, the death rate among females was 3.5 times that for males. Among Kurdish refugees on the Turkey-Iraq border in 1991, however, the death rate among males and females was approximately equal.[6]

Causes of Death

The most common reported causes of death among refugees during the early influx phase have been diarrheal diseases, measles, acute respiratory infections, and other infectious diseases.[10] Epidemics of severe diarrheal disease have been increasingly common; cholera epidemics have occurred in refugee camps in Malawi, Zimbabwe, Swaziland, Nepal, Bangladesh, Turkey, Afghanistan, Burundi, and Zaire. Cholera case-fatality rates in refugee camps have ranged between 3 and 30 percent. In addition, outbreaks of dysentery caused by *Shigella dysenteriae* type 1 have been reported since 1991 in Malawi, Nepal, Kenya, Bangladesh, Burundi, Rwanda, Tanzania, and Zaire. Dysentery case-fatality rates have been as high as 10 percent in young children and the elderly. In the Goma area of eastern Zaire, between 40,000 and 45,000 Rwandan refugees may have died from cholera or dysentery (80 to 90 percent of all deaths) during the month following their arrival in mid-July 1994.[8]

Measles epidemics have caused high death rates among refugees. For example, during a three-month period of 1985, more than 2,000 measles-associated deaths were documented in the Ethiopian refugee camp of Wad Kowli in eastern Sudan.[11] Since 1990, measles outbreaks have been reported among new refugees in camps in Nepal, Zimbabwe, and Malawi, contributing to high death rates in those camps. Large refugee camps for Somalis in Ethiopia, Iraqis in Turkey, and Rwandans in Tanzania and Zaire have been spared measles epidemics, probably because measles vaccination coverage rates in the refugees' countries of origin were relatively high.

Malaria has been reported as a major cause of death in camps in Thailand (1979), Malawi (1988–1993), eastern Sudan (1988), western Ethiopia (1991), and Kenya (1992). High malaria-specific death rates among refugees have been associated with movements from areas of low malaria endemicity through or into areas of high endemicity, and with the development of chloroquine resistance. Refugees in camps in Somalia, Ethiopia, and Kenya have experienced outbreaks of hepatitis E virus infection with attack rates between six and eight percent, and case-fatality rates among pregnant women between 14 and 17 percent.[12] Between March and October 1991, one in five deaths in the Somali refugee camp of Liboi in Kenya were attributed to this disease. Outbreaks of meningococcal meningitis have been reported in refugee camps in Thailand (1980), Sudan (1985), Ethiopia (1988), Malawi (1991), Burundi (1994), and Zaire (1994).

Nutritional Deficiencies

The impact of communicable diseases on the health of refugees has often been exacerbated by a high prevalence of protein-energy malnutrition that dates from prolonged food shortages before they became refugees. Local farmers may not have planted crops as extensively as usual due to uncertainty created by armed conflict. The supply of seeds and fertilizer may have been disrupted; irrigation systems may have been damaged by the fighting; and crops may have been intentionally destroyed or looted by armed soldiers. The resulting food shortages may have caused prolonged hunger and eventually have driven families from their homes in search of relief.

Since weight is more sensitive to sudden changes in food availability than height, nutritional assessments during emergencies focus on measuring weight-for-height. Moderate to severe acute malnutrition is defined as a weight-for-height more than two standard deviations below the mean of the CDC/NCHS/WHO reference population (Z-score less than -2).[13] All children with edema are classified as having severe acute malnutrition. As a screening measurement, the mid-upper arm circumference (MUAC) may also be used to assess acute undernutrition, although there is not complete agreement on which cutoff values should be used as indicators. Field studies indicate that a MUAC between 12.0 cm and 12.5 cm correlates with a weight-for-height Z-score of -2; the lower figure (12.0 cm) is more appropriate in children less than two years of age.[14]

The prevalence of acute malnutrition among children less than five years of age has been as high as 50 percent among Ethiopian refugees in eastern Sudan (1985), 45 percent among Sudanese refugees arriving in Ethiopia during 1990, 29 percent among Somali refugees in Kenya in 1991, and 48 percent among Mozambicans in Zimbabwe (1992).[6] In some settings, refugee children who were adequately nourished upon arrival in camps have developed acute malnutrition due either to inadequate food rations or to severe epidemics of diarrheal disease. In the Hartisheik refugee camp in eastern Ethiopia, for example, the prevalence of acute malnutrition increased from less than 10 percent to almost 25 percent during a six-month period in late 1988 and early 1989 due to inadequate food rations.[15] In early 1991, the prevalence of acute malnutrition among Kurdish refugee children aged 12 to 23 months increased from less than 5 to 13 percent during a two-month period following a severe outbreak of diarrheal disease.[16] The prevalence of acute malnutrition was between 18 and 23 percent in Rwandan refugee camps in eastern Zaire, following the severe cholera and dysentery epidemics during the first month after the influx.[8]

In addition, high incidence rates of several micronutrient deficiency diseases have been reported in many refugee camps, especially in Africa. Young refugee and displaced children are at high risk of developing vitamin A deficiency because food rations usually contain inadequate vitamin A. In addition, common infectious diseases such as measles and diarrhea may deplete their body stores of the vitamin. In 1990, more than 18,000 cases of pellagra, caused by food rations deficient in niacin, were reported among Mozambican refugees in Malawi.[17] Numerous outbreaks of scurvy (vitamin C deficiency) were documented in refugee camps in Somalia, Ethiopia, and Sudan between 1982 and 1991. The prevalence of scurvy was higher among females and the elderly and was highly associated with the period of residence in camps, a reflection of the time exposed to rations lacking in vitamin C.[18]

Internally Displaced Persons

Although reliable data on the internally displaced are difficult to gather, death rates may be considerably higher in these populations than among refugees. In Liberia, for example, the annual CMR among internally displaced persons in Monrovia was estimated in 1990 to be 85 per 1,000—almost six times the normal CMR in that country.[6] By contrast, death rates among Liberian refugees in Côte d'Ivoire and Guinea were relatively low. In Southern Sudan, civil war has resulted in mass population displacement, hunger, and—during 1993—death rates up to 15 times those reported in nonconflict times.[20] (See Table 14-4.)

While the main causes of death among internally displaced persons have been similar to those among refugee populations, prevalence rates of acute malnutrition among the internally displaced have tended to be extremely high. In southern Somalia during 1992, the prevalence of acute malnutrition among children younger than five

Table 14-4. Mean crude monthly mortality rates[a] (CMRs) for internally displaced persons, 1990–1994.

Country	Date	Baseline CMR	Internally Displaced Persons CMR
Liberia[b]	January—December 1990	1.2	7.1
Iraq[c]	March–May 1991	0.7	12.6
Somalia[d] (Merca)	April 1991–March 1992	2.0	13.8
Somalia (Baidoa)	April–November 1992	2.0	50.7
Somalia[c] (Afgoi)	April–December 1992	2.0	16.5
Sudan[c] (Ayod)	April 1992–March 1993	1.6	23.0
Sudan[c] (Akon)	April 1992–March 1993	1.6	13.7
Bosnia[c] (Zepa)	April 1992–March 1993	0.8	3.0
Bosnia[e] (Sarajevo)	April 1993	0.8	2.9

[a]Deaths per 1,000 per month.

[b]Médecins Sans Frontières (Belgium).

[c]Centers for Disease Control and Prevention, Atlanta, GA (USA).

[d]Médecins Sans Frontières (France).

[e]Médecins Sans Frontières (Holland).

years in displaced persons camps in Marka and Qorioley was 75 percent, compared with 43 percent among town residents.[21] Among the displaced in southern Sudan, in March 1993, approximately 70 percent of children were acutely malnourished.[20]

Refugees and internally displaced persons in Bosnia and other parts of former Yugoslavia have perhaps suffered most from intentional injuries inflicted during the course of bitter interethnic fighting. An estimated 200,000 civilians have died during the last three years of conflict (1992 to 1995)—more than 15,000 in Sarajevo alone.[22] Population surveys in southern and central Somalia determined that between 4 and 11 percent of deaths between April 1992 and January 1993 were caused by war-related trauma.[23] Many displaced persons who sought refuge in Angolan towns such as Cuito, Huambo, Benguela, and Melanje were killed during fierce fighting in 1993 and 1994.

Sexual assault of displaced women has been increasingly common; for example, reports from the former Yugoslavia estimate that at least 20,000 Bosnian, Serbian, and Croatian displaced women have been raped.[24] The Office of the United Nations High Commissioner for Refugees (UNHCR) documented 192 cases of rape of Somali refugee women in Kenyan camps during a seven-month period during 1993; in addition, several thousand unreported rapes were estimated to have occurred.[3]

Response to Population Displacement Emergencies

Epidemiologic data have documented those health problems that consistently cause most deaths and severe illnesses among refugees and internally displaced populations, and have identified young children and women as being at highest risk. Most deaths are preventable using currently available and affordable measures. Relief programs, therefore, must channel all available resources toward identifying, treating, and preventing cases of measles, diarrheal disease, malnutrition, acute respiratory infection (ARI), and, where prevalent, malaria, especially among women and young children.

Initially, refugees may suffer severe anxiety or depression, compounded by complete dependence on the generosity of others for survival. If refugee camps are located near borders or close to areas of continuing armed conflict, the desire for security is an overriding concern. Since most refugees and internally displaced people tend to be women and children—up to 80 percent—the first priority of any relief operation is to ensure adequate protection.

To diminish the sense of helplessness and dependency, refugees should be given an active role in the planning and implementation of relief programs. Nevertheless, giving total control of the distribution of relief items to so-called refugee "leaders" may be dangerous. For example, leaders of the former, Hutu-controlled Rwandan government took control of the distribution system in Zairian refugee camps in July 1994, resulting in diversion of relief supplies to young male members of the former Rwandan Army. Surveys indicated that households headed by single women had diminished access to food and shelter material, which led to elevated malnutrition rates among children in those households.[8]

The critical elements of a relief program in response to sudden population displacement are clean water, food, sanitation, and shelter. UNHCR recommends that at least 15 to 20 liters of potable water be provided daily to each person. Although there is a consensus on the minimum quantity and quality of food required by these populations for survival, the timely provision of adequate food supplies remains a critical issue in many parts of the world, especially in Africa. In addition to the minimum caloric requirement of 2,000 kilocalories per person per day, adequate micronutrients need to be provided in ration foods, through fortification of ration cereals or through routine supplementation (especially of vitamin A). General rations should consist of familiar and culturally acceptable foods, and adequate cereal grinding mills, cooking utensils, and cooking fuel need to be provided. Food should be distributed, preferably by women—who have been shown to be fairer than men—to family units, with special care taken to ensure that socially vulnerable groups in the community receive their fair share.

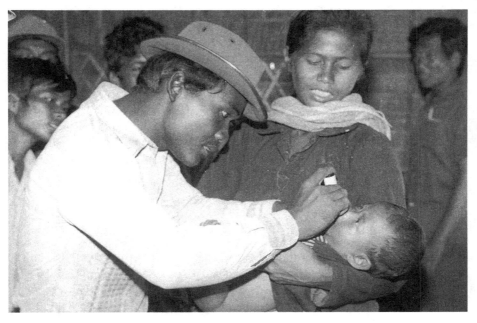

Figure 14-4. Public health worker administers oral polio vaccine to a child in Khao-I-Dang camp for Cambodians in Thailand (Photograph by Barry S. Levy).

Beyond the provision of the above basic needs, the following elements of a public health program should be established as soon as possible:

1. A *health information system,* including surveillance of mortality, nutritional status, and morbidity from diseases of public health importance.
2. *Diarrheal disease control,* including oral rehydration therapy (ORT) in a supervised setting, appropriate treatment of dysentery, community hygiene education, and cholera preparedness.
3. *Immunization,* including measles immunization for children 6 months to 12 years of age immediately; provision of other WHO Expanded Program on Immunization antigens (diphtheria-pertussis-tetanus, oral polio vaccine, and BCG [Bacille Calmette-Guerin]) later, when the emergency subsides; and identification of sources for meningitis vaccine. (Figure 14-4)
4. *Basic curative care,* including an emphasis on maternal and child health; establishment of a referral system; development of an essential drugs list; preparation of standard treatment guidelines (at least for diarrhea, malaria, and ARI); and selection, training, and deployment of community health workers.
5. *Selective feeding programs,* including supplementary feeding for vulnerable groups, such as young children, pregnant and lactating women, and the elderly;

therapeutic feeding for severely malnourished children; and the provision of micronutrient supplements to vulnerable groups.

6. *Endemic disease control and epidemic preparedness,* comprising establishment of surveillance, including standard case definitions; development of standard case management protocols; agreement on policies for prevention (including vaccination and prophylaxis); identification of a laboratory to confirm index cases of epidemic diseases; identification of sources of relevant vaccines; establishment of reserves of essential medical supplies (ORT, intravenous solutions, and antibiotics); identification of treatment sites, triage systems, and training needs; identification of expert assistance for epidemic investigation; development of environmental management plans; and implementation of community education and prevention programs.

Innovative and culturally appropriate programs of counseling, support, and rehabilitation are often necessary to address the needs of people who have experienced the violence of shelling, land mines, and sexual assault. Also, there is a need to develop specialized approaches to caring for unaccompanied children, such as those Rwandan children in the camps of eastern Zaire and Tanzania during 1994.

Once the emergency relief phase is over, new challenges arise. Public health programs need to be community-based and integrated with other development programs that aim to minimize dependency on the outside world, restore dignity to stressed communities, and prepare for eventual repatriation to their homelands. Training of community health workers, particularly women, should be the cornerstone of these longer-term programs. New, and sometimes sensitive, issues such as family spacing and the prevention of infection with the human immunodeficiency virus (HIV) need to be addressed through community development processes.

Relief management decisions need to be based on sound technical information, coordinated action, information sharing, and careful evaluation of the impact and effectiveness of interventions. Responsibilities for the implementation of relief programs should increasingly be shared with proven, competent, and experienced indigenous and foreign nongovernmental organizations (NGOs) (see Chapters 19 and 20). However, the core group of international relief agencies with appropriate experience and technical competence in emergency management remains small and overstretched. The public health needs of displaced populations cannot be adequately addressed by traditional, Western-style curative care in expensive, difficult-to-manage hospital settings. Therefore, there is an urgent need for relevant training programs in emergency public health for NGO personnel and limited operational research to develop effective and innovative approaches to emergency health problems.

Recent emergencies have followed a predictable pattern of political unrest, civil war, human rights abuses, food shortages, and, finally, mass population displacement. There has been almost no preparedness for these emergencies within the public health community. Agencies involved in health development projects should integrate preparedness planning into all aspects of public health programs. Health information systems should incorporate plans to simplify and focus on major health problems in the event of emergencies. Immunization, diarrheal disease control, and community health worker training programs should likewise incorporate emergency contingency plans.

Finally, greater attention needs to be given to the early prevention of conflict situations that give rise to mass population displacement. Early warning systems have been in place in disaster-prone regions for the past decade; however, their warnings have often been ignored. Determined diplomacy applied to warring parties early in a conflict might preclude the need for later military toughness, with all the associated problems that were witnessed in Somalia, Bosnia, and elsewhere.

REFERENCES

1. Convention and Protocol Relating to the Status of Refugees. Geneva, Switzerland: United Nations High Commissioner for Refugees; 1968. Publication HCR/INF/29/Rev.3.
2. United Nations High Commissioner for Refugees. *The state of the world's refugees.* Geneva, Switzerland, 1993.
3. U.S. Committee for Refugees. *World refugee survey, 1995.* Washington, D.C.: U.S. Committee for Refugees, 1994.
4. Centers for Disease Control and Prevention. Famine-affected, refugee, and displaced populations: Recommendations for public health issues. *MMWR* 41 (RR-13), 1992.
5. Toole, M.J. and Waldman, R.J. An analysis of mortality trends among refugee populations in Thailand, Somalia, and Sudan. *Bull. World Health Organ.* 67:381–388, 1989.
6. Toole, M.J. and Waldman, R.J. Refugees and displaced persons: War, hunger, and public health. *JAMA* 270:600–605, 1993.
7. Centers for Disease Control and Prevention. Public health consequences of acute displacement of Iraqi citizens: March-May 1991. *MMWR* 40:443–446, 1991.
8. Goma Epidemiology Group. Public health impact of Rwandan refugee crisis. What happened in Goma, Zaire, in July 1994? *Lancet* 345:339–344, 1995.
9. Centers for Disease Control and Prevention. Mortality among newly arrived Mozambican refugees, Zimbabwe and Malawi, 1992. *MMWR* 42:468–469, 475–477, 1993.
10. Toole, M.J. and Waldman, R.J. Prevention of excess mortality in refugee and displaced populations in developing countries. *JAMA.* 263:3296–3302, 1990.
11. Shears, P., Berry, A.M., Murphy, R. and Nabil, M.A. Epidemiologic assessment of the health and nutrition of Ethiopian refugees in emergency camps in Sudan. *British Medical Journal* 295:314–318, 1987.
12. Centers for Disease Control and Prevention. Enterically transmitted, non-A, non-B hepatitis—East Africa. *MMWR* 36:241–244, 1987.
13. World Health Organization Working Group. Use and interpretation of anthropometric indicators of nutritional status. *Bull. World Health Organ.* 64:929–941, 1986.
14. Gorstein, J., Sullivan, K., Yip, R., de Onis, M., Trowbridge, F., Fajans, P. and Clugston, G. Issues in the assessment of nutritional status using anthropometry. *Bull. World Health Organ.* 72:272–283, 1994.
15. Toole, M.J. and Bhatia, R. A case study of Somali refugees in Hartisheik A camp, eastern Ethiopia: Health and nutrition profile, July 1988–June 1989. *Journal of Refugee Studies* 5: 313–326, 1992.

16. Yip, R. and Sharp, T.W. Acute malnutrition and high childhood mortality related to diarrhea. *JAMA* 270:587–590, 1993.

17. Centers for Disease Control and Prevention. Outbreak of pellagra among Mozambican refugees—Malawi, 1990. *MMWR* 40:209–213, 1991.

18. Desenclos, J.C., Berry, A.M., Padt, R., Farah, B., Segala, C., and Nabil, A.M. Epidemiologic patterns of scurvy among Ethiopian refugees. *Bull. World Health Organ.* 67:309–316, 1989.

19. Toole, M.J. and Miller, D.S. Hunger in the midst of war. *Encyclopaedia Britannica Medical and Health Annual.* 156–181, 1994.

20. Centers for Disease Control and Prevention. Nutrition and mortality assessment—southern Sudan, March 1993. *MMWR* 42:304–308, 1993.

21. Manoncourt, S., Doppler, B., Enten, F., et al. Public health consequences of civil war in Somalia, April 1992. *Lancet.* 340:176–177, 1992.

22. Toole, M.J., Galson, S. and Brady, W. Are war and public health compatible? *Lancet* 341:935–938, 1993.

23. Boss, L.P., Toole, M.J., and Yip, R. Assessments of mortality, morbidity, and nutritional status in Somalia during the 1991–1992 famine. *JAMA* 272:371–376, 1994.

24. Amnesty International. Bosnia and Herzegovina: Rape and sexual abuse by armed forces (Amnesty International report EUR 63/01/93). New York: Amnesty International, 1993.

V

The Impacts of Specific Military Conflicts on Public Health

15

Public Health
and the Vietnam War

MYRON ALLUKIAN, JR., and PAUL L. ATWOOD

To mention Vietnam in the United States today is to invoke painful memories of the 10-year military conflict that began in Southeast Asia—over 9,000 miles away—three decades ago, in an impoverished nation the size of New Mexico. Relatively few Americans think of Vietnam as a country instead of a war—including veterans, few of whom saw more than one or two of the nation's 70 provinces.

The impact of the Vietnam War, also known as the "Second Indochina War" or the "American War" (as it is called by the Vietnamese), exemplifies the consequences of armed conflict. Consider the following: Vietnam suffered 3,000,000 war deaths, millions more wounded or maimed, immense population dislocations, the most massive bombing campaign in the history of warfare, and defoliation of an area the size of Massachusetts.[1,2] Over 58,000 U.S. military personnel died, 313,616 were wounded, and about 10,000 lost at least one limb—more loss-of-limb injuries to U.S. military personnel than in World War II and Korea combined.[3]

It is sometimes difficult to distinguish between the consequences in Vietnam of the war with the United States, and the effects of the First Indochina War with France. Matters were complicated by Vietnam's conflicts with China and Cambodia, which began shortly after U.S. withdrawal. Further compounding the difficulties of analysis are the effects of the U.S. trade embargo, the inexperience of Vietnam's socialist government in economic management, the devastation of Vietnam's infrastructure, numerous natural disasters, the effects of a century of colonial exploitation, and questions about the reliability of data.

Background

History

Vietnam, which means "Land of the South," had conflicts with China, directly to its north, for 2,000 years, and with France for a century preceding U.S. involvement.[4] After the French defeat at Dienbienphu in May 1954, Vietnam, which then had a population of about 24 million, was separated temporarily at the 17th Parallel by the Geneva Accords of July 21, 1954, into two republics: The Democratic (Communist) Republic of Vietnam (DRV) in the north (62,066 square miles), and the Republic of Vietnam in the south (67,108 square miles).[4,5,6] About 928,000 Vietnamese, primarily Catholics, soon moved from northern to southern Vietnam.[7] Essentially refugees, these people strained already inadequate services in the South. The Accords also provided for reunifying elections to be held throughout both territories in 1956. With the approval of the United States, South Vietnam later refused to participate in these reunifying elections, seeking to separate permanently. In 1955, the United States established the Southeast Asia Treaty Organization (SEATO), by which it promised to defend any nation in the region from attack by "foreign" communist governments.[8]

Many Vietnamese on both sides of the 17th Parallel did not approve of this permanent division, and in the South a guerrilla insurgency, led by southern communists, began. This armed movement, known as the National Liberation Front but called the Viet Cong (V.C.) by U.S. forces, was successful because, in contrast to the South Vietnam government, it had an extensive network of committed support among peasants in the countryside. The government of South Vietnam was in danger of collapsing. The United States first responded by committing American advisers to the Army of the Republic of South Vietnam (ARVN), about 12,000 by 1962. The Gulf of Tonkin Resolution was adopted by Congress in August 1964 in response to two alleged attacks on U.S. naval ships by North Vietnamese in international waters. This resolution gave President Lyndon Johnson authority to use armed force in Vietnam. The United States initiated large-scale bombing of the north in 1964, which it escalated throughout 1965. U.S. Marines landed in Danang in March 1965, the first American combat troops in Vietnam.[4] The People's Army of Vietnam (PAVN) of the North then became committed to the goal of forcible reunification of Vietnam. By 1968, over 540,000 U.S. troops were in South Vietnam, in a war they could not carry to North Vietnam for fear of antagonizing China.[9] Unable to win without virtually annihilating the country they were sent to "save," and facing a very determined fighting force, U.S. troops were withdrawn in March 1973. In April 1975, the troops of the Viet Cong and PAVN captured Saigon. After the communist victory, the members of the ARVN and their families, who were seen as agents of foreign occupation, were severely persecuted. Many were imprisoned and over a million sought exile.

Demographics

In 1965, the total population of Vietnam was estimated to be 34.8 million; in 1975, it was 43.4 million.[10] The populations of North and South Vietnam were about 26 million people each in 1979, when the first modern nationwide census was done.[11] With a total population of 52.7 million, Vietnam was the 13th largest country in the world.[10] Average life expectancy was 66 years, 63.6 years for men and 67.9 years for women. The literacy rate was about 85 percent. Vietnam also had 55 to 60 minority groups that made up 15 percent of the population. Most were of Chinese descent or were aborigines. Located on the Gulf of Tonkin and the South China Sea, with China to the north, and Laos and Cambodia to the west, Vietnam is a tropical country with a 1,400-mile coastline. Most of the population is centered in two major river deltas, the Red River Delta in the north and Mekong River Delta in the south. Both deltas are quite fertile. They contain about 24 percent of Vietnam's total land, where 62 percent of its population lives. Another 19.2 percent of Vietnamese live in urban areas. The rest of Vietnam consists of mountains, high plateaus, and jungle.[10]

The Immediate Effects of the War

Over 12 million tons of high explosives were discharged by the United States in Vietnam—5 million tons of bombs and 7.4 million tons of artillery shells. Over 1,000 pounds of explosives per person were discharged in South Vietnam, the territory of the U.S. ally, where the most intensive bombing of the war took place[2,12] (see Figure 15–1). More bombs were dropped by the United States in Vietnam than were discharged by all combatants during World War II. This resulted in massive destruction and over 10 million war victims, about 25 percent of the population of North and South Vietnam.[7] Aside from the estimated 3,000,000 people killed, victims included refugees and evacuees, those suffering from physical and mental disabilities, orphans, and elderly people whose children were killed.

Reliable data do not exist on the immediate effects of the war because of poor recordkeeping, biased perspectives, destruction of records, and massive population shifts as millions became homeless and refugees. Estimates vary according to the source. Table 15-1 provides estimates of casualties and destructive impacts due to the war. The estimated 3,000,000 war deaths among civilians and military personnel of both North and South Vietnam represented 7.7% of the population. If the United States had the same proportion of deaths, war invalids, and refugees for its population of 205 million in 1970 as did Vietnam, there would have been about 15.8 million American deaths, 2.3 million war invalids, and 45 million refugees.

All five of North Vietnam's industrial centers were demolished. All 29 of its provincial capitals were bombed, as were 2,700 of its 4,000 villages[12] (see Figure 5-2).

Figure 15-1. In 1965, wounded and shocked civilian survivors of the battle at Dong Xoai outside of fort-bunker where they survived the ground fighting and air bombardments of the previous two days (Source: AP/Wide World Photos).

Virtually every railway and highway was destroyed. An accurate count of the irrigation dikes and water conservancy projects destroyed is impossible, though the devastation was extensive.

In South Vietnam, 9,000 of 15,000 rural villages were destroyed or damaged, resulting in millions of people becoming homeless, displaced, and forced into urban areas[13]. Consequently, Saigon's population swelled from 1.4 to 4.2 million. In 1975, South Vietnam was burdened with 800,000 war orphans (with another 500,000 in the North), 400,000 war cripples, 600,000 prostitutes, 500,000 drug addicts, and 3,000,000 unemployed people.[12]

In Saigon, the number of juvenile delinquents brought to trial before the juvenile court increased more than fivefold, from 1,040 in 1965 to 5,700 in 1975.[6] According to a 1978 report, 360,000 disabled war victims were collecting government compensation.[12] A 1987 report estimated that 300,000 Vietnamese were still disabled, incapable of working, and totally dependent on the government for their livelihoods.[14] Of

Table 15-1.   The immediate effects of the Vietnam War on Vietnam, 1965–1975

34,800,000 total population in 1965
43,400,000 total population in 1975
3,000,000 deaths (civilian and military)
3,200,000 wounded (Vietnam, Laos and Cambodia)
1,000,000 widows (South Vietnam)
360,000–500,000 war invalids
800,000 orphans (South Vietnam)
300,000 military personnel missing-in-action (MIAs)
83,000 amputees (South Vietnam)
15,000 Amerasian children
10,000,000 refugees and evacuees (South Vietnam)
1,900,000 cattle killed
20,000,000 bomb craters
150,000–600,000 tons of unexploded munitions.

this population, approximately 60,000 were amputees in need of devices and rehabilitation, though only 15 percent could be provided prostheses.

At the end of the war, there were about 150,000 to 600,000 tons of unexploded bombs and land mines across Vietnam[15,16] (see Chapter 10). In an initiative from 1975 to 1977 to remove them, the Vietnamese suffered an additional 12,000 deaths and 20,000 other casualties.[17]

Between 1975 to 1984, the Vietnamese government cleared about 59,000 land mines from the central province of Quang Tri alone. Since 1985, in Quang Tri Province, there have been 449 serious injuries and 25 deaths due to those deadly weapons left behind. These figures do not reflect true numbers since many deaths and injuries were not reported or investigated.[18]

Health Services During the War

South Vietnam

Health services for the South Vietnamese in the early part of the war were abysmal. In 1965, there were only 800 physicians, 500 of whom were in the military, while 150 treated only private, paying patients. This situation left 150 doctors to treat over 15 million people, a physician-to-population ratio of less than 1 to 100,000.[19] Of the 28 provincial hospitals with surgical suites, only 11 (39 percent) were being used, due to lack of medical personnel.

U.S. Senate hearings held in 1967 found that the war had brought even limited public health programs to a halt and that medical care for civilians was severely compromised.[19] Not one of 43 provincial hospitals in South Vietnam was considered up to minimal standard for a developing country. Almost all hospitals lacked electricity, drinking water, and sanitation facilities. The medical logistics system had broken down, and even soap was not available in many hospitals. There was a serious shortage of surgeons. In hospitals, hundreds of wounded South Vietnamese were living in sheds and corridors, on floors, and sometimes in open courtyards, awaiting surgery that might be delayed for one to two years. Conditions of extreme overcrowding existed in some hospitals with two or three patients to a bed. Often hospitals were virtually closed at night and on weekends because medical personnel were unavailable or unwilling to work. With some 36,000 amputees awaiting prosthetic devices and only a few hundred a month being produced, most people needing such devices could expect delays of years. No means had been developed to get the war-injured to hospitals; for those who did reach hospitals, the lapse of time from injury to admission was 24 to 36 hours. Estimates of those civilians killed outright or who died before reaching hospitals were from 20,000 to 50,000 per year. Civilian medical programs in South Vietnam were inadequate to meet even the peacetime needs of the country. Destruction of villages, uncontrolled movement of refugees, and squalid conditions in refugee camps had broken the natural barriers to the spread of disease, causing a rising incidence of tuberculosis, intestinal parasites, leprosy, and malaria as major causes of morbidity, and also marked increases in the incidence of cholera, plague, and human rabies.[19,20,21]

Although much health assistance was provided to South Vietnam by the United States and other countries beginning in 1964, it was not until 1969 that a major government initiative was implemented, so that each province would have at least one adequate general hospital for both military personnel and civilians.[21] A much-needed hospital manager training program was also implemented in 1968.[22] In spite of the program to expand hospital facilities, clinical pediatric services remained seriously inadequate up to 1975. Preventive services for children under age 15 were also inadequate, as indicated by the percentage of those *not* vaccinated for diphtheria, pertussis, and tetanus (83 percent), polio (82 percent), tuberculosis (70 percent), and smallpox (50 percent).[6]

The infant mortality rate was 100 per 1,000 live births. Life expectancy at birth was 54 years for males and 60 years for females. For the South Vietnamese, average family size was 5.8 children, as compared to 3.9 for Korea, 2.0 for Japan, and 1.9 for the United States.[6] In the South Vietnamese budget for 1973, the equivalent of US$870 million (53 percent) went to national defense, while less than 1 percent went to public health. U.S. aid to South Vietnam that year amounted to $2.5 billion, of which 76 percent was directed to the military and 0.5 percent to public health.[15]

Dental care was also inadequate in South Vietnam, which had a dentist-to-population ratio of less than 1 to 100,000. There were about 150 dentists in the country, 70 in the military and most of the rest practicing in Saigon. Another 5,000 ''sidewalk dentists,'' with little or no educational background, also practiced ''dentistry,'' but their efforts were considered more detrimental than helpful.[23]

North Vietnam

In contrast, health services in North Vietnam during the war appeared to be better organized and more effective, although documentation is limited. This was primarily due to North Vietnam, beginning in 1954, making access to health services and preventive medicine a national priority, and establishing a socialized health service that had mass vaccination campaigns for cholera, typhoid, smallpox, plague, tuberculosis, and polio.[24,25] The effectiveness of these programs is not known. By 1965, about 66 percent of rural villages were served by their own assistant doctor, a nurse with three years of practical experience and two years of additional training.[26] In contrast, in South Vietnam health services had deteriorated in rural areas by 1965, so that it was "almost impossible to effectively manage, control, direct, or support any kind of medical supply."[21]

Despite great constraints during the war, North Vietnam continued to make health services a high priority. By 1974 there were 5,566 community health centers or infirmaries, a 28-fold increase from the 200 in 1955.[27] Polyclinics and specialized clinics also increased in number from 51 in 1955 to 441 in 1974. Also added were 58,000 hospital and 46,000 infirmary beds, although these did not satisfy minimum standards. There was a major emphasis on primary care and prevention throughout the health care system. Efforts were made to ensure that each family had an assigned "health activist," or health promoter, who ensured family sanitation, immunization, proper medication, home visitation, and health education. By 1973, there were 7,000 physicians, for a physician-to-population ratio of 1:3,500, in addition to 20,000 assistant physicians.[28] About 71 percent of the doctors were primary care physicians, and most deliveries were done by midwives in the villages, sometimes with the aid of assistant physicians. In 1972 there was, on average, one dentist for 6,000 people, an inadequate number to serve the population's needs. All health care was free, as was training and education for health care personnel.

Despite wartime conditions, the North Vietnamese seem to have developed an impressive health care system with a major focus on prevention and public health at the family and community level. In 1973, malnutrition was rare in North Vietnam, and cholera, plague, smallpox, malaria, and sexually transmitted diseases were controlled. The malaria reduction program, which was begun in 1957, had reduced rates of infection (slide positivity) from 5.6 percent in 1958 to 0.3 percent in 1964. However, as a result of the war, the slide positivity rate increased to 0.7 percent by 1973.[27] Trachoma had also been greatly reduced in incidence.[28]

The bombing of North Vietnam resulted in the destruction of many health facilities such as 533 (10 percent) of the community health centers, 94 (28 percent) of the district hospitals, 28 (60 percent) of the provincial hospitals, and 24 research and specialized hospitals.[27] Bach Mai Hospital in Hanoi, the largest diagnostic and therapeutic institution in North Vietnam with over 1,000 beds, was bombed three times in 1972, resulting in the deaths of 31 people, including a physician and other health personnel.[28] Due to a comprehensive evacuation plan and air raid shelters, patient and other civilian casualties, including children, were kept low in North Vietnam. From 1965 to 1968, about 34 million individual shelters, thousands of group shelters, and about 30,000 miles of trenches were built.[7]

The Effects of Herbicides: Immediate and Long-Term

In addition to the use of explosives, between 1961 and 1971 the United States military sprayed almost 19 million gallons of herbicides over approximately five million acres of farmland and forest in South Vietnam, over one-third of the total land mass.[29,30,31] These chemical defoliants were used to deprive the Viet Cong and the North Vietnamese Army (NVA) of food crops and jungle cover, and to denude the perimeters of U.S. base camps to prevent enemy infiltration. The largest proportion of chemicals sprayed came from the herbicide Agent Orange, a source of great controversy, then and now, in Vietnam and in the United States. The use of Agent Orange came under heavy criticism from the American Academy for the Advancement of Science (AAAS) because its active ingredient 2,4,5-trichlorophenoxyacetic acid (2,4,5-T) had been shown to cause birth defects in laboratory animals.

The AAAS Herbicide Assessment Commission reported in 1970 that 20 to 50 percent of South Vietnam's mangrove forests, vital to marine life, had been ''utterly destroyed,'' and that half of the commercial hardwood trees and many rubber trees on Vietnam's famed plantations had been killed[32] (see Figure 5-3). Shortly thereafter, it was discovered that 2,4,5-T was contaminated with 2,3,7,8-tetrachlorodibenzo-p-dioxin (2,3,7,8-TCDD), or dioxin, which is one of the deadliest toxicants and is now known to be a carcinogen.[33,34,35] Because 2,4,5-T had been shown to be a teratogen, the use of Agent Orange in Vietnam was stopped by the Department of Defense in 1970.[36]

An AAAS team traveled to Vietnam and demonstrated easily measurable amounts of dioxin in fish and in human milk. Simultaneously, Dr. Ton That Tung, a recognized specialist in hepatic surgery and Vice Minister of Health in North Vietnam, found a large increase in the rate of primary liver carcinoma, and later of hydatidiform mole and choriocarcinoma. Dr. Tung's study showed that the offspring of spouses of North Vietnamese soldiers who served in the South were more likely to suffer abnormalities, such as anencephaly, oral clefts, and stillbirths, than the offspring of wives of soldiers who served north of the 17th parallel, where herbicides were never used.[37]

Studies in the United States and Europe have since demonstrated increased risk for soft-tissue sarcomas and malignant lymphomas due to dioxin exposure, either as a result of military service in Vietnam or from exposure to agricultural herbicides contaminated with TCDD. In 1991, the U.S. Congress passed a bill providing permanent disability benefits to Vietnam veterans suffering from soft-tissue sarcomas and non-Hodgkin's lymphomas.

The case for a causal connection between dioxin and teratogenicity rests on epidemiological studies since experimental evidence is lacking. At the International Herbicide Conference held in Ho Chi Minh City (formerly Saigon) in 1983, a consensus was reached among scientists that the only positive medical effects demonstrated by internationally accepted studies were in the field of reproductive abnormalities.[38] In studies conducted by the Centers for Disease Control[39] and the U.S. Air Force,[40] a strong risk relationship was shown between service in Vietnam and exposure to Agent Orange and spina bifida, cleft lip, congenital neoplasms, and coloboma (an eye anomaly)—although not anencephaly, the deformity seen most often in Vietnam.

The Institute of Medicine (IOM) of the National Academy of Sciences completed in 1994 an exhaustive review of studies of Agent Orange and its potential effects on the health of Vietnam veterans in the United States. This review found sufficient evidence of association with soft-tissue sarcoma, non-Hodgkin's lymphoma, and Hodgkin's disease, and limited suggestive evidence of association with some respiratory cancers, prostate cancer, and multiple myeloma.[41] The IOM also made numerous recommendations for further studies, but none to be conducted in Vietnam. A 1995 study showed that dioxin blood levels among southern and central Vietnamese living in sprayed areas was six times greater than for northerners in unsprayed areas. In addition, the mean dioxin level in adipose tissue in these areas was three times greater than in the United States, where there is dioxin in the environment from industry. This finding suggests that dioxin may be persistent in the environment and in the food chain of some Vietnamese, putting them at increased risk for cancer.[42,43] In 1996, the IOM published an update on Agent Orange, which added spina bifada as well as acute and subacute peripheral neuropathy to the category of limited/suggestive evidence of an association.[44]

While the direct health effects of herbicide spraying in Vietnam remain a matter of dispute, other forms of damage do not. About 14 percent of southern Vietnam's merchantable timber (eight percent of Vietnam's total), the primary source of housing materials and an important source of foreign exchange, was destroyed completely. About 30 more years will be required to make up this loss. Prior to the Second Indochina War, rubber production accounted for 60 percent of exports and employed over 100,000 people. By 1973, 40 percent of plantation trees had been destroyed, while overall production was reduced by 70 percent. By 1983, rubber export in the form of latex had reached only half of pre-war levels, and full reattainment of production appears many years away.[12] The reduction of such valuable export commodities limits Vietnam's capacity to earn foreign currencies, which, in turn, has deleterious effects upon investment in public health.

Herbicides were directed extensively at the coastal mangrove forests, the primary breeding grounds for shrimp and many fish, staples in the Vietnamese diet. Despite efforts to boost production in this area, the annual marine catch has been declining.

It is impossible to determine at this stage whether this decline is due to disruptions in the food chain from chemical contamination, although this seems likely. Such declines contributed to malnutrition problems after the war.

Post-War and Long-Term Effects of the War

Once the war ended and Vietnam was reunified in 1975, it had to cope with the results of the war: millions of dead, wounded, disabled, unemployed, and orphaned individuals, and traumatized families, together with massive destruction of homes, villages, the environment, and Vietnam's infrastructure. With an agenda for rebuilding under socialist principles, the ravaged nation had few friends or allies. Unhappy with the forcible reunification of Vietnam by communist troops in 1975, the United States extended an existing embargo with North Vietnam to the entire country. Hanoi also quickly lost the support of its erstwhile ally, China, over territorial issues and Vietnam's opposition to the Khmer Rouge regime in neighboring Cambodia. Since most of the other nations of Southeast Asia were aligned with or economically dependent upon the United States, most also participated to some extent in the embargo. The result was that Vietnam had to attempt its reconstruction primarily with limited Soviet assistance. Nations that had long opposed American intervention in Vietnam, like Sweden and Finland, provided some aid, but this too was limited because of U.S. opposition to such assistance.[45]

Malaria, tuberculosis, leprosy, hemorrhagic fever, trachoma, cholera, plague, sexually transmitted diseases, and parasitic diseases were all reported to be serious public health problems in South Vietnam after the war.[27] Malaria was reported to be the most serious public health problem in 1976, with 75 percent of the population living in malarial areas with varying levels of endemicity. Tuberculosis was also a major problem; one survey reported nine cases per 1,000 for individuals over age 10 years, a rate two times greater than in neighboring countries.[27] About 80,000 to 160,000 cases of leprosy were estimated, and in some areas there were 55 infected cases of leprosy per 1,000 people. The prevalence of trachoma was 75 percent in the northeastern provinces and 57 percent in the Mekong Delta, according to a 1971 survey, with an incidence of active trachoma of 47 percent and 34 percent in those areas, respectively. Although Vietnam had a well-developed (but economically poor) health care delivery system in the North, this was not true for the South.

Already one of the poorest countries in the world, Vietnam had to develop governmental structures and public health institutions over half of its territory, struggle to overcome its appalling losses, and endure isolation from world markets and humanitarian aid as a result of the U.S.-imposed embargo. Simultaneously, it embarked upon a war with the Khmer Rouge in neighboring Cambodia in order to stop Khmer incursions into Vietnamese border territories and persecution of ethnic Vietnamese in

Cambodia. In the process, Vietnam rid Cambodia of one of the bloodiest regimes in modern history—those responsible for the "killing fields," something no other government attempted. Yet, Washington accused Vietnam of attempting "military conquest" in Cambodia as the United States tightened the embargo further. In 1979, Vietnam also became involved in a war with China over disputed territories, which resulted in the exodus of most of Vietnam's commercialy vital ethnic Chinese population. About 483,000 ethnic Chinese left Vietnam during 1978 and 1979 alone.

After reunification in 1976, the government of Vietnam began a massive relocation of at least 5,000,000 people as part of its security effort.[13] The primary purpose of this relocation was to break up the existing social order and to raise class consciousness by downgrading the middle and upper classes through communication and education programs. In addition, at least 700,000 people a year were placed in reeducation camps to educate and/or coerce certain social classes of people to accept or conform to the new social norms. In 1982, there were still about 120,000 Vietnamese in these camps.

Because of the change in government, massive relocation, and social ostracism, many middle-class Vietnamese fled their native land. Since 1975 about 1.5 million people have left Vietnam,[46] of whom about 910,640, or 86.5 percent, reached a destination. About 142,150 refugee "boat people" were lost at sea. Of those refugees reaching a destination, 596,600 (66 percent) were of Chinese ancestry, and 310,400 (34 percent) were ethnic Vietnamese.[10]

While the revolutionaries who waged war against the United States were successful in winning their goal of reunification of Vietnam and of maintaining political independence, their abilities at running the government and the economy was sorely tested, especially given Vietnam's isolation from the "community of nations." Subsequently, the rigidly Stalinist model of economic growth proved unsuccessful, and throughout the 1980s famine broke out in various provinces due to a combination of destruction from the war, poor government practices, and natural disasters. Once the "rice bowl of Asia," Vietnam could no longer feed itself.

The United States rebuilt ravaged Germany and Japan after World War II, spending more to restore these nations than the war cost the United States. By comparison, the Pentagon never provided Hanoi with maps of mine fields in South Vietnam to enable the Vietnamese to disarm these weapons of war that, coupled with enormous quantities of unexploded ordnance, continue to kill innocent people more than 20 years after the peace was signed. Vietnam desired normalization of relations, but the U.S. government continued to use the issue of POW-MIAs to exact political concessions similar to those that might have been imposed had the United States won the war. Meanwhile approximately 300,000 Vietnamese remain missing in action, compared to 2,261 U.S. soldiers (less than 4 percent of U.S. soldiers who were killed).[47] (By contrast, there are still over 78,000 American MIAs from World War II, or 19 percent of the over 405,000 killed, and over 8,000 MIAs from the Korean War, or 15 percent of those killed.)

The U.S. Trade Embargo:
The Long-Term Effects of War by Other Means

During the peace negotiations held between the United States and North Vietnam in 1972–1973, President Richard Nixon promised U.S. participation in the reconstruction of Vietnam. In a secret memorandum sent to Premier Pham Van Dong on February 1, 1973, a specific figure of $3.25 billion was promised, and a Joint Economic Commission began planning for the reconstruction of ports, water facilities, agriculture, and transportation.[48] However, no dollar figure for such reconstruction was included in the formal Paris Agreements signed in July 1973. Nixon's promise has never been kept. Indeed, from 1975 when Vietnam was forcibly reunited under communist rule until 1994, a trade embargo was imposed against Vietnam. (See also Chapter 17 and box on pp. 156–58.) President Bill Clinton lifted the embargo in 1994 and normalized relations between the two nations in 1995. The embargo had played a significant role in the difficulties Vietnam faced in recovering from decades of war. It also froze Vietnamese bank accounts in the United States and was made even more stringent by the Reagan Administration. Probably the most significant effect of the embargo was to keep Vietnam poor and isolated since many U.S. allies also participated in economic sanctions against Hanoi. Though poor planning and bureaucratic rigidities on the part of Hanoi also hampered Vietnam's recovery, even the World Bank praised Vietnam's ability to raise social indices against overwhelming odds.[49]

Population

Despite its relatively small geographic area, Vietnam in 1994 was the 13th most populous nation, with about 73 million people, mostly concentrated in the northern and southern deltas of the Red and Mekong rivers.[50] Nearly 39 percent of the people are under 15 years of age, while approximately 50 percent have been born since 1975, the year Vietnam was reunified.[51] Thus, most of Vietnam's citizens have no memory of the destruction and chaos that attended the "American War."

Nevertheless, despite losses to war, famine, and migration, Vietnam's population has increased rapidly, owing to high fertility rates and moderate-to-low mortality. The infant mortality rate fell from 156 per 1,000 live births in 1960 to 83 per 1,000 in 1979; it dropped by another 50 percent or so by 1989 due to a solid commitment to health care by the government.[52] Additionally, the fertility rate in Vietnam fell from 5.1 children in 1979 to 3.8 in 1989.[53,54] According to the 1979 census, Vietnam's population was about 52.7 million people, of whom 52 percent were female, and 70 percent were below the age of 30.[11] For the age group 20 to 64 years, 11.6 million, or 53.4 percent, were female, and there were about 1.5 million more females than males.[11] This large population imbalance is a result of almost three decades of war with the United States and France. This has resulted in more women in the labor force and single mothers having children out of wedlock, a situation still common in the 1990s. Vietnam has one of the lowest ratios of males to females in the world, especially in the age groups above 35, a fact clearly related to the loss of men during the war and the large-scale migration out of Vietnam following the war.[52] This imbalance of sexes has contributed to fertility decline, but exactly what weight can be attributed to this factor remains unclear. In cooperation with the United Nations Fund for Population Activities (UNFPA), the DRV has introduced Western birth control measures, although availability is limited due to supply and training, and the population growth rate has fallen from 3.1 percent during the period 1960–1976 to 2.16 percent currently.[52] Economic devastation caused by the war and emigration have also played major roles in the falling growth rate. Despite these factors, the population will reach 80 million by the year 2000 and will approach 100 million by 2015 at present growth trends. This will further stress the economy and the health care system.[52]

During the war years, the population of Vietnam increased due to a continuing decrease in the infant mortality rate. The war did not appear to increase infant mortality, except possibly in high-intensity combat areas. However, it is very difficult to determine the impact of the Vietnam War on infant mortality since reliable data from that era are not available.[55]

Nutrition

Vietnam, with a subsistence agricultural economy, was an important rice exporter until the beginning of the war in 1965. After the war, food shortages were estimated to be one to two million tons a year, resulting in basic foods being rationed, which, in turn, caused longstanding nutritional deficits.[56] Even though food production is now increasing, differentials in productivity remain wide between regions, so populations in some provinces continue to suffer chronic malnourishment and even famine. The proportion of malnourished children is 45 percent for weight-for-age and 57 percent for height-for-age rates—comparable to those in Bangladesh,[52] with 80 percent of these children in the one- to three-year-old group.[57] While short-term acute food deficits appear throughout Vietnam, the chronic problem is undernutrition. One-fifth of all infants born in 1990 weighed less than 2,500 grams at birth.[52] Food deficits begin at birth and continue for most Vietnamese throughout life due to low caloric intake and to cultural beliefs in the inferiority of colostrum as a food, with resultant early weaning. Infants are introduced to solid foods relatively early—at two to three months of age—greatly increasing the rate of infection due to malnutrition. Traditional dependence on rice as a staple of diet has long contributed to caloric, lipid, and micronutrient deficiencies, especially of vitamin A, iron, and iodine, which are increasing throughout Vietnam. However, peasants in the western mountainous regions of southern Vietnam, where defoliation was significantly greater than elsewhere in the South (no herbicide spraying was done on North Vietnamese territory) and destruction of the triple-canopy tree cover has increased flooding and soil erosion, have half the protein intake of their counterparts elsewhere. Adult malnutrition, therefore, is shaped in part by the unavailability of productive arable land due to defoliation by herbicides, natural disasters, and poor economic performance.

Health Care under the Socialist System

Vietnam was able to provide better health care services than some of its equally poor Southeast Asian neighbors, which had not suffered the ravages of war. For example, the average per-capita income in Vietnam today is $220 as compared with $2,085 in Thailand, which has been the recipient of steady U.S. investment since the 1950s.[58] Vietnam does not have adequate medical and dental equipment due to the embargo and the state of the economy. Vietnam now provides one doctor for every 2,857 people; Thailand, one for every 4,361 people. Vietnam's average life expectancy of 65 years was almost one decade longer than for Bangladesh in 1989, although both nations are nearly equally poor[59] and both have devoted the same percentage of their GNP (0.7 percent) to health care. Vietnam's achievements in health indicators are far better than most countries at its income level. Vietnam's infant mortality rate is better than neighboring countries that have four times its Gross National Product.[52] Nevertheless, there are economic impediments compromising health care, and these good survival rates are not evenly distributed throughout Vietnam, particularly with respect to the nutritional status of children. Owing to income differentials throughout Vietnam, infant mortality rates are three times higher in the poorest provinces as compared to the richest. While adult literacy averages 88 percent nationwide, it is only 66 percent in the poorest province.

North Vietnam had developed a free, but highly centralized, five-tier health system, which was financed entirely by state funds. However, this system was weakened by the staggering demand put on it during the decade following the war's end, by the outflow of doctors and other medical personnel from South Vietnam to the West, and by the underfinancing of the health sector due to intrinsic economic weakness. After 1975, there was also a severe shortage of medical and dental equipment, supplies, and pharmaceuticals in Vietnam due to the U.S. trade embargo and the overburdened economy. For example, prior to 1975, drugs valued at about $60 to $65 million were imported into Vietnam each year, but this dropped to $20 to $25 million a year from 1975 to 1988, or about $0.30 to $0.50 per capita in drug consumption.[58] In 1991, Vietnam's Ministry of Health did a survey of rural health centers in six provinces in the north; only 49 percent had a usable sterilizer, and 58 percent had a usable scale to weigh infants.[60] With the adoption of market mechanisms and open policy for foreign investment, by 1993 drug imports were at $132 million per year, or $1.05 per capita, and local drug production increased dramatically, resulting in an uncontrolled market with nonessential drugs, irrational drug use, extensive overprescription, and profiteering.

Impact of Economic Reform on Health Services

Economic reform in Vietnam is hailed by Western nations and the World Bank as a first step in Vietnam's reintegration into the "community of nations." Market mechanisms have replaced central planning. In line with World Bank guidelines, Vietnam has arrested inflation, stabilized its currency, and reduced foreign trade imbalances. Agriculture has been privatized: Peasants no longer work on farming collectives. Now, families produce for a predominantly export market and get to keep approximately 10 percent of the crop. While this system has raised food production substantially and growth in personal income has averaged more than five percent annually, these advances hide growing imbalances across the nation.[52,61]

More than half the population remains below the official poverty level, with incomes declining among the poorest.[61] As a result of reforms essentially dictated by Western financial institutions, 500,000 soldiers have been released from service and 800,000 public-sector workers have been laid off.[52] Meanwhile, in line with economic retrenchment, prices have risen, while wages have been cut. Rapidly changing economic and social conditions are producing an "extremely dynamic epidemiological and health transition."[63] Physicians and pharmacists have also been allowed to establish private practices, producing higher prices for health care both in private practice and in state-run clinics. Health care professionals have left state institutions to work in private practice. While health care has improved for those with disposable income, for most Vietnamese who live in poverty, health conditions have worsened and access to quality care has diminished. Thus, the wealthiest quintile of households has 4.4 times the income of the lowest and spends 4.6 times as much on health expenditures. Public expenditures on health have decreased from 6.1 percent to 4.4 percent of Vietnam's budget, although the total size of the budget has grown.[63] Underinvestment in state-supported medical schools and other training facilities thus continues, with the consequence that these institutions lack qualified instructors and teaching aids. While the government has decided to raise salaries of health-care workers, in line with World Bank recommendations to attract physicians, nurses, and pharmacists back into the public sector, this increase has been made possible only by laying off many employees. At present, of the 9,788 doctors who graduated between 1977 and 1988, 2,715 remain unemployed.[58] The collapse of the public-sector health network, in tandem with growing poverty in the bottom half of Vietnamese society, is also producing an upsurge in the incidence of disease. While childhood immunization rates remain high (70 to 75 percent), malnutrition contributes strongly to increased incidence of diarrheal disease and respiratory tract infection. Malaria and tuberculosis remain widespread.

Cardiovascular diseases and cancer are said to be increasing, although reliable figures are nonexistent.

The World Bank recommends strengthening of the public health sector, but this will be possible only by heavily taxing the private sector. Vietnam has avoided taxing the private sector, or implementing fair labor standards, child labor laws, and environmental standards that are commonplace in the West. The absence of such standards is the primary reason that Western capital wishes to invest in Southeast Asia.[64]

Assistance for Vietnam

There were important exceptions to the isolation of Vietnam after 1975. Many nongovernmental organizations, including religious groups and some nations that provided humanitarian aid to either North or South Vietnam during the war, continued in these efforts. Many, including some U.S. Vietnam veterans groups, took the lead to help restore and rebuild Vietnam. They helped build clinics, houses, and schools; assisted in population planning, nutrition, and education; and provided prosthetics for disabled Vietnamese.

In August 1987, Vietnam and the United States agreed to improve cooperation to address the humanitarian concerns of both governments.[65] This became known as the "Vessey Initiative," after General John W. Vessey, Jr., former Chairman of the Joint Chiefs of Staff, who was the Special Presidential Emissary to Hanoi for POW/MIA Affairs, and who was key to these discussions. The U.S. government chose not to provide assistance directly to Vietnam or through specific NGOs, due to legal and policy constraints, until November 1989, when President George Bush hailed a "new openness" with the Vietnamese. Over some opposition, the U.S. government decided to send Vietnam more than $250,000 in surplus medical equipment, taken from excess and obsolete stock, as a goodwill gesture for help in accounting for the 1,705 American MIAs.[66] In December 1989 in New York, a conference on Vietnam with about 100 NGOs from the United States was held,[65] which helped improve NGO activity in Vietnam. The Vietnamese government soon began granting six-month, multiple-entry visas to American NGOs.

Some groups, including American veterans groups, have also been in the forefront to help restore diplomatic relations between the United States and Vietnam, as the most rational and effective means to heal the wounds of both sides. In 1990, as president of the American Public Health Association (APHA), Myron Allukian, a Vietnam veteran, went to Vietnam to visit health departments, clinics, schools, and hospitals in Ho Chi Minh City (Saigon), Hue, Danang, and Hanoi. Upon his return, he wrote an open letter to President Bush urging normalization of relations and the promotion and encouragement of humanitarian aid.[67] In 1990, APHA formed a Vietnam Caucus, and in 1991 the APHA Governing Council adopted a policy statement calling for normalization of relations with Vietnam, the promotion of humanitarian aid, and additional resources for U.S. Vietnam veterans. The International Council of the International Physicians for the Prevention of Nuclear War (IPPNW) also adopted a resolution urging all nations to assist Vietnam through the United Nations, to end other embargoes, and to normalize relations. In February 1994, after a 62–38 vote by the U.S. Senate approving a non-binding resolution, President Clinton lifted the U.S. trade embargo. In January 1995, the United States and Vietnam opened diplomatic "liaison offices" in each other's capitals, 20 years after the fall of Saigon. In August 1995, the United States and Vietnam formally restored full diplomatic relations, ending three decades of hostility.

The Effects of the War in the United States

While the major focus of this chapter has been on the health effects of the Vietnam War on Vietnam, the consequences in this country were so profound that they must be mentioned. The following represents a kaleidoscopic view of the impact of the war on the United States:

> The dead. The injured. POW-MIAs. Agent Orange. Post-traumatic stress disorder (PTSD). Shameful treatment of veterans. Homelessness. The Vietnam Memorial. Civil disobedience. The Pentagon Papers. Student unrest and the killing of student demonstrators at Kent State. Draft resistance and draft-card burnings. Flight to Canada. Families torn apart. The rioting at the 1968 Democratic National Convention. The downfall of a U.S. president. The collapse of the War on Poverty. Vietnamese "boat people." Amerasian children abandoned in Vietnam. Distrust of government, and cynicism toward power and authority.

Many of these effects and public reactions still affect our people, policies, and national psyche today.

The Vietnam War cost the United States at least $130 billion in direct costs, and at least that amount in indirect costs, which continue to this day.[3] The United States also lost President Johnson's War on Poverty, both economically and politically, since we could not afford two wars simultaneously. As federal funds were redirected toward the war in Vietnam, public health programs originally designed for the poor in the U.S. suffered cutbacks. Furthermore, the war in Indochina spurred serious inflation, which further affected low-income citizens.

Just as public health problems affect the poorest Americans disproportionately, so the burden of the Vietnam War was borne mainly by soldiers from low-income families. Twenty-six million young men reached draft age during the war in Vietnam, but only 10.9 million served in the military as a result of draft deferrals available to those who could afford college or graduate school.[68] Of these, about 2.6 to 3.8 million served in Vietnam. Dropping the usual entry criteria, the army enlisted over 300,000 young men under a special program called "Project 100,000" between 1966 and

1972. Eighty percent of these recruits were African-American, reading below sixth-grade level and often suffering from learning disabilities. They were promised benefits after the war. More than one-third served in combat. They had double the death rate of other soldiers, and were so disabled physically or psychologically that they were never able to use the G.I. Bill for housing or college. About 80,000 men recruited under this program were discharged with less than honorable discharges, receiving no benefits.[69] Many of these veterans are homeless, of whom 40 percent have serious mental illness[70] and 10 percent suffer from post-traumatic stress disorder (PTSD).[71] The needs of homeless veterans far exceed the Veterans Administration's capacity to serve these needs.

The official U.S. estimate of the number of U.S. deaths in Vietnam is 58,196, but this does not include many who were killed in Laos and Cambodia (who were there "illegally"), nor does it count all servicemen who were killed in accidents outside the official combat zone, or trainees killed by "friendly fire" at home bases. It does not count those who have died since the war, often as a result of wounds incurred in Vietnam, or by self-destructive behavior owing to PTSD. Over 20,000 Vietnam veterans have taken their own lives.[72] No accurate accounting of U.S. civilians killed in Vietnam, including U.S. Agency for International Development workers, Central Intelligence Agency operatives, missionaries, and Red Cross nurses, has ever been made. The probability of getting killed in Vietnam for U.S. troops who served there was 85 per 1,000, compared with 31 per 1,000 for those who served in World War I, World War II, and the Korean War.[73]

Over 300,000 Americans were wounded, with 153,300 classified as seriously wounded. While only 2.6 percent of the wounded reaching hospitals died, as a result of rapid helicopter evacuation techniques and advanced medical facilities, some 10,000 servicemen lost at least one limb, more than in World War II and Korea combined. Over 700,000 veterans suffer from severe PTSD, many of whom have been hospitalized for long periods and have lost much work time. Closely associated with these disorders are acute drug and alcohol abuse, violent or antisocial behavior, high divorce rates, broken families, and homelessness.[74–77] It has been estimated that over 1.5 million veterans may eventually need psychiatric care.[77] A comprehensive study of Vietnam veterans by the Centers for Disease Control found that during the first five years after discharge from the military, veterans had a 45 percent excess in deaths, due primarily to external causes such as motor vehicle injuries, homicides, and suicides.[78] In addition, about 15 percent reported having symptoms of combat PTSD. There was a higher prevalence of alcohol abuse or dependence, anxiety, and depression.

The use of herbicides in Vietnam affected not only the Vietnamese but also U.S. servicemen. In 1984, as a result of a class action suit brought by U.S. Vietnam veterans and their families against the manufacturers of Agent Orange, the corporations involved agreed to a settlement fund of $184 million for disabled veterans and their children.[79] The effect of Agent Orange on U.S. soldiers is still controversial in our country. It is tragically ironic that the son of Admiral Elmo Zumwalt, who ordered the use of Agent Orange in Vietnam, not only served in Vietnam, but may have died as a result of his exposure to the herbicide. The admiral's grandson was born with a developmental disability, which some people believe may be due to dioxin exposure.

The ramifications of the war in Vietnam are widespread in our society, though concentrated among the poor and working-class populations. Finally, the Vietnam War also affected the credibility of our presidents and government in general, creating deep distrust and resentment, which, in turn, has seriously affected our society's ability to solve numerous pressing problems. As former Secretary of State under President Nixon, Henry Kissinger, admitted:

> Vietnam is still with us. It has created doubts about American judgment, about American credibility, about American power—not only at home but throughout the world. It has poisoned our domestic debate. We paid an exorbitant price.[4]

In his memoir, *In Retrospect: The Tragedy and Lessons of Vietnam,* which was released in April 1995, former U.S. Defense Secretary Robert S. McNamara asserted 30 years after his stewardship of the Vietnam War, "We were wrong, terribly wrong. We owe it to future generations to explain why."[80]

The Vietnam Memorial, popularly known as "The Wall," has been the most visited monument in Washington, DC, since it was unveiled in 1982. Inscribed on it are 58,196 names of U.S. military personnel killed during the War. The Wall has reminded Americans of the sacrifices made during the War and has helped to heal the nation. However, the immense losses to Vietnam, Laos, and Cambodia remain almost invisible in the U.S.

Opponents of the Vietnam War used the slogan, "War is hazardous to the health of children." The Vietnam War has been hazardous and destructive to generations of Americans and Vietnamese.

REFERENCES

1. National Academy of Sciences, National Research Council, Committee on the Effects of Herbicide in Vietnam. *The effects of herbicide in Vietnam, Part A—summary and conclusions.* Washington, D.C.: U.S. Government Printing Office, 1974.
2. Stockholm International Peace Research Institute. *Ecological consequences of the Second Indochina War.* Stockholm: SIPRI, 1976.
3. Brennan, J.S. (ed.), *The Vietnam War: An almanac.* New York: World Almanac Publications, 1985.
4. Karnow, S. *Vietnam: A history.* New York: Penguin Books, 1983.
5. World Bank, *Vietnam: Population, health and nutrition sector review.* July 30, 1993.
6. Dan, P.Q. *The Republic of Vietnam's environment and people,* 1st ed. Republic of Vietnam, Saigon, 1975.
7. Wiesner, L.A. *Victims and survivors: Displaced persons and other war victims in Viet-Nam, 1954–1975.* Westport, CT: Greenwood Press, 1988.

8. U.S. Department of State. The SEATO Treaty. *American foreign policy, 1950–1955.* Washington, DC: U.S. Government Printing Office, 1975, I, pp. 912–916.

9. Baritz, L. *Backfire.* New York: Ballantine Books, 1985, p. 146.

10. Bannister, J. The Population of Vietnam, International Population Reports, Series P-95, No. 77, U.S. Department of Commerce, Bureau of the Census, October 1985.

11. Vietnam Population, 1979, Central Census Steering Committee, Hanoi, 1983.

12. Westing, A.H. The environmental aftermath of warfare in Viet Nam. *Nat. Resources J.* 23: 372–387, 1983.

13. Cima, R.J. *Vietnam: A country study.* Federal Research Division, Library of Congress, Washington, D.C.: U.S. Government Printing Office, 1989.

14. Vessey, J.W. The problem of the disabled in Vietnam. U.S. Department of State, Washington, D.C., Oct. 13, 1987.

15. Relief and rehabilitation of war victims in Indochina. IV: South Vietnam and regional problems. Hearing before Subcommittee to Investigate Problems Connected with Refugees and Escapees. Committee on the Judiciary, U.S. Senate, 93rd Congress, 1st session, Washington, D.C.: U.S. Government Printing Office, Aug. 1, 1973.

16. Bonacci, M.A. *The legacy of colonialism in Southeast Asia.* Washington, D.C.: The Asia Resource Center, 1990.

17. Muller, R. Personal communication with the Peoples' Committee on War Crimes, Hanoi, 1993. Vietnam Veterans of America Foundation, November 1994.

18. Monan, J., Landmines and underdevelopment: A case study of Quang Tri Province. Oxfam Hong Kong, 1995.

19. Civilian casualty and refugee problems in South Vietnam. Findings and recommendations, Subcommittee to Investigate Problems Connected with Refugees and Escapees. Committee on the Judiciary, U.S. Senate, 90th Congress, 2nd session, Washington, D.C.: U.S. Government Printing Office. May 9, 1968.

20. Cavanaugh, D.C., Dangerfield, H.G., Hunter, D.H., Joy, R.J.T., et al. Some observations of the current plague outbreak in the Republic of Vietnam. *Amer. J. Public Health* 58(4): 742–752, 1968.

21. Craddock, W.L. United States medical programs in South Vietnam. *Military Medicine* 135(3):186–191, 1970.

22. Camp, E. A retrospective report: Health care in South Vietnam. *Hospitals, J. Amer. Hosp. Assoc.* 50:55–58, 1975.

23. Revsin, M.E. Vietnam dental education project: A five year report. *J. Amer. Dental Assoc.* 84:1049–1062, 1972.

24. Shellard, E.J. Health services in Vietnam. *Medicine and War* 8(3):169–174, 1992.

25. Ladinsky, J. and Levine, R.E. The organization of health services in Vietnam. *J. Public Health Policy* 6:255–268, 1985.

26. Quinn, J.S. Shortages confront Vietnam's health care. *Indochina issues.* Center for International Policy, Indochina Project, April 1986.

27. World Health Organization, Report on the Democratic Republic of Vietnam, February 26, 1976.

28. Relief and rehabilitation of war victims in Indochina. III. North Vietnam and Laos. Hearing before Subcommittee to Investigate Problems Connected with Refugees and Escapees. Committee on the Judiciary, U.S. Senate, 93rd Congress, 1st session. Washington, D.C.: U.S. Government Printing Office, July 31, 1973.

29. Westing, A.H. (ed.). *Herbicides in war: The long-term ecological and human consequences.* London: Taylor and Francis, 1984, p. 5.

30. Sidel, V.W. Farewell to arms: Impact of the arms race on the human condition. *PSR Quarterly* 3(1):18–26. 1993.
31. Cecil, P.F. *Herbicide warfare: The ranch hand project in Vietnam.* New York: Praeger, 1986.
32. Herbicides in Vietnam: AAAS study finds widespread devastation. *Science.* 171(3966):43–47, 1971.
33. Sterling, T.D. and Arundel, A. Review of recent Vietnamese studies on the carcinogenic and teratogenic effects of phenoxy herbicide exposure. *Int. J. Health Serv.* 16:265–278, 1986.
34. Hardell, L., Eriksson, M., Lenner, P. and Lundgren, E. Malignant lymphoma and exposure to chemical substances, especially organic solvents, chlorophenols, and phenoxy acids. *Br. J. Cancer* 43:169–176, 1981.
35. Hoar, S., Blair, A., et al. Agricultural herbicide use and risk of lymphoma and soft-tissue sarcoma. *JAMA* 255:1141–1147, 1986.
36. Constable, J.D. and Hatch, M.C. Reproductive effects of herbicide exposure in Vietnam: Recent studies by the Vietnamese and others. *Teratog. Carcino. Mutag.* 5:231–250, 1985.
37. Hatch, M.C. Dioxin, teratogenicity and reproductive function. In Atwood, P.L. (ed.), *Agent Orange: Medical, scientific, legal, political and psychological issues.* Boston: The William Joiner Center for the Study of War and Social Consequences, 1993, pp. 30–34.
38. Nguyen, C., et al. Reproductive epidemiology: Symposium summary. In A.H. Westing (ed.), *Herbicides in War.* London: Taylor & Francis, 1984. pp. 133–134.
39. Centers for Disease Control. Health status of Vietnam veterans. III. Reproductive outcomes and child health. *JAMA* 259:2715–2717, 1988.
40. Air Force Health Study. An epidemiologic investigation of health effects in Air Force personnel following exposure to herbicides. Reproductive outcomes. Brooks AFB: USAF School of Aerospace Medicine. A1-TR-1992-0090.
41. Institute of Medicine: National Academy of Science. *Veterans and Agent Orange: Health effects of herbicides used in Vietnam.* Washington, D.C.: National Academy Press, 1994, p. 6.
42. Schecter, A., Dai, L.C., et al. Agent Orange and the Vietnamese: The persistence of elevated dioxin levels in human tissues. *Am. J. Public Health* 85(4):516–522, 1995.
43. Dwyer, J.H. and Flesh-Janys, D. Editorial: Agent Orange in Vietnam. *Am. J. Public Health* 85(4):476–478, 1995.
44. Institute of Medicine, National Academy of Science, Veterans and Agent Orange—Update 1996, Washington D.C. Pre-publication Copy, National Academy Press, 1996, pp. 1–5.
45. United Nations Fund for Population Activity. Program Review and Strategy Development Report: Vietnam. 1993.
46. United Nations Population Fund. Vietnam: Program Review and Strategy Development Report, New York, 1991.
47. Branigan, W. U.S. recovers MIA remains in Vietnam: Hopes for more fade. *Washington Post,* Feb. 9, 1993.
48. Charny, J. and Spragens, J. *Obstacles to recovery in Vietnam and Kampuchea: U.S. embargo of humanitarian aid.* Boston: Oxfam America, 1985, pp. 30–31.
49. World Bank. Vietnam: Population, health, and nutrition sector review. September 1993.
50. Khanh Hoa, D.T. Vietnam population profile and transition (unpublished conference paper). Presented at: Implications of Vietnam's Economic Reform for the Health Sector, Harvard University, Nov. 18–19, 1994.
51. United Nations Economic and Social Council. Country Programme Recomendation: Vietnam. Feb. 3, 1988.
52. World Bank. Vietnam: Population, Health and Nutrition Sector Review. July 30, 1993.

53. *Statistical data of Vietnam, 1976–1989.* Hanoi: Statistical Publishing House, 1990.

54. Feeney, G. and Xenos, P. *The demographic situation in Vietnam: Past, present, prospect.* Honolulu: East-West Center, 1993.

55. Savitz, D.A., Nguyen, M.T., Swenson, I.E. and Stone, E. Vietnamese infant and childhood mortality in relation to the Vietnam War. *Am. J. Public Health* 83:1134–1138, 1993.

56. Kaufman M. Vietnam, 1978: Crisis in food, nutrition and health. *J. Amer. Diet Assn.* 74: 310–316, 1979.

57. Hiebert, L.G. Malnutrition among children. *Indochina Issues 65.* Center For International Policy.

58. Phong, N.K. The changing structure of health care (unpublished conference paper). Presented at: Implications of Vietnam's Reform for the Health Care Sector, Harvard University, Nov. 18–19, 1994.

59. World Bank. *Social indicators of development, 1994.* Baltimore: Johns Hopkins University Press, 1994.

60. Tuan, T. Ministry of Health, Department of Planning and Finance Community Research Unit, Hanoi Medical School, 1992.

61. Gellert, G.A. The influence of market economics on primary health care in Vietnam. Letter from Ho Chi Minh City. *JAMA* 273 (19):1497–1502, 1995.

62. Socialist Republic of Vietnam. State Planning Committee. *Statistical abstract: Vietnam living standard survey, 1992–1993.* Hanoi: General Statistical Office, 1994.

63. Chen, L.C. and Hiebert, L.G. From socialism to private markets: Vietnam's health in rapid transition. Working Paper Series, No. 94.11. Center For Population and Development Studies, Harvard University School of Public Health, October 1994.

64. Charny J. and Spragens, J. Obstacles to Recovery in Vietnam and Kampuchea: U.S. Embargo of Humanitarian Aid. Boston: Oxfam America, 1985.

65. Twining, C. Personal written communication to Dr. Myron Allukian, U.S. Department of State, Office of Vietnam, Laos and Cambodia, Aug. 14, 1990, 17 pp.

66. *Boston Globe,* Nov. 9, 1989.

67. Allukian, M. An open letter to the President. *The Nation's Health,* August 1990; and *J. Publ. Health Policy* 12(1):10–13, 1991.

68. Baskir, L. and Strauss, W. *Chance and circumstance: The draft, the war, and the Vietnam generation.* New York: Alfred A. Knopf, 1978.

69. Hsiao, L. Project 100,000: The Great Society's answer to military manpower needs in Vietnam. *Vietnam Generation* 1(2):14–37, 1989.

70. Rosenheck, R., Frisman, L. and Chung, A.M. The proportions of veterans among homeless men. *Am. J. Public Health* 84:466–469, 1994.

71. U.S. General Accounting Office. *Homelessness: Demand for services to homeless veterans exceeds VA program capacity.* Report to the Chairman, Committee on Veterans Affairs, U.S. Senate, Washington, D.C., February 1994.

72. Bullman, T. and Kang, H.K. A study of suicide among Vietnam veterans. *Federal Practitioner,* March 1995.

73. Staff Report: Medical evaluation of the prisoners of the Vietnam War. *Nutrition Today,* May/June 1973, pp. 24–30.

74. Stanton, M.D. Drugs, Vietnam and the Vietnam veteran: An overview. *Am. J. Drug Abuse* 3(4):557–570, 1976.

75. Decoufle, P., Holmgreen, P., Boyle, C.A. and Stroup, N.E. Self-reported health status of Vietnam veterans in relation to exposure to herbicides and combat. *Am. J. Epidemiol.* 135(3):312–323, 1992.

76. Goldberg, J., Eisen, S.A., True, W.R. and Henderson, W.G. Health effects of military service: Lessons learned from the Vietnam experience. *Ann. Epidemiol.* 2:841–853, 1992.

77. Walker, J.I. and Cavenar, J.O. Vietnam veterans: Their problems continue. *J. Nervous and Mental Disease* 170(30):174–180, 1982.

78. Centers For Disease Control. *Health status of Vietnam veterans: Vietnam experience study.* CDC, U.S. Department of Health and Human Services, Public Health Service, Vol. I., Synopsis, January 1989.

79. Schuck, P.H. *Agent Orange on trial: Mass toxic disasters in the courts.* Cambridge: Harvard University Press, 1986.

80. McNamara, R.S. *In retrospect: The tragedy and lessons of Vietnam.* New York: Random House, 1995.

16

Public Health and War in Central America

PAULA BRAVEMAN, ALAN MEYERS, THOMAS SCHLENKER, and CURT WANDS

Belize, Guatemala, El Salvador, Honduras, Nicaragua, and Costa Rica constitute the fertile Central American isthmus. While Nicaragua and El Salvador have experienced the most intensive and widespread military conflicts, no country in the region escaped serious direct or indirect consequences of war during the 1980s. This chapter discusses the economic and social effects of war in Central America, as well as changes in health and health care. Economic sanctions intended to produce destabilization are also weapons of war, and their effects are discussed. (See also box on pp. 156–58 and Chapter 17.)

The term ''low-intensity conflict'' (LIC) has been used to describe recent Central American wars. With LIC, small-scale, guerilla-style methods avoiding full engagement are applied over time to wear down the enemy and win over populations, rather than to acquire new territory. Civilians are often targeted. The LIC strategy permitted the United States to wage war in Central America without significant direct deployment of U.S. ground troops. LIC's coordinated actions are of ''low intensity'' only for the attacker, not the victim. As shown by data discussed here, widespread and sustained use of LIC can inflict overwhelming damages in small, poor nations.

That militarism is a destroyer of the public health is obvious. It takes its toll in direct and indirect ways, including social and economic dislocations, reduced social spending, and stunted societal development due to war-related restriction of civil liberties and redirection of priorities. However, examination of the factors that created the conditions for war and the conditions prevailing in the ''post-war'' period in Central America reveals another issue: Economic exploitation is almost always backed by the implied or explicit threat of superior force. Because, after an initial invasion or expropriation, the threat is often implied rather than stated openly, it is often unacknowledged, sometimes even by its victims. Victims can internalize an ideology according to which they are less worthy, hard-working, or capable, and hence deserve exploitation; racism adds a convenient rationale for an unjust order backed by aggression, and fatalistic religious beliefs can also promote acceptance of injustice. The implicit or explicit threat of use of force is as unjust as the ultimate use of that force and may account for more total damages to health than do implemented acts of military aggression. Thus, in this chapter, we discuss the health effects of the economic exploitation of Central America that has been backed implicitly or explicitly by centuries of threatened or implemented use of force by international and domestic elite groups.

Overview of the Region Before the Most Recent Wars

Central America's population of about 27 million[1] is predominantly young, with a high birth rate and limited life expectancy. Spanish-speaking *mestizos* of mixed European and indigenous ancestry generally predominate numerically, politically, and economically. Main regional exports are coffee, cotton, sugar, and bananas. El Salvador, Guatemala, and Costa Rica are the only nations with some manufacturing capacity. Despite its wealth of natural resources, Central America is impoverished, most people living without basic material needs being met. Around 1980 the proportion of the region's people without basic needs satisfied was 64 percent.[2] About 50 to 70 percent of income was in the hands of the richest 20 percent of the population.[2]

Armed colonizers from Spain seeking mineral riches and land invaded during the 16th through 18th centuries. Indigenous peoples were murdered, enslaved, driven off their land, or killed by new diseases. During the conquest, and especially during the 19th century with the entrenchment of national oligarchies following independence from Spain, the land was increasingly concentrated under fewer owners and turned from subsistence toward export crops. Foreign, mainly U.S., investment in all export enterprises became extensive. Major U.S. corporations, such as United Fruit, Standard Fruit, and railroad companies, and large investors such as the Rockefellers, had substantial holdings in Central America by the early 20th century.[3,4] The isthmus also was a desirable location for a transoceanic canal necessary to the U.S. role in world trade. For the United States during the 20th century, the region has been a nearby source of raw materials and a market for manufactured goods that cannot be produced locally. Although small-scale conflicts have arisen without foreign direction or financing, the major wars that have afflicted the isthmus in recent decades have been largely financed by the United States to protect its strategic interests in the region.[3,5]

Organized civil unrest, often with anti-imperialist elements, emerged by the early 20th century, responding to extreme inequities in land ownership and poor working conditions and pay on the largely U.S.-owned plantations.[3–5] United States investor-owners feared expropriation if populist movements succeeded. The local landowners and governments dependent on U.S. companies became increasingly repressive. Increasing repression and continuing economic exploitation, in turn, fueled more popular rebellion. Full-scale wars of resistance developed by the late 1970s.

War and Public Health in El Salvador

Creating the Conditions for War in El Salvador

Conflict in El Salvador, as in the rest of Central America, begins with the *conquistadores'* confiscation of arable land in the 16th century. In 1881, the national government, representing the nascent planter oligarchy, abolished traditional indigenous communal land tenure, forcibly evicting thousands from their lands to plant coffee for export. A 1932 uprising for land reform was suppressed in a massacre of 10,000 to 30,000 people by the Salvadoran military. The status quo was maintained by military governments for the next 50 years.[6]

El Salvador is primarily agricultural, but densely populated. Maldistribution of land and wealth is extreme. Before the onset of war in the 1980s, 90 percent of farms were half or less the size needed for a family's subsistence; 60 percent of rural families earned less than the minimum needed to buy food.[7] Six families held more land than 133,000 small farmers.[7] In 1985, 92 percent of the rural population lived in poverty, with 60 percent in extreme poverty; 22 percent had access to potable water.[8] A 1968–1972 study by the Pan American Health Organization revealed exceedingly high child mortality in rural El Salvador, particularly from diarrheal disease and nutritional deficiency.[9] Studies by the U.S. Centers for Disease Control found chronic undernourishment among about one third or more of young children in rural northern El Salvador in 1978.[10,11]

During the 1970s Catholic priests began to organize peasants to improve their living conditions and gain labor rights. Landowners' ''death squads'' responded violently; leaflets urged Salvadorans to ''be a patriot, kill a priest.''[12] In the mid-1970s, unions coalesced; following a military coup in October 1979, hundreds of unarmed unionists were killed by the Salvadoran military.[13] On November 27, 1980, moderate political opposition leaders were surrounded by military forces while conducting a press conference in a high school; their mutilated bodies were found the next day.[14] Many felt there was no alternative left but armed revolution. The Farabundo Marti National Liberation Front (FMLN) formed in 1980. In January 1992, following 12 years of war, a peace accord was signed between the government and the FMLN. FMLN forces were demobilized that year, and the FMLN became a legal political party.

Effects of War in El Salvador

Nearly 1.5 percent of the Salvadoran population, 70,000 persons, were killed between 1980 and 1992; most were unarmed people killed by armed government forces and allied death squads.[8] Life expectancy declined from 56.6 years in 1970–1975 to 50.7 years in 1980–1985.[8,15]

The 1992 peace accords mandated the creation of a commission to investigate "serious acts of violence" since 1980. The commission's findings agree with those of human rights organizations and diplomats who for years have maintained that violence against unarmed civilians was a systematic policy of the Salvadoran government.[14,16,17] Recently released U.S. government documents confirm that the civilian assassination campaigns were planned by Salvadoran government officials with the full knowledge of the Reagan and Bush Administrations.[18]

Torture of captured rebel combatants, their suspected civilian supporters, and others identified with social change was an official but systematic policy of the Salvadoran government forces; reportedly, U.S. military advisers participated in "torture classes."[19] A 1985 study of imprisoned men and women found that 100 percent reported being tortured while in the custody of governmental paramilitary forces. Reported torture techniques included electric shock and application of acid;[20] suspension from body parts; beating; partial asphyxiation; tooth extraction; and sexual assault.[21]

A census of war-injured persons by international agencies[22] counted 30,854 persons, of whom 21 percent were over age 60 years and 48 percent were female; 59 percent of the females were between 44 and 70 years old. Thirty-two percent were excombatants (59 percent had served with the Salvadoran military, 41 percent with the FMLN). Twelve percent were mentally disabled, and 98 percent physically disabled; half had 50 percent or greater disability.

During the war, the rebel movement controlled up to one-third of the countryside.[23] The government strategy was to starve, terrorize, and kill the civilians in areas under rebel control in order to depopulate these regions and deprive the rebels of civilian support. Anyone living in "free fire zones" was bombed and strafed from the air, including with napalm.[24] In "hammer and anvil" operations, one military force would move through the region, forcing the fleeing inhabitants into a second force stationed on the far side.

Civilians captured in the "conflicted zones" were often publicly tortured to death.[25] On May 14, 1980, a group of at least 600 unarmed civilians, mostly women and children, were killed by the military while fleeing into Honduras, where Honduran troops blocked their path.[26] On March 18, 1981, 7,000 refugees were massacred while fleeing into Honduras.[27] In December 1981, between 733 and 926 civilians, including 280 children, were massacred by the military in El Mozote. The perpetrators of this and many other massacres were an elite battalion trained in the United States.[28]

About one million Salvadorans (20 percent of the population) fled the country, most to the United States as undocumented immigrants, or to refugee camps in neighboring countries; about 500,000 (10 percent) were displaced within the country.[8,29] The largest camps were in Honduras, supervised by international relief agencies. Of the internally displaced, nearly half did not register with the government, fearing persecution as suspected supporters of the opposition. These undocumented refugees were denied access to U.S. relief, which flowed only through Salvadoran government channels. The refugees' crude mortality was 22.4 per 1,000, three times higher than the general population.[8,29]

Medical neutrality was systematically violated by the Salvadoran military, which routinely abducted, tortured, and murdered health workers who served the poor and others believed to be sympathetic to the opposition.[30,31,32] The FMLN maintained mobile hospitals in the conflicted zones, which were regularly attacked and destroyed by the Salvadoran military.[33] On April 15, 1989, a "special operations" unit of the Salvadoran air force attacked an FMLN field hospital, killing a patient, two nurses, and a doctor. An autopsy of one of the nurses showed that she had been executed. The official post-war commission concluded that the air force had "deliberately attacked medical personnel."[34] In 1980, a public health delegation from the New York Committee for Health Rights in El Salvador reported that "death squads and uniformed forces have repeatedly entered hospitals and clinics and shot patients, doctors, nurses, and medical students in cold blood. These assassinations are frequently preceded by the cruelest forms of dismemberment and brutality." The delegation documented 11 armed incursions into medical centers, and the murder of nine physicians, seven medical students, and one nurse between October 1979 and July 1980.[35]

In January 1983, a medical mission sponsored by the National Academy of Sciences, the Institute of Medicine, the American Association for the Advancement of Science, and others visited El Salvador to investigate violence by the government against health professionals. They reported "the repression of human beings by the systematic use of terror in ways that are hideous." Thirty-two health workers had "disappeared," as did the senior obstetrician at the public maternity hospital within one month of hosting the delegation.[36] In June 1985, the government's "special anti-terrorist commandos" attacked a hospital in San Salvador, where a strike by workers was underway. Patients and hospital staff were bound and handcuffed; one died.[21] No evidence of violation of medical neutrality by the FMLN was found by a delegation from Physicians for Human Rights in 1989.[30]

One of the most difficult-to-measure consequences of war is the survivors' psychologic trauma. Psychiatric visits rose from the eighth to the third most common reason to seek medical care between 1978 and 1981.[15] Health care providers working with Salvadoran refugees have observed many war-traumatized children who appear to have lost the ability to speak.[29] (See Chapters 2 and 12.)

About 7.5 percent of the population utilizes private health services and hospitals, and another 12.5 percent, mostly salaried workers, have access to the Social Security system's health services. According to government figures, only 37 percent of the population receives public medical care outside Social Security.[8] The war consumed 36 percent of the national budget in 1986;[8] from 1976 to 1986, the share of the total government budget devoted to health fell from 10.6 to 7.1 percent, and per-capita spending by the Ministry of Health fell by nearly one-third.[37] In 1990, the share of gross domestic product (GDP) devoted to public health was 42 percent of its 1981 level.[38] Costs charged to patients for use of the public system rose 61 percent in constant dollars between 1977 and 1989.[38] Patients hospitalized for surgery in the public hospital had to bring their own surgical materials, sutures, food, soap, and toilet paper.[8] There was a waiting list of 20,000 for elective surgery at the major public hospital in San Salvador.[8]

The United States provided approximately $500 million a year in aid to the Salvadoran government throughout the 1980s; contrary to the Reagan Administration's claim that military aid comprised only one-fourth of this amount, a group of U.S. congressional representatives found that only 15 percent of U.S. aid was spent on development, the "vast majority" of the remainder being used to support the war effort directly.[39]

Medical education has suffered as a direct consequence of the war. In June 1980, the Salvadoran military invaded the campus of the national university, murdering students and professors, including medical school faculty. The military occupied the campus for the next four years, during which time they looted and destroyed the teaching facilities.[36] In 1985, there were 3.2 physicians, 2.1 nurses, 0.4 dentists, and 95 government soldiers per 10,000 inhabitants.[8]

Prospects for the Future in El Salvador

With the end of large-scale armed conflict, the hope for peace in El Salvador is strong. However, there has been a resurgence of death squad activity: In the first two years after the accords went into effect, 24 FMLN members were murdered, including candidates for elective office.[40] The government has resisted the dissolution of the paramilitary National Police.[41] And the maldistribution of land and wealth, which lies at the root of the suffering, ill health, and violence, continues.

War and Public Health in Guatemala

Guatemala has the largest population in Central America, with about 9.6 million people in 1992, as well as the greatest endowment of natural resources, including oil. It resembles other Central American nations in its social and economic inequities, the grinding poverty of the majority of its people, and its long history of repression, rebellion, and war. However, unlike the rest of the Central American isthmus, where indigenous peoples have been assimilated or exterminated, the indigenous peoples of Guatemala, predominantly Mayan Indians, have survived as a distinct cultural group and still constitute more than half of the population. They have suffered the violence of state repression for centuries, as eloquently recounted by the 1992 Nobel laureate, Rigoberta Menchu.[42]

The Conditions for and Effects of War in Guatemala

Fifty-nine percent of all and 71 percent of rural Guatemalans lived in extreme poverty in 1989.[43] A wealthy elite controls most of the economy. The army controls major banking, utility, and transportation institutions.[44] Some 400 U.S. firms have investments in the country, including 17 of the top 20 U.S. pharmaceutical companies and all of the top 10 U.S. pesticide manufacturers.[45] In 1991, Guatemala had a $319 million negative trade balance with the United States.[46]

Basic grain production has failed to keep up with population growth, and nontraditional crops for export have taken up increasing proportions of land. The U.S. government program ''Food For Peace'' provides basic grains to the Guatemalan government, which sells them commercially, generating cash income for the Guatemalan government but doing little to meet the basic needs of the population. Malnutrition among children under age five is estimated at 58 percent, with higher rates among Indians and the largely rural population of the Western Highlands.[45] Kwashiorkor is still seen among weaned preschool-age children. Vitamin A deficiency has been reported in 19 percent of women and 9 percent of children. The resulting eye disease is most prevalent in preschool-age children, leading to blindness in one of six afflicted.[45] Hypothyroid goiter caused by iodine deficiency is endemic. Malnutrition is the result of the poverty of subsistence farming in Guatemala, in which peasant farmers have been driven off better land onto plots too small and/or infertile to support their families. Wars, and especially the ''scorched earth'' strategy of the government's counterinsurgency campaigns of the 1980s, have driven additional thousands off even these tiny plots into the jungles and mountains, further restricting access to land for subsistence farming.

In 1954, the elected government of Jacobo Arbenz was overthrown by a U.S. CIA-directed coup, following Arbenz's attempt to nationalize unused land of the United Fruit Company and turn it to domestic food production. In the mid-1960s, guerilla struggles by disaffected army officers in the Eastern provinces were crushed by government forces assisted by U.S. military personnel. Civilian populations were attacked in the areas involved. In the 1970s, more resilient guerilla movements with broader support among both Ladino (mixed European and indigenous ancestry) and indigenous people formed in the Western provinces and coalesced in 1982 into the National Revolutionary Union of Guatemala (URNG).

Life expectancy at birth in Guatemala is 63.4 years, compared to 69.5 years for Latin America as a whole and 75.3 years for the United States.[47] Rural mortality is 33 percent higher than urban, and Indian mortality is 50 percent higher than that of Ladinos.[48] The 1985–1990 infant mortality rate (IMR) is estimated at 59 per 1,000 live births.[49] Paralleling declining infant mortality rates in other Central American countries, Guatemala's IMR has fallen by 50 percent since 1950.[49] Declining national IMRs during times of war have been demonstrated in other countries as well; the aggregate IMR for the Vietnamese nation declined overall during the Vietnam War, although an adverse effect was shown in those Vietnamese provinces most intensely affected by the war.[50] Guatemala's postneonatal mortality rate of 34.0 per 1,000 live births in 1986 was the highest of any country in Latin America, as was the mortality rate of children aged one to ten years.[49] The leading reported causes of death were infectious diseases, malnutrition, and accidents. The single most frequent cause of death for all males in Guatemala in 1981 was homicide;[48] most of this is believed directly related to armed conflict rather than crime or noncombatant accidents.

Health services in Guatemala are unevenly distributed. Although 65 percent of the population live in rural areas, 80 percent of all health services are located in the capital, where there are 28 doctors per 10,000 inhabitants, compared to 1.1 per 10,000 in the Western Highlands.[45] In 1984, 3.7 percent of the GDP was expended on health; 89 percent of this went to the public sector, including the Ministry of Health, Social Security health care for salaried workers, and the military health system. The military receive the best public services; the wealthy use 59 well-equipped private hospitals. Nongovernmental organizations have attempted to fill the void in rural health services.

As in El Salvador, health care workers who organize and serve the poor are often considered subversive. From 1980 to 1985, over 137 violations of medical neutrality were documented by the U.S.-based Guatemala Health Rights Support Project.[51] Medical and nursing personnel and community health promoters were shot, "disappeared," or driven into exile. Many professionals were killed for treating patients suspected of antigovernment activities. Patients were killed in ambulances and in their hospital beds. None of these incidents has been subjected to judicial inquiry.

During the 1980s, tens of thousands of peasants driven from their villages by the military formed communities in remote jungle regions. Village health promoters, sanitation practices, and community gardening helped to ameliorate the difficult living conditions. However, vaccines and medications are scarce, and the health promoters lack training and supervision. In the early 1980s, nearly 50,000 rural poor fled into southern Mexico. Currently 129 official refugee camps exist in that area, while thousands more individuals are living among the Mexican population. The Mexican government operates clinics for the refugee camps.

Prospects for the Future in Guatemala

Public health care has deteriorated precipitously in recent years. In early 1993, all nonemergency public hospital patients were discharged due to lack of resources. The Guatemalan military took over the administration of public hospitals in October 1993.[52] For several years, refugees have been voluntarily repatriated to Guatemala with United Nations assistance; their fate is unknown. A negotiated return of 2,480 refugees in January 1993 included an agreement with the Guatemalan government granting the refugees rights to land and protection against persecution by the military, but no reports are available on compliance. As in El Salvador, economic conditions and distribution of power and wealth in Guatemala are unchanged from those that have previously engendered armed conflict.

War and Public Health in Nicaragua

Creating the Conditions for War in Nicaragua

The U.S. Navy invaded Nicaragua four times during the 1850s in response to anti-U.S. protests; the Marines intervened in 1912 to help overthrow a nationalist president. The Marines occupied Nicaragua almost continuously from 1912 until 1933,[5] when the first Somoza was installed by the withdrawing occupation forces as head of the U.S.-trained and U.S.-equipped National Guard. Somoza murdered the populist and anti-imperialist leader Sandino and ousted the president in 1936.[5] The Somozas ruled the country virtually as their private estate for the next 50 years, relying on the population's fear of the National Guard.

Health, education, and development in general were neglected.[53] In the 1970s, approximately 50 percent of the population was illiterate; infant mortality in 1977 was estimated at 121 and 200 per 1,000 births overall and in rural areas, respectively.[54] Measles, polio, neonatal tetanus, and malnutrition were major causes of morbidity and child mortality.[53] No single agency coordinated public health activities.[55] About 90 percent of public health resources were allocated to about 10 percent of the population, primarily urban publicly employed persons.[55] The wealthy received their medical care in other countries.

Changes in Health and Health Care in the 1980s

In 1979, a popular insurrection led by the Sandinistas ended the half-century of rule by the Somozas. Improvement in health was a major focus. All public health agencies were consolidated under the Ministry of Health, and regional planning was introduced. Emphasis was placed on universal coverage with basic, low-technology curative and preventive services at the local level, and on improved education and sanitation, rather than investment in hospitals. The new government faced formidable obstacles, including lack of infrastructure and trained personnel, a high foreign debt, and the emerging regional economic crisis.

Despite these obstacles, and with substantial aid from donor countries and international organizations, community-based health facilities and services expanded rapidly in the early 1980s, especially in the previously neglected rural regions. Health spending as a percentage of the national budget increased by more than 50 percent between 1977 and 1981.[56] From 1977 to 1984, ambulatory visits per person almost doubled overall, and they increased by over 400 percent in community-based sites. Substantial increases occurred in the proportion of children receiving immunizations and acute care, and in pregnant women receiving prenatal and obstetric care. Hospitalizations and surgeries increased by 30 to 40 percent.[56] Significant investment was made in training health professionals, including paraprofessionals and technicians as well as physicians and nurses.[57] The first national school of public health in Central America was established in Managua in 1982.[58]

The "Contra" War and Its Impact on Health

The "Contra" war began soon after the Sandinistas came to power. It accelerated markedly after 1981 when the United States assumed a major role in what had previously been episodic attacks on the Sandinista army by small, independent groups of Nicaraguans. U.S. policy toward the new government crystallized in relation to early Sandinista policies calling for major land reform and use of anti-imperialist rhetoric. The United States began to finance and organize the "Contras" into a unified fighting force. Overt and covert military operations and economic sanctions gathered momentum. The war continued until the Sandinistas were voted out in 1990.

Medipaz, a Nicaraguan medical group affiliated with the International Physicians for the Prevention of Nuclear War, estimates that due to military combat between 1980 and 1989, a total of 61,884 people were killed, injured, or kidnapped, with 40,000 handicapped, including civilians and combatants. Over 16,470 children were orphaned; 347,513 persons were displaced, and over 99,000 were expatriated to Mexico and Central America from 1984 to 1990.[59] Few families escaped one or more casualties. Anxiety disorders, depression, and psychiatric illness attributed to war and the accompanying social dislocation were widespread.[56,59,60] A military draft was instituted in 1983; 250,000 performed military service from 1983 to 1990.[59] Many boys were sent to live with relatives in the United States to escape the draft.

The "Contras" had a systematic policy of terror. They regularly used rape, torture, mutilation,[61] and attacks on civilians,[62] especially targeting civilians on agricultural cooperatives or in villages supportive of the Sandinistas. Health workers and teachers were often targeted.[60,62,63] Interrupting services was intended to help erode popular support for the government. Malaria control programs, immunization programs, and health posts had to be closed down in many rural zones. By the late 1980s, malaria re-emerged in some zones along with epidemics of measles and other vaccine-preventable illnesses that had diminished markedly by the mid-1980s.[60] A new rural hospital was closed. Medicines and medical supplies were destroyed, most dramatically in the 1983 bombing of the port of Corinto.

The Indians of Nicaragua's Atlantic Coast suffered especially. Somoza had not invested in services or development but also had not interfered much with the zone's political and cultural life. The non-Spanish-speaking and non-Catholic peoples of the Atlantic Coastal Area had always felt limited connection with Nicaragua's government and majority population, whom they often referred to as "the Spaniards." The Sandinistas were initially insensitive to Indian concerns, promoting a literacy campaign and education in Spanish. The army, in response to "Contra" rebels operating in the zone, forcibly relocated many indigenous peoples from ancestral lands. A group of Indians resisting relocation was massacred in 1981; troops involved were punished by the government, but the damage had occurred. Many Indians fled to Honduras; others joined "Contra" bands. Combat casualties and displacement from traditional communities and sources of livelihood severely affected Indian health and well-being. During the 1980s, the Sandinista government publicly acknowledged the mistakes and attempted to address Indian concerns. In 1987, an agreement granted limited political autonomy for indigenous peoples. Many people returned from Honduras, only to face devastating Hurricane Juana in 1988.

The war's indirect economic effects also took a serious toll on health. Military costs increasingly sapped resources. Allocation to health as a proportion of the total budget continued to increase until 1988, with severe declines thereafter.[64] Special facilities and programs for war casualties interrupted development of a comprehensive and prevention-focused health system. Mobilization of health personnel to war zones created strains for those mobilized and their families, and also for urban staff facing increased patient loads. Stress, fatigue, and consequent demoralization contributed to attrition of health professionals.[56]

Early work in popular health education and community participation lost ground. Many young people who had previously volunteered in health campaigns were in the military; others were at school or working at night to make household ends meet under wartime belt-tightening. Training of health volunteers shifted from community-oriented preventive programs to a focus on first aid and civil defense. Education overall and education of health professionals was disrupted by the draft, social dislocation, and wartime economic conditions.

The war's effects on health via effects on the economy were at least as devastating as the direct health effects of military action. Land was not cultivated because many rural zones were unsafe; displaced persons from the besieged rural zones flocked to cities unable to provide jobs, housing, clean water, or sanitation. As agricultural production plummeted, unemployment rose and export earnings fell, exacerbated by the continuing decline of world prices for Nicaragua's agricultural commodities.

However, in addition to these indirect economic consequences of military actions, the war on Nicaragua was openly fought with economic sanctions. From 1981 until the Sandinistas left office in 1990, the United States blocked all major development loans from the large multilateral lending agencies and successfully influenced some individual donor countries as well. This had a crippling effect on investment in transportation, agriculture, schools, clean water, and sanitation projects that were essential to improve health. The Soviet-bloc nations and Cuba diminished support during the later 1980s as they faced internal crises, in part over their inability to satisfy their own populations' material needs. The United States, which had been Nicaragua's major trading partner, imposed a trade embargo in 1985. By the late 1980s, most hospital, transportation, and agricultural equipment that was U.S.-manufactured became nonfunctional for lack of spare parts.

Post-War Nicaragua: The Early 1990s*

Elections in 1990 resulted in victory for Violeta Chamorro, presidential candidate of the U.N.O., a coalition of parties with little ideological common ground except their desire to defeat the Sandinistas. It was clear that the United States would continue the war and economic sanctions if the Sandinistas stayed in power. The U.N.O. created expectations that the country would be flooded with U.S. aid if the Sandinistas were voted out. Sandinista economic experiments had not been successful, and the international discrediting of socialist economic models undoubtedly was another major factor. The vote appeared to be a resounding cry of "enough war; enough economic adversity." With substantial indirect campaign support from U.S. agencies such as the National Endowment for Democracy, the U.N.O. achieved 51 percent of the vote by pooling the votes for numerous parties. Because 42 percent of the vote went to the Sandinista Party, Chamorro considered it necessary to agree that Sandinistas would lead the army and police.

For most of the population in 1995, the high hopes of some voters in 1990 have not been met, although relief over the end of the war is universal. The United States has periodically withheld much of the limited aid promised, pressuring Chamorro to exclude the Sandinistas from power and take a harder line against strikes and demonstrations by labor and peasant groups. Unrest appears to grow, however, in the face of severe austerity measures instituted to control hyperinflation and restructure the foreign debt. Even after massive restructuring and debt forgiveness, debt payments continue to consume half of Nicaragua's export earnings.[66] While wartime hyperinflation is now under control, real wages in 1992 were about half their June 1990 value.[64] As a result of a massive contraction in the public sector including the military, and negligible private investment, 50 to 60 percent of the economically active population are now unemployed or underemployed.[64,67] Crime, juvenile delinquency, prostitution, and harmful drug use have increased.[59] Seventy percent of Nicaraguans now live in extreme poverty.[59] Most of the Sandinista-instituted public subsidies of transportation, food, education, and utilities have been eliminated. Many workers cannot afford bus fare to go to work; many children are no longer in school because of lack of bus fare, inability to buy formerly free uniforms or school supplies, or families' need for extra income from child labor. The poor cannot afford previously nominal fees for sanitation services. The public health care infrastructure put in place in the 1980s is deteriorating, not because of a change in policy from within the health sector, but primarily because of lack of funds. Another factor may be demoralization among personnel who in the 1980s had felt involved in a meaningful social experiment.

Small-scale paramilitary operations continue, with an ironic twist: Former "Con-

*This section was adapted from: Braveman, P. Book Review: *Health in Nicaragua* (by R. Garfield and G. Williams, Oxford University Press). *Journal of Public Health Policy,* 14:360–363, 1993.[65]

tras'' disgruntled over the government's failure to provide land sometimes join forces with former or present Sandinistas disgruntled over lack of government credits to small farmers.[66,67] Arms left over from the 1980s are widely available. However, such paramilitary operations appear not to have substantial foreign financing; thus, damages from direct military action are limited in comparison with the previous decade's toll. Prospects for the future are uncertain; the unstable environment has not attracted foreign capital or investment by wealthy Nicaraguans. The increasingly desperate majority is unlikely to suffer in silence.

Final Remarks

During the 1980s, Honduras became largely a military base for U.S. operations in El Salvador and Nicaragua.[3,68] The role of the Honduran military was strengthened by U.S. investment in increasing militarization of the economy and society.[69] Military leaders suppressed local insurgencies organizing around land reform, plantation working conditions, and human rights abuses.[3,68] Costa Rica experienced massive immigration of poor Nicaraguans fleeing war there; this economic burden coincided with Costa Rica's beginning to feel the consequences of the high debt incurred to invest during the 1970s in social infrastructure, including schools, roads, housing, sanitation, and public health services.[70]

Although we have focused on the sites of the larger-scale conflicts, war produced region-wide damages to health and development during recent decades in Central America. Open military conflict may be less in the current post-Cold-War period. However, especially given the stunting of regional economic development by decades of war, there is increasing involvement of global international monetary interests. Inequities within countries are likely to widen, with war-weary populations kept under control—at least until the next round of social explosions—by the implied or explicit use of police or army force. The recent memories of war may make impoverished populations even more susceptible to appeals to clutch at peace—even without justice.

REFERENCES

1. The World Bank. *World development report 1993: Investing in health.* Washington, DC: Published for the World Bank by Oxford University Press, 1993.
2. Pan American Health Organization. *Priority health needs in Central America and Panama.* Washington, DC: PAHO, 1984.
3. Burbach, R. and Flynn, P. (eds.). *The politics of intervention: The United States in Central America.* New York: Monthly Review Press, 1984.
4. Morgan, L.M. *Community participation in health: The politics of primary care in Costa Rica.* New York: Cambridge University Press, 1993.
5. Barry, T. and Preusch, D. *The Central America fact book.* New York: Grove Press, 1986.
6. Arnson, C. *El Salvador: A revolution confronts the United States.* Washington, D.C.: Institute for Policy Studies, 1982.

7. Simon, L.R., Stephens, J.C. and Diskin, M. *El Salvador land reform 1980–1981—Impact Audit.* Boston: Oxfam America, 1982.
8. Instituto de Derechos Humanos de la Universidad de Centroamerica. La salud en tiempos de guerra. *Estudios Centroamericanos* 46:653–671, 1991.
9. Puffer, R.R. and Serrano, C.V. *Patterns of mortality in childhood.* Washington, D.C.: Pan American Health Organization, Scientific Publication No. 262, 1973.
10. Stetler, H.C., Trowbridge, F.L. and Huong, A.Y.: Anthropometric nutrition status and diarrhea prevalence in children in El Salvador. *Am. J. Trop. Med. Hyg.* 30:888–893, 1991.
11. Trowbridge, F.L. and Newton, L.H. Seasonal changes in malnutrition and diarrheal disease among preschool children in El Salvador. *Am. J. Trop. Med. Hyg.* 28:135–141, 1979.
12. Lernoux, P. *Cry of the people: United States involvement in the rise of fascism, torture, and murder and the persecution of the Catholic Church in Latin America.* New York: Doubleday, 1980.
13. McClintock, M. *The American connection, Volume 1: State terror and popular resistance in El Salvador.* London: Zed Books, 1985.
14. White, R. The problem that won't go away. *New York Times Magazine,* July 18, 1982.
15. Garfield, R.M. and Rodriguez, P.F. Health and health services in Central America. *JAMA* 254:936–943, 1985.
16. Amnesty International. *El Salvador: "Death squads"—a government strategy.* London: Amnesty International, 1988.
17. Thomsen, J.L., Gruschow, J. and Stover, E. Medicolegal investigation of political killings in El Salvador. *Lancet* 1:1377–1379, 1989.
18. Krauss C. U.S. aware of killings, worked with Salvador's rightists, papers suggest. *New York Times,* Nov. 9, 1993.
19. Bonner, R. U.S. advisers at "torture class," Salvadoran says. *New York Times,* Jan. 11, 1982.
20. Gordon, E. and Mant, A.K. Clinical evidence of torture: Examination of a teacher from El Salvador. *Lancet* 1:213–214, 1984.
21. Allen, T., Kandel, S., Stephens, S., Thorburn, K.M. and Wuerker, M.C. *El Salvador update: Counterterrorism in action.* Boston: Unitarian Universalist Service Committee, 1987.
22. CEE (European Economic Community), PNUD, Cooperacion Canadiense, COPAZ. Censo nacional de lisiados y discapacitados a consecuencia del conflicto armado en El Salvador: Informe de resultados. San Salvador: European Economic Community, September 1993.
23. Americas Watch: *Draining the sea.* Sixth supplement to the report on human rights in El Salvador. New York: Americas Watch, March 1985.
24. Biddle, W. Salvadoran army possesses napalm. *New York Times,* Sept. 30, 1984.
25. Hoge, W. Soldiers are villains in Salvadorans' tales of horror. *New York Times,* June 5, 1981.
26. Blundy, D. Victims of the massacre that the world ignored. *Sunday Times* (London), Feb. 22, 1981.
27. Blundy, D. The innocents caught in Lempa River massacre. *Sunday Times* (London), April 26, 1981.
28. Massacre of hundreds is reported in El Salvador. *New York Times,* Jan. 28, 1982.
29. Lundgren, R.I. and Lang, R. "There is no sea, only fish": Effects of United States policy on the health of the displaced in El Salvador. *Soc. Sci. Med.* 28:697–706, 1989.
30. Geiger, H.J., Eisenberg, C., Gloyd, S., Quiroga, J., Schlenker, T., Scrimshaw, N. and Devin, J. A new medical mission to El Salvador. *N. Engl. J. Med.* 321:1136–1140, 1989.
31. Graham, P.J. Health personnel terrorized in El Salvador. *Med. J. Austr.* 1:648, 1981.
32. Hellquist, L. Violence against doctors in El Salvador and Guatemala. *Lancet* 1:1360, 1982.

33. Secret radio and doctors keep moving. *New York Times,* Dec. 26, 1985.
34. Betancur, B., Planchart, R.F. and Buergenthal, T. Report of the Commission on the Truth for El Salvador. New York: United Nations, April 1993.
35. Guttmacher, S., Hubbard, F., Lear, W., Sagan, L. and Warner, A. Abuses of medical neutrality: Report of the Public Health Commission to El Salvador, July 1980. *Int. J. Health. Serv.* 11:329–337, 1981.
36. Gellhorn, A. Medical mission report on El Salvador. *N. Engl. J. Med.* 308:1043–1044, 1983.
37. Fiedler, J.L. Recurrent cost and public health care delivery: The other war in El Salvador. *Soc. Sci. Med.* 25:867–874, 1987.
38. Fiedler, J.L. Increasing reliance on user fees as a response to public health financing crises: A case study of El Salvador. *Soc. Sci. Med.* 36:735–747, 1993.
39. Leach, J., Miller, G. and Hatfield, M. U.S. aid to El Salvador: An evaluation of the past, a proposal for the future. Washington, D.C.: Arms Control and Foreign Policy Caucus, February 1985.
40. Associated Press: U.N. plans investigation. *New York Times,* Nov. 9, 1993.
41. Salvador is said to renege on police pledge. *New York Times,* Nov. 11, 1993.
42. Menchu, R. *I, Rigoberta Menchu.* London: Verso, 1984.
43. INE-FUNDAP: Perfil de la pobreza en Guatemala. Guatemala City, 1991.
44. Painter, J. *Guatemala: False hope—false freedom.* Catholic Institute for International Relations/Latin America Bureau of London, 1987, pp. 47–51.
45. Barry, T. *Inside Guatemala.* Albuquerque, N.M.: The Inter-Hemispheric Education Resource Center, 1992.
46. U.S. Embassy. Guatemala: Economic trends. April 1992.
47. U.S. Department of Commerce. *Statistical abstract of the United States, 1992.*
48. Pan American Health Organization. Health conditions in the Americas 1981–1984, Vol II. Washington, D.C.: PAHO, Scientific Pub. No. 500, 1986.
49. Pan American Health Organization. Health conditions in the Americas, Health of children and adolescents, 1990. Washington, D.C.: PAHO, Scientific Pub. No. 524, 1990.
50. Savitz, D.A., Thang, N.M., Swenson, I.E. and Stone, E.M. Vietnamese infant and childhood mortality in relation to the Vietnam War. *Am. J. Public Health* 83:1134–1138, 1993.
51. Wands, C. *Guatemala: Health care and hope.* Guatemala Health Rights Support Projects, 1985.
52. *La Hora, El Grafico, Prensa Libre* (Guatemalan newspapers), Oct. 17, 1993; CERIGUA News Agency Report, Oct. 22, 1993.
53. Halperin, D.C. and Garfield, R. Developments in health care in Nicaragua. *N. Engl. J. Med.* 307:388–392, 1982.
54. Behm, H. and Primante, D. Latin American Center for Demographic Studies (CELADE), Series A, No. 1036. San Jose, Costa Rica: CELADE, December 1977.
55. Braveman, P. Primary health care takes root in Nicaragua. *World Health Forum* 6:368–372, 1985.
56. Braveman, P. and Siegel, D. A health system developing under conditions of war: Nicaragua. *Int. J. Health Services* 17(1):169–79, 1987.
57. Braveman, P.A. and Mora, F. Training physicians for community-oriented primary care in Latin America: Model programs in Mexico, Nicaragua, and Costa Rica. *Am. J. Public Health* 77(4):485–490, 1987.
58. Braveman, P.A. and Roemer, M.I. Health personnel training in the Nicaraguan health system. *Int. J. Health Services* 15(4):699–705, 1985.

59. Medipaz. *The war in Nicaragua: The effects of low-intensity conflict on an underdeveloped country.* Managua, Nicaragua: Medipaz, 1993.

60. Siegel, D., Baron, R. and Epstein, P. The epidemiology of aggression: Health consequences of war in Nicaragua. *Lancet* 1:1492–1493, 1985.

61. Cabestrero, T. *Blood of the innocent: Victims of the Contras' war in Nicaragua.* Maryknoll, N.Y.: Orbis Books, 1985.

62. The Americas Watch Committee. *Human rights in Nicaragua 1986.* New York: The Americas Watch Committee, 1987.

63. Garfield, R.M., Frieden, T. and Vermund, S.H. Health-related outcomes of war in Nicaragua. *Am. J. Public Health* 77:615–618, 1987.

64. Blumenthal, G. *Health and social sectors in Nicaragua.* Helsinki, Finland: Health and Social Development Cooperation Group; National Agency for Welfare and Health in Finland, 1992.

65. Braveman, P. Book Review: *Health in Nicaragua* (by R. Garfield and G. Williams, Oxford University Press). *J. Pub. Health Policy,* 14:360–363, 1993.

66. Envio. Neoliberalism in Central America: More than an economic plan. *Envio* (Universidad Centroamericana, Managua, Nicaragua) 11(129):32–40, 1992.

67. Correos de Centroamérica 29(3):1–15, 1993.

68. Shepherd, F. with Cohn, B., Roberts, C. and Benton, E. *From banana cases to Contra bases: A chronology of U.S.–Honduran relations, January 1977 to July 1986.* Washington, D.C.: Central American Historical Institute, 1986.

69. Honduras voters picking president. *New York Times International,* Nov. 29, 1993.

70. Frieden, J. *On borrowed time.* Report on the Americas 1985; 19:25–33, 1985.

17

Public Health and the
Persian Gulf War

ERIC HOSKINS

War has always been disastrous for civilians, and the Persian Gulf War was no exception. Yet the image that has been perpetuated in the West is that the Gulf War was somehow "clean" and fought with "surgical precision" in a manner that minimized civilian casualties. However, massive wartime damage to Iraq's civilian infrastructure led to a breakdown in virtually all sectors of society. Economic sanctions further paralyzed Iraq's economy and made any meaningful post-war reconstruction all but impossible. Furthermore, the invasion of Kuwait and the subsequent Gulf War unleashed internal political events that have been responsible for further suffering and countless human rights violations. The human impact of these events is incalculable.

In 1996, more than five years after the end of the war, the vast majority of Iraqi civilians still subsist in a state of extreme hardship, in which health care, nutrition, education, water, sanitation, and other basic services are minimal.

As many as 500,000 children are believed to have died since the beginning of the Persian Gulf War, largely due to malnutrition and a resurgence of diarrheal and vaccine-preventable diseases. Health services are barely functioning due to shortages of supplies and equipment. Medicines, including insulin, antibiotics, and anesthetics, are in short supply. The psychological impact of the war has had a damaging and lasting effect on many of Iraq's estimated eight million children.

Iraq before the Gulf War

Prior to the war, Iraq was described by the United Nations as a high-middle-income country with a modern social infrastructure. Since the early 1960s, Iraq has evolved from a largely rural, agricultural society to one where 70 percent of the country's 20 million citizens now live in urban areas. Fifty-three percent of workers were employed in agriculture in 1960, but by 1990 only 12 percent were.[1] Meanwhile, oil, which accounts for more than 90 percent of export earnings, has dominated all areas of the Iraqi economy since the early 1960s, if not earlier. It was this almost singular reliance on oil that, following the Iraqi invasion of Kuwait, made Iraq particularly vulnerable to the effects of economic sanctions.

Before the 1991 Gulf War, Iraq's investment in its own economic and social development had a visible impact on the living conditions and health status of the civilian population. Iraq's medical facilities and public health system were well developed. There were more than 250 hospitals, with an extensive network of primary health care facilities. Since the 1960s, all health indices had shown dramatic improvement. Between 1960 and 1990, life expectancy had climbed from 49 to 67 years, a level comparable to many Latin American countries, including Brazil and Mexico.[2] By 1990, nearly all urban dwellers and 72 percent of rural residents had access to clean water. By then, 93 percent of Iraqis had access to health services.[3]

With the start of the Iran-Iraq war in 1980, military expenditures increased from roughly 10 percent of the country's gross national product (GNP) to more than 30 percent. Health expenditures, meanwhile, were reduced to just 0.8 percent of GNP, which is below the average for less developed countries.[4] Yet despite this decrease in health spending, the previous trend of improvement in health continued throughout the 1980s. Between 1977 and 1990, Iraq's infant mortality rate (IMR) declined by nearly 50 percent from 70 to 39 deaths per 1,000 live births.[2] During the 1985–1989 period, the proportion of fully immunized one-year-olds increased from 15 to 84 percent.[5]

Although dramatic improvements in health care occurred during (and despite) the Iran-Iraq War, Iraq's economy and labor force suffered. The eight-year war left Iraq in near financial ruin due to massive losses in oil revenue, a foreign debt of nearly $100 billion, and depletion of foreign currency reserves. Out of a total work force of five million, approximately one million men were mobilized for the war, more than 100,000 died, and many tens of thousands were injured or captured. The resulting labor shortage contributed to even greater economic stagnation, forcing increasing numbers of women into the workplace and extending Iraq's reliance on foreign workers.

As damaging as the Iran-Iraq War was, its institutional impact was mainly economic. Iraq's health, education, and other social programs continued to advance throughout the 1980s. This has, particularly in the area of health, made it somewhat easier to separate the effects of the 1991 Gulf War from those of the earlier Iran-Iraq War. Observers familiar with Iraq agree that the August 2, 1990 Iraqi invasion of Kuwait unleashed a conflict far more devastating than anything ever before experienced in modern-day Iraq. In fact, the Gulf War erased many of Iraq's social and economic achievements of the previous two decades.

The 43-Day War

On August 2, 1990, Iraqi forces invaded Kuwait. International condemnation of Iraq led to the imposition of economic sanctions on August 6. Iraq's refusal to withdraw from Kuwait, coupled with failed diplomatic efforts, quickly led to the largest mobilization of troops since the Vietnam War. On January 17, 1991, the Gulf War began with a relentless Coalition bombing campaign that was aimed at eliminating Iraq's military capacity. Coalition forces were comprised of military personnel, and equipment from 28 countries led by the United States and including, among others, Canada, Great Britain, France, Egypt, and Saudi Arabia. An estimated 25 percent of all sorties flown by Coalition aircraft penetrated deep into Iraq's heartland, often targeting elements of the civilian infrastructure, such as bridges, electricity plants, and sites of other essential services.

Coalition forces dropped more than 80,000 tons of explosives during the Gulf War. Despite allied claims that the war was fought "surgically" to minimize civilian casualties, only seven percent of all bombs dropped on Iraq were so-called "smart" or laser-guided bombs, and, of these, more than 20 percent missed their target. Overall, nearly 75 percent of all bombs dropped on Iraq missed their intended targets. The Coalition's overwhelming superiority in air power resulted in massive numbers of Iraqi military deaths, estimated at between 50,000 and 100,000, compared to several hundred on the Coalition side.[2,4]

Civilian wartime casualties were estimated by compiling data from hundreds of extensive interviews and direct eyewitness reports. Middle East Watch, an independent human rights agency, has estimated that between 2,500 and 3,000 Iraqi civilians were killed during the air campaign.[6] This estimate is further supported by a United Nations report of March 20, 1991, which estimated that 9,000 homes throughout the country were destroyed or damaged beyond repair during the war[7] (Figure 17-1).

It soon became clear, however, that the considerable number of deaths occurring during the war would rapidly be overshadowed by escalating post-war deaths due to damage of the life-sustaining civilian infrastructure (Figure 17-2), in particular destruction of Iraq's electricity-generating power plants. Continued economic sanctions further compromised civilian well-being and prevented any meaningful post-war relief or reconstruction.

Post-War Displacement and Unrest

From March to May 1991, nearly two million Kurds, the vast majority of them women and children, fled northern Iraq for greater safety in Iran and Turkey. The conditions of their flight, together with the harsh climate and poor living conditions in refugee camps, led to high death rates due to inadequate shelter, malnutrition, and disease.

Figure 17-1. Damage caused by wartime aerial bombardment of a civilian neighborhood in the Old Market area of Baghdad as photographed in March 1991 (Photograph by Eric Hoskins).

An estimated 10,000 to 30,000 Kurds died in refugee camps along the Iran-Iraq and Turkey-Iraq borders.[8,9]

In May and June, many refugees began returning to northern Iraq, under the auspices of the Coalition forces' ''safe haven'' repatriation. However, few Kurds were able to return home and most remained displaced in new camps or returned to villages destroyed by Iraqi forces during the 1980s. Conditions of ill-health and deprivation continued, while the United Nations mounted a massive relief effort to try to improve the displaced Kurds' conditions of shelter, food, sanitation, and health care.

The Coalition forces' creation of a separately administered Kurdish autonomous region in northern Iraq led to further repercussions from Baghdad, including a near-total embargo of goods flowing to the north, and further military pressures. By 1996, conditions had improved somewhat, as relief efforts placed more emphasis on rebuilding local economies and on reconstruction. However, the lack of a political solution for the Kurds continues to threaten their health and well-being, and their situation remains tenuous.

Meanwhile, with international attention focused on the Kurdish north of Iraq, the largely Shiite population in southern Iraq was experiencing a similar plight. For several weeks during March 1991, a Shiite uprising in the south led to many thousands of civilian deaths (Figure 17-3). Furthermore, an estimated 50,000 civilians fled to the

Figure 17-2. Two women collecting drinking water from a polluted tributary of the Tigris River near Basra, southern Iraq, as photographed in August 1991. The lack of electricity and wartime damage to the water infrastructure prevented purification and pumping of clean water to most parts of the country (Photograph by Eric Hoskins).

marshes around the Tigris and Euphrates rivers where they lived (and many died) under conditions of extreme deprivation.

The Economic Impact of War and Sanctions

The effects of the Gulf War need to be considered together with the impact of more than six years of internationally mandated economic sanctions. Even before the war, the trade embargo against Iraq, which began in August 1990 following Iraq's invasion of Kuwait, had resulted in hyperinflation, food rationing, and deterioration in health care. By January 1991, the Iraqi economy had been weakened by sanctions, so the

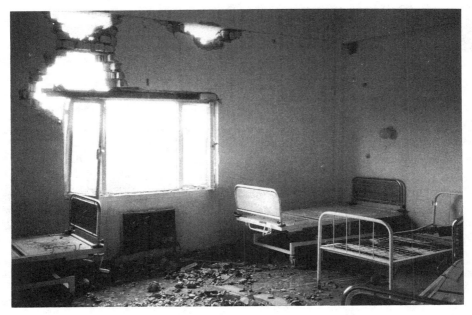

Figure 17-3. The pediatric ward of Kerbala General Hospital in southern Iraq, as photographed in April 1991. The hospital was badly damaged during civil disturbances that followed the war (Photograph by Eric Hoskins).

country was vulnerable to the effects of the air campaign. While the war caused extensive damage to the economic infrastructure, including oil refineries, electricity-generating plants, bridges, and telecommunications, sanctions have made comprehensive post-war reconstruction nearly impossible. (See also box on economic sanctions on pp. 156–58.)

Now, after more than six years of economic sanctions, most Iraqi civilians are living in extreme poverty. Many households are dependent on handouts, having long since exhausted their financial reserves. Families have been forced to sell personal belongings, even clothing, in order to make ends meet. Some Iraqis, desperate to obtain much-needed cash for their families, have reportedly even sold one of their own kidneys for transplant (for $1,000). Hyperinflation and unemployment have reduced family incomes to less than five percent of pre-war levels, and most people have become dependent on food rations. Many children and women are receiving only two-thirds of their daily caloric needs.

Impact on Trade

United Nations Security Council Resolution 661—the sanctions resolution passed unopposed on August 6, 1990—effectively eliminated any possibility that Iraq could generate sufficient trade revenue to sustain its domestic infrastructure and material needs. The economic embargo prevented, among other things, the unmonitored sale of Iraqi oil, which accounted for more than $10 billion in annual revenue (62 percent of GNP) during the pre-sanctions period. More than five years after the war, Iraq, citing infringement on its sovereignty, had still not agreed to the terms of United Nations Security Council Resolution 706, which permitted the limited sale of oil for the purchase of humanitarian supplies. The balance of Iraq's export earnings had been historically generated from the sale of dates, gas, and chemical fertilizers—all banned from trade under existing sanctions legislation.

Iraq relies heavily on imported food. Before the imposition of sanctions, approximately 70 percent of Iraq's food supply was imported. The United Nations Food and Agriculture Organization (FAO) estimates that more than seven million metric tons of food must be imported each year—in addition to Iraq's domestic production of approximately three million metric tons—at a total cost of nearly US$3 billion.[10,11] Food imports all but disappeared following the August 1990 imposition of sanctions; from then until March 1991, it was illegal under existing sanctions legislation to import *any* food into Iraq. Security Council Resolution 661 (August 6, 1990) stated that food was permitted only "in humanitarian circumstances." Such circumstances were not judged by the Security Council to have occurred in Iraq until April 3, 1991, at which time the prohibition of foodstuffs was lifted.

After the war's end, although the importation of food became legal, in practice it remained problematic. Medicines, although in principle exempt from sanctions, were also in short supply. From 1991 to 1993, the amount of food and medicine imported by the United Nations and other aid agencies was less than five percent of the total humanitarian needs of the civilian population. Furthermore, Iraq claimed to lack the currency required to purchase badly needed medicines and food—although this has been disputed by the West.

Apart from medicine and food, Security Council approval was also granted on a case-by-case basis for items considered to be of urgent humanitarian and civilian need. A modest supply of reconstruction materials, particularly for the water and sanitation systems, has been imported after such approval. However, many companies, fearing repercussions, refuse to engage even in such legal trade with Iraq. Orders of millions of dollars worth of medicine, food, and water and sanitation equipment, paid for by Iraq before August 1990, have been cancelled or delayed.

Although Iraq was able to utilize some of its estimated $4 billion in overseas frozen assets for the purchase of humanitarian supplies, albeit under very strict conditions, this action was prohibited in 1992. Repeated offers by the United Nations to permit Iraq to channel funds, including those from the sale of oil, through an account administered and supervised by the United Nations had until recently been refused by the Iraqi government. In May 1996, Iraq accepted United Nations Security Council Resolution 986 (April 14, 1995), authorizing the limited sale of Iraqi oil. Of the up to $2 billion generated every six months, just over one-half is earmarked for humanitarian supplies, such as food and medicine, while the balance will be spent on war reparations (30 percent), relief to the three predominantly Kurdish governments, and UN administrative costs in Iraq.

Impact on Industry

Most of Iraq's industrial base was heavily dependent on the importation of sophisticated machinery, equipment, spare parts, and raw materials procured abroad. With the imposition of sanctions, these resources rapidly became unavailable, and industrial production suffered.

The loss of electricity, together with more widespread infrastructural damage due to the war, made continued industrial activity difficult. Consequently, post-war production has decreased by more than 50 percent. Industrial unemployment following the war has been estimated at more than 70 percent.

Impact on Agriculture

Agricultural disruption was caused both by the embargo and the war. The embargo led, for example, to a lack of fertilizers, the inability to apply pesticides by aerial spraying, the lack of replacement parts for irrigation, and a lack of harvesting and processing equipment. The war caused, among other things, damage to power stations, disruption of transportation, and the displacement of populations including migrant workers. The combined impact of sanctions and war contributed to a reduction in the post-war 1991 crop harvest by an estimated 25 to 30 percent of the 1990 level.[1] Since then, harvests have still not reached pre-war levels of production.

Impact on Employment and Wages

Damage to Iraq's economy has resulted in escalating unemployment and layoffs. Underemployment is commonplace since the demand for trained technical and professional personnel has diminished. Engineers and technicians, for example, can be seen selling vegetables and cigarettes on street corners and in markets. The demobilization of Iraq's army has added hundreds of thousands of potential workers to an already burgeoning workforce. Many women, children, and elderly people have entered the workforce in order to increase family incomes in the face of increasing hardship. Child labor has increased, as sons and daughters drop out of public school to contribute to the family's income.

Wages have increased since the imposition of sanctions, but have not kept pace with inflation. During 1993, average monthly salaries for civil servants ranged from 200 to 500 dinars, two to three times their August 1990 levels. However, Iraq's food price index increased by nearly 75-fold over the same period of time. Average food prices in 1995 were 4,000 to 5,000 times August 1990 levels. Meanwhile, average

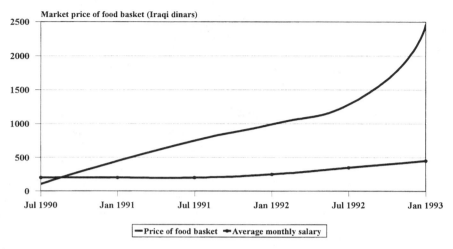

Figure 17-4. Increase in price of Iraqi monthly food basket for a family of six compared to average monthly salary, July 1990–January 1993. By July 1995, the price of the monthly food basket had increased to 194,460 Iraqi dinars and the average monthly salary, to 5,000 Iraqi dinars. The food basket, yielding approximately 3,000 daily kcal per person is comprised per person per month of: 13 kg flour, 3.75 kg rice, 1.050 kg oil, 1.5 kg lentils, 2.75 kg sugar, 0.2 kg tea, 2 kg meat, and 1 kg milk. (Source of food prices: World Food Program, 1993).

real earnings have fallen to less than five percent of their pre-sanctions level, as measured by their power to purchase food.

Figure 17-4 shows the rapid increase in the price of an Iraqi food basket compared to the negligible rise in average monthly salary levels.

Annual per-capita income was estimated at US$335 in 1988 (using the free market exchange rate) and fell to $65 in 1991, and $44 in 1992. These levels are far below the international poverty line of US$100 that has been established by the World Bank. Based on personal income and calorie-purchasing power, the prevalence of poverty is now greater in Iraq than in India.[1] At such low incomes, even considering more than one wage-earner per household, most Iraqi families are unable to generate the funds necessary to meet their basic minimum requirements of food and other essential commodities.

Impact on Household Economy

The damaging effects of sanctions become even more visible upon entering the household of an Iraqi family. Many families already suffer economically from the loss of one or more male wage-earners, killed during the Iran-Iraq War or the Persian Gulf War. Frequently, the woman is the single-parent head of the household and the main generator of income. Whereas 50 percent of family income was spent on food in 1988, almost all middle-class families during the post-war period have been forced to spend all their income on food and other essential commodities.

A monthly food basket for a family of six (providing 3,000 kilocalories per person per day), which cost only 100 dinars in July 1990, cost nearly 2,500 dinars in January 1993 and nearly 200,000 dinars in July 1995. Even taking into account the provision of government food rations (providing approximately 1,100 kilocalories per person per day and roughly 37 percent of daily energy needs), a family of six would still need approximately 125,000 dinars monthly to purchase the shortfall in food. The average monthly salary in July 1995 was approximately 3,000 to 5,000 dinars. Although life-sustaining, the government food ration is inadequate both in terms of quality of food (nutrients) and overall quantity (total caloric content). In addition, some families sell part of their ration on the free market as a means of earning dinars in order to purchase medicines or other essential goods. Even with its distribution shortfalls and the inadequate caloric and protein value of the food distributed, the government food rationing system remains the key to preventing widespread hunger and malnutrition among the civilian population.

Infrastructural Damage—Water and Sanitation

During the air war, all significant electricity-generating plants in Iraq were either totally destroyed or badly damaged, thereby reducing Iraq's capacity to generate electricity to an estimated four percent of pre-war capacity. Similarly, many oil refineries, fuel storage facilities, water pumping stations, and chemical treatment plants were badly damaged by Coalition air strikes. Since Iraq, prior to the war, had been a highly mechanized, electricity-dependent society, the impact of such damage was immediate and profound. A surge in water-borne and sewage-related infectious diseases led to many thousands of post-war civilian deaths, particularly among children. Meanwhile, economic sanctions have prevented repair to Iraq's water and sanitation systems.

Impact on Water Supply

Prior to the Gulf War, in 1990, nearly all urban dwellers and 72 percent of rural residents had access to clean water. From the early hours of the war, the supply of water to Iraqi households was either stopped or greatly reduced. The lack of electricity resulted in a total paralysis of the water purification and supply networks. In addition, a number of water supply and treatment facilities were directly damaged by air bombardment. During a World Health Organization/UNICEF mission in February 1991, the available piped water supply was reported to be between 0 and 15 liters per person per day in Baghdad, less than five percent of the pre-war supply. Throughout Iraq, most people were forced to obtain untreated water from rivers and stagnant ponds.

Even with the gradual post-war restoration of electricity, most water-pumping and water-treatment facilities remained inoperable, or functioned on a very irregular basis. Fluctuations in returning power burned out many pump motors. Spare parts, largely imported, were not available, nor permitted until late March 1991—and then only on a slow case-by-case basis if approved by the United Nations Sanctions Committee.

The low pressure within the gradually recuperating system prevented water from entering many homes. In response, civilians frequently dug their way down to street water mains, broke into the pipes, and inserted plastic hosing to withdraw water. These practices not only further reduced the overall pressure in the system but facilitated the entry of contaminants and raw sewage, contaminating the entire water system downstream from the break. Breakage of pipes in this way occurred on almost every street in southern Iraq.

Further damage to the water supply system, in both the north and south of the country, was caused by the destruction and looting that took place during the unrest of March and April 1991. Tanker trucks used for the distribution of water were often stolen or destroyed. Water testing laboratories were looted of equipment and reagents. Pumping and purification stations were vandalized and burned.

The damage to the water infrastructure was so vast, and the parts so expensive to procure, that it will take years and hundreds of millions of dollars before the water supply network can be rehabilitated to pre-war levels. Without proper reconstruction and repair, it is expected that ad hoc repairs made with substandard or cannibalized spare parts will eventually break down and that the water supply will slowly deteriorate. In 1993, two years after the end of the war, the national water supply was estimated at only 50 percent of pre-war levels. Even in 1996, most families continue to consume contaminated water from the damaged systems or from untreated local sources.

The end result of the damage to Iraq's water purification and supply system has been the dramatically increased rates of infectious diseases, including cholera and other diarrheal illnesses, related to the contaminated water supply.

Impact on Sewage and Sanitation Services

Before the outbreak of war, the major urban centers and most cities on the Tigris and Euphrates rivers had modern sewage treatment systems, while smaller towns and cities relied on older systems consisting of open sewers and septic tanks. With the onset of war, Iraq's sewage collection and treatment system suffered from many of the same difficulties as did the water sector. Since 1991, sewage treatment, also electrically driven, has remained below 50 percent of pre-war capacity.

Iraq's flat topography means that sewage lifting stations are essential to physically move sewage to plants for treatment and eventual discharge into rivers. Many sewage-lifting stations are no longer functioning, and lakes of sewage have formed in residential areas, increasing the risk of epidemics.

During 1995, approximately half of all sewage produced by Baghdad's four million people was discharged untreated into the Tigris, which downstream becomes the principal source of drinking water for most of the densely populated governorates in southern Iraq. Other treatment facilities around the country are in a similar state, or not functioning at all due to a shortage of spare parts or due to damage inflicted during the war.

The system of garbage collection broke down, and huge piles of garbage accumulated in streets and residential areas throughout Iraq. During 1993, it was estimated that Iraq's solid waste collection and disposal system was operating at less than 25 percent of pre-war capacity. At that time, only 18 out of 152 garbage collection vehicles remained in service in the three northern governorates of Dohuk, Erbil, and Sulaimaniyah.

The weakened sewage and sanitation infrastructure, caused by wartime Coalition bombing and years of economic sanctions, is a major health risk to the civilian population. Post-war Iraq has experienced an increase in infectious diseases associated with poor sanitation, including cholera, polio, and typhoid, as well as other water- and sanitation-related diseases, which had reached greatly reduced levels prior to the war.

Health and Disease

The breakdown of health, water and sanitation, and other essential social services which followed the Gulf War led to a dramatic upsurge in infectious disease and malnutrition. Shortages of medicines made treatment difficult and contributed to high rates of ''delayed mortality,'' which greatly surpassed the number of civilian casualties occurring during the war itself.

Medical Services

Both during and after the war, physical damage was sustained by many health facilities. The Iraqi Ministry of Health in Baghdad was badly damaged following a direct hit by a cruise missile. Several hospitals were hit by poorly targeted free-falling bombs, while many facilities had windows shattered during near misses. During the post-war unrest, both government and rebel troops often occupied hospitals because of their strategic worth and because they were generally modern, well-equipped facilities. Such occupation frequently led to violent exchange of gunfire and artillery, and hence massive damage to health facilities.

In the immediate post-war period, hospital personnel were unable to find transport to work. Medicines stored in Baghdad could not reach outlying areas due to the lack of fuel for transport. Hospitals lacked electricity, water, and sanitation, which further limited their usefulness. Hundreds of community-level health centers were closed. Hospitals effectively became empty shells, unable to provide even basic medical or surgical care. By the end of the war, therefore, all but the most rudimentary diagnostic and therapeutic capabilities of Iraq's health care system had been eliminated.

Medicines

Despite exemptions for ''supplies intended strictly for medical purposes,'' as mentioned in United Nations Security Council Resolution 661, supplies of basic medicines began to be in short supply even before the onset of war. Iraq historically imported nearly $500 million worth of medicines and medical supplies each year. Many suppliers, with the onset of the embargo, refused to ship orders to Iraq, fearing legal or political repercussions from their governments. With Iraqi overseas assets frozen, suppliers were also reluctant to ship without being sure that they would get paid.

Sanctions led to shortages in medicines, vaccines, syringes, anesthetics, and materials used for surgery, radiology, and laboratory and diagnostic tests. As early as February 1991, medical stocks were at one-sixth of normal levels, with the supplies of many essential medicines having been completely exhausted.[12] During the first days of the war, the break in electricity destroyed all refrigerated and frozen vaccines, medicines, and laboratory reagents.

A shortage of insulin led to deaths of children and adults with insulin-dependent diabetes. Children with treatable cancers, including leukemia, were unable to find anticancer drugs. X-ray films, laboratory reagents, sutures, intravenous fluids, and antibiotics were also in short supply. After the war began and most laboratory reagents were destroyed by the power outage, there was no screening of transfused blood for the human immunodeficiency virus (HIV) and hepatitis B virus (HBV). Disposable syringes, needles, and surgical gloves were in short supply and were repeatedly reused. A shortage of anesthetics led to deferral of most nonemergency surgery. The setting of bones and, in some cases, leg amputations were sometimes performed without anesthesia.

International organizations, overwhelmed by the acute need for drugs and medical supplies, focused on medicines and supplies for children with infectious diseases. However, this meant that chronic diseases, as well as illnesses specific to the adult population, including the elderly, were not given adequate attention. As a result, an increase in deaths due to stroke and heart attack was observed as antihypertensive and antianginal medicines were no longer available in Iraq.

Infant and Child Mortality

In August 1991, the Harvard-based International Study Team conducted the most comprehensive assessment of child deaths due to the Gulf War and its aftermath. The team surveyed more than 9,000 households in nearly 300 population centers throughout Iraq and estimated mortality rates; the infant mortality rate rose from 33 deaths per 1,000 live births pre-war to 93 post-war (1991), accounting for 33,000 excess deaths between January and August 1991; the under-five mortality rate rose from 43 pre-war to 129 post-war (1991), accounting for 47,000 excess deaths between January and August 1991.[13]

It was estimated that 111,000 civilians died in 1991 from health effects. Of these deaths, 70,000 were of children under 15 years of age, while another 8,500 were of people more than 65 years old. It was also estimated that 56,000 military personnel and 3,500 civilians died during the war, while post-war violence accounted for another 35,000 deaths. Therefore, an estimated total of 205,500 Iraqis died as a direct consequence of the Gulf War. Seventy percent of these deaths were among civilians. Furthermore, 30 times more civilians died after the war (due to war-related health effects) than during the military conflict.[2]

A 1995 study conducted by the United Nations Food and Agriculture Organization (FAO) found that health conditions in post-war Iraq had deteriorated even further. The mortality rate for children under five was found by FAO to be five times higher than in the immediate pre-war period. In absolute terms, it estimated that approximately 500,000 more children than expected died in the five-year period following the war.[14]

Infectious Diseases

The breakdown in water and sanitation that occurred during the Gulf War was responsible for outbreaks of cholera, typhoid, acute gastroenteritis, malaria, meningitis, brucellosis, measles, polio, hepatitis, and other infectious diseases. Contaminated water supplies and poor sanitation created health conditions that enabled diarrhea to emerge as the leading child killer during the post-war period. During both 1991 and 1992, mortality due to diarrhea was estimated at more than three times the 1990 levels.[15]

Cholera, which during the 1980s was scarcely detected, reached epidemic levels in 1991 with nearly 1,000 confirmed cases. Typhoid also spread rapidly, and during 1991 the number of cases more than doubled compared to 1990. In Sulaimaniyah, monthly reported typhoid cases increased from 426 cases in January 1992 to 2,180 cases in January 1993.

Post-war environmental hazards, including poor hygiene and contaminated water, resulted in outbreaks of hepatitis A, especially in urban areas. Hepatitis B became more prevalent due to the reuse of disposable syringes and needles, and the lack of testing of blood supplies for HBV. Poor hygiene has also led to increases in the prevalence of intestinal parasites and scabies.

An upsurge in acute respiratory infections occurred due to the poor post-war living conditions, crowding, and increased exposure to harsh climates. The lack of meaningful medical treatment and the higher prevalence of malnutrition increased the proportion of such infections resulting in death. The incidence of malaria increased due to the lack of aerial and ground spraying, while large areas of stagnant water became breeding grounds for mosquitos.

Vaccination Services

Before the Gulf War, Iraq's Expanded Program on Immunization (EPI) had made significant progress. The Ministry of Health and UNICEF reported high levels of immunization for all vaccines. By 1990, coverage had reached levels greater than 80 percent of eligible children.[16,17]

Within a few days of the start of the Gulf War, a collapse of the primary health care services brought Iraq's vaccination services to a halt. Refrigerated and frozen vaccines were destroyed by the war-time breakdown in electricity that occurred with the onset of war. Iraq's only syringe factory was destroyed during Coalition bombardment. With the gradual post-war restoration of electricity, unstable electric current and frequent electricity cuts damaged many refrigeration units. Post-war unrest generally destroyed what was left of the refrigeration units, syringes, and other vaccination materials.

In all parts of the country, vaccine services were suspended from January until March 1991. This suspension of services led to a massive backlog of hundreds of thousands of unvaccinated children and women who were left susceptible to infection. It was not until late 1991 that vaccine programs were again reestablished at near pre-war levels.

The reduction in vaccine coverage, combined with poor post-war water supply and sanitation, led to a resurgence of vaccine-preventable diseases. For polio, previously in sharp decline with only 10 cases reported in 1989, there were 186 cases in 1991, and 120 in 1992. Diphtheria increased from 96 reported cases during 1989, to 369 cases in 1992. In 1992, a measles epidemic swept through Iraq with almost 20,000 reported cases.

Recent vaccination campaigns have reduced the risks of full-scale epidemics. However, the Expanded Program on Immunization (EPI) has been weakened due to the war and sanctions and will require considerable material input before it can regain its pre-war status and capacity.

Maternal Health and Prenatal Care

More than 750,000 babies are born each year in Iraq. Since the Gulf War has undermined the health care system's ability to provide mothers with adequate prenatal care and delivery services, the impact has been considerable on maternal and perinatal mortality, as well as on the incidence of severe complications resulting from inadequate care.

A shortage of nitrous oxide and other general anesthetics used during cesarean sections led to an increase in maternal and perinatal deaths. The prevalence of anemia during pregnancy increased because women's diets were deficient in iron and folic acid; this, in turn, led to complications of pregnancy and low-birthweight infants (less than 2.5 kilograms). The percentage of low-birthweight babies increased from four percent in August 1990 to 17 percent in late 1992 and 22 percent in 1995.

Even if hospital delivery services can be restored to pre-war levels, the underlying socioeconomic conditions, poverty, and malnutrition have increased the risks of child-birth. It is likely that the current prevalence of nutrient-deficient mothers, low-birthweight infants, and malnourished children will result in retarded mental and physical development of many thousands Iraqi children.

Nutrition

Following the imposition of sanctions in August 1990, food became increasingly scarce and costly. By early January 1991, supplies of many essential commodities (including wheat, rice, vegetable oil, and sugar) were scarce and very tightly con-trolled. Food prices were already 5 to 20 times their pre-sanctions levels.[10] During the war, the lack of transport, communication, and electricity led to a collapse of the country's normal mechanisms for food distribution. The result was an acute food deficit that continued for the duration of the war and compelled most families to rely on hoarded food stocks.

In the post-war period, limited food imports, decreased domestic production, and increasing food prices restricted the population's access to essential food. Malnutrition quickly emerged as one of the biggest threats to Iraqi children. In June 1991, UNICEF indicated an "alarming and rising incidence of severe and moderate malnutrition among the population of children under age five."[18] Its concern was echoed by the FAO report of July 1991 warning that Iraq was "approaching the threshold of extreme deprivation." In July 1993, two years after the war, the FAO warned that "a vast majority of the Iraqi population" was facing "persistent deprivation, severe hunger, and malnutrition", and that "large numbers of Iraqis now have food intakes lower than those of the populations in the disaster-stricken African countries."[19] In August 1995, the FAO reported that the level of child malnutrition in Baghdad was similar to that seen in Ghana and Mali. FAO wrote that "there is a strong possibility of an outright collapse of the food and agricultural economy."[20]

Post-War Nutritional Surveys

Several nutritional surveys were carried out in post-war Iraq during 1991 and are summarized in Table 17-1. The surveys differ in the methodology used, the location, and characteristics of the surveyed children. For these reasons, they should be viewed

Table 17-1.   Early post-war nutritional studies[a]

Study Authors	Survey Date	Survey Location	Number of Children	Age Group Surveyed	Weight-for-age[b] (percent)	Height-for-age[c] (percent)	Weight-for-height[d] (percent)
Helen Keller, Save the Children, UNICEF	May 1991	Basra	231	<6 years	40	18	10
Tufts University	June 1991	Basra/Amara	680	<5 years	26	39	4
UNICEF Basra	July/ August 1991	Basra	742	<5 years	22	21	7
International Study Team	August 1991	National (300 sites)	2,902	<5 years	12	22	3
Catholic Relief Services	December 1991	Baghdad	315	<5 years	17	9	11
UNICEF Tehran	May 1991	Kurdish camps in Iran	900	<5 years	32	29	not measured

[a]Percentage malnutrition indicated is moderate and severe (< −2 standard deviations from the reference median). Although not reported here, most of the above studies also found levels of mild malnutrition (< −1 standard deviation) of approximately 25 percent in addition to the percentages of moderate and severe malnutrition shown in the three columns at the right of this table.

[b]Weight-for-age = Underweight = an indicator of acute and/or chronic malnutrition, reflecting stunting and/or wasting.

[c]Height-for-age = Stunting = an indicator of chronic or long-standing malnutrition, reflecting decreased skeletal growth.

[d]Weight-for-height = Wasting = an indicator of acute malnutrition, reflecting weight loss or short-term growth failure.

as individual case studies and not considered representative of the situation in Iraq as a whole. An exception to this is the survey by the International Study Team, which was a representative national survey of nearly 3,000 children in 300 randomly selected locations throughout Iraq. Levels reported in the table are combined percentages for both moderate and severe malnutrition.

Baghdad Nutritional Study

UNICEF conducted a study examining the same cohort (group) of children over a prolonged period of time, attempting to assess, separately, the nutritional impact of sanctions and war. The data reflect changes in nutritional status among a population of Baghdad children observed over a three-year period, beginning in 1989.[21,22] It was carried out at the Sheikh Omar Health Center, which serves an area populated largely by families of low socioeconomic status. Using weight-for-age (percentage under-

Table 17-2. Baghdad post-war nutritional survey[a]

| Study Date | Number of Children (1-3 years) | Weight-for-age (Children 1–3 years) | | Nutritional Status Compared to WHO Reference (Z-score) |
		Mild (percent underweight)	Moderate to Severe (percent underweight)	
January 1989–August 1990 (Pre-sanctions)	620	13	8	−0.19
August–December 1990 (Sanctions, pre-war)	1060	19	10	−0.57
January–May 1991 (Sanctions, war)	1412	33	11	−0.82
March 1992 (Sanctions, post-war)	1259	31	12	−0.78

Source: Al-Hadi, A., and Obeid, O., 1992. (Both references 21 and 22.)

[a]Moderate and severe malnutrition refers to children with malnutrition < -2 standard deviations from the median of standard reference curves. For the pre-sanctions period, nutritional levels were almost identical to World Health Organization (WHO) standards for an adequately nourished population. A negative number in the table indicates a nutritional status that is worse than the WHO standard. The larger negative values indicate a worsening nutritional status.

weight, as an indicator of both acute and/or chronic malnutrition), the team found the results shown in Table 17-2 (see Figure 17-5).

If one includes mild malnutrition in the analysis, malnutrition among children less than three years of age increased during both the pre-war period of sanctions (August–December 1990) and the wartime and immediate post-war period (January–May 1991). Although one year following the war nutritional conditions had improved somewhat, they were still considerably worse than before the imposition of sanctions and still worse than the pre-war sanctions period. More recently, in 1995, FAO reported a four-fold increase in wasting for the city of Baghdad compared with 1991 estimates. Prevalence estimates for stunting and underweight had also risen dramatically. It is important to note that malnutrition makes both children and adults more vulnerable to contracting and dying from other diseases.[23]

The post-war government ration was also deficient in micronutrients, including vitamins A, D, B_{12}, riboflavin, iron, folic acid, and iodine. Numerous cases of iron deficiency anemia were detected, and nutritional surveys confirmed a high prevalence of anemia in both children and pregnant women. The incidence of iodine deficiency (manifested by goiter) increased, as did that of rickets (vitamin D deficiency).

The post-war nutritional status of the country as a whole can be characterized by an overall nutritional deficit. Most people have, for many years, been consuming a diet deficient in calories, protein, and essential vitamins and nutrients. Although the caloric intake has been adequate to prevent overt starvation, it has most certainly led

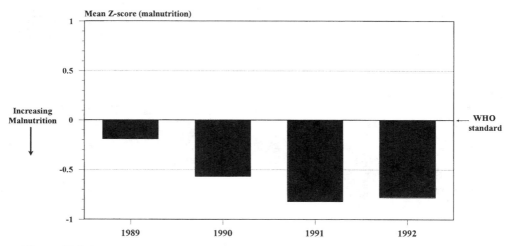

Figure 17-5. Increase in weight-for-age malnutrition among children 1–3 years of age in Baghdad, 1989–1992 (Source: UNICEF, Baghdad).

to a chronic state of nutritional deficiency, making both adults and children more susceptible to illness and death.

Nutritional status is determined by a combination of one's access to nutritious foods, the ability to care for oneself—or in the case of children, the mother's ability to spend time caring for the physical well-being of her child—and access to health care. War and sanctions have compromised all three of these determinants of nutritional status. The result has been an overall reduction in the level of nutrition of most Iraqi civilians, which has greatly increased morbidity and mortality. Recovery from the low level of nutrition, even with the 1996 "sale-of-oil" agreement, is likely to be slow.

Women

Iraqi women have shouldered considerable burdens as a result of the Persian Gulf War. More than 10 percent of married Iraqi women are widows. Many are single parents and sole wage-earners, having to cope with severe economic difficulties. Work for them is more difficult to find, and more women have had to join the informal working sector, selling such items as fish, vegetables, or tea. Mothers are preoccupied with satisfying their children's and family's needs, and household chores have become more time-consuming. Their health suffers because of nutritional problems, a lack of prenatal care, and shortages of medicines. Despite all these difficulties, Iraqi women must be credited with holding together the basis of Iraqi society—the household.

During the Iran-Iraq War, women were often left solely responsible for the household, including elderly relatives and young children. After the Persian Gulf War, hundreds of thousands of men were decommissioned from the military and returned home. Most have remained unemployed and without any income, which has increased the burden on the women's ability to provide for the family.

Securing adequate quantities of food became a main preoccupation for Iraqi women. Mothers often went hungry and gave their share of food to their children. Many families became totally dependent on government rations and charity. By August 1991, many Iraqi families had already used up their savings and were forced to sell their personal belongings. Forty-eight percent of families surveyed by the International Study Team in 1991 had incurred heavy debts.[24] This increased the dependency and vulnerability of many women and their families, sometimes leading to begging or, in more extreme cases, prostitution.

Sixty percent of women interviewed by the International Study Team indicated that they suffered from psychological problems including depression, anxiety, headache, and insomnia. Often anxieties manifested themselves as physical problems, including weight loss, menstrual irregularity, difficulty breastfeeding, and other illnesses.

Daily chores, such as purchasing and preparing food, became more time-consuming than before the crisis. New chores such as waiting in line for water and collecting firewood (especially in northern governorates) added to women's burden in the household. Mothers stood in line for hours, waiting for medicines or medical consultations for their children. Male frustration at inability to find employment often led to family conflict. Marital breakups were reported to have increased during the post-war period.

In the concluding paragraph of its women's study,[25] the International Study Team reported: ''Iraqi women have experienced this whole crisis not only as victims, but also as crucial actors who have sustained the family and the society. The basis of the Iraqi society, the home, has been held together by their ingenuity and strength—despite their own economic, social, emotional and psychological deprivation.''

Children in Especially Difficult Circumstances

Psychological Impact

The Gulf Crisis has left many lasting psychological scars on the minds of Iraqi children. For many of them, the war and its aftermath have taken away their hope for the future and have left them feeling anxious, fearful, and uncertain. (See also Chapter 12.)

In August 1991 and again in 1992, 214 children of primary school age were interviewed by child psychologists expert in the impact of conflict on children. Two-thirds of the children interviewed did not even believe they would survive to become adults. The study revealed the level of psychological stress and pathological behavior to be the highest ever recorded by the psychologists in over 10 years of experience in conflict-affected areas.[26] Their findings led the researchers to conclude that post-war Iraqi children were ''the most traumatized children of war ever described.''

Disabled Children

The Iran-Iraq War and, more recently, the Gulf War have added thousands of victims to the numbers of physically handicapped children in Iraq, especially amputees. Unexploded ordnance, land mines, and the use of anti-personnel bombs have in particular affected Iraqi children. It is estimated that thousands of children have lost their limbs, many in the northern governorates, due to exploding land mines and other ordnance.

Apart from death, there is no other effect of war upon children more profound or long-lasting than being maimed or incapacitated. Such injuries not only affect the physical and emotional development of the child, but also long-term prospects as an adult for work, marriage, social life, self-support, and dignity. The wounded, permanently damaged child becomes a burden not only for the family, but for society as a whole.[27] In addition, the economic embargo has made procurement of supportive and rehabilitative materials needed for recovery difficult.

Displaced Children

Tens of thousands of children in the northern governorates of Dohuk, Erbil, and Sulaimaniyah, and many in southern Iraq, are still displaced from their homes. They and their parents eke out an existence that is often wholly dependent on foreign aid and local charity. Their access to health and education is severely limited. Many have only temporary shelter. With them are the many thousands of children who have returned with their parents to towns and villages that were levelled by Iraqi forces during the 1980s. These children also lack the basic necessities of life and reside in makeshift shelters, often with no source of clean water, with minimal food, and with minefields surrounding them.

The Environment

Oil Spills

The first oil spill reportedly occurred on January 22, 1991, when oil was discharged into the ecologically fragile northern Gulf waters. At least three other spills followed, in total covering hundreds of square kilometers of Gulf water, as well as more than 500 kilometers of coastline. An estimated four million barrels of oil were spilled, making the Gulf spill possibly the worst on record. The oil has severely affected the Gulf's wildlife and marine biology, which includes many fragile and endangered species. Human populations were also put directly at risk when their source of water, the many desalination plants along the Gulf coast, was directly affected.

Oil Fires and Atmospheric Effects

More than 500 burning oil fires blackened skies and released thousands of tons of contaminants into the atmosphere, leading to unquantifiable health risks to human and wildlife populations (Figure 5-4). During their emission, oil fires in Kuwait were creating approximately ten times as much air pollution as all industrial and power plants in the United States.[28] Tons of sulfur dioxide and nitrogen oxide released by the burning oil wells came into contact with water droplets, turning into sulfuric and nitric acids and falling to the earth as acid rain. Other toxic chemicals, including benzene (a known carcinogen), toluene, and xylene were dispersed into the atmosphere. Fortunately, the oil fires were all extinguished by November 1991. However, by then, fumes from burning an estimated more than one billion barrels of oil had been discharged into the atmosphere. Furthermore, between 35 and 150 million barrels of oil had been spilled over as much as 60 percent of Kuwait's surface area, forming large shallow black lakes of crude. Much of this spilled oil will also evaporate with its toxic components into the atmosphere. The risk of groundwater contamination is high.[29]

In early February 1991, the National Oceanographic and Atmospheric Administration (NOAA) detected unusually high amounts of soot in the air in Hawaii. Beginning in late January 1991, there were Iranian reports that ''black rain'' was falling in that country. Traces of soot were also found in rain falling in the Himalayas. Toxic particulate matter was deposited heavily over Kuwait and southern Iraq, adversely affecting crops and livestock. In November 1991, nine months after the end of the war, levels of carcinogenic and mutagenic gases, at levels tens of times higher than WHO safety levels, were found.[28]

Chemical and Nuclear Arsenals

Before the Gulf War, Iraq possessed a formidable stockpile of chemical and biological weapons, as well as a growing covert nuclear weapons program. Any use of these weapons would have had not only tragic human consequences (see Chapters 7 and 8), but also far-reaching political manifestations. Although there exists no public evidence of the deliberate use, by Iraq, of chemical weapons during the Gulf War, it is generally believed that such agents were used by Iraqi forces during the Kurdish uprising of March 1991. In 1994, allegations of Iraq's use of chemical weapons—this time against Coalition forces—came from American Gulf War veterans suffering from unexplained illnesses contracted during service in the Gulf.

During the Gulf War, Coalition forces admitted to destroying more than 20 of Iraq's chemical and biological facilities. On January 22, 1991, chemical protection units along the Saudi-Kuwaiti border detected chemical agents in the air, assumed to be the result of bombardment of chemical factories or weapons stockpiles.[8] Similar reports of chemical releases came from other military and anti-chemical units situated in the region. Sites identified by Coalition forces as being part of Iraq's nuclear weapons program were also specifically targeted and destroyed during the Gulf War. By destroying such sites, Coalition forces risked both radioactive and toxic environmental contamination.

Ordnance Hazards

Tens of thousands of tons of bombs were dropped on Iraq during the Gulf War. Many were cluster bombs, which dispersed into hundreds of smaller bomblets. Unexploded bombs still litter the landscape of the Gulf Region. In addition, thousands of land mines were scattered in southern Iraq, Kuwait, and northern Kurdish regions. Unexploded ordnance regularly leads to civilian deaths and injuries, with thousands of casualties estimated to have occurred since the end of the war.

Coalition forces also used radioactive, depleted uranium in many shells and armor-piercing projectiles. Depleted uranium is a radioactive byproduct of the enrichment process used to make atomic bombs and nuclear fuel rods. Used because of its exceedingly high density, hence its effective penetrating capability, between 40 and 300 tons of uranium remain scattered throughout much of southern Iraq and Kuwait. Toxic, like lead, the uranium can become airborne and may be both inhaled and ingested. It can concentrate in the kidneys, lungs, and bones, causing illness. Although low in radioactivity, internalized particles remain for life, constantly emitting low-level radiation to the surrounding tissues. In addition to the direct health risks, it is possible that the depleted uranium may have contaminated soil and drinking water in Iraq and Kuwait. If this is the case, Iraqis and Kuwaitis could be exposed to the radioactive and toxic effects of depleted uranium for generations to come.

Gulf War Syndrome

More than 25,000 American veterans, and a smaller number of British soldiers, have contracted unexplained illnesses since serving in the Gulf War. Known as Gulf War syndrome, signs and symptoms include fatigue, dizziness, joint and muscle pain, weight loss, diarrhea, and rashes. There are also reports of increased levels of illness and congenital disorders in infants born of Gulf War veterans. Although there is, as yet, no firm scientific explanation for Gulf War syndrome, several have been proposed. They include possible side effects of vaccines administered to military personnel prior to service in the Gulf, effects of anti-nerve-gas pills, exposure to contaminants from burning oil fires, contact with chemical and/or biological agents, inhalation of particulates derived from depleted uranium used in Coalition weapons, or possibly parasitic infection (leishmaniasis) endemic to the region. If Gulf War syndrome is a result of exposure to a toxic environmental contaminant, there may be, in the Gulf Region itself, many more thousands of civilian victims of this illness.

REFERENCES

1. Dreze, J. and Gazdar, H. Hunger and poverty in Iraq, 1991. *World Development.* 20:921–945, 1992.
2. Osborne Daponte, B. A case study in estimating casualties from war and its aftermath: The 1991 Persian Gulf War. *PSR Quarterly* 3:57–66, 1991.
3. United Nations Children's Fund. *State of the world's children.* Oxford, England: Oxford University Press, 1992.
4. Haines, A. and Doucet, I.L. Persian Gulf War: The human tragedy. *Medical and Health Annual.* London, England: Encyclopedia Britannica, 1993.
5. Sayegh, J. *Child survival in wartime: A case study from Iraq, 1983–1989.* Baltimore, Maryland: Department of Population Dynamics, The Johns Hopkins School of Hygiene and Public Health, 1992.
6. Middle East Watch. *Needless deaths in the Gulf War.* New York: Human Rights Watch, 1991.
7. United Nations. Report to the Secretary-General on humanitarian needs in Kuwait and Iraq in the immediate post-crisis environment by a mission to the area led by Mr. Martti Ahtisaari, Under-Secretary-General for Administration and Management, dated 20 March 1991. New York: United Nations, 1991.
8. Arkin, W.M., Durrant, D. and Cherni, M. *On impact: Modern warfare and the environment: A case study of the Gulf War.* Washington, D.C.: Greenpeace, 1991.
9. Centers for Disease Control. Public health consequences of acute displacement of Iraqi citizens—March–May 1991. *MMWR* 40:443–446, 1991.
10. Congressional Research Service. CRS report for Congress: Iraq's food and agricultural situation during the embargo and the war. Washington, D.C.: Library of Congress, February 1991.
11. El Dessouky, F. *Basic food import requirements of Iraq for one year (1991/92).* Baghdad, Iraq: United Nations Food and Agricultural Organization, 1992.
12. Taylor, C. and Reid, R. *Children as victims of war.* New York: United Nations Children's Fund, 1991.
13. Ascherio, A., Chase, R., Cote, T., Dehaes, G., Hoskins, E., Laaouej, J., Passey, M., Qaderi, S., Shuqaidef, S., Smith, M. and Zaidi, S. Effect of the Gulf War on infant and child mortality in Iraq. *N. Engl. J. Med.* 327:931–936, 1992.
14. Zaidi, S., and Smith Fawzi, M. Health of Baghdad's children. *Lancet* 346:1485, 1995.
15. United Nations Children's Fund. Children and women in Iraq: A situation analysis. Baghdad, Iraq: United Nations Children's Fund, March 1993.
16. United Nations Children's Fund, World Health Organization. National cluster surveys. Baghdad, Iraq: United Nations Children's Fund, 1985–1989.
17. United Nations Children's Fund, World Health Organization, Economic and Social Commission of Western Asia, Iraq Ministry of Health. Iraq immunization, diarrhoeal disease, maternal and childhood mortality survey 1990. Amman, Jordan: United Nations Children's Fund, 1990.
18. United Nations Children's Fund. Malnutrition in Iraq: Executive summary of field reports. Baghdad, Iraq: United Nations Children's Fund, June 1991.
19. United Nations Food and Agricultural Organization. Special feature: Food supply situation and crop outlook in Iraq. Rome, Italy: Food and Agricultural Organization, July 1993.

20. United Nations Food and Agriculture Organization. *Evaluation of food and nutrition situations in Iraq*. Rome: FAO, 1995

21. Al-Hadi, A. and Obeid, O. Report on the changes in the nutritional status of Iraqi children between 2 January 1989 and 26 May 1991. Baghdad, Iraq: United Nations Children's Fund, February 1992.

22. Al-Hadi, A. and Obeid, O. Report on the nutritional status of Iraqi children: One year following the Gulf War and sustained sanctions. Baghdad, Iraq: United Nations Children's Fund, March 1992.

23. Grant, J.P. Nutritional security: An ethical imperative of the 1990s. Unpublished paper presented at the International Conference on Nutrition, Rome, Italy, December 1992.

24. International Study Team. Health and welfare in Iraq after the Gulf crisis: An in-depth assessment, October 1991.

25. Bhatia, B., Kawar, M. and Shahin, M. Unheard voices: Iraqi women on war and sanctions. In *Change: Women and society*. London: Calverts Press, March 1992.

26. Raundalen, M. and Dyregrov, A. *The long-term impact of the Gulf War on the children of Iraq*. Bergen, Norway: Research for Children, February 1992.

27. Consultative Group on Early Childhood Care and Development. *Protecting children from the scourge of war*. New York: UNICEF, October 1991.

28. Medical Educational Trust. *Continuing health costs of the Gulf War*. London: Medical Educational Trust, April 1992.

29. Greenpeace. *Findings of Greenpeace on-site study of the environmental impacts of the Gulf War*. London: Greenpeace, December 1991.

VI

The Roles of Public Health Professionals and Organizations in War

18

The Roles and Ethics of Health Professionals in War

VICTOR W. SIDEL

Ethical conflicts occur whenever the health professions and war intersect. This chapter deals with four general types of potential ethical conflict:

1. Conflict between the obligation of military health personnel to provide medical care and other health services to members of the military force of which they are members and the medical obligation to serve others—such as members of opposing military forces and civilians—who need their services.
2. Conflict between the obligation of military health personnel to "conserve the fighting strength" and the medical obligation to respond to the special needs or rights of individual military personnel under their care, even if such response hinders the "fighting strength."
3. Conflict between "combatant" and "noncombatant" roles for health personnel.
4. Conflict between the national obligation to serve one's country through service in a military force and the international obligation to prevent war or to prevent specific actions by the military force of one's own country.

The history of physician involvement with military forces is a long one. Homer praised the efforts of the sons of Asclepios in providing surgical care before the gates of Troy,[1] and Hippocrates, recognizing the battleground as an important training ground for surgeons, urged that "he who would become a surgeon should join an army and follow it."[2]

But health personnel had relatively little to offer military forces until the eighteenth century. Since then rapid developments in military weaponry and concurrent advances in medical technology and in techniques for evacuation of casualties have made de-

Excerpted and adapted from: Sidel, V. W. Warfare: Medicine and War. *Encyclopedia of bioethics (second edition)*, Warren T. Reich, editor-in-chief, Vol. 5, pp. 2533–2538. Copyright 1995 by Warren T. Reich. Used by permission of Macmillan Reference USA, a division of Simon & Shuster.

ployment of medical resources increasingly important to armies and their commanders for the treatment of casualties. Perhaps even more important, developments in public health made its practitioners useful in the prevention of disease. To the armies of the czar, for example, Peter the Great brought the *feldsher,* modeled on the *feldscherer* (field barber-surgeon) of the Prussian armies. In the New World, deplorable medical care during the American Revolution caused bitter political conflicts over the management of hospitals and health care for soldiers. The increase in the number of military casualties during the wars of the nineteenth century and the extraordinary increase in both military and civilian casualties during the wars of the twentieth century, together with dramatic improvements in the ability to treat casualties successfully and to prevent illness, led to changes in the types of ethical issues that arise and an increase in their number.

Military Obligations versus Health Professional Obligations

As a member of the military forces of a nation, the military health professional is charged with the mission of protecting the strength of the military force. As a member of the health professions, on the other hand, the practitioner is generally obligated to provide public health and preventive services for all impartially and to care for all the sick and wounded who need his or her services, setting those priorities on the basis of the urgency and effectiveness of health and medical needs. Hippocrates, often called "the father of medicine," apparently rejected the principle that physicians have an obligation in war to succor "enemies" as well as "friends." The evidence is found in Plutarch's *Lives,* in a reference to "Hippocrates' reply when the Great King of Persia consulted him, with the promise of a fee of many talents, namely, that he would never put his skill at the service of Barbarians who were enemies of Greece."[3]

Just before the start of the U.S. Civil War, the American Medical Association (AMA) selected, as the model for a commemorative stone carving for placement in the Washington Monument, then being built in the District of Columbia, the painting *Hippocrates Refuses the Gifts of Artaxerxes,* portraying Hippocrates's dismissal of the emissaries of the king of Persia (Figure 18-1). The inscription the AMA selected was *Vincit Amor Patriae,* "Love of Country Prevails."[4]

In a time of "unjustifiable and monstrous rebellion," a phrase used contemporaneously by one of its leaders, the AMA probably meant by its use of the painting and the inscription to applaud the refusal to provide medical services for enemies. Indeed no evidence can be found that in the pre–Civil-War United States there was a great deal of sympathy for evenhanded medical care in time of war.[5]

Figure 18-1. Hippocrates refuses to treat Persian soldiers suffering from the plague during the Persian War against Greece. (Painting by Anne-Louis Girodet de Roucy: *Hippocrate refusant les présents d'Artaxercés* [Hippocrates refuses the gifts of Artaxerxes], 1792)

Physicians as Impartial Healers

The physician's responsibility to treat those in medical need on both sides did not burn itself into either public or medical consciousness until the late 1860s, in the aftermath of the Crimean War and the U.S. Civil War. Leadership in raising this new consciousness was assumed by nurses and by others who were not physicians, such as Florence Nightingale, who served as a nurse in Turkey and the Crimea from 1854 to 1856, and Dorothea Dix, whose work in bringing humane care to mental patients in the United States led President Abraham Lincoln to invite her to organize the U.S. Army Nursing Corps and to become the first Superintendent of Nurses in the U.S. Army. (See Chapter 23 for a description of the role of public health nurses in attempts to prevent World War I.)

Henri Dunant, a Swiss banker who was an eyewitness at the Battle of Solferino in 1859, organized medical services for the Austrian and French wounded. A few years later, he helped initiate an international conference in Geneva that led to the founding of the Red Cross and its national affiliates. The conference adopted a Convention for the Amelioration of the Condition of the Wounded and Sick in Armed Forces in the Field. Fourteen signatory nations pledged to regard the sick and wounded, as well as personnel, facilities, and transport for their care, as neutrals on the battlefield. For his efforts, Dunant was awarded the first Nobel Peace Prize.

Two contemporaneous events in the United States influenced future codifications and applications of international law and their bearing on medicine. Francis Lieber, a German-born philosopher-lawyer-historian, was commissioned by the Union forces in the Civil War to draft a code of conduct for armies in the field. The resultant Lieber Code was promulgated in May 1863 as General Order No. 100 by the Union Army. Closely related to this development was the 1865 trial of Captain Henry Wirz, a physician who served as commandant of the infamous Confederate prison at Andersonville, Georgia. He was charged with a series of offenses alleging inhumane regard for prisoners under his charge. His plea of "superior orders" mitigating the negligence of duty with which he was charged was disallowed, and Wirz was convicted and sentenced to be hanged.

During the 80 years following the first Geneva treaty on treatment of war casualties, three other related international agreements were negotiated in the Hague and in Geneva. The Convention for the Amelioration of the Wounded, Sick, and Shipwrecked Members of Armed Forces at Sea dealt with the care of casualties of naval warfare. The Convention Relative to the Treatment of Prisoners of War regulated the treatment and repatriation of prisoners. The Convention Relative to the Protection of Civilian Persons in Time of War prohibited deportation, taking of hostages, torture, and discrimination in treatment. These three agreements, plus the original Geneva accord, were codified in a single, formal document in Geneva in 1949; together, they are called the Geneva Conventions. Agreed to at that time by 60 nations, the 1949 conventions were declared binding upon all nations according to "customary law, the usages established among civilized people . . . the laws of humanity, and the dictates of the public conscience".[6]

Under the conventions, medical personnel are given certain specific protections by an explicit separation of their medical role from the combatant role. Medical personnel and treatment facilities are designated as immune from attack, and captured medical personnel are to be promptly repatriated. In return, specific obligations are required of medical personnel:

1. Regarded as "noncombatants," medical personnel are forbidden to engage in or be parties to the acts of war.
2. The wounded and sick—soldier and civilian, friend and foe—must be respected, protected, treated humanely, and cared for by the belligerents.
3. The wounded and sick must not be left without medical assistance, and only urgent medical reasons authorize any priority in the order of their treatment.
4. Medical aid must be dispensed solely on medical grounds, "without distinctions founded on sex, race, nationality, religion, political opinions, or any other similar criteria."
5. Medical personnel shall exercise no physical or moral coercion against protected persons (civilians), in particular to obtain information from them or from third parties.

Such duties are imposed clearly, permitting no exceptions, and are given priority over all other considerations. Thus, the Geneva Conventions formalized the recognition that, while professional expertise merits special privileges, it likewise incurs very specific legal as well as moral obligations.[7] That special role of health professionals is now embodied in the public expectations and in the ethical training of health professionals in most societies. It is also embedded in the World Medical Association's Declaration of Geneva, which is administered as a "modern Hippocratic Oath" to graduating classes at many medical schools. At least one school of public health envisions an analogous role for public health professionals. At the annual commencement of the School of Public Health at Columbia University, the dean has established the custom of handing each graduate a copy of the Universal Declaration of Human Rights with the diploma.

There is, however, evidence of deviation from these principles. An example of the erosion of the principle of equal medical care for "enemies" occurred in the United States during the Cold War. The medical society of Maryland and the AMA refused to criticize a Maryland psychiatrist who testified voluntarily before the Un-American Activities Committee of the U.S. House of Representatives in 1960 about information he had obtained in the course of treatment of an employee of the National Security Agency (NSA). His patient, together with another NSA employee with whom the patient had allegedly had a sexual relationship, later defected to the USSR. The psychiatrist, clearly without his patient's permission, provided to the committee information given to him by his patient, and the material was leaked to the press by the committee. To a petition by a group of Maryland psychiatrists and other physicians asking that the psychiatrist be censured, the medical society responded that "the interests of the nation transcend those of the individual."[8]

Obligations to Enhance Military Strength versus the Needs of Individual Military Personnel

Military health professionals must accept different priorities than do their civilian colleagues.[2] The primary role of the military health professional is expressed in the motto of the U.S. Army Medical Department: "To conserve the fighting strength."[9] In describing this role, a faculty member of the Academy of Health Sciences at Fort Sam Houston in 1988 cited as "the clear objective of all health service support operations" the goal stated in 1866 by a veteran of the Army of the Potomac in the U.S. Civil War: ". . . [to] strengthen the hands of the commanding general by keeping his Army in the most vigorous health, thus rendering it, in the highest degree, efficient for enduring fatigue and privitation [sic], and for fighting."[10]

Principles of triage unacceptable in civilian practice may be required, such as placing first emphasis on patching up the lightly wounded so they can be sent back to battle. For example, "overevacuation" (the presumed excessive transfer of personnel to a safe area rather than back to the military operation) is cited as "one of the cardinal sins of military medicine."[9] Violation of patient confidentiality unacceptable in civilian practice may be required. Medical personnel may be required to administer experimental drugs or immunizations to troops without their free and informed consent.[11]

Combatant versus Noncombatant Roles for Health Personnel

Perhaps history's most dramatic attempt to meld these conflicting obligations was made by the Knights Hospitallers of St. John of Jerusalem, members of a religious order founded in the eleventh century. With a sworn fealty to "our Lords the Sick," the Knights defended their hospitals against "enemies of the Faith," becoming the first organized military medical officers. They were "warring physicians who could strike the enemy mighty blows, and yet later bind up the wounds of that same enemy along with those of their own comrades."[7]

A more recent example of erosion of the distinction between combatant and noncombatant roles was demonstrated in a U.S. Army exhibit at the 1967 AMA Convention. It was titled "Medicine as a Weapon" and featured a photograph of a Green Beret (Special Forces) Aidman handing medicine to a Vietnamese peasant.[12] Dr. Peter Bourne, who had been an Army physician working with the Special Forces in Vietnam, wrote that the primary task of Special Forces Medics was "to seek and destroy the enemy and only incidentally to take care of the medical needs of others on the patrol."[12]

In 1967, Howard Levy, a dermatologist drafted into the U.S. Army Medical Department as a captain, refused to obey an order to train Special Forces Aidmen in dermatological skills. He refused specifically on the grounds that the aidmen were being trained predominantly for a combat role and that crosstraining in medical techniques eroded the distinction between combatants and noncombatants. For this refusal he was charged with one of the most serious breaches of the Uniform Code of Military Justice: willfully disobeying a lawful order. Tried by a general court-martial in 1967, Levy admitted his disobedience, saying he had acted in accordance with his ethical principles. The physicians who testified for the defense "argued that the political use of medicine by the Special Forces jeopardized the entire tradition of the noncombatant status of medicine."[13] They agreed with Levy that a physician is responsible for even the secondary ethical implications of his acts; that he must not only act ethically himself, but also anticipate that those to whom he teaches medicine will act ethically as well. Although Levy was a medical officer, the court-martial panel did not include a physician. Levy was given a dishonorable discharge and sentenced to three years of hard labor in a military prison; his appeals were not successful.[13,14]

Inside or outside the armed forces, health professionals may also be involved in war-related research and development, such as work on biological weapons or on the radiation effects of nuclear weapons. In such work, it is said to have been common practice to concentrate physicians into "principally or primarily defensive operations."[15] But work on weapons and their effects can never be exclusively defensive, and at times the distinction is quite arbitrary. The question arises whether there is a special ethical duty for health professionals (because of their ethical obligation to "do no harm") to refuse to participate in such work, or whether in situations that do not involve patient care health professionals simply share the ethical duties of all human beings.[16]

The noncombatant role of health professionals in military service is an ambiguous one, even if frank combatant activities are eschewed. Military health professionals, like all members of the armed forces, are limited by threat of military discipline in the extent to which they can publicly protest what they believe to be an unjust war. The issue of what is a "just war," which has been debated for over two millennia, can be touched on only briefly here.[17,18] There are generally held to be two elements in a just war: *jus ad bellum* (when is it just to go to war?), and *jus in bello* (what methods may be used in a just war?). Among the elements required for *jus ad bellum* are a just grievance and the exhaustion of all means short of war to settle the grievance. Among the elements required for *jus in bello* are protection of noncombatants and proportionality of force, including avoiding use of weapons of mass destruction such as chemical, biological, and nuclear weapons, and massive bombing of cities. Membership in the armed forces, even in a noncombatant role, usually requires self-censorship of public doubts about the justness of a war in which the armed forces are engaged.

In addition, health professionals, like other human beings, may consider themselves pacifists. "Absolute pacifism" opposes the use of any force against another human being, even in self-defense against direct, personal attack. The argument underlying this position, for many of its adherents, is that the use of force can only be ended when all humans refuse to use it, and that acceptance of one's own injury or even death is preferable to use of force against another. More limited forms of pacifism, such as "nuclear pacifism," hold that the use of certain weapons of mass destruction in war is never justified, no matter how great the provocation or how terrible the consequences of failure to use them. It has been suggested under the term "maternal pacifism" that women, because of their nurturing roles, have a special responsibility to oppose the use of force.[19] (See box.)

When a group is threatened with genocide, as the Nazis attempted in World War II, many who might otherwise adopt a pacifist or limited pacifist position believe that force may be justified. Their shift in position is based on the threat to the very survival of the group, a threat that makes the pacifist argument—that current failure to resist will lead to future diminution in violence—seem untenable.

Women in Military Service

Mary-Wynne Ashford and Yolanda Huet-Vaughn

Despite the suffering women experience in war (see Chapter 13) and despite the estimate that 70 percent of the workers for peace and social justice in the world are women (see Chapter 23), it is clear that women do not unanimously oppose war. It is simplistic to suggest that women are by their biologic nature more peace-loving than men. Women have, even without taking combat roles, supported wars by working in war industries, serving in support positions in the armed forces, working as nurses on the front lines, encouraging their husbands and sons to enlist, and voting for leaders who take their countries to war. U.S. women led the "yellow ribbon" campaign in support of the Persian Gulf War. Women leaders, such as Margaret Thatcher, have shown themselves as ready to go to war as any of their male counterparts.

In most countries, the possibility of women taking combat roles is rejected by the military because of the assumption that women lack the necessary physical strength. The increasing participation of women in military service has forced reevaluation of this position and a recognition that in modern technological warfare, physical strength may not be a critical factor. Some analysts have suggested that a continuing concern in the military is: "If you let the women in, then who are the men protecting and who can they feel superior to?"[1]

The question of combat roles brings out at least two positions among feminists. One position holds that women are entitled to equal opportunities for jobs that pay well, offer education and advancement, and offer the possibility to give one's life for one's country. Therefore, not only should women be able to serve in combat alongside men, but they have a patriotic duty to do so. The other position holds that the equality being offered is like an equal opportunity to serve in slavery. This position maintains that women should work to end the entire war system, which they see as a classic case of patriarchy, and that women should not support either men or women in combat roles.

In fact, women have participated in civil wars, nationalist wars, and anti-colonial movements. Women were mobilized in the French and Russian revolutions, and in wars of liberation, such as in Nicaragua and South Africa. In the Vietnam War, 10,000 American women served in the armed

1. Dyer, G. Anybody's son will do. In *War.* Toronto: National Film Board of Canada, 1983.

There is considerable debate whether health professionals, because of a special dedication to preservation of life and health, have a special obligation to serve or to refuse to serve in a military effort. That position is made more complex by definition of the military role as "noncombatant." Many military forces nonetheless permit health professionals, like other military personnel, to claim conscientious objector status. In the United States, conscientious objection is defined as "a firm, fixed, and sincere objection by reason of religious training and belief to: (1) participation in war in any form, or (2) the bearing of arms." Religious training and belief is defined as "belief in an external power or being or deeply held moral or ethical belief to which all else is subordinate and . . . which has the power or force to affect moral well-being."[20] The person claiming conscientious objector status must convince a military hearing officer that the objection is sincere.

forces, not including 7,000 more who served as nurses.[2] Some of those servicewomen have described their tour of duty in Vietnam as among the best experiences of their lives, much as some men describe their war experience. There were 32,340 American servicewomen in the Gulf; 15 American women died—11 in combat and four otherwise.[3]

The effects of women serving in military forces are very complex, both on the women and on the military. Their abilities to carry out combat duties may lead to undermining the machismo associated with combat roles.[3] For example, as women show themselves capable of being fighter pilots, the definition of the fighter pilot as the prototype of masculinity is seriously eroded. For some feminists, this is an important means to effect change from within the system. On the other hand, morale of women in the Armed Forces suffers from the sexist attitudes of some of their male colleagues. In World War II, rumors were spread that the members of the American Women's Army Corps were prostitutes provided particularly for the officers.[2]

Biological arguments to exclude women from war zones appear to be weak, except possibly with respect to the physical strength required to serve in the infantry. In terms of medical problems, women who serve in war zones have, in addition to typical gynecological complaints, slightly different patterns of illness from their male counterparts. Studies of female Gulf War veterans show that one-fourth of all visits to medical units were for gynecological problems related to menstrual dysfunction, vaginitis, pregnancy, pelvic pain, abnormal cytology, and contraceptive needs.[4] Although these problems are predictable in a population of healthy young women, it appears that the military was not prepared for the medical conditions specific to women. Many of the women who were diagnosed as pregnant had requested a pregnancy test before deployment, but were denied.[5] Abnormal Pap smears or colposcopy results forwarded from the United States caused frustration because complete gynecological services were not available in the field hospitals. Ectopic pregnancy posed a significant risk among active-duty women. Rates as high as one in 27 pregnancies were reported,[4] but field hospitals did not have the capability to do ultrasound or laparoscopy. Women complained of less than optimal facilities for perineal hygiene, which, combined with the desert heat and the uniforms worn daily, probably accounted for the many cases of fungal vaginitis. Three-fourths of all diagnoses among women were considered to be orthopedic problems and acute minor illnesses.

2. Elshtain, J.B. and Tobias, S. *Women, militarism and war: Essays in history, politics and social theory.* Savage, Maryland: Rowman and Littlefield, 1990.

3. Cooke, M. and Woollacott, A. Postscript. In Cooke, M. and Woollacott A. (ed.), *Gendering war talk.* Princeton: Princeton University Press, 1993.

4. Hines, J.F. Ambulatory health care needs of women deployed with a heavy armor division during the Persian Gulf War. *Military Medicine* 157:219–221, 1992.

5. Markenson, G. and Raez, E. Female health care during Operation Desert Storm: The Eighth Evacuation Hospital experience. *Military Medicine* 157:610–613, 1992.

Obligations to Serve in War versus to Prevent War

As wars kill an increasing percentage of civilians with so-called conventional weapons and threats of the use of weapons of mass destruction continue, what form of service is appropriate for the ethical health professional? One response was suggested in the late 1930s by John A. Ryle, then Regius Professor of Physic at the University of Cambridge:

It is everywhere a recognized and humane principle that prevention should be preferred to cure. By withholding service from the Armed Forces before and during war, by declining to examine and inoculate recruits, by refusing sanitary advice and the training and command of ambulances, clearing stations, medical transport, and hospitals, the doctors could so cripple the efficiency of the staff and aggravate the difficulties of campaign and so damage the morale of the troops that war would become almost unthinkable.[21]

During the Vietnam War more than 300 American medical students and young physicians brought Ryle's vision a step closer to reality by signing the following pledge:

> In the name of freedom the U.S. is waging an unjustifiable war in Viet Nam and is causing incalculable suffering. It is the goal of the medical profession to prevent and relieve human suffering. My effort to pursue this goal is meaningless in the context of the war. Therefore, I refuse to serve in the Armed Forces in Viet Nam; and so that I may exercise my profession with conscience and dignity, I intend to seek means to serve my country which are compatible with the preservation and enrichment of life.[12]

Ryle's vision is a variation on that of Aristophanes in his comedy *The Lysistrata,* written in 411 B.C., just before the probable time of Hippocrates's refusal to treat the Persians (circa 400 B.C.). The title character, an Athenian woman, ends the second Peloponnesian War by organizing the wives of the soldiers of both Athens and Sparta to refuse sexual intercourse with their husbands while the war lasts. The Athenians and Spartans make peace quickly and go home with their wives.[22]

Some health professionals have refused to support war by refusing to serve in the armed forces. In one of the most dramatic examples, Yolanda Huet-Vaughn, a captain in the U.S. Army Medical Service Reserve, refused to obey an order for active duty in the Persian Gulf. In her statement, she explained:

> I am refusing orders to be an accomplice in what I consider an immoral, inhumane, and unconstitutional act, namely an offensive military mobilization in the Middle East. My oath as a citizen-soldier to defend the Constitution, my oath as a physician to preserve human life and prevent disease, and my responsibility as a human being to the preservation of this planet, would be violated if I cooperate.[5]

The reasons Huet-Vaughn gave for her action were quite different from the reasons given by Levy. Levy refused to obey an order that he believed required him to perform a specific act that would violate the Geneva Conventions; Huet-Vaughn refused to obey an order she believed required her to support a particular war that she felt to be unjust and destructive to the goals of medicine and humanity.

One of the questions Huet-Vaughn's action raises is whether health professionals have a special ethical responsibility, in view of their obligation to protect the health and the lives of their patients and the people of their communities, to refuse to support a war they believe will cause major destruction to the health and environment of both combatants and noncombatants.[5,23] If a health professional considers service in support of a particular war unethical, may—or, indeed, must—that person refuse to serve, even if that objection does not qualify for formal conscientious objector status? Furthermore, is there an ethical difference if the service is required by the society—as in a "doctor draft"—or if the service obligation has been entered into voluntarily to fulfill an obligation in return for military support of medical training or for other reasons? And is military service indeed a "voluntary obligation" if enlistment, as it is for many poor and minority people, is prodded by lack of educational or employment opportunities or, as for many health professionals, by the cost of education or training that in other societies would be provided at public expense?

While few health professionals are willing or able to take an action such as that taken by Huet-Vaughn, other actions are available to oppose acts of war considered unjust, to oppose a specific war, or to oppose war in general. One is acceptance of a service alternative consistent with an ethical obligation to protect health and prevent illness, or to care for those wounded or maimed, without simultaneously supporting a war effort. Opportunities for service in an international corps such as Médecins du Monde or Médecins Sans Frontières (see boxes in Chapter 20) are limited, but health professionals may wish to demand that their nation redirect some of the billions of dollars it spends annually on preparation for war to the United Nations or the World Health Organization to help fund an international health service to treat the casualties of war.

Other health professionals may wish, as individuals and particularly in groups, to help to prevent war by contributing to public and professional understanding of the nature of modern war, the risks of weapons of mass destruction, and the nature and effectiveness of alternatives to war. Among the groups organized for this purpose are the International Physicians for the Prevention of Nuclear War, whose U.S. affiliate is Physicians for Social Responsibility and whose U.K. affiliate is Medical Action for Global Security (see Chapter 22). In the interest of public health, health professionals may need to consider new forms of national service and to contribute in a broader sense to their nation and their planet.[24] (Women may have special concerns related to participation in military service; these are discussed in the box accompanying this chapter.)

In the broader context of medical ethics, it is widely accepted that opposition to war does not permit the ethical health professional to refuse care to victims of war he or she is in a position to serve and that such care does not presume support by the professional of the war being fought. The ethical dilemmas arise when the professional actively supports the war effort by membership in a military medical service or by assigning priority to patient care based on military demands rather than patient needs. These issues and those associated with the role of the health professional in peace-making and peace-keeping, often grotesquely distorted by the fervor that may accompany war and preparation for war, require dispassionate analysis and action in times of peace.

REFERENCES

1. Homer. *The Iliad.* Translated by Robert Fagles. New York: Viking Penguin, 1990.
2. Vastyan, E.A. Warriors in white: Some questions about the nature and mission of military medicine. *Texas Reports on Biology and Medicine* 32:327–342, 1974.
3. Plutarch. *Lives.* Vol. 2. Translated by Bernadotte Perin. Cambridge, Mass.: Harvard University Press, 1914.
4. Stacey, J. The cover. *Journal of the American Medical Association* 260:448, 1988.
5. Sidel, V.W. Quid est amor patriae? *PSR Quarterly* 1:96–104, 1991.
6. Geneva Conventions of 1949. In *Human rights documents: Compilation of documents pertaining to human rights.* Washington, DC: Government Printing Office, 1983.
7. Vastyan, E.A. Warfare: I. Medicine and war. In W.T. Reich (ed.), *Encyclopedia of Bioethics,* pp. 1695–1698. New York: Macmillan, 1978.
8. Sidel, V.W. Confidential information and the physician. *New England Journal of Medicine* 264:1133–1137, 1961.
9. Bellamy, R.F. Conserve the fighting strength. *Military Medicine* 153:185–186, 1988.
10. Rubenstein, D.A. Health service support and the principles of war. *Military Medicine* 153:145–146, 1988.
11. Annas, G.J. Changing the consent rules for Desert Storm. *New England Journal of Medicine* 326:770–773, 1992.
12. Liberman, R., Gold, W. and Sidel, V.W. Medical ethics and the military. *The New Physician* 17:299–309, 1968.
13. Langer, E. The court-martial of Captain Levy: Medical ethics v. military law. *Science* 156:1346,1349, 1967.
14. Glasser, I. Judgment at Fort Jackson: The court-martial of Captain Howard B. Levy. *Law in Transition Quarterly* 4:123–156, 1967.
15. Rosebury, T. Medical ethics and biological warfare. *Perspectives on Biology and Medicine* 6:312–323, 1963.
16. Sidel, V.W. Biological weapons research and physicians: Historical and ethical analysis. *PSR Quarterly* 1:31–42, 1991.
17. Walzer, M. *Just and unjust wars.* New York: Basic Books, 1977.
18. Seabury, P. and Codevilla, A. *War: Ends and means.* New York: Basic Books, 1989.
19. Ruddick, S. *Material thinking.* Boston: Beacon Press, 1989.
20. Department of Defense. Directive 1300. 6, Aug. 20, 1971. Washington, DC.
21. Ryle, J.A. Foreword to *The doctor's view of war,* edited by H. Joules. London: George Allen and Unwin Ltd, 1938, pp. 7–10.
22. Aristophanes. *The Lysistrata.* Translated by Benjamin Buckly Rogers. Cambridge, Mass.: Harvard University Press, 1979.
23. Geiger, H.J. Conscience and obligation: Physicians and just war. *PSR Quarterly* 1:113–116, 1991.
24. Lown, B. Nobel Peace Prize lecture: A prescription for hope. *New England Journal of Medicine* 314:985–987, 1986.

19

The Role of Nongovernmental Organizations in Responding to Health Needs Created by War

BARBARA SMITH

The effectiveness of nongovernmental organizations (NGOs) in responding to public health needs created by war was arguably fostered by governments themselves. The Red Cross, the NGO that established the framework that most NGOs have since followed, was founded in the 1860s and involved lengthy negotiations with governments. The new international laws and treaties developed to facilitate the work of the Red Cross were as much political as they were humanitarian. Political agreements included those that enabled the Red Cross to have access to people on both sides of a conflict, to cross lines of confrontation unharmed and without being required to pay in any way for this movement, to import necessary life-sustaining items and to distribute them according to need only, and to enjoy protection from any aggression in the course of its duties.

The Red Cross implemented this mandate by remaining silent on issues of the conflict, gained access to soldiers and civilians by remaining in the background, and developed a quiet form of diplomacy to ensure its own security as it moved through war-affected areas. In general, NGOs were reactive organizations that moved in behind governments to try to manage whatever health problems were left in the wake of political and military conflict.

Although hundreds of NGOs have developed since the founding of the Red Cross, almost all the NGOs have adopted this model of unobstrusive work that has been so successful for the Red Cross. This model is predicated on the idea that proactive involvement in conditions that create the disaster of war will preclude neutral humanitarian intervention later. NGOs have perceived themselves as nonpolitical entities that meet the health needs of populations solely by providing direct services in the field to those people to whom they are able to gain access.

Recently, however, NGOs have begun to exercise the political power that they seemed to have had all along. In the 1970s, the huge scale of the wars for which the NGO community was asked to provide services and the increasingly devastating effect these wars had on the health of civilians resulted in the creation of a new model of NGO work. According to this new model, NGOs have begun to see their political power as a tool to focus attention on and alleviate public health problems. NGOs found they could operate in dangerous and disputed areas, with or without consent of the warring parties, their home governments, or the United Nations, the acknowledged lead agency in most situations that involve NGOs.

In addition, NGOs began distributing their own analyses of war situations and began making their own calls for intervention by governments in the service of the health needs of civilians. No longer did NGOs limit themselves to trying to solve the catastrophes after they occurred; NGOs began to wield both the technical as well as the political power needed to effect improvements in the status of civilian populations during war.

U.S.–Based NGOs and Their Motivations

The Red Cross model is, above all, based on the idea of neutrality. The circumstances that created the war are ignored by the Red Cross, which instead spends great effort in attending to the wounds and illnesses of people on any side of a conflict. As far as possible, the Red Cross and similar NGOs will go wherever they must and do whatever risky activities are necessary to ensure that public health needs are being met. NGOs work quietly and do not embarrass any political entity through bad publicity. Access to populations and prisoners is gained by discretion; improvements in the conditions for war-affected people are made by quiet diplomacy. The Red Cross movement itself is loudly promoted, but the actual program activities in times of war are rarely made known.

Most U.S.–based NGOs followed this model until the 1970s. NGOs worked quietly in the field with small discrete projects. They willingly agreed to work under the formal supervision of an international group, often the UN. Soliciting the attention of the press was seen as unseemly or as mercenary in the NGO community. NGOs shunned grants from governments, preferring private donations in an effort not to be seen as partisan.

However, in the 1970s, the notion arose that an NGO could provide humanitarian relief and at the same time strongly advocate human rights by directly criticizing political activities. NGOs increasingly found that they did not always need to rely on the UN to supervise or coordinate their activities. Indeed, some NGOs were flexible and fast enough that they could arrive at the scene of an emergency sooner than the UN or other large agencies.

In areas of extreme danger and limited access, ''cross-border operations'' were organized to provide services to civilians almost completely isolated by the war. These infrequent operations were often surreptitious, planned and executed with minimal control by the UN, Red Cross, or any government.

Over time, NGOs developed their capabilities to gain attention from and to speak through the media, and to use political pressure. In 1994, during the Rwandan crisis, 16 NGOs signed a petition demanding action against the Hutu military apparatus by the former government, which was savagely controlling the camps. They threatened to leave if this action was not taken. This petition was signed and made public despite the potential risk of the Hutu military acting against NGO staff. The U.S. Undersecretary for African Affairs called a meeting to hear the NGOs at the State Department immediately after the release of this statement.

In addition to using a public voice, NGOs are also accepting much government assistance, such as financial and logistical support, while still maintaining an independent stance.

One of the reasons for this increased funding and independence is that NGOs have proven themselves to be irreplaceable in the actual implementation of humanitarian aid. Whereas governments and militaries can provide the security and logistics for humanitarian aid, they are not inclined to meet all the needs of war-affected people. The distribution and efficient use of the relief supplies—and the community organizing that sustains the humanitarian effort—are almost solely the responsibility of NGOs. Often NGOs can function alone. When governments and international agencies do become involved, the NGOs are still the indispensable link in actually reaching the people. In the last several years, NGOs have been routinely consulted by U.S. government agencies, included on policy-making field assessments, and afforded much higher visibility by governments and the media.

The change has affected the way many NGOs conduct their business. NGOs in the past, because they were expected to do such difficult work in areas where no one else could help, were rarely criticized. In the past, "we did the best that we could under the circumstances" was widely accepted as being good enough. Often the work of the NGOs was judged by how hard their staff members worked, how noble was their effort, how difficult were the working conditions, and how many beneficiaries could be served with meager resources.

Now, NGOs come under stricter scrutiny for the quality of their programs. As NGOs are viewed more professionally, so are they held to higher standards. Nowhere has this been more striking than in the Centers for Disease Control and Prevention (CDC) role in reviewing the operations around Goma, Zaire, in 1994 (Chapter 14). No one can argue that the conditions in Goma were some of the most disastrous that have ever confronted the NGO community, but this fact did not obviate the point that some unnecessary mistakes were made and that improvements were possible. Though CDC staff members have often served as consultants to review humanitarian actions, this review by CDC in Goma seemed to reflect the new role of NGOs. NGOs were assessed as professional providers of services that had a duty to bring people who had been adequately trained to implement programs in the most effective ways known.

Despite the enormous effort the NGOs made in responding to cholera, no laudatory review was given. Due to the lack of water and some other factors, CDC publicly reported, not a single case of cholera was prevented by the NGO efforts in Goma, Zaire, in July and August, 1994. Many NGOs have responded professionally to such evaluations. For example, an American consortium of over 100 NGOs, called Interaction, is now redoubling efforts to make training more available to NGO field workers and to improve coordination with the U.S. military to ensure better programs on the ground.

The new model of NGO functioning seems to be integrating both flexibility and accountability needs. The CDC report on Goma, Zaire, and the NGO response to it certainly makes this point. One of the reasons for this new accountability is that NGOs are so much more visible and have reserved for themselves a more public role.

The Specific Case of War

NGOs have helped institutionalize effective public health measures that protect people involved in a war and remain in use afterward. The first effective NGO, the Red Cross, initially occupied itself with the health needs of combatants. Picking up wounded soldiers and civilians caught in crossfire and visiting prisoners of wars occupied most of its efforts for many decades. Indeed, during these times civilians were generally protected from the actual battles. What public health needs were created by war were generally confined to the health crises in which the military found itself. These public health crises were, however, substantial.

In the U.S. Civil War, more soldiers died of preventable public health problems than of battlefield injuries. Overcrowding and lack of sanitation facilities became a central burden for the military. Morbidity and mortality increased markedly, affecting morale as well as the physical ability of the military to engage in battle.

Seemingly simple public health measures instituted by Red Cross nurses during war still have a profound influence on public health techniques today. Routine handwashing, human waste disposal, wound care, vector control, and ventilation, all of which proved to be powerful in protecting soldiers, have come to benefit civilians as much as the military. While the NGOs did not invent such techniques, the Red Cross had a pivotal role in enforcing their institutionalization in U.S. public health programs.

Although Red Cross personnel were in areas where civilians were under siege for long periods of time, they still mainly concerned themselves with the soldiers. Techniques used were those that would benefit the soldiers as much as anyone else. However, as civilians became increasingly victimized, if not targeted by warring governments, NGOs, including the Red Cross, began attending to the needs of civilians during war. Shelters were erected to protect the health and security of civilians. Tracing and mailing services were established to reunite families. Techniques used were mainly for the benefit of the civilians. The use of oral rehydration therapy (ORT) is a recent example of NGO concentration on techniques that serve the needs of civilians in war more than those that directly benefit the combatants. Developed in 1960, ORT is the technique credited with saving thousands of people during the Bangladesh floods in 1969. In ORT a simple mixture of clean water, salt, sugar, and potassium and other electrolytes is used to replace the fluids lost during bouts of serious diarrhea and dehydration. ORT rapidly saves lives and is very inexpensive. Although the UN has strongly promoted ORT, it is the NGOs who implement a large portion of ORT programs during war. NGOs directly contributed to the widespread use of ORT in all types of disasters. ORT, however, benefits mostly civilians because during war dehydration is most often a problem of civilians. Soldiers and other military personnel usually retain access to any clean water and medicine that is available in a war zone.

Limitations of NGOs in War

In many countries, the Red Cross is the only NGO present, either by law or because a country cannot financially support any other groups. In recent years, Red Cross groups have become formally organized to meet the needs of civilians as well as the military. The Red Cross is therefore indispensable in serving the needs of a country that cannot provide enough social services through its own institutions, particularly during wartime. However, the Red Cross is always in danger, despite legal prohibitions against it, of serving the interests of national governments during crises. Local employees can be pressured to show ''patriotic'' favoritism to their own military institutions. For example, in a town in Croatian-held Herzegovina in 1993, the Red Cross headquarters was filled mostly with soldiers, although the person nominally in charge was a middle-aged woman. The military had keys to the Red Cross warehouse. This scenario is repeated across the globe.

Therefore, while functioning chapters of the Red Cross exist in almost every nation that goes to war, this geographic and logistical advantage does not in itself create a complete humanitarian operation. Outside NGOs are often necessary to create alternative distribution systems that can be monitored independently of the government. This is one reason the Red Cross movement maintains in Switzerland the International Committee of the Red Cross (ICRC), which acts in times of war and is not subject to the supervision of national Red Cross groups.

NGOs that come from the outside are less likely to respond to pressure to serve the host government. If a host government asks an international NGO to leave, then it loses access to the essential services brought by the NGO. Harassment of or injury to international Red Cross or other NGO workers usually brings adverse publicity to the host government, if not a withdrawal of services.

Nonetheless, creating NGO distribution systems that bypass governments and sometimes bypass the UN and the Red Cross, which have formal political arrangements with host governments, carries risks. Increasingly, however, NGOs are accepting such risks and attendant criticisms. In addition, the enormity of the disaster that befalls civilians requires governments to turn to outside NGOs to fill their needs during war because, as civilians are increasingly targeted during war, national Red Cross chapters cannot fill all the health needs of the civilians affected by war.

Such reliance on expatriates for the integrity of war-relief programs is not without problems. Public health practices are all tied in with culture. International NGOs, without much knowledge of the culture they have entered, can make mistakes—large and small—that affect their ability to improve the health of the civilians. One of the most frequent mistakes of NGOs is to hire local employees who speak the same (usually European) language and who are confident and energetic enough to work the same long hours as the NGO international staff members. Young people hired into positions of authority in international NGOs may often be required to supervise and monitor the behaviors of elders, who may have previously held power in the community before war disrupted community life. The elders can resist the NGO's program, and young employees may be fearful or too respectful of their elders to insist that they follow the NGO's plans. Enormous tensions can build in such a situation; an expatriate NGO can easily misunderstand why its young staff member is failing to do his or her job. Often, programs that have good intentions can thus get bogged down.

Another problem is that NGOs often bring in programs they developed in their headquarters based on sound public health principles proven to protect the health of many of people. However, in most cultures, people will not fully cooperate with programs in which they have had no input and that do not reflect their cultural concerns. Sanitation and health education programs particularly require cultural sensitivity. NGOs are attempting to address these issues. Computer software packages are available for NGOs to generate health education images of people who dress and look like people in many different cultures. Multiple types of latrines and human waste systems have been developed not only to take into account the area's terrain, but also the cultural acceptance of these facilities.

A third problem NGOs have faced has arisen from their disregarding the usual demographics of civilians in war. Four-fifths of civilians so victimized by war that they must flee are women and children. Public health programs have increasingly developed a model of care for children under five years of age and for pregnant women, but otherwise services are predominantly used by men. Routine out-patient department (OPD) care is usually most accessible to men. Policy decisions are made by men. Food distribution, shelter materials, and living quarters favor men. As a result, malnutrition rates are often highest among women and children. The physical safety of women and children is not assured. And women and children generally live in the least desirable areas that have the fewest resources.

It has not been until the last decade that this state of affairs has received much attention. Currently, single women, who in every culture seemingly do not receive fair access to essential life-sustaining supplies or to public health programs, have been identified as a vulnerable group. Single women with children are now considered as vulnerable as disabled people. UN guidelines have been developed to try to equalize the treatment women receive in war zones. Although the stated policies of all NGOs and government groups call for focusing on the public health needs of women and children, these guidelines are often not implemented. Many relief workers have never heard of them.

Occasionally, the administrative structure of NGOs weakens their position in bringing public health care to victims of wars. Often positions in NGOs, with the exception of Red Cross jobs, are not well paid. NGOs cannot always attract the most experienced people for the job at hand, nor can they keep people in the field for sufficiently long periods of time. A high turn-over rate ensures that the quality of the programs varies greatly. Tasks that should be institutionalized have to be repeatedly reinvented as new staff members attempt to resolve the same issues that met their predecessors. These tasks include generating training and educational materials for the refugees, developing and using financial accounting procedures, and working with the media.

Although some U.S.–based NGOs would not choose to have formal working relationships with the military, others would say that in order to access needed logistics in times of war, there is no substitute to working with the military. However, the coordination among U.S.–based NGOs and the military can be tortuous during actual emergencies, and it can take more than a month to get NGO supplies airlifted to the site of emergencies such as Goma. Although the spirit of cooperation among the military and NGOs is increasing in the United States, the massive bureaucracy involved with getting airlift space, and the U.S. commitment to assist the United Nations before assisting NGOs, contributed in Goma to a minimally effective response from U.S.–based NGOs at the start of the crisis.

The story, however, has been quite different in the former Yugoslavia. U.S. agencies were given full access to cargo space and were the lead agencies providing services there, except for supplying food. In utilizing military logistics capacity, U.S. NGOs built on the model that others had forged. IRC, in particular, became one of the largest distributors of non-food items in the war zone as a result of coordinating with the military.

The limitations of this model—the rapid withdrawal of services after the emergency phase has ended but long before all life-sustaining needs have been met, and its lack of focus on sanitation (logisticians generally take on the sanitation responsibilities)—are balanced by the strengths of other NGOs whose mandate calls for remaining in the areas of need as long as necessary. These NGOs, however, would become increasingly marginalized if they did not also have a visible and rapid-acting emergency program.

The Evolution of the International Rescue Committee

The International Rescue Committee (IRC) is an NGO that has undergone several transformations in its public health role. Originally founded to rescue likely victims of Nazi persecution, IRC at first did not establish a public health role for itself in serving victims of war. However, as the refugee problem grew in the 1950s to include Hungarians in Austria, Poles in Sweden, and others elsewhere, IRC began operating medical clinics in countries of first asylum. These clinics were geared to attending to acute medical problems, but not to creating a system to protect the public health. IRC continued its assistance to victims of war in Vietnam by operating highly technological clinics and surgical services that met some medical needs of the refugees. But still it did not seek to meet the public health needs of the population.

IRC's goal remained to resettle as many war victims as possible. The creation of the UN High Commissioner for Refugees (UNHCR) position in 1951 formally distinguished war victims or victims of persecution who left their homeland as refugees from those who did not flee as refugees (see Chapter 14). IRC's mandate was to assist refugees. As it became the largest organization in the United States devoted to refugee assistance, it tried to serve these people as well as possible, but found it could do little for the people who remained in their own countries. This started to change in the 1960s when, responding to the U.S. role in Vietnam, IRC began medical programs there. After the withdrawal of the French, IRC began to supply sanitation items and medicine in South Vietnam. By the 1960s, plastic surgery was provided as well as curative medical services.

Seeing its role in curative and rescuer services, IRC also helped gain funding for ORT in Bangladesh and reacted to the partition of Pakistan by developing 28 clinics and hospitals. These clinics were the seeds of IRC's imminent role in public health, implemented without heavy reliance on clinics. However, at that point still a small NGO, IRC did not suspect that the numbers of refugees requiring public health services would soon be in the hundreds of thousands.

IRC kept steadfastly to the Red Cross model work in discrete, low-profile programs, not calling attention to itself, involving volunteers with the best of intentions and skills, and placing them in short-term roles. This model was, in many instances, highly effective. In Vietnam alone, IRC taught over 100,000 people to read and to write, resettled more people than almost any other organization, and was flexible enough to meet many rapidly changing needs. But few people had ever heard of IRC, and the organization prided itself on getting by with even less than anyone thought was possible. One of the defining moments for IRC came when Vietnamese "boat people" landed in Malaysia, Hong Kong, and other Southeast Asian countries. IRC remained committed to these refugees as it had since 1954. (In the beginning it was the only foreign NGO, other than the Red Cross, allowed to work in Malaysia.) But on these borders no small discrete clinic program would do.

In addition, multiple NGOs throughout the world arrived to assist as well—another unusual sight for IRC workers, who were used to working in relative obscurity. Here, the old model was tried again: Clinics were erected by every NGO in Thailand. In Malaysia, Vietnamese-staffed clinics were erected in the prison-like camps that the government had set up to try to prevent any destabilization by the Vietnamese presence there. Public health and sanitation programs were also started, but almost no one

Figure 19-1. Pediatric ward operated by a nongovernmental organization at Khao-I-Dang camp for Cambodians in Thailand (1980) (Photograph by Barry S. Levy).

had enough experience with large-scale relief operations. Enormously large tracts of land were cleared to accommodate the refugees, with no thought of how the removal of all vegetation would cause erosion, flooding, and standing water with attendant malaria and sanitation problems (see Figure 14-1). Other consequences of inexperience increasingly occurred. The death rate soared. It took many months to stabilize the camps on the Thai-Cambodian border.

What was learned, however, was that NGOs would have to be prepared to attend to the public health needs of hundreds of thousands of refugees on very short notice. The refugees' needs in medical care, public health services, social services, safe water, and sanitation would have to be met in areas where the countries of first asylum were hostile to their presence, where local health facilities were soon overwhelmed by the new demand, and where highly preventable illnesses would become the leading causes of death (Figures 19-1 and 19-2). In response, IRC, along with other NGOs, learned some important lessons: Local health structures must be supported to win the cooperation of the local government; refugees, many of whom have no previous training, must be quickly prepared to offer services for their own group due to the many people requiring assistance. Resettlement would become less of an option and long-term programs would have to be supported if IRC would be true to its mandate to help refugees until they did not need the help anymore.

IRC began to receive increased funding from U.S. government sources to augment

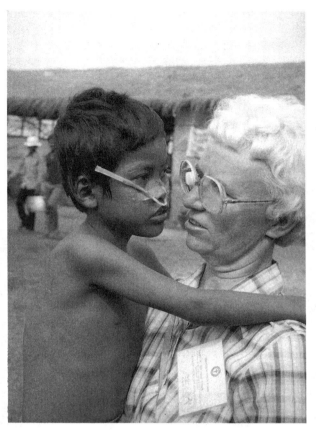

Figure 19-2. Nongovernmental organization worker and orphan boy in Khao-I-Dang camp for Cambodians in Thailand (1980). The boy was unable to see after having witnessed his parents' executions (Photograph by Barry S. Levy).

the substantial private support it enjoyed. Public health programs of this type demanded many fewer highly skilled doctors—once the backbone of IRC assistance; instead they required nurses, logisticians, sanitarians, and others concerned with providing public health services.

In general, IRC was able to find widespread support for whatever kind of program was needed, but the change from curative to public health and institution-building programs generated its share of controversy within IRC. Until the end of the 1980s, IRC remained true to its original belief that quiet work that did not draw attention to itself was most effective. IRC's decentralized decision-making process gave enormous responsibility and opportunity to creative and motivated people who did not necessarily have the professional credentials to undertake the job assigned to them.

The IRC model for public health included the following elements: consistent, long-term commitment; outreach home-visiting of the weakest people, instead of relying on them to be strong enough to bring themselves to the overcrowded clinics; training refugees from the start, to help meet their own needs; supporting local structures and not duplicating services for refugees; and emphasizing sanitation. Perhaps IRC's last attempt to duplicate the model of hospital-based treatment was in the famine in Sudan and Ethiopia in 1984, where hospitals were erected at a time that death rates were surpassing those of the Biafra famine. It was only after the abandonment of the hospital-based model that death rates fell quickly.

IRC is perhaps most widely known for instituting mother and child health (MCH) clinics immediately during the emergency phase of war and for training refugees to be public health officials (Figure 19-3). The training of refugees makes many more people available to help civilians than if only expatriates were performing the work.

While this institutionalization of MCH services is not at all controversial among NGOs, the refugee training emphasis from day one is unusual. IRC held steadfastly to the utility of this approach and found itself vindicated in Goma, where despite lack of resources, the death rate in IRC's public-health catchment areas was quickly one-third lower than those elsewhere in the camp. Sanitation is also a priority of IRC, but one that is, unfortunately, not glamorous to fulfill. IRC has devoted a large portion of logistical capacity and staffing levels to this need. The results have been borne out in quickly lowered death rates.

All NGOs have been confronted with increasingly terrifying public health consequences of war. Among the most well known are events in Rwanda and Zaire in 1994. In looking for sites for shallow wells in Rwanda, IRC staff came across mass graves. In trying to construct latrines in the volcanic rock in Goma, IRC found that the crevices that had to be used for latrines had unretrievable dead bodies at their bottoms. In the worst of these situations, communities did not show concern for the large number of their own people who died, even for members of their own families. Such a situation occurred in Goma, where well-fed and well-paid militia members who controlled the money that was taken from Kigali before the collapse of the Hutu government watched quietly as members of their community died of starvation. Food had to be purchased from these militia. Another example occurred in Somalia, where there was no limit to the number of people who were being sacrificed to the battles between warlords.

Situations like these require difficult moral decisions, which must be made in order to assist. The Red Cross decided that in Somalia in 1992, it would pay exorbitant ''Security Fees'' to local gangs who provided protection, ''cash facilitation fees'' in order to prevent armed robbery, and landing fees in order to bring in the relief supplies. The Red Cross was forced to allow open pilferage of supplies. Some NGOs were forced to put thousands of people on the payroll with no chance of firing anyone lest their own lives be placed in jeopardy. Local militia fired weapons into NGO compounds, and some were so careless with their guns that bullets were shot into relief vehicles.

Figure 19-3. Cambodian public health workers listen attentively during a public health course at Khao-I-Dang camp for Cambodians in Thailand that was presented by nongovernmental organizations (1980) (Photograph by Barry S. Levy).

Another distasteful situation occurred in Goma. NGOs from many nations threatened to leave Goma with the public health needs being far from met, because of the moral implications of organizing a relief effort that would be wholly controlled and abused by the Hutu militia, who were killing refugees and threatening expatriates in order to ensure their power over all activities.

The complicated moral and political terrain of recent war situations has undermined the idea that UN bodies should be the leaders and coordinators of medical relief in war situations. When UNHCR was not present in Somalia in 1992, the political and medical relief decisions fell to the NGOs. UNHCR for the first time, in responding to world outrage about its absence, entered into a collegial relationship with IRC, instead of the donor-grantee supervisory relationship, under which the UN usually works. IRC and UNHCR jointly implemented a cross-border program from Kenya into the Gedo region in Somalia.

Elsewhere, the UN has had to move from its coordinating and donor status to implementing programs on its own. Nowhere has this been more evident than in the Sarajevo airlift. Operated in cooperation with UN Protection Forces and UNHCR staff, food sustaining over 300,000 people was provided for almost three years. Far from increasing the status of UNHCR in the world community, as may be deserved since it was the only body capable of doing such a massive task, it had to delegate other of its usual responsibilities to NGOs, which stepped de facto into coordinating roles, offering security advice and general information to other NGOs in Split (although not assuming responsibility for security).

The UN, being directly connected to the governments, must be more generous and gracious in fulfilling the requests of the host government in terms of the distribution of its supplies. Food from the airlift was given directly to the Bosnian government, which distributed it fairly enough to have kept its population from starving, but also fed its army with it, which was clearly not intended. In addition, the UN could not protect the NGOs from having to give a portion of the relief goods to Serbian armies, whether they had need for them or not. Indeed, the UN had to forfeit a percentage of its commodities to the Serb forces as well. While this may not have directly affected public health work in Bosnia, the position of the UN ebbs and wanes with situations like this, creating an increased role for NGOs in all sectors.

Important political meetings that included representatives of the Bosnian Serb army, the Bosnian government, and the UN also included representatives of NGOs. Public health concerns, such as availability of water and gas, were discussed at these meetings, with NGOs having some influence on decisions. In the past, NGOs would never have been invited to such meetings, but would have carried out the decisions that the UN made. NGOs now acknowledge the UN role as the lead agency, but they operate under the assumption that the UN may not always be able to fulfill this mandate very rapidly. Further complicating this scene, war increasingly displaces people in their own countries and creates refugees who cross borders.

The UNHCR cannot generally respond to emergencies within a country—Bosnia-Herzegovina being a notable exception—but must wait for people to flee across borders. A Department of Humanitarian Affairs (DHA) was created by the UN to act as a coordinating body in emergencies and to handle displaced persons. This creates confusion of leadership in war zones involving the two UN agencies and dilutes their power. NGOs increasingly act independently and enter areas where no UN agency has an active role. In the Abkhazian region of Georgia, for example, a small DHA staff was headed by a native of Sarajevo. Trying to assist the victims of that conflict, he said, "was worse than what is going on in Sarajevo."

IRC has yet to test its own political weight with governments. Some groups are much less reluctant to use their political power in seeking to influence the conditions creating public health consequences of war. IRC also remains devoted to the idea of individual cases and each person's right to seek his or her own freedom. IRC has not abandoned its resettlement or advocacy efforts.

Other public health conditions occur when the local people refuse to sacrifice unlimited numbers of people for political or economic gain. Malawi was perhaps one of the finest examples of local response to a refugee crisis in the last 25 years. Malawi, although it was one of the poorest and most repressive countries in Africa at the time, shared absolutely every resource it had to protect the health of the Mozambican refugees flooding its already crowded country. In several districts, refugees outnumbered local people. Malawians allowed Mozambicans to live on what had been their garden plots, knowing full well that if the Mozambicans did not farm they would not eat and any food that was given away was given only to the Mozambicans. Only in the later years of this refugee crisis, which lasted from 1986 to 1994, did donors attend to the needs of Malawians. Had the Malawians not reacted so humanely, starvation and public health crises could have reached the same proportions as they did in Somalia, Sudan, and Rwanda. Malawi was a very good opportunity for NGOs to implement good public health programs in relative safety and to have the opportunity to find that hard work and organized programs actually will reduce death rates and prevent public health tragedies.

IRC continues to develop public health approaches to war, emphasizing refugee training and sanitation principles. However, IRC has also had its role in war limited by the policies of governments. For example, IRC has not intervened for the needs of Iraqi citizens whose health structures have been destroyed by war. A Harvard study conducted soon after the Persian Gulf War documented the disastrous consequences the war had on children's health status in Iraq (see Chapter 17).

Conversely, when the United States openly supported the Mujahadeen in their resistance to the Russian-backed government of Afghanistan, IRC found itself the recipient of almost unlimited funding for public health and other programs for Afghan refugees in Pakistan. The three million people displaced by that war required large-scale intervention. IRC used this money to ensure the health protection of all the refugees and granted girls and women access to medical care and to literacy programs. Local opposition to these programs led to the assassination of local IRC employees who were committed to the integrity of IRC programs and also to death threats to IRC international staff members.

IRC's massive projects for the former Yugoslavia have been concentrated in the territory controlled by Bosnian and Croatian government forces. Relatively small programs for the need have been implemented or funded for the Serbian-held territory, despite the fact that the public health concerns in the Bosnian Serb–held territory keep mounting as the army takes more of the limited resources for itself.

The Changing Role of NGOs during War

NGOs play an increasingly central role in alleviation of the public health consequences of war. This role has arisen out of the difficulty of coordination among UN bodies and the sometimes slow pace at which the UN can mobilize. For better or for worse, when a crisis of war affects a large population, NGOs frequently have programs already running before the UN becomes fully operational. There is increasing recognition that NGOs are irreplaceable in their willingness to go into insecure areas and provide health services in areas deemed too dangerous for armies. This has afforded the NGO community respect from the public and international institutions in general.

The voice of NGOs must now be sought in making policies. Without this input, NGOs might not agree to go to the field and do the actual work, and there will be no relief effort. The UN role of both funding and coordinating is being replaced, in part, by NGOs, which have the mobility and resources to run highly effective programs without the help of the UN. Coordination of health programs in times of war is still an accepted role of the UN. Although many NGOs see their role as broader, they participate voluntarily in UN efforts as an invited ''implementing partner'' of the UN.

The NGO community is rapidly becoming more professional, more sensitive to and knowledgeable about public relations concerns, and more coordinated with government and military structures. NGOs are exercising their political power, which they never perceived to any large extent before. As a result, the public health status of populations affected by war is increasingly affected by decisions of NGOs.

20

Effective Humanitarian Aid: Our Only Hope of Intervention in Civil War

JAMES C. COBEY, ANNETTE FLANAGIN,
and WILLIAM H. FOEGE

Despite the dissolution of the Soviet Union and other totalitarian regimes, the world has yet to see a ''peace dividend.'' Instead of two superpowers competing for sole possession of the best economic and political system, we now see numerous ethnic groups trying to found nations, define separate identities, and vent long-standing resentments. These seemingly sudden and unprecedented conflicts have centuries-old historical roots.[1]

Today, of the many armed conflicts underway in the world, 32 have each produced more than 1,000 battlefield deaths, the majority occurring within the boundaries of individual countries. Since World War II, the number of civilian deaths has surpassed military fatalities in most wars and conflicts.[2] In Cambodia, for example, half the landmine casualties in 1991 were civilian.[3] The International Human Rights Law Institute of DePaul University in Chicago, estimates that there have been 140,000 to 150,000 war fatalities in the former Yugoslavia in only the last few years. Fifty percent of these deaths are considered civilian, and one-third of those have been women and children. These wars and civil conflicts have also resulted in an ''epidemic of mass migration''—with more than 43 million refugees and internally displaced persons in the world today.[4] In response to the dramatic increases in civilian war casualties, refugees, and displaced persons, thousands of relief agencies have organized to provide humanitarian assistance. These include multilateral organizations such as those spon-

Excerpted and adapted from: Cobey, J. C., Flanagin, A., and Foege, W. H., Editorial: Effective humanitarian aid. *JAMA* 270:632–634, 1993. Copyright 1993, American Medical Association.

Médicins Sans Frontières (MSF)

Barry S. Levy and Victor W. Sidel

Médecins Sans Forntières (MSF, or Doctors Without Borders) was founded in 1971 by physicians who believed that populations in danger had a right to humanitarian assistance, and that this right supersedes the sovereignty of the state.

According to its charter, MSF offers assistance to populations in distress, to victims of natural or man-made disasters, and to victims of armed conflict, without discrimination with regard to race, religion, creed, or political affiliation. It observes strict neutrality and impartiality in the name of universal medical ethics and the right to humanitarian assistance, and demands full and unhindered freedom in the exercise of its functions.

Its basic objective is rapid and effective intervention in cases of extreme emergency and crisis, and it has progressively widened its range of expertise and increased the means of intervention at its disposal.

Most emergencies to which it responds are related to intra- and inter-state conflict. A minority are natural disasters. In addition, it carries out long-term operations in many countries where medical facilities are insufficient or nonexistent.

In armed conflicts, it sends medical teams composed of doctors, specialized nurses, and logistics experts, along with specially designed pre-packaged equipment for immediate operational efficiency, to sites that have already been assessed by reconnaissance teams. These interventions can be delicate and complex. Technical problems are often further complicated by problems of security and difficult living conditions for personnel. In cases of prolonged conflict, medical assistance—primary health care, nutrition, and prevention—may be extended to displaced populations. In refugee camps, MSF has provided primary health care, immunization, and nutrition services as well as water, waste-processing, and training of local personnel.

In most cases MSF works with the knowledge and agreement of the government in power. However, in keeping with its positions that the rights of populations in danger supersede claims of national sovereignty, MSF has launched a small number of "cross-border" operations, such as in Afghanistan in the 1980s, where MSF medical teams worked within the country without the permission of the Russian-backed Afghan government.

MSF has been determined to remain independent and neutral. Although it receives funding from governments in Western Europe, Asia, and North America, it relies on private funds for almost half of its revenues, which ensures that it can respond to emergencies without first having to apply for funding from a government donor. The solid funding base, strong training activities, volunteers who put themselves on call for departure within 48 hours notice, and a well-developed logistical capability allow MSF to react quickly and autonomously.

MSF operations deploy from Belgium, Spain, France, Holland, Luxembourg, and Switzerland. Nineteen offices in the United States, Canada, Japan, Sweden, and the United Kingdom also raise funds and recruit. It has liaison agencies in Geneva and New York, and an international office in Brussels.

sored by the United Nations (UN), government agencies that provide bilateral aid, and international and indigenous nongovernmental organizations (NGOs). Since the international community has so far been powerless to stop war, humanitarian aid through these organizations has often been the only possible way to help the victims of war (see boxes).

Médecins du Monde (MDM)

Victor W. Sidel and Barry S. Levy

The goal of Médecins du Monde (MDM) is to respond to medical emergencies arising from natural and political catastrophies. MDM was created in 1980 by a group of French doctors in response to the exodus of Vietnamese refugees, and now has a permanent staff of over 200, with its main office in Paris. It works with a large group of medical and non-medical volunteers throughout the world. There are currently MDM affiliate organizations located in Cyprus, Greece, Hungary, Italy, Japan, Spain, Sweden, Switzerland, and the United States.

The work of MDM is based on a "Duty to Intervene," which includes:

- Individual medical practitioners and private non-governmental relief agencies have the duty and right to intervene on behalf of communities in distress without governmental authorization.
- The obligation to help people who are suffering is a responsibility that transcends cultural, social, and national borders.
- Medical assistance and humanitarian aid supersede considerations of national sovereignty.
- Physical suffering and related anguish must not be accepted as the inevitable price of the functioning of nations.

Two types of operations are conducted by MDM throughout the world:

- Short-term operations intended to meet the immediate medical and humanitarian needs of crisis situations. Thirty short-term missions were conducted in 1994.
- Long-term projects which are designed to develop solutions to medical and sanitation problems. In 1994, 40 long-term missions were operational in the field.

Overall, MDM coordinates more than 40 missions each year, ranging from disaster relief to long-term public health programs, from emergency aid and immunization campaigns to construction of medical faculties and training of health workers.

Doctors of the World (DOW) is the U.S. affiliate of MDM, with headquarters in New York City. In collaboration with MDM, DOW sends volunteer doctors and other members of the health care community on missions of international medical assistance. DOW's missions in early 1996 included:

- Distributing health and nutrition commodities in Kosovo in former Yugoslavia.
- Implementing a multi-faceted program to provide health care to homeless, poor, and socially vulnerable children in St. Petersburg, Russia.
- Implementing a women's and children's mental health project in the West Bank and Gaza Strip.
- Implementing the Apaporis Indian Health Project in Amazonas, Colombia, in a remote part of the Amazon jungle to bring desperately-needed medical assistance and to build permanent health clinics for the Apaporis Indian population.
- Providing emergency assistance to the people of Chiapas, Mexico.
- Operating the New York City Human Rights Clinic for torture victims seeking political asylum in the United States.

The Geneva Conventions and the History of Humanitarian Relief

The modern tradition of humanitarian relief in wartime dates back to 1859 when Henri Dunant, a Swiss citizen, was horrified by the sight of soldiers dying on the battlefield from lack of medical attention in Solferino, Italy. Four years later, Dunant and others founded the International Committee of the Red Cross (ICRC).[5] In 1864 the first Geneva Conventions were promulgated. Since then a number of amendments have been added to the Conventions; the last version, the Geneva Conventions of 1949,[6] followed the atrocities exposed during the Nuremberg trials. More than 170 governments have signed the Conventions, which specify the rights of prisoners of war and civilians in occupied territories and give relief agencies access to wounded civilians and soldiers who lay down their arms. In 1977, additional protocols were added to the Conventions.[7] However, these protocols have not been ratified by the United States and many other countries primarily because of concern about the inclusion of the following passage: armed conflicts in which people fight ''against colonial domination and alien occupation and against racist regimes in the exercise of their right of self-determination.''[7] Governments that have not signed the additional protocols argue that it may be difficult to distinguish a freedom fighter in a war of liberation from a terrorist. Contradictory interpretations of the Geneva Conventions by relief agencies, governments, and the UN have hindered the provision of effective aid in countries in civil war. For example, Somalia's lack of a recognized sovereign government and loss of civil order resulted in disrupted and delayed aid by all relief agencies.[8]

Effective Aid

Effective aid can be given by either neutral or partisan groups. Neutral groups, exemplified by the ICRC, try to work on both sides of a conflict and avoid making public statements about the conflict. The ICRC can give effective aid as long as the warring parties recognize it as being neutral. For example, the ICRC's neutrality allowed it to keep working in Ethiopia in the late 1980s when other respected relief organizations, such as Médecins Sans Frontières, were forced to evacuate after publicizing governmental actions. The ICRC has also served as an effective intermediary between victims of conflict and warring governments and authorities.

The various relief agencies that work under the auspices of the UN, such as the United Nations High Commissioner for Refugees (UNHCR), the World Food Program, the United Nations Children's Fund (UNICEF), and others, provide an immense amount of assistance worldwide. However, these agencies can only be as neutral as UN member states allow.

Many people feel it is unethical to be neutral in a conflict and support relief only for the victimized or the more democratic party. In some conflicts, the side supported has turned out, on coming to power, to be just as unethical as its opponents. The United States has changed its backing of local factions a number of times in Somalia, Mozambique, and Angola. Supporting one side may result in a quicker end to the conflict, but the partisan agency may also be forced out of the action by the opposing side.

Both neutral and partisan aid organizations have advantages. Groups such as Amnesty International, Human Rights Watch, and Physicians for Human Rights are needed to help document the existence of human rights abuses,[9] but neutral organizations are needed to continue care in many civil wars in which unconditional humanitarian assistance is the only hope for most refugees and displaced persons.

Effective aid must be aimed at recipients' needs, not donors' whims. During war, the most vital commodities are water, food, sanitation, and shelter.[4] We know that basic sanitation may save more lives than high-tech medical care, but this fact is often ignored.[10] As Toole and Waldman[4] point out, preventable diseases such as diarrhea and acute respiratory tract infections are the most common causes of death among refugees and displaced persons. During armed conflict, acute injuries also need focused attention and treatment.

To make the best use of limited resources during armed conflict, emergency medical relief personnel must specifically target the effects of war (Figures 20-1 and 20-2) rather than work to increase the level of medical technology above its antebellum state, a common temptation for relief groups. An economy stable and wealthy enough to maintain new technology is rarely present during a war. For example, Western ophthalmologists arrived in war-torn Cambodia in 1979 to perform cataract operations for a civilian population that had never had treatment for cataracts and would not until political and economic stability fostered development of a medical infrastructure. In general, only durable and locally repairable surgical supplies and equipment should be donated during war. Complex surgical care for one person can impede the treatment of many other victims by consuming too much limited time and resources. Clearly, public health programs that decrease mortality from starvation, preventable diseases, and treatable war injuries deserve priority.

Aid should be sent only to requesting organizations familiar with local needs. Good early surveys by epidemiologists rather than by well-meaning journalists can minimize the secondary dilemma of dealing with massive unsolicited shipments of inappropriate supplies.[11] Too many well-meaning private voluntary organizations, often newly formed, collect used clothing and sample medications in small quantities and send them via airlifts to the disaster site, thereby clogging the system with supplies that frequently must be destroyed.[12] Professional organizations handling supplies call this problem "the second disaster." In general it is far more efficient and effective for established NGOs, UN agencies, and the ICRC to buy supplies locally rather than ship them from abroad. The Pan-American Health Organization (PAHO) has started

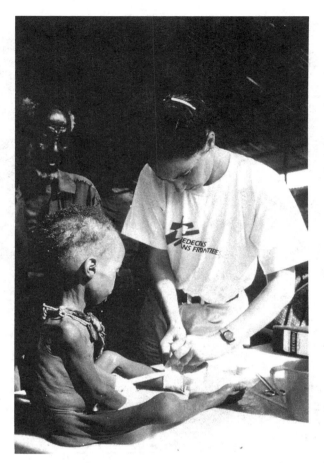

Figure 20-1. Médecins Sans Frontières (Doctors Without Borders) worker attends to a Somali child in clinic on Kenya-Somalia border (Photograph by Roger Job; Source: Médecins Sans Frontières).

a computer system for supply management called SUMA to try to sort and distribute supplies appropriately in disasters.

Many donors want to be sure their money will be used for actual food or necessities for war victims rather than for administration or transportation, but in fact, the cost of such logistics is far higher than that of food or water. Transporting clean water may require a fleet of trucks and even road building. Delivering food to Ethiopia, for example, sometimes required airlifts. It is important to remember that the administrative infrastructure is often destroyed in war before shortage of tangible commodities occurs.

How can we provide effective and appropriate aid to victims of war and at the

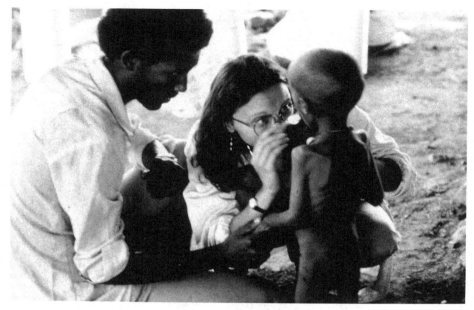

Figure 20-2. Médecins Sans Frontières worker attends to child in Ethiopia (Source: Médecins Sans Frontières).

same time ensure the safety of aid workers and volunteers? There is no simple answer. Standardized mortality and morbidity surveillance systems should be established to provide the basis for all early interventions.[4,10,13] These systems should include crude death rate analyses as well as rapid assessment and diagnostic procedures that are continuously monitored and amended as the situation changes. Relief programs must be based on scientifically sound public health strategies.[14] But the science of humanitarian aid is still in its infancy, and holding relief volunteers accountable to the same rigorous standards we demand of scientists working in fully funded and safe laboratories is difficult to justify. Funding for research into reliable surveillance systems, valid assessment tools, and effective intervention strategies is sorely needed.

The Limitations of Humanitarian Aid

The limitations of humanitarian assistance include competition for scarce funds, trained personnel, and material resources; logistical problems, such as inadequate, nonexistent, or poorly coordinated supply transport systems and communication abilities that impede rapid response capacities; inadequate security for relief workers; and a seemingly erratic response from the public and national leaders to pleas for aid and funding. For example, in 1990, the UNHCR's cost for caring for the world's refugees amounted to $540 million.[15] In 1992, the costs more than doubled, reaching $1.1 billion. In 1993, they reached $1.3 billion. The UNHCR costs are a fraction of worldwide aid expenditures. Many relief administrators fear that funding will decrease in response to increased demands and resultant "donor fatigue."

One might argue that relief agencies should collaborate to make better use of existing resources. Yet such collaboration may cause bureaucratic bottlenecks, reduce responsiveness, and politicize aid.[16] Each group may be operating under its own agenda. At times, different groups compete to make their care of starving children seem more media-friendly in order to raise funds. If one group has a religious affiliation, conflicts may arise with other agencies about the type of aid given.

Internal and external politics also hamper effective assistance—especially during civil war. Local authorities may play relief agencies off one another. Combatants often conduct war by denying food and basic medical care directly or indirectly to civilian populations.[17] The Biafran conflict was decided in 1970 by starvation as well as by military action. In 1992, in Somalia, tons of donated food were held hostage in Mogadishu by warlords as thousands of civilians died daily.[8] Some of the most desperate people, mostly displaced citizens persecuted by their own governments, are not even within reach of relief agencies. For example, the UNHCR has legal authority to protect and assist the world's 18 million refugees, but has no such authority over some 25 million internally displaced persons[4] (see Chapter 14).

The free press, and particularly television, has both mediated and obfuscated public response to humanitarian crises. The camera's presence in Somalia and Bosnia engendered much support for aid in those countries, while its absence in Sudan, Liberia, Angola, and other war-torn countries reminds us that our world resources are indiscriminately focused.

Ideally, a single international or nongovernmental organization could coordinate all humanitarian aid and provide constant surveillance of all relief efforts. But the political and logistical obstacles to such a plan are formidable. Various organizations coordinate and distribute food or medical care in specific countries, but there is no universal measure of accountability for such aid. In countries with sovereign governments—that is, those recognized by the UN—the local government, preferably through one person, should coordinate all incoming aid. Strengthening the host government's coordinating ability and supporting local relief groups may help stabilize relief efforts after expatriate volunteers have gone home.[18] However, in countries without sovereign governments or in newly formed nations fighting to keep their autonomy, an independent body is needed to coordinate relief efforts. Recently in Bosnia and Somalia, the UN appointed specific agents to coordinate relief. The UNHCR has served this role in Bosnia, while three agencies have done so at different times in Somalia. The UN's efforts in these countries, while successful in many respects, have been plagued by all the limitations described above. For example, an outbreak of measles in Somalia could have and should have been prevented. In addition, the UN is not deemed neutral by many recipient nations and has been accused of being a Trojan horse for Western political intervention—even though such accusations are used by some governments to distract the world from human rights abuses taking place in their countries.

Perhaps the ICRC could be given a stronger role in coordinating aid, as it has proved effective in protecting victims of civil war as well as negotiating between warring authorities. But an officially recognized coordination role might diminish the ICRC's neutrality, the key to its successful interventions.

In recent conflicts and disasters, armies have been used to help deliver aid. For example, in Bangladesh, the U.S. armed forces helped in the relief logistics after the 1991 cyclone.[19] United States troops, followed by UN forces, have policed Somalia to allow relief workers to distribute food and have provided medical care. There is no question that the initial military presence facilitated relief efforts in Somalia. Yet six local UN workers were killed in July 1992, and, in June 1992, 24 Pakistani UN troops lost their lives while trying to keep peace—the largest UN troop casualty in a single incident since 44 UN troops were killed in the Congo in 1961.[20] In Bosnia, UN forces were trying to create safe areas for giving aid. Yet relief corridors continued to be blocked and hospitals continued to be bombed. Despite their expertise and logistical skills, neither UN military forces nor those from any single country are perceived as neutral, and they have been unable to negotiate an end to ethnic fighting. While a military force may be needed to keep peace and allow relief to be dispersed, it cannot serve as an effective aid coordinator.

No matter who takes the central coordinating role in a given crisis, lessons should be learned from previous interventions.[16] We should recognize that certain NGOs or the ICRC respond faster and more effectively in specific situations. Because of the large numbers of aid organizations and the constancy of the challenges they face, a clear division of labor among all the players is essential. As Minear aptly states, ''The world does not have the luxury of gearing up from scratch for each new emergency.''[16]

Conclusions

Acknowledging all the limitations we have discussed, we support a recent report on humanitarian intervention[21] that calls for the UN to act ''more promptly and routinely'' to offer humanitarian assistance to all people in need—whether refugee or displaced—without waiting for consensus from international leaders or the mass media. The report suggests that the following criteria[21] should determine UN action:

1. The number of persons affected by the humanitarian emergency
2. The immediacy and severity of the threat to life
3. The number of refugees or displaced persons who have been forced to flee
4. A pattern of significant human rights abuses
5. The inability or unwillingness of the government to cope with the crisis

We urge that the UN take on this role. The newly created UN Department of Humanitarian Affairs is a step in the right direction, but it remains to be seen if this office will be given the resources and authority to establish an effective early warning system and take timely, decisive action to provide effective aid.

Authorized or not, televised or not, effective humanitarian aid is difficult to provide amid intense warfare. Given that we do not have the solution for ending war, offering effective humanitarian relief to the victims of war will remain a priority—and perhaps the only avenue for hope. Obtaining a ceasefire for the purpose of providing humanitarian relief may provide an opportunity to negotiate a more long-lasting peace. In El Salvador and Lebanon, for example, ceasefires were negotiated to allow for immunization of children.[16] We believe that the health needs of starving and war-maimed children can be used to halt the violence fueled by oppressive governments or age-old ethnic hatreds.

Ethnocentricity is a learned behavior, and as Einstein said, "Nationalism is . . . the measles of humankind."[22] Today, he might expand nationalism to include ethnic hatred.

The greatest advance in public health during war would be to stop the fighting. But this indisputable point raises a host of thorny philosophical questions. When and where should we intervene and who should intervene? The developed world is often accused of watching humanitarian abuses and atrocities without acting, yet intervention may also be seen as interference or "neo-colonialism." Should the United Nations send forces to make or keep peace by using weapons? When should international forces intervene in either international or domestic wars? If an international police force intervenes, should it stay neutral or should it support one side? Again, in a civil war, how does one determine who is carrying out terrorist activities against a legitimate government and who is seeking well-deserved independence, ethnic autonomy, or removal of an oppressive government? By encouraging local and ethnic identities, will we cause the world to become more fragmented, and would that fragmentation help the causes of peace or war? But given the fact that we do not have the solution for ending war, offering relief will remain a priority.

Finally, all relief agencies must realize that they are guests in a foreign land and that the national or local government has the final say on what type of aid is given. Local authorities have been known to play relief agencies off against one another for their own benefit. Strengthening the host government's coordinating ability and supporting the infrastructure of local relief groups may do more long-term to stabilize the relief efforts after the expatriate groups have gone home.[18] Long-term development after a war will depend on local resources and the citizens' optimism that they can improve their condition far more than on foreign donations. One can argue that the side with the best human rights record will probably be best for post-war development of the country, but for development to proceed, all citizens must feel that there is a "level playing field."[23] Since each culture has a different definition of human rights— an issue of cultural relativism—we must recognize that some people may never gain the confidence or ambition to try to change their lives and develop their country. The more confusing the politics of a conflict, the safer it may be to be neutral, remembering that true humanitarian relief is unconditional.

REFERENCES

1. Flanagin, A. and Foege, W.H. Health, human rights, and humanitarian assistance: A call for papers, *JAMA* 268:3480–3481, 1992.
2. Garfield, R.M. and Neugut, A.I. Epidemiologic analysis of warfare: A historical review. *JAMA* 266:688–692, 1991.
3. Stover, E. and McGrath, R. *Land mines in Cambodia—The coward's war.* Boston, Mass: Physicians for Human Rights, 1991, p. 2.
4. Toole, M.J. and Waldman, R.J. Refugees and displaced persons: War, hunger and public health. *JAMA* 270:600–606, 1993.
5. Federation and International Committee of the Red Cross. *Red Cross and Red Crescent: Portrait of an international movement.* Geneva, Switzerland: International Committee of the Red Cross, 1989, p. 5.
6. International Committee of the Red Cross. *The Geneva Conventions of August 12, 1949.* Geneva, Switzerland: International Committee of the Red Cross, 1981.
7. International Committee of the Red Cross. *Protocols Additional to the Geneva Convention of 12 August 1949.* Geneva, Switzerland: International Committee of the Red Cross, 1977, p. 4.
8. Flanagin, A. Somalia's death toll underlines challenges in post–Cold War world. *JAMA* 268:1985–1987, 1992.
9. Geiger, H.J. The role of physicians in conflicts and humanitarian crises: Case studies from the field missions of Physicians for Human Rights, 1983–1993. *JAMA* 270:616–620, 1993.
10. Yip, T. and Sharp, T.W. Acute malnutrition and high childhood mortality related to diarrhea: Lessons from the 1991 Kurdish refugee crisis. *JAMA* 270:587–590, 1993.
11. Cobey, J. Donation of unused surgical supplies: Help or hindrance. *JAMA* 269:986, 1993.
12. de Ville de Goyet, C. Post-disaster relief: The supply-management challenge. *Disasters* 17:169–171, 1993.
13. Lee, L.E., Fonseca, V., Brett, K.M., et al. Active morbidity surveillance after Hurricane Andrew—Florida, 1992. *JAMA* 270:591–594, 1993.
14. Colins, S. The need for adult therapeutic care in emergency feeding programs: Lessons from Somalia. *JAMA* 270:637–638, 1993.
15. Lewis, P. UN refugee official seeks pledges from donors. *New York Times.* June 20, 1993, p. 2.
16. Cahil, K.M. (ed.). *A framework for survival: Health, human rights and humanitarian assistance in conflicts and disasters.* New York: Council on Foreign Relations and Basic Books, 1993.
17. McCrai, J. and Zwi A.B. Food as an instrument of war in contemporary African famines: A review of the evidence. *Disasters* 16:299–321, 1993.
18. Bossert, T.J. Can they get along without us? Sustainability of donor-supported health projects in Central America and Africa. *Soc. Sci. Med.* 30:1015–1023, 1990.
19. Shears, P. Health effects of the 1991 Bangladesh cyclone: A comment. *Disasters* 171:166–168, 1993.
20. Lind, M. Alboutros. *The New Republic.* June 28, 1993, pp. 16–20.
21. Weissbrodt, D. Additional comments: Humanitarian intervention and the erosion of national

sovereignty. In *Refugees in the 1990s: New strategies for a restless world.* Minneapolis: American Refugee Committee, 1993 (suppl.).

22. Dukas, H. and Baensch, H. *Albert Einstein: The human side.* Princeton, N.J.: Princeton University Press, 1979, p. 38.

23. Harrison, L. *Underdevelopment is a state of mind: The Latin American case.* Lanham, Md.: Madison Books, 1985, p. 3.

VII

Can War and Its Public Health Impacts Be Prevented?

21

Education for Peace

LELAND MILES

The focus of attention at the sixth triennial meeting of the International Association of University Presidents (IAUP) in 1981 in Costa Rica was the University for Peace, which was then being constructed there under the auspices of the United Nations and the United Nations Economic and Social Council (UNESCO). The case to be made in this chapter is that every university should be a university for peace, not just the one in Costa Rica.

All major problems have become international, including hunger, poverty, pollution, disease, overpopulation, depletion of fossil fuels, and potential environmental collapse. Such problems transcend national borders and can only be resolved by international cooperation. Universities, however, have not radically altered their curricula to reflect these changes. Neither the ''professional'' education of industrialized nations nor the understandably vocational education of developing countries makes much effort to focus on global problems, among which the most dangerous is the widening gap between the wealth of the major powers and the poverty, hunger, and disease of the Third World.

Although our world is shrinking, most universities continue to produce global illiterates. Such graduates are educationally disadvantaged not because of some economic hardship or because they are unable to read or write, but because they are globally blind. They will be at a disadvantage in a world dominated by global forces. Most of the career life of today's graduating seniors will be spent in the twenty-first century. Yet at most institutions they continue to receive an obsolete twentieth-century education.

Global illiterates are dangerous because they see military strength as the way to peace. Such a view holds that more advanced weapons are the way to fend off war. But advanced weapons do not address the economic causes of war and the competition for limited resources. Albert Einstein once said, ''Peace cannot be kept by force. It can only be achieved by understanding.''—understanding that leads to cooperation and a sharing of resources between the ''haves'' and ''have-nots.''

On our shrinking planet, there can be no relevant education that is not international.

It is not enough to be a proficient engineer, a competent accountant, or even a liberal arts graduate aware of one's own national heritage. Many Western institutions are fond of claiming that they educate students for the "real world." But the real world is no longer just the marketplace or executive suite. Today it encompasses the whole human family.

Flaws of the Academy

Why have educators failed to change in a changing world? There are at least three long-standing flaws in the academy, which work against change: departmental structure, misunderstanding of international education, and the narrow education of faculty.

Departmental Structure

University departments, which have been single-disciplinary units since medieval times, are incapable of addressing multidisciplinary international problems, such as environmental problems. A department is not organized to address multifaceted problems. Many university presidents have recognized this weakness.

Misunderstanding of International Education

Foreign students on campus, faculty exchange programs, and international relations clubs provide a favorable environment for international education, but they do not constitute such education. The essence of international education is a curriculum with an internationalized general education core that is required of all students, and that provides them with a common international experience. Such a curriculum would be far different (and far more exciting) than the traditional liberal arts core, with its parochial distribution requirements—such as a little history here, a little philosophy there. The truly international curriculum would be interdisciplinary, problem-oriented, issue-based, and team-taught. There would be cross-cultural offerings in religion, ethics, history, anthropology, literature, sociopolitical and economic systems, philosophy, and law. Students would be introduced to the emergence of nation-states, the concepts of nationalism and revolution, the pros and cons of technology, various notions of progress, the difference between developing and developed nations, and human evolution and race prejudice. They would learn about the historical roots of modern problems and their possible future directions. The aim of such a sequence of courses would be to create new attitudes among future leaders: a sense of interdependence, a crosscultural awareness, a bias against stereotyping, a global perspective, and an orientation toward peace as the only common security for everyone.

The Narrow Education of Faculty

If we are to believe a host of relevant studies (see Bibliography), few of the world's institutions of higher learning have even the rudiments of an international education program as defined above. Such a program would require a radical transformation of undergraduate curricula. Most faculties do not have the temperament to make such extensive alterations. Individual faculty members might be nonconformists, but when a faculty operates as a group, there is no organization more resistant to change. This resistance is not so much intellectual as temperamental, and stems from the way doctoral students are educated. Many of them continue to be trained in a narrow spectrum of one country—often their own or a country similar to theirs in culture. Moving a faculty with that type of training toward an international curriculum is like moving a cemetery or picking up an elephant. It can be done, but it is difficult.

Curricular Reform: A Failure

Faculty are often part of the problem, not part of the solution. For example, the IAUP, inspired by the founding of the University for Peace in 1981, decided to hold symposia in various parts of the world for the purpose of developing prototype internationalized curricula, similar to the cross-cultural program described above, that could serve as possible models for faculty at member institutions. Each of IAUP's regional councils agreed to hold such a symposium, but only the North American Council (NAC) actually did. It held three week-long symposia, each of which brought together about 20 or so leaders from academia, business, government, and the media.

The assigned objective for each symposium was to create an ideal 36-hour general education core, designed to produce graduates with global perspective and intercultural awareness. Gonzaga and Central Michigan Universities developed similar cores, emphasizing three components: international mobility, global perspective with emphasis on interdependence, and peace orientation. Central Michigan's syllabus urged that "instruction should generate curiosity about other people and places," that global education should begin in kindergarten, and that the teaching of peace "must be analytical rather than propagandistic," with emphasis on conflict resolution. Florida International, on the other hand, moved away from specific disciplines and adopted an interdisciplinary approach. This resulted in a core of six components: environment, human (social) problems, political/economic issues, regional conflicts, student service, and foreign language. The detailed outlines for these general education cores were published in 1984 in *Lux Mundi* (IAUP's semiannual journal) and were strenuously compared and debated at the IAUP triennial conference in Bangkok later that year.

But then nothing else happened. None of the prototype material ever got introduced into the curricula of even the three institutions that had sponsored the symposia. To push for such changes would, of course, have aroused controversy and opposition. As one of the involved professors later said of himself and his colleagues, "We were theoretical heroes, but practical cowards." So the products of the IAUP symposia languish, but they still represent a tremendous resource for any institution that seeks to internationalize undergraduate education.

The IAUP/UN Commission: A Success

By comparison, the IAUP/UN Commission on Disarmament Education, drawn from the academic, security, business, and other communities, has had considerable success with a more limited mission. Formed by the IAUP and the UN Center for Disarmament Affairs in 1991, the Commission's mandate was to find ways to expand teaching in disarmament. After a year of assessing the field, the Commission reached the following conclusions:

- Most academic work in disarmament is conducted in the West.
- Even in the West, much academic material has been rendered obsolete by the disintegration of the former Soviet Union.
- There is little or no academic, civilian, or military constituency for arms limitations in developing countries.

In 1992, on the basis of this assessment, the 160-person Commission formed three teams of scholars and practitioners to develop new disarmament curricula for universities, especially in the developing world. These teams were headed by Steven Spiegel of UCLA (for graduate and undergraduate modules), Victor Sidel of Albert Einstein Medical College (for professional schools, especially those in health sciences), and by Edward Page of Business Executives for National Security (for universities interested in the linkage among arms control, environment, and economy). This material was first presented at IAUP's 10th Triennial Conference in Kobe, Japan, in July, 1993, and was then introduced to 14 "lead universities" in Southeast Asia (the Philippines and Thailand), East Africa (Uganda, Kenya, and Tanzania), and Latin America (Mexico, Argentina, Chile, and Peru). The pilot effort in developing countries was funded by the W. Alton Jones Foundation and the U.S. Institute of Peace.

Each of the 14 institutions committed to adapt, teach, and evaluate the Commission's experimental modules by the spring of 1995. To achieve that goal, each appointed a "host professor" or "fellow" and a faculty committee to work with an experienced Commission "mentor." By August 1994, Commission mentor/scholars had made initial visits to all of these universities.

As the Commission's mentors visited the overseas institutions, they were greeted with much enthusiasm. When Professor Spiegel arrived at Philippine Women's University in Manila, he was asked, unexpectedly, to give the keynote address for the founding of the institution's new Peace Institute. The audience was in the hundreds, including a university president and faculty team from 200 miles away. Faculty members from Asia, Africa, and Latin America asked for regional seminars so they might work jointly with fellow institutions to adapt the Commission's material to their own regions and cultures, and to the special needs of their own institutions.

In Mexico, at the Universidad del Valle, the faculty not only adapted the material, but quickly launched a course with 30 students and five guest professors. They also distributed their disarmament syllabus to branch campuses. In Argentina, a small private institution, the University of Palermo, and a huge public institution, the University of Buenos Aires, took the unprecedented step of working together on a team-taught disarmament course. In Chile, four universities created an informal consortium for the purpose of jointly creating a common course drawn from the Commission's materials.

More recently, universities in China, Central America, and South Africa asked to participate in the Commission's project through their political science, government, health sciences, and sociology programs. The U.S. Arms Control and Disarmament Agency (USACDA) expressed its support by awarding the Commission an unprecedented $100,000 grant for this later phase in disarmament education.

The USACDA grant greatly accelerated the Commission's work. By April 1996, 49 partner universities were involved from 26 countries. Seventeen mentor/scholars from the Commission were working with 60 host professors abroad. Almost 90 courses or programs were underway, serving 2,600 students, with 100 courses and 3,000 students projected by fall 1997. From these statistics let me extract two fairly typical case histories.

President Corporal-Sena heads Bicol University at Legazpi City in a rural province of the Philippines. Her campus library is weak; her faculty willing but unsophisticated. Despite these drawbacks, she put together a competent cross-disciplinary faculty team, inserted Commission modules into four existing courses, and launched a Master's program in Peace and Security Studies in the fall of 1995. The first classes included military officers, judges, lawyers, and teachers.

Joseph Kalunga is President of Evelyn Hone College in Lusaka, Zambia. Dr. Kalunga was one of the 12 "students" at the 1994 IAUP/UN International Seminar on Arms Control and Disarmament. He returned to Lusaka, digested the curricular materials distributed at the seminar, transformed them to meet the needs and culture of his country, and then proposed that his government approve a required three-year program in peace and disarmament for the entire 16-member public college system. The government not only approved, but joined Kalunga in planning two faculty workshops as preparatory steps toward introducing the program in 1996.

Such case studies stress an important point. Statistics on the Commission's progress, however impressive, do not capture the drama, spirit, and human dimension of what is happening. Behind the statistics are many talented, inspired, and determined people who are pushing disarmament education in developing countries, not because they will be rewarded monetarily, but because they believe its time has come.

As the Commission enters 1996, it is planning to include new partners from the Balkans and Middle East, and to initiate a chain reaction of surrogate replication by key institutions in selected nations such as Chile, Zambia, and the Philippines. During the 1996–1999 period, the Commission plans to expand its work in China and Japan; explore new countries like India, Indonesia, Korea, Vietnam, and those in Central and Eastern Europe; and create new disarmament material for training those in professions like law, journalism, and education. With adequate funding, the potential for this curricular project is great.

Reform Secrets

Given the usual problems in intercultural communication and the different culture of timeliness in developing countries, no one would have thought that this much progress could have occurred this fast. Why are so many Third World faculty using the Commission's material, while their U.S. counterparts have shown so little interest in similar material developed by the 1983 IAUP symposia?

There are many answers, but only a few are presented here. First and foremost, the Commission's effort is far more modest than the earlier IAUP attempt to reform the total undergraduate curriculum. By contrast, the effort now is simply to introduce new international material into existing curricula. Also, unlike prior disarmament syllabi based on superpower confrontation, the IAUP/UN Commission material focuses on regional conflict, conventional arms, the arms trade, the dangers of nuclear proliferation among small countries, emergence of biological and chemical weapons in Third World states, the health and environmental impact of such weapons, peace economics and defense conversion, relation of peace to economic and environmental improvement, civilian control of the military, and peace-building techniques like mediation, negotiation, preventive diplomacy, and confidence building.

These regional themes, presented to successive classes of students, can help build an academic, and then a political, military, and civilian constituency for arms limitation, which is the *sine qua non* for achieving social justice in developing countries. Thus, such material is seen as highly relevant for countries like Guatemala and South Africa, which are just emerging from civil strife, or struggling to do so. Small wonder then that faculty from less-developed countries regard the IAUP/UN curricula as an opportunity to positively influence the future course of their countries, and to improve the quality of life for their people.

Another reason for the Commission's success, however, in combination with the other factors mentioned, is the modular approach. By "module" is meant a 2- to 5-week academic unit that can be inserted into an already existing course, or combined with similar modules to form a new course or even a new program. This approach recognizes that in academia, the introduction of any new material is difficult, and likely to be opposed by the individual professor, the department, or a university curricular committee. The modular approach provides a psychological and "political" solution to such opposition.

To start with the introduction of one or two modules into an already existing course is not threatening to the individual professor and does not require departmental or committee approval. Moreover, modules provide flexibility—that is, they can be arranged in all kinds of combinations, and can therefore be adapted to regional, cultural, and institutional needs. In short, the modular approach wisely starts with the acorn; the 1983 symposia naively started with the oak.

By way of verifying the "acorn approach," many of the Commission's "partner" institutions have moved through an increasingly discernible sequence of workshops, modules, courses, and programs. That is, an institution typically begins with one or more orientation workshops for faculty, then cautiously integrates a few Commission modules into already existing courses. Once students are receptive and faculty comfortable, the institution moves more boldly toward a full-fledged course, created by linking interrelated Commission modules. At first this course is made elective, then later required.

Ultimately, the more venturesome universities take the leap to multicourse degree programs at the baccalaureate or master's level. For example, at Philippine Women's University, this process has led to the integration of Commission modules into 12 undergraduate areas (1994), then an elective course "Introduction to Peace and Development" (May 1995), and more recently to a Bachelor of Arts program entitled "International Studies in Peace and Development" (January 1996).

Health Programs and the Acorn Approach

The wisdom of the "acorn" approach is nowhere better illustrated than in work with health science schools. Of all the professionals that should be drawn to disarmament teaching, medical, public health, and similar faculty should be foremost. Many people might still be mystified by how one bomb, in little more than one second, could have devastated a city like Hiroshima. But as arms control specialists and health professionals know—in large part through the work of the International Physicians for the Prevention of Nuclear War (IPPNW) and its U.S. affiliate, Physicians for Social Responsibility (PSR)—the destruction was caused by heat, blast, and radiation of incredible dimensions (Chapters 6 and 22).

The fearful thing to face today is that the Hiroshima bomb was a mere toy compared with the nuclear leviathans still stockpiled by at least five nations, despite the fall of the Soviet Union and the various arms reduction treaties achieved bilaterally by the United States and Russia, or multilaterally by the United Nations. The danger now comes not from deliberate action of the one remaining superpower, but from miscommunication, technological failures, plutonium stockpile theft, "outlaw state" dictators, and nuclear or similar terrorism (Chapter 22). There is a special danger from chemical and biological weapons, which can bring horrors worse than Hiroshima, yet the manufacture of such weapons of mass destruction is difficult to detect even with sophisticated monitoring devices (Chapters 7 and 8). The silent epilogue to Hiroshima's "Peace Memorial" video is still valid. "If there is another Hiroshima," it says, "there will be no one left to record the sadness."

Although nuclear weapons still pose a serious threat to humankind, medical and other health professional schools have been slow to introduce disarmament materials. To some extent this is understandable, because the curricula have been very rigid. But now the situation is changing. Building on earlier work by PSR and IPPNW, an international, interdisciplinary team of the IAUP/UN Commission began by developing a disarmament curriculum for these schools.

This curriculum features 18 modules that can stand alone, be inserted in other courses, or be sequenced to comprise one or more courses. Among these are modules on medical ethics and war, the role of health professionals in the prevention of war, and a sequence of four modules on nuclear weapons: nature and threat, short-term health effects, long-term health problems of survivors, and environmental consequences. Other modules include health consequences of chemical, biological, and conventional weapons; psychological consequences of the arms race; and underdevelopment (poverty and hunger) as both consequence and cause of the arms trade. Each module contains a detailed substantive outline accompanied by extensive readings and issues for student discussion. The list of modules is shown in the box.

In 1993, after an initial presentation at the IAUP triennial meeting in Kobe, Japan, Dr. Sidel, one of the Commission's team leaders, made a major address on the subject at the IPPNW World Congress in Mexico City. IPPNW and PSR then printed the entire curriculum (now titled, "Medicine and Peace"), in a loose-leaf binder to allow for frequent updating, and distributed it to every medical-school dean in the United States and to medical leaders abroad. This dissemination was reinforced in meetings with IPPNW affiliates all over the world, including those in Japan, Australia, Canada, China, Malaysia, the Netherlands, New Zealand, the United Kingdom, and Vietnam (Figure 21-1).

The results of this broad communication are just beginning to be realized. In the United States and Europe, a few medical schools have begun to adapt parts of the IAUP/UN material. In Tanzania, the medical dean of Muhimbili University said that he could adapt "only" five of the disarmament modules, given the rigidity of his curriculum. In Thailand, almost all of the medical school and public health deans in Bangkok have discussed the curriculum. In East Africa, three institutions are moving toward such commitments; in South Africa, three are awaiting funding; and in Nigeria, the University of Ibadan will be attempting to develop an interdisciplinary syllabus based on the material, drawing on scholars from medicine, political science, and sociology.

The merits of the modular concept are illustrated by Moi University in Kenya, where for some years a conventional medical course had been taught in "Injury and Trauma." After becoming a host professor for the Commission, Peter Nyarang'o continued to maintain the title and broad outline of this course. But he changed the course

"Medicine and Peace"

A model curriculum for medical schools prepared by the Commission on Arms Control Education, co-Sponsored by the International Association of University Presidents and United Nations Centre for Disarmament Affairs, in association with the International Physicians for the Prevention of Nuclear War (IPPNW) and Physicians for Social Responsibility (PSR). The curriculum has been translated into Spanish and is being translated into other languages.

 I. The Physician's Role in War: Aesculapius and Mars

 II. The Physician's Role in Promoting Peace: Medicine and the Prevention of War

 The Physician's Role in Promoting Peace: Conflict Management and Conflict Resolution

 III. The Nature of the Arms Race and Arms Control

 IV. Nuclear Weapons: History of the Nuclear Age

 Nuclear Weapons: The Nature of Nuclear Weapons and the Threat of Nuclear War

 Nuclear Weapons: Short-term Health Effects of Use of Nuclear Weapons

 Nuclear Weapons: Long-term Health Problems of Survivors

 Nuclear Weapons: Environmental Consequences of Nuclear War

 V. Chemical and Biological Weapons: Health Consequences of Production and Use

 VI. "Conventional" and "Low-Intensity" Warfare: Health Consequences

 VII. Environmental Consequences of the Arms Race

 VIII. Psychological Consequences of the Arms Race

 IX. Economic Consequences of the Arms Race

 X. "Underdevelopment" as a Consequence and as a Cause of the Arms Race

 XI. Towards World Order: Classic Conceptions

 Towards World Order: International Conflict as Human Conflict: Aggression, Violence, and War

 Towards World Order: Interdependence and Alternative Futures

 Towards World Order: Post-Cold-War International Politics and the Revival of the United Nations

Copies of this curriculum may be obtained from IPPNW and PSR. Addresses are provided in the Appendix.

substance dramatically by introducing IAUP/UN modules on the health impact of nuclear, biological, and chemical weapons.

Such encouraging developments would probably not be taking place if the Commission had required that participating institutions adopt the total "Medicine and Peace" curriculum. This "all-or-nothing" approach would have achieved the same results as the "core curricula" advocated by the 1983 IAUP symposia—no takers. Instead, institutions working with the Commission are asked to adapt the material to their own needs, and to use one or more modules in any way they think best for their own regions and culture. The result, in health programs and elsewhere, is self-evident.

Figure 21-1. Faculty member Ted Conna, M.D., Assistant Professor of Psychiatry and Co-Director of the Central Massachusetts Chapter of Physicians for Social Responsibility (second from left) and second-year medical students (left to right) Chris Rohan, Rachel Inker, and David Feinbloom at the University of Massachusetts Medical School use the Medicine and Peace Curriculum as a basis for discussing the roles of physicians in war and peace (Photograph by Bruce M. Fiene).

The Promotion of Survival

The Preamble to the UNESCO Charter states that "wars begin in the minds of men. It is therefore in the minds of men that we must construct the defenses of peace." Former President Rodrigo Carazo of Costa Rica put it more bluntly: "If you want peace, educate for peace," he said. The big problem is, how and where do we begin this process of peace education?

Ideally, the process should start with elementary school. That is where some children first learn to distrust anyone who looks different than they do. One thinks of Ray Bradbury's parable in the *Martian Chronicles*. An astronaut lands on a strange planet. With his ray gun he kills a huge spider, because the creature seems repellant. Unfortunately, the spider is part of a superrace, which takes revenge by destroying the human race.

Someday there might be a global peace education program for elementary or high school students, if admirable groups like Educators for Social Responsibility have their way. Meanwhile, the next best locus for peace education is the universities, especially those in developing countries, where there has been little or no constituency for arms control, whether military or academic. After all, future wars may be led by today's university students. If we can sensitize them to the need for arms limitations, we can inspire a movement of irresistible force.

Pierce Corden of the U.S. Arms Control and Disarmament Agency, after describing the development of the atomic bomb, recently made this comment: "We invented a chain reaction for war. Can we now create a chain reaction for peace?" The answer is, "Yes." If even one professor teaches peace to only 10 students a year, and some of them then teach it directly or by example in subsequent years, a network of peace-oriented citizens, government officials, and military officers emerges, bound together by a common cause, and insisting that the cause be heard. If we ever achieve world peace, it will likely be seen in retrospect as nothing more than a mosaic of individual peaces, motivated by the common cause of disarmament.

In the last analysis, the IAUP/UN Commission seeks to promote survival. It seeks to create university graduates who will give civilization a chance to continue. H. G. Wells said, "Human history becomes more and more a race between education and catastrophe." The chief motivation of every university, not just the one in Costa Rica, should be to help education win that race against catastrophe and for a peace based on social justice.

BIBLIOGRAPHY

Background

America's crisis in international competence. Prepared by American Institute for Foreign Study and National Council on Foreign Language and International Studies. Greenwich CT, 1982.

Jacobson, C.G., et al. *World security: The new challenge.* Niagara Falls: Dundurn Press (for Pugwash Canada), 1994.

Miles, L. *Costa Rica's University for Peace.* National Association of Foreign Student Advisors Newsletter, January 1982.

Miles, L. Hiroshima revisited: Reflections on war and peace. *Dialectics and humanism* (Polish Academy of Sciences), Nos. 3–4, 1985.

Spiegel, S. *World politics in a new era.* Fort Worth: Harcourt Brace College Publishers, 1995.

Wendon, A. and Schaffaer, C. *Language and peace.* London: Dartmouth Press, 1994.

Weston, B.H. *Toward post-Cold War global security.* Santa Barbara: Nuclear Age Peace Foundation, 1994.

Global Education

Eichenberg, R.C. and Klare, M. The President's conference on the responsibilities of the university in the nuclear age: A draft curriculum for arms control education. Prepared for the Talloires Conference, 1988.

Jamison, C.W. Can we change our thinking? Santa Barbara: Nuclear Age Peace Foundation, 1993.

Krieger, D. (ed.). Security in the nuclear age: A course outline. Santa Barbara: Nuclear Age Peace Foundation, 1993.

Krieger, D. (ed.). A student's guide to global responsibility. Santa Barbara: Nuclear Age Peace Foundation, 1993.

Miles, L. Universities for peace: The benign conspiracy. Vital Speeches of the Day, March 1, 1992.

Muller, R. *A world core curriculum.* New York: UNESCO, 1981.

The Talloires Declaration of University Presidents on the Responsibility of Universities in the Nuclear Age. 1988.

Peace and Disarmament Education

Daffern, T. A global overview of trends in universities in peace and world order studies. Prepared for the IAUP/UN Commission on Disarmament Education, New York, 1992.

Frolich, M., et al. *Learning to live in security.* Swedish pilot project on peace, disarmament, security, and development. Paris: UNESCO, 1991.

Klare, M. College peace studies. A guide to undergraduate peace studies programs at colleges and universities in the United States. Amherst, MA: Five College Program in Peace and World Security Studies, 1992.

Lall, B., and Fine, L. Reference guide: Peace studies in graduate education in New York. Studies in Intercultural Education. New York: New York University, 1988.

Miles, L. and Pettigrew, E. Peace lessons: Skills can be taught. *International Herald-Tribune,* April 28, 1993.

Peace education. New York: United Nations Association, 1995.

Reardon, B.A. *Comprehensive peace education.* New York: Teachers College Press, 1988.

Reardon, B.A. with Nordland, E., et al. *Learning peace: The promise of ecological and cooperative education.* Albany: State University of New York Press, 1994.

Strasser, J. and Ringler, D. *Dilemmas of war and peace.* An integrated audio-print course. Vol. 1, preview kit. Vol. II, A listener's guide. Madison: Annenberg/CPB Project and University of Wisconsin, 1993.

The Talloires guide: A transnational and transdisciplinary curriculum on global peace and security. Stockholm: Uppsala University, 1990.

Thomas, D.C. and Klare, M.T. (eds.). *Peace and world order studies: A curriculum guide,* 5th edition. Boulder CO: Westview Press, 1990.

IAUP/UN Commission on Disarmament Education

Global arms control issues: A model curriculum for undergraduate students. Prepared by Steven L. Spiegel et al. for the IAUP/UN Commission on Disarmament Education. Revised and expanded, 1994.

IAUP and UN support global program for arms control education. *Chronicle of Higher Education,* July 21, 1993.

Lux Mundi. Journal of International Association of University Presidents, November 1991–1995. (Contains articles on various phases of IAUP/UN Commission's work, including projects/project leaders, international seminars, curricular replication, progress since 1/95.)

Medicine and peace: A model curriculum for medical students. Prepared by Victor W. Sidel *et al.* for the IAUP/UN Commission on Disarmament Education, International Physicians for the Prevention of Nuclear War, and the Physicians for Social Responsibility. Revised 1995.

Peace, ecology, and development in Latin America. Adaptation of a Swarthmore College Syllabus. Prepared by Miguel Diaz-Barriga, et al. for the IAUP/UN Commission on Disarmament Education. 1994.

22

Preventing Nuclear War

LACHLAN FORROW and ERNESTO KAHAN

On July 16, 1945, a nuclear explosion shattered the quiet darkness of the New Mexico desert, and on-looking physicists watched with a mixture of awe and horror as the first atomic mushroom cloud rose thousands of feet above the desert floor. J. Robert Oppenheimer, leader of the Manhattan Project, reported later that he immediately recalled words of the Bhagavad Gita: "I am become death, destroyer of worlds."[1] Twenty-one days later, a second nuclear explosion obliterated within seconds most of the Japanese city of Hiroshima, killing over 100,000 people, almost all civilians. The impact on the medical care personnel of Hiroshima was movingly described by John Hersey[2] (see box). Three days later, another 70,000 civilians were killed when a third nuclear explosion destroyed most of the city of Nagasaki (Chapter 6). Every nuclear warhead built up to that time had then been used.

During the 1950s, first the United States and then the Soviet Union tested weapons based on the principle of nuclear fusion rather than nuclear fission—hydrogen or thermonuclear bombs. These weapons had the potential for an explosive force 1,000 times greater than that of the nuclear bombs dropped on Japan.

In 1962, in a series of articles published in the *New England Journal of Medicine,* a group of Boston physicians described the potential medical consequences of a thermonuclear attack on Boston. They estimated that following such an attack more than 2,000,000 people in the Boston area would die and 1,500,000 more would be injured, but would survive. Most physicians would be killed and their medical facilities destroyed, the disposal of corpses would be difficult or impossible, and the risks of epidemic disease would be high. Given the inability of the medical profession to respond to this devastation in any effective way, the authors concluded that "physicians, charged with the responsibility for the lives of their patients and the health of their communities, must also explore a new area of preventive medicine, the prevention of thermonuclear war."[3]

Over five decades since the first test in New Mexico, the governments of the United States, the former Soviet Union, Great Britain, France, and China built tens of thousands of nuclear warheads and conducted over 1,200 nuclear test explosions. By

From *Hiroshima*[2]

John Hersey

The lot of the majority of physicians of Hiroshima—with their offices and hospital destroyed, their equipment scattered, their own bodies incapacitated in varying degrees, explained why so many citizens who were hurt went untended and why so many who might have lived, died. Of the one hundred fifty doctors in the city, sixty-five were already dead and most of the rest were wounded. In the biggest hospital, that of the Red Cross, only six doctors were able to function, and only ten nurses. The sole uninjured doctor on the Red Cross Hospital staff was Dr. Sasaki. . . .

Dr. Sasaki worked without method, taking those who were nearest him first, and he noticed soon that the corridor seemed to be getting more and more crowded. Mixed with the abrasions and lacerations which most people in the hospital had suffered, he began to find dreadful burns. He realized then that casualties were pouring in from outdoors. There were so many that he began to pass up the lightly wounded; he decided that all he could hope to do was to stop people from bleeding to death. Before long, patients lay and crouched on the floors of the wards and the laboratories and all the other rooms, and in the corridors, and on the stairs, and in the front hall, and under the portecochere, and on the stone front steps, and in the driveway and courtyard, and for blocks each way in the streets outside. Wounded people supported maimed people; disfigured families leaned together, many people were vomiting. . . .

In a city of two hundred and forty-five thousand, nearly a hundred thousand had been killed or doomed at one blow; a hundred thousand more were hurt. At least ten thousand of the wounded made their way to the best hospital in town, which was altogether unequal to such a trampling since it had only six thousand beds, and they had all been occupied. The people in the suffocating crowd inside the hospital wept and cried for Dr. Sasaki, and the less seriously wounded came and pulled at his sleeve and begged him to go to the aid of the worse wounded. Tugged here and there in his stockinged feet, bewildered by the numbers, staggered by so much raw flesh, Dr. Sasaki lost all sense of profession and stopped working as a skillful surgeon and a sympathetic man; he became an automaton, mechanically wiping, daubing, winding, wiping, daubing, winding.

the mid-1980s, their arsenals contained more than 50,000 nuclear warheads, many of them fusion weapons with the explosive force of more than 1,000 Hiroshima bombs. Collectively, these weapons threatened the equivalent of 1,000,000 Hiroshima explosions, with the force of more than three tons of TNT for every man, woman, and child on the planet. On several occasions, including especially the Cuban Missile Crisis of 1962, political and military leaders seriously considered initiating a nuclear attack.[4]

In the 1980s, a series of scholarly reports by organizations such as the World Health Organization (WHO)[5] and the Institute of Medicine (IOM) of the U.S. National Academy of Sciences[6] summarized previously existing scientific knowledge about the short-, medium-, and long-term health effects of nuclear war, and also identified several previously unsuspected, but likely, effects of nuclear warfare. These have been summarized in most authoritative detail by the Scientific Committee on Problems of the Environment (SCOPE) Environmental Effects of Nuclear War (ENUWAR) Project,[7] in which approximately 100 physical and atmospheric scientists and an additional 200 agricultural and ecological scientists from more than 30 countries spent two years assessing the overall global consequences of nuclear war. Their conclusion was that the distant global effects of a large-scale nuclear war would likely far exceed the morbidity and mortality in areas near the nuclear explosions themselves. The most common cause of death would be mass starvation resulting from massive disruption of both ecological and agricultural systems and transportation and industrial infrastructure. An earlier study by WHO[5] concluded that several hundred million human fatalities would likely occur in the United States and the Soviet Union following a nuclear war between the superpowers. The SCOPE-ENUWAR report suggested that the overall global casualties from such a conflict would be between one and four billion lives, with most of the victims dying far from the explosions themselves, in conditions more like those fitting current images of Ethiopia and the Sudan than of Hiroshima and Nagasaki.

In 1995, some years after the end of the Cold War, the concern among military experts and the general public about the risk of large-scale nuclear war diminished considerably as the two nuclear superpowers, the United States and Russia, no longer targeted their weapons at each other. Nevertheless, widespread concern has remained about the future political situation in the former Soviet Union, and military experts have observed that these weapons can be reset to their previous targets within a very short period (as little as 10 to 15 minutes). Even if all arms control treaties that were in place by 1995 were fully implemented (by the year 2003), nearly 20,000 of the previous 50,000 nuclear warheads would remain—the equivalent power of 200,000 Hiroshima bombs.

Furthermore, in the mid-1990s concern about the dangers of nuclear weapons heightened in the context of rising terrorist activity, which included the fertilizer-bomb that killed 168 people in Oklahoma City, fatal bombings in Paris and in Israel, and the nerve gas release in the Tokyo subway system. For years, many experts had concluded that the only significant barrier to the construction of a nuclear weapon by terrorist groups was the difficulty in obtaining weapons-usable fissile material. Following the collapse of the former Soviet Union, increasing evidence suggested that hundreds of tons of such material were being kept under inadequate security, with several well-documented cases of theft of small amounts of both plutonium and enriched uranium.[8]

The burn, blast, and radiation effects of even an inefficiently-constructed nuclear weapon, with less than 10 percent of the yield of the Hiroshima bomb, would cause fatal or near-fatal injuries almost immediately to most individuals within 600 meters of the explosion. In the aftermath, many more people would almost certainly die because of the inability of emergency personnel to find and transfer them safely to medical facilities capable of providing adequate treatment for the extraordinarily complex problems resulting from simultaneous burn, blast, and radiation injuries. In addition, fallout would leave several square kilometers contaminated by dangerous levels of radiation.[9]

The spectrum of possible nuclear war thus ranges from the explosion of a relatively small warhead, such as a Hiroshima-type bomb, to the global devastation predicted by the SCOPE-ENUWAR studies. Prevention of nuclear war must encompass this full range.

Public Health Responsibilities

Health workers have a central and urgent professional responsibility for helping to prevent nuclear war because:

- Health workers have a professional responsibility to treat disease and to reduce mortality.
- The use of nuclear weapons in war would cause death and illness on a massive and, in the case of large-scale war, unprecedented scale.
- Health workers would be unable to intervene effectively in the human injury and death expected following a nuclear attack.
- Prevention is the only way to reduce mortality where treatment is ineffective.
- The use of nuclear weapons is possible, or even probable, in the decades ahead.
- Efforts by health workers could help prevent nuclear war.[10]

Although a comprehensive analysis of the etiology of nuclear war might identify many contributing factors, a conceptual framework could include the following six steps:

1. Development of knowledge of the physics and technology involved in building a nuclear weapon.
2. Obtaining fissile materials, such as weapons-grade uranium and plutonium.
3. Construction, testing, and stockpiling of the weapons.
4. Development and maintenance of plans for use of the weapons.
5. Development of political or military situations in which actual use is seriously considered.
6. Actual use.

In the 1960s and then again in the 1980s, massive civil defense plans were proposed and, to a variable extent, implemented in the United States, the Soviet Union, and other countries. Detailed plans prepared by the U.S. Federal Emergency Management Agency (FEMA) claimed that with effective evacuation over a period of four to seven days, proper sheltering, and other civil defense measures, 80 percent of the U.S. population could survive a large-scale nuclear attack. After detailed scrutiny, the FEMA claims were widely discredited. Accepting as reasonable the survival of 80

Figure 22-1. Physicians for Social Responsibility billboard in 1980s in Philadelphia (Source: Physicians for Social Responsibility [PSR]).

percent of the U.S. population is, it was argued, accepting as reasonable the deaths of 45 million people.[11] Furthermore, these plans did not take into account the environmental and agricultural devastation predicted by the SCOPE-ENUWAR studies. After a vigorous public debate involving many physicians and public health workers, President Ronald Reagan, who had initially proposed $4.1 billion for the FEMA program, concluded that "a nuclear war can never be won and must never be fought" (Figure 22-1).

Current efforts therefore focus on preventing nuclear war, mainly by two approaches: for states that already possess nuclear weapons, the doctrine of nuclear deterrence; for states that do not (yet) possess nuclear weapons, the nuclear nonproliferation regime, which has been enshrined in the Nuclear Non-Proliferation Treaty (NPT).

The doctrine of deterrence has been analyzed in considerable detail by many scholars, with conflicting views over whether its dominant effect has been to prevent nuclear war or to drive a relentlessly escalating arms race.[12] As Bernard Lown has warned, "In order for it to be effective, nuclear deterrence must operate perfectly and forever. No such expectations are permissible for any human activity."[13] Figure 22-2 illustrates the relationship between the threat of nuclear war, regional wars (in which so-called conventional weapons are used), civil wars, terrorism, ethnic or national conflicts, and societal violence.

The process by which a conflict might generate the use of nuclear weapons may

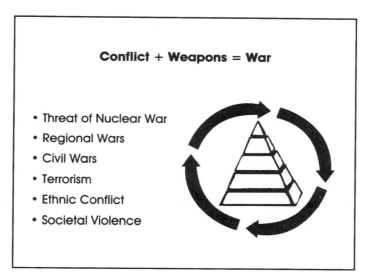

Figure 22-2. The pyramid of conflict and the cycle of violence (Source: International Physicians for the Prevention of Nuclear War [IPPNW]).

be termed ''a spiral of false security.'' In this process, a logical chain of events takes place following the decision to create a nuclear arsenal. The starting point of the spiral is the decision to use nuclear weapons as a means of deterring attack by others. For advanced technological nations, this is not a complicated decision, owing to the availability of plutonium and the readily accessible knowledge of how to construct nuclear weapons. But once a nation's adversaries know that nuclear weapons are being used as a deterrent—and they must know in order for the deterrent to be effective—this information sparks a chain reaction that can increase the danger of nuclear war, either by intention or by accident.

Similarly, the NPT which, with over 180 signatories, is the most widely accepted treaty, has been hailed by some as the most important vehicle for controlling the spread—and therefore preventing the use—of nuclear weapons. Others, however, have condemned the treaty—at least as it has been implemented—for its perpetuation of a world of nuclear ''haves'' and ''have-nots,'' in which the latter will inevitably seek to become the former.

Both prevention approaches aim to lower the probability of the use of nuclear weapons, but each envisions a world in which several nuclear weapons states continue to possess thousands of nuclear warheads. (In parallel with their status in the UN Security Council, the United States, Russia, France, Great Britain, and China are often referred to as the ''permanent five.'') With 20,000 weapons currently expected to remain in place by the year 2003, then even with one out of 100,000 chance in any given year that any specific warhead would be used—whether because of a government's carefully planned military strategy, or as a result of miscalculation or terrorism—the risk of actual nuclear devastation rises rapidly over time. Increasingly, physicians, public health workers, lawyers, military leaders, and others have therefore called for abolition of nuclear weapons as the only plausible permanent approach to the prevention of nuclear war.

Role of Health Professionals

As in other areas, the role of public health professionals in the prevention of nuclear war can be analyzed in terms of three levels of activity: primary, secondary, and tertiary prevention. "Primary prevention" is often used to refer to efforts aimed at preventing the disease—that is, war—itself; "secondary prevention" refers to preventing or minimizing the effects of the disease after it has already begun; and "tertiary prevention" refers to the treatment or amelioration of the effects of the disease, including rehabilitation of affected individuals.[14]

Unfortunately, efforts by health professionals to address health problems related to war too rarely include such a comprehensive approach, as illustrated in an exercise that was performed in Israel to train staff in dealing with affected people after a chemical warfare attack. Although this was purely an exercise, the medical staff were affected both emotionally and professionally in two profound ways:

1. They were all made aware of the enormity of such a possibility and the severity of the effects on the population with which they would have to deal.
2. Since the available medical skills and resources were always inadequate to deal with the number of potential casualties, physicians would have to establish extremely difficult triage priorities.[15]

During the preparation for the exercise, the emphasis regarding medical duties was placed on treatment (tertiary prevention), with a complete absence of discussion of primary or even secondary prevention. This was despite the fact that a paper discussed for technical purposes in one of the preparatory lectures for this exercise[16] concluded that physicians must be active concerning the inadvisability of developing, stockpiling, and using chemical and biological weapons. This conclusion was ignored by the government of Israel.

Many health personnel would have to attempt to take care of those affected if nuclear, chemical, or bacteriological warfare occurs. And most, if not all, would have been trained to ask the questions: "Why did this happen? Could it have been prevented?"[17] Posing such questions is clearly the first step in formulating an effective public health program. However, none of the dozens of physicians and nurses who participated in the exercise, or the military representatives in charge, suggested that these questions might be a part of the solution to the problem.

Fortunately many health workers have responded vigorously to the threat of nuclear war by engaging in activities that contribute in important ways to the primary prevention of nuclear war. These activities have fallen into three general categories: research, education, and advocacy. Through such research efforts as those culminating in the publication of the 1962 articles in the *New England Journal of Medicine* and in the WHO and SCOPE-ENUWAR reports of the broad health and environmental effects of large-scale nuclear war, public health workers and colleagues in related disciplines have helped ensure that any discussions about nuclear weapons are solidly based in scientific knowledge. These efforts appear to have made a major contribution to debates about policies such as those related to civil defense.

More recently, the International Physicians for the Prevention of Nuclear War (IPPNW), a federation of 83 national affiliates that was founded in 1980, published in partnership with the Institute for Energy and Environmental Research a series of three books on the health and environmental problems associated with nuclear weapons. *Radioactive Heaven and Earth*[18] describes in detail the health and environmental effects of nuclear weapons testing in, on, and above the earth. *Plutonium: Deadly Gold of the Nuclear Age*[19] reviews the hazards of plutonium production, including the dangers of handling and storing radioactive waste. *Nuclear Wastelands: A Global Guidebook to Nuclear Weapons Production and Its Health and Environmental Effects* was published in 1995.[20] Together with early reports of the expected effects of nuclear warfare, these three books provide a comprehensive analysis of the significant health and environmental problems associated with preparations for nuclear warfare—even if it never again takes place.

Organizations such as IPPNW and its national affiliates have also mounted vigorous educational campaigns to ensure that political and military leaders, as well as the general public, are informed of the conclusions of these research activities. IPPNW's work was recognized in 1984 by UNESCO, which honored the federation with its Peace Education Prize, citing "especially remarkable activity to inform public opinion and mobilize the conscience of mankind for peace." The following year, IPPNW was awarded the 1985 Nobel Peace Prize in Oslo. In its citation, the Nobel Committee again stressed the importance of IPPNW's educational efforts:

[IPPNW] has performed a considerable service to mankind by spreading authoritative information and by creating an awareness of the catastrophic consequences of nuclear warfare. . . . This in turn contributes to an increase in the pressure of public opposition to the proliferation of nuclear weapons and to a redefining of priorities, with greater attention being paid to health and other humanitarian issues. Such an awakening of public opinion . . . can give the present arms limitation negotiations new perspectives and a new seriousness.[21]

In the 1980s, IPPNW and other organizations of health professionals moved beyond research and educational activities to advocacy for specific steps that, in their judgment, would reduce the likelihood of nuclear war. The areas of concern, described

Figure 22-3. IPPNW members march in Paris in 1995 to protest French nuclear testing (Source: Dr. Jacques Mongnet and Dr. Abraham Behar, IPPNW/France).

below, can be related to the first five of the six steps in the etiologic pathway toward nuclear war, which was described earlier in the chapter.

1. *Development of knowledge of the physics and technology involved in building a nuclear weapon.* This knowledge cannot be "disinvented," and all preventive efforts must therefore focus on other steps.

2. *Obtaining fissile materials, such as weapons-grade uranium and plutonium.* IPPNW and its affiliates have advocated a ban on production and stockpiling of all weapons-usable fissile materials; IPPNW also advocates placing existing fissile materials under secure international control. Transport of such materials should be for the sole purpose of final storage under international control or preparation for such storage. As long as weapons-usable material exists and is not fully secure, the possibility of theft and illicit construction of a nuclear warhead will remain, even if all nation-states agree to dismantle their arsenals.

3. *Construction, testing, and stockpiling of weapons.* A cornerstone of global advocacy for the prevention of nuclear war has been a campaign by health professionals to permanently end all nuclear test explosions (Figures 22-3 and 22-4). In part, as a result of lobbying efforts by health professionals, all nuclear weapons states except for China and France have observed a testing moratorium since 1993. IPPNW and

Figure 22-4. Members of the American Public Health Association demonstrate at nuclear weapons underground test site in Nevada in 1986 (Source: American Public Health Association [APHA]).

other organizations have urged not only a ban on production of any additional nuclear weapons, but also the destruction of all existing stockpiles of nuclear weapons as rapidly as possible.

4. *Development and maintenance of plans for use of the weapons.* IPPNW and organizations such as the International Association of Lawyers Against Nuclear Arms (IALANA) and the International Peace Bureau (IPB) concluded that the effects of the use of nuclear weapons on medical personnel and medical facilities would constitute a violation of the Geneva Conventions of 1949 and therefore a clear violation of international law. IPPNW and its partner organizations thus worked closely with representatives to the World Health Assembly, the governing body of the World Health Organization, to support a resolution instructing the Director-General of WHO, under WHO's authority as an agency of the United Nations, to request the following advisory opinion from the International Court of Justice (Figure 22-5), located in The Hague: ''In the view of the health and environmental effects, would the use of nuclear weapons by a state in war or other armed conflict be a breach of its obligations under international law, including the WHO constitution?''

In May 1993, the World Health Assembly adopted this wording for its historic resolution (WHA46.40, Health and Environmental Effects of Nuclear Weapons). WHO officially submitted the question to the Court in August 1993, and in September, the Court requested written statements on the issue from WHO member nations. By the time of the extended deadline of September 1994, the Court had received statements from 37 nations. With the exception of those from nuclear powers and their allies, the statements urged the Court to respond positively to the request. In addition, over 100 million people around the world, 43 million in Japan alone, signed petitions opposing nuclear weapons, and a selection of these were accepted by the Court as evidence.

In December 1994, the United Nations General Assembly resolved to request the International Court of Justice urgently to render its advisory opinion on the following question: Is the threat or use of nuclear weapons permitted in any circumstance under international law? Thus, it formally asked the Court if even threatening to use nuclear weapons should be considered illegal.

On July 8, 1996, the Court rendered its advisory opinions. The Court declined to rule on the question raised by WHO but used health arguments in its rulings on the question raised by the UN General Assembly. The court unamnimously declared that "there is an obligation to pursue in good faith and to bring to a conclusion negotiations leading to nuclear disarmament in all its aspects . . ." By a split vote, the Court declared that "the threat of use or use of nuclear weapons would be contrary to the rules of international law applicable in armed conflict, and in particular the principles and rules of humanitarian law." The only exception to this sweeping declaration of illegality, some members of the Court held, was threat or use "in an extreme circumstance of self-defence, in which the very survival of the State would be at stake."

5. *Development of political or military situations in which use of nuclear weapons is seriously considered.* Health professionals have worked together across political chasms to address common health problems and, in so doing, to help diffuse the political and social tensions among nations that increase the risk of war, including nuclear war. This work has included activities, ranging from medical exchange programs between the United States and the Soviet Union at the peak of the Cold War to health confrences such as those among Israeli, Palestinian, Egyptian, Jordanian, and other health workers that began in 1995.

In early 1995, IPPNW integrated all of its research, educational, and advocacy activities under a single program, Abolition 2000, with a single concrete goal: that there be by the year 2000 a signed global treaty committing the world to the permanent elimination of nuclear weapons according to a fixed timetable. By the end of 1995, hundreds of other nongovernmental organizations had joined an Abolition 2000 network. In addition, the government of Australia had established the Canberra Commission, made up of 15 of the world's leading experts on nuclear weapons and disarmament, charged with preparing a report to the United Nations by August 1996 on the practical steps required to achieve the complete elimination of nuclear weapons.

Figure 22-5. The International Court of Justice in the Hague, which issued an advisory opinion on the use or threat of use of nuclear weapons in response to a request by the General Assembly of the United Nations. This request was brought about by the International Physicians for the Prevention of Nuclear War and other groups (Source: United Nations/DPI/82584).

Long-term Primary Prevention of Nuclear War: Addressing Violence and Its Roots

Even if the ambitious goal of a signed treaty for the complete elimination of nuclear weapons were accomplished, and even if that treaty were implemented early in the twenty-first century, efforts to prevent nuclear war would not end. Given the fact that knowledge of how to construct a nuclear weapon will never be lost, these efforts must address underlying reasons why any individuals or nations might seek nuclear weapons to further their security or other interests.

As expressed in IPPNW's "Pyramid of Conflict" (Figure 22-2), these efforts must address the underlying patterns and causes of violence at all levels of society, including their roots in poverty and in equality, lack of freedom and development, and the capacity of the human species for ethnocentrism, prejudice, hatred, and violent conflict. As David Hamburg has written:

> The evolution that is distinctively human centers around our increasing capacity for learning, for communication chiefly by language, for cooperative problem solving, for

complex social organization, and for advanced toolmaking and tool using. These attributes have gotten us here by enormously enhancing our capabilities, not only to adapt to the widest variety of habitats, but also to modify our habitats profoundly in ways that suit our purposes.

Now we are challenged as never before to find ways in which these unique capacities can be used to prevent us from destroying ourselves and especially to prevent the final epidemic; to prevent that will make possible the search for a decent quality of life for everyone on the planet. If we have lost our sense of purpose in the modern world, perhaps this perspective can help us regain it.[19]

REFERENCES

1. Cited in Newhouse, J. *War and peace in the nuclear age.* New York: A.A. Knopf, 1989.
2. Hersey, J. *Hiroshima.* New York: A.A. Knopf, 1946, pp. 24–26.
3. Sidel, V.W., Geiger, H.J. and Lown, B. The physician's role in the post-attack period. *New England Journal of Medicine* 266: 1137–1145, 1962.
4. Ellsberg, D. Introduction. *Protest and survive,* Thompson, E.P. and Smith D. (eds). New York: Monthly Review Press, 1981.
5. World Health Organization. *Effects of nuclear war on health and health services.* Geneva: WHO 1984, 1987.
6. Institute of Medicine. *The medical implications of nuclear war.* Washington, DC: National Academy of Sciences, 1986.
7. Pittock, A.B., et al. *Environmental consequences of nuclear war: Volume I, Physical and atmospheric effects.* Harwell, M.A. and Hutchinson, T.C. *Environmental consequences of nuclear war: Volume II, Ecological and agricultural effects.* Scientific Committee on Problems of the Environment (SCOPE) 28, Chichester and New York: John Wiley and Sons, 1985, 1986.
8. Allison, G. et al. *Avoiding nuclear anarchy.* Cambridge, MA: MIT Press, 1996.
9. Rotblat, J. *Nuclear radiation in warfare.* London: Taylor and Francis, 1988.
10. Cassel, C. and Jameton, A. Medical responsibility and thermonuclear war. *Ann. Intern. Med.* 97(3):426–432, 1982.
11. Leaning, J. and Keyes, L. (eds.). *The counterfeit ark: Crisis relocation for nuclear war.* Cambridge, Mass.: Ballinger/Harper & Row, 1984.
12. Abrecht, P. and Koshy, N. (eds.). *Before it's too late.* Geneva: World Council of Churches, 1983.
13. Lown, B. *Never whisper in the presence of wrong.* Cambridge, MA: International Physicians for the Prevention of Nuclear War, 1993.
14. Last, J.M. *A dictionary of epidemiology.* New York: Oxford University Press, 1993, p. 84.
15. Kahan, E. Primary, secondary and tertiary prevention of genocidal weapons. *Medicine and War.* 7:9–15, 1991.
16. Sidel, V.W. and Goldwyn, R.M. Chemical and biologic weapons—a primer. *New Engl. J. Med.* 274(1):21–27, 1966.
17. Rose, G. Sick individuals and sick populations. *Int. J. Epidemiol.* 14:32–38, 1985.
18. Special Commission of International Physicians for the Prevention of Nuclear War and the Institute for Energy and Environmental Research. *Radioactive heaven and earth: The health and environmental effects of nuclear weapons testing in, on, and above the earth.* New York: Apex Press, 1991.

19. Special Commission of International Physicians for the Prevention of Nuclear War and the Institute for Energy and Environmental Research. *Plutonium: Deadly gold of the nuclear age.* Cambridge, Mass.: International Physicians Press, 1992.

20. Makhijani, A., Hu, H., and Yih, K. (eds.) *Nuclear wastelands: A global guidebook to nuclear weapons production and its health and environmental effects.* Cambridge, Mass.: MIT Press, 1995.

21. Norwegian Nobel Committee. Citation for 1985 Nobel Peace Prize. Oslo: Norwegian Nobel Committee, 1985.

22. Hamburg, D. Introduction. *Institute of Medicine: The medical implications of nuclear war.* Washington: National Academy of Sciences, 1986.

23

Nurses and the Prevention of War: Public Health Nurses and the Peace Movement in World War I

ELIZABETH TEMKIN

Since the Crimean War, when Florence Nightingale's care of wounded British soldiers marked the beginning of modern nursing practice, war has been recognized as a catalyst for the advancement of the nursing profession. Historically, wars have led to new opportunities, better education, and increased status for nurses. Nevertheless, nursing has a rich heritage of leaders who have understood that war and health could never coexist.

In the United States, World War I coincided with the rise of public health nursing, and the rise of a new type of nurse. The pioneers of public health nursing were socialists and feminists with a progressive spirit of social reform. In diagnosing their patients' ailments, they searched not only for the immediate physiologic causes, but for the underlying economic and political causes. Militarism, they realized, was a health hazard. During World War I, three nurses in particular—Margaret Sanger, Lillian Wald, and Lavinia Dock—made peace activism a fundamental part of their work to improve the public's health. This chapter will highlight these nurses' writings and actions on behalf of peace and will examine the characteristics of early public health nursing that fostered a spirit of activism.

Photographs of Margaret Sanger typically showed her looking solemn. Her supporters often told her to "lighten up," but she would reply, "I am the protagonist of women who have nothing to laugh at."[1] The women Sanger was referring to were the obstetrical patients she nursed through repeated unwanted pregnancies. Her experiences led her to open the first birth control clinic in America and to found the American Birth Control League, which later became the Planned Parenthood Federation. Sanger once vowed that she would not get involved with peace activism because

Figure 23-1. Illustration published in 1917. (Source: *Birth Control Review,* June 1917).

she feared that the birth control movement would suffer if she did not focus on it exclusively. But to Sanger, war and women's lack of control over fertility were so intertwined that she disregarded her vow. The journal she founded and edited, the *Birth Control Review,* was filled with essays and cartoons devoted to pacifism. In her autobiography, recounting how she and her co-workers sold the *Review* in the streets, Sanger told a story of how Americans' obsession with the war blinded them from recognizing the birth control movement:

> During the war, it was astonishing how many men, in and out of uniform, mistook Birth Control for British Control. ''We don't want no British control here!'' they exclaimed. [We] would correct them, ''Birth Control,'' and someone would call, ''Oh, that's worse!''[1]

Sanger argued that war and birth control were inherently at odds (Figure 23-1). In a militaristic state, women would forever be consigned to the role of ''mere breeding machines . . . grinding out cannon fodder.''[2] Women were denied access to contraception precisely because the state needed them to reproduce a vast army to justify national expansion and to fight its wars. In an essay titled, "Battalions of Unwanted Babies the Cause of War," she wrote:

> In every nation of militaristic tendencies, we find the reactionaries demanding a higher and still higher birthrate. Their plea is, first, that great armies are needed to defend the country; second, that a huge population is required to assure the country its proper place among the powers of the world. . . . As soon as the country becomes overpopulated, these reactionaries proclaim loudly its moral right to expand . . . and to take by force such room as it needs.[3]

Sanger pointed out that the European War began among the countries with the highest birthrates. Once German mothers were conscripted to bear children out of "patriotic duty," Germany's claim to new territory was inevitable.[3]

In America, as well, the breeding of healthy babies was becoming the subject of unprecedented government concern. As a wartime handbill from the Maternity Center of New York announced, "baby saving" was "now a serious problem of national security." During the war, vast strides were made in maternal-child health care, culminating in the Sheppard-Towner Maternity and Infancy Protection Act of 1921, which designated federal funding for state-run maternal and infant care clinics. While women reformers initiated such acts to boost maternal-child welfare, officials approved them to boost the war effort.[4] Most reformers saw the clinics as a great innovation in public health, but Sanger vigorously opposed them. She argued that state-run maternal care was designed to "keep the slaves in ignorance," for at the clinics "the poor woman is taught how to have her seventh child, when what she wants to know is how to avoid bringing into the world her eighth."[5,6] The Sheppard-Towner Act confirmed that the "traditional after-the-war duties for women" consisted of three commandments: breed, breed, and breed (Figure 23-2). The post-World-War-II generation known as "baby-boomers" is testimony to the recurrent validity of this cartoon.

Sanger recognized that war was not only a struggle between nations, but also a struggle between classes, since men killed in combat were disproportionately from the working class. As Sanger saw it, war was an inevitable process "imposed upon the workers" to correct the imbalance between a growing population and a static food supply.[2,3] Birth control, she argued, could replace war as the restorer of equilibrium between food supply and human demand, only without coercion or bloodshed. A policy of reproduction based on "quality, not quantity" would end the need for war and change the moral climate that allowed war to flourish. Once women limited births and stopped "mak[ing] life cheap," human life would become "too valuable to be sacrificed on the battlefield."[2,3] It was up to each woman to usher in an era of peace by practicing contraception and refusing to be "a victim of unwilling motherhood and the handmaiden of militarism."[2]

Like Sanger, Lillian Wald envisioned a form of nursing that treated personal ills by correcting social ills. Wald invented the term "public health nurse" to describe a

Figure 23-2. "The New Vision," an illustration published in 1918. (Source: *Birth Control Review,* December 1918).

new type of nurse, whose mission was no less than to "bring . . . human beings to a higher level."[7] In 1895, Wald established the Henry Street Nurses Settlement in the immigrant community of New York's Lower East Side. Wald believed that nurses could best diagnose and serve the needs of a community by living within it. The role of the public health nurse was to promote both the physical health and social cohesion of a neighborhood. When World War I broke out, Wald became a key figure in a new wing of the American peace movement: the wing of social reformers who believed that, as self-proclaimed "experts in social relations," they were best equipped to solve international problems.[8]

Wald spoke frequently about the connection between her work as a nurse and her work as a peace activist. In a front-page interview in a 1914 issue of the *New York Evening Post,* Wald explained the basis of pacifist sentiment among social reformers like herself: "Today a vast army of trained men and women are at work in our large cities. . . . In its broadest conception their work is teaching the sanctity of human life, and . . . the doctrine of the brotherhood of man. . . . War is the doom of all that it has taken years of peace to build up." Wald expressed the same idea by saying, "When militarism comes in at the door, democracy flies out of the window."[9]

In September 1914, Wald and a group of other social reformers met at the Henry Street Settlement to discuss how to stem the tide of militarism that was threatening both the funding and the spirit of their projects. Out of that meeting was born the

American Union Against Militarism, a group which, according to one journalist, "put the fist in pacifist."[10] Over the next year, with Wald as president, membership in the UAM rose from 15 to 15,000.

The UAM's first major effort was in response not to the war erupting in Europe, but the war threatening to erupt between the United States and Mexico. In 1916, Mexico was in a state of civil war between the government forces, led by Venustiano Carranza, and opposing factions, led by Pancho Villa and Emiliano Zapata. In retaliation for the U.S. government's support of Carranza, Villa led a series of raids across the border, killing American civilians. Against Carranza's wishes, President Wilson sent an American expedition to pursue Villa. In June 1916, American troops led by Captain Morey clashed with Carranza's forces in the town of Carrizal. Twelve U.S. soldiers were killed. The *New York Times'* headline proclaimed, "American Cavalry Ambushed by Carranza Troops," and the paper concluded that "war between the United States and Mexico seems inevitable."[11] That is when the founder of public health nursing rushed in to save the day.

Wald and the other members of the UAM recognized the power of the press to manipulate public opinion through the use of words like "ambush." In fact, a letter left by Captain Morey revealed that the "ambush" had actually been provoked by the Americans. In publicizing Morey's letter, the press managed to gloss over this minor detail, instead sensationalizing the "thrilling tale" of how Morey lay wounded in a ditch and "risked death in the desert alone."[11] Trusting that if Americans knew the facts about the incident, the war frenzy could be dampened, the UAM placed full-page advertisements in all the major newspapers across the country. The ads contained the complete text of Morey's letter and claimed, "If this is true—and it seems impossible to doubt it—we submit that the Carrizal episode does not constitute a just cause of war." The ads urged readers to write their Congressmen to oppose a war that would be a "blot upon American history."[11]

Amazingly, the ploy worked. Woodrow Wilson's biographer wrote that, as a result of the ads, "Wilson was immediately overwhelmed with a flood of telegrams, letters, and petitions. . . . Not slowly, but almost at once, good sense returned to the official circles in Washington."[12] The UAM organized roundtable discussions between Mexican and American citizens, paving the way for official deliberations between the two governments, in which the United States agreed to withdraw all troops from Mexico. To Wald, averting a war was all in a day's work for a public health nurse. As she pointed out, problem-solving through conference instead of violence, while novel to world leaders, was practiced by her clients at the settlement house every day[13] (see Chapter 25).

The UAM's efforts to stop America's entrance into World War I were less successful, but equally creative. In April 1916, Wilson made a tour of midwestern cities to rally support for increased military preparedness. In one speech, Wilson challenged those who disagreed with him to "hire large halls" and state their views. The UAM took Wilson's suggestion literally and hired Carnegie Hall for the first of a series of mass meetings to tour 11 cities. At the end of the tour, a delegation from the UAM met with President Wilson to inform him of the antimilitarist spirit they witnessed throughout the country. At this meeting, Wald questioned Wilson's policy of peace through preparedness, commenting that military buildup logically leads to war. Wilson answered, "Well, logically, Miss Wald, but I have not the least regard for logic."[11] Eleven months later, the United States entered the war.

With the country at war, pacifists had to choose between continuing to oppose the war or supporting U.S. intervention with the hope of a quick and lasting peace. This dilemma led the UAM to dissolve into factions, but its legacy lives on today. One splinter group of the UAM established a legal bureau for the preservation of civil rights during wartime; this group is now the American Civil Liberties Union.[13]

While Wald and Sanger combined nursing and peace activism in their individual efforts, Lavinia Dock worked to make peace a priority of nurses as a group. Dock was one of the core group of nurses at the Henry Street Settlement. She was the first nurse to write a book on sexually transmitted diseases, and her writing reflected a public health focus on prevention. Dock was also a leader of the movement to professionalize nursing and was one of the founders of the organizations that became the American Nurses Association (ANA), the National League for Nursing, and the International Council of Nurses. For Dock, professionalization was not merely a matter of gaining prestige or leverage for nurses, but was a means to create a large, vocal lobby on issues of social justice.

Dock was committed to the teachings of the anarchist Petr Kropotkin. Considered the major anarchist theorist of the nineteenth century, Kropotkin envisioned free association and voluntary mutual aid as the basis for a moral society. While today the ANA is not often considered an anarchist organization, that was the spirit in which Dock founded it, claiming that free association in professional organizations would unite nurses into "a moral force on all the great social questions of the day."[14] When the great social question was war in Europe, Dock used her monthly column in the *American Journal of Nursing* to rally nurses into a united voice for peace.

Dock was often the sole voice of dissent in a journal that extolled the new opportunities war was creating for nurses. Dock recognized that nurses' role of healing soldiers so that they could return to battle was of dubious moral value (see Chapter 18). She wrote in her column: "Does it not seem that the very work of the Red Cross . . . is a tacit giving of a moral support to war which every human being should refuse to give? Does it not make war more tolerable, more possible, and, by mitigating, keep it bolstered up and alive?"[15] Although Dock's column, the "Foreign Department," was the most logical place for news from Europe to appear, Dock refused to include it. She explained to her readers that her column "intends to boycott this particular war. The only mention it will draw from us will be denunciation of 'war' as a specimen of man's stupidity."[15]

Dock was not using the word *man* in its generic sense here. She was a prototype of the new feminist wing of the peace movement, which emerged as a powerful force

Women and the Peace Movement

Mary-Wynne Ashford and Yolanda Huet-Vaughn

The actions of groups of women in the peace movement are quite different from actions taken by mixed groups or groups of men. Women analyze the causes of war differently, and from their different perspective, they have developed different governance structures, decision-making methods, and strategies. Women offer a new viewpoint on the centuries-old problem of war, at a time when the urgency to prevent war has become more compelling than ever before.

In general, women see the patriarchal organization of society as a major factor that contributes to the war system. Virginia Woolf wrote in 1938 of the importance of seeing the connections between patriarchy and militarism, patriarchy and fascism, and patriarchy and war.[1] While some authors feel that women oppose war because their maternal role makes them innately peaceful, the support many women give to war efforts undermines this idea. Woolf believed that women's strong convictions came from their being outside the sphere of power and wealth. Women reject the system of one person's having power over another, and speak of "power to" instead of "power over." Women see grave dangers in promoting patriotism and nationalism, often quoting Woolf's statement: "As a woman I have no country. As a woman I want no country. As a woman, my country is the whole world."[2]

Because of their opposition to patriarchal organization, and their desire to ensure that all voices are heard, women try to organize and govern their groups with a minimum of hierarchy. Often there is no designated leader, and, when there is, the role of the leader is to facilitate, not to control.

1. Pierson, R.R. "Did your mother wear army boots?" Feminist theory and women's relation to war, peace and revolution. In Sharon, M., Holden, P. and Ardener, S. (eds.), *Images of women in peace and war.* London: Macmillan Education, 1987.

2. Woolf, V. *Three guineas.* New York: Harcourt Brace and World; the Hogarth Press, 1966 (orig. 1938).

at the start of the war. (See box for another perspective on women and the peace movement.) Less than a month after war was declared, 1,500 women, including Dock and Wald, marched down New York's Fifth Avenue in a Women's Peace Parade. Feminist pacifists emphasized the gender differences that made men prone to violence and women suited to peacekeeping. They claimed that women have an innate gift for nurturing and cooperation, while men are naturally aggressive. Many of Dock's writings on the prevention of war sound remarkably like her writings on the prevention of syphilis. Indeed, according to Dock, both problems had a common root: If men could simply be taught to control their impulses for sex and violence, syphilis and war could be eradicated. Nurses could take the lead in modeling alternations to nationalism. In her column in the *American Journal of Nursing,* she implored her colleagues serving as military nurses to reject a veteran's label upon returning home: "I hope we shall not have "Mexican War Nurses" or "European War Nurses" or any kind that applaud and foster the war spirit—blight of nations. Surely women should now give men a new lead, not follow them in their old barbarous customs."[15] Dock saw the ballot as the ultimate tool to project women's values onto the country's politics and morals. Recognizing suffrage and peace as linked issues, Dock campaigned mil-

Women use consensus decision making, stressing the full participation by each member. The strength of a leaderless movement was shown by the actions of Women Strike for Peace, during the early 1960s, when women all over the United States participated in ever-changing demonstrations against atmospheric testing of nuclear weapons:

> With no paid staff and no designated leaders, thousands of women in different parts of the country, most of them previously unknown to each other, managed to establish a loosely structured communications network capable of swift and effective direct action on a national and international scale.[3]

Because of women's position outside power structures, when women take action to oppose war and militarism, they must devise their own methods to attract attention to their protest. Mothers of the Plaza de Mayo in Argentina stood in silent witness for the "disappeared," their presence alone accusing the government of torture and murder. The women wore white scarves embroidered with the names of their sons and daughters who had disappeared after they were seized by the military.

The women of Greenham Common aroused enormous controversy for their actions through the 1980s when they camped outside the U.S. missile base at Greenham Common. The women lived in plastic shelters in the mud and rain, refusing to develop any system of hierarchy or leadership, some staying for weekends, others for years. The women were frequently jailed for obstructing the actions of the military, for cutting through the fence, and for such actions as dancing on the missile silo. Such actions were powerful because they challenged the symbolic strength of the base, with its secrecy and security systems. The women made fun of the cruise missile maneuvers carried out in the middle of the night by following the vehicles and publicizing their route and destination. Although the Greenham women faced scathing criticism from the media, they inspired thousands to take up nonviolent protest in other countries.

The UN conferences on women in 1975, 1980, and 1985 raised issues of women's rights and the interdependency of equality, development, and peace. Women have criticized the failure of governments to implement the Forward Looking Strategies of 1985, and they have lobbied intensely to have women's perspectives addressed at all UN conferences, because women's issues cut across all others.

3. Elshtain, J.B. and Tobias, S. *Women, militarism and war; Essays in history, politics and social theory.* Savage, Maryland: Rowman and Littlefield, 1990.

---

itantly for suffrage and was jailed three times for civil disobedience. In an article titled, "What Will Nurses Do About War?" written shortly after the passage of the Nineteenth Amendment, Dock proclaimed nurses' moral obligation to use their votes for peace: "We shall share the responsibility for future horrible mass murders by bullets, poison gas, and perhaps even disease germs, if we do not align ourselves with those men and women who are throwing their political and personal influence against the war system. Which side are we going to take?"[15]

The stories of Sanger, Wald, and Dock raise the question: What was responsible for the spirit of peace activism among the pioneers of public health nursing? In other words, which came first, the public health nursing or the peace activism?

On one hand, the activism—if not peace activism specifically—came first. Public health nursing was established by women who were challenging social structures. New professions like public health nursing were invented by a generation of middle-class women who had just been granted access to higher education, but were still denied entrance to male professions.[16] These women carved out a professional niche for themselves by founding institutions such as settlement houses and birth control clinics.

In choosing communal living with women in a settlement house over marriage, and a career over domestic life, they defied the norms prescribed for their gender and class. As one settlement house worker told a reporter, settlement house life was part of "the revolt of the daughters, . . . the revolt against a conventional existence" and the life that "the majority of well-to-do American women have to live."[17] Public health nursing also represented a revolt against the subservience required in hospital nursing. Lillian Wald commented, "There may be some souls so humble and so meek that the old-time position of women nurses—namely that of blind obedience in the treadmill—is all that they may desire," but she demanded the independence and autonomy that public health nursing offered.[17] For these women challenging convention and authority on so many levels, challenging government military policy was a natural progression. In this sense, activism came first, and public health nursing was created to accommodate the rebellious impulses of its leaders.

On the other hand, public health nursing came first, in that it fostered a spirit of activism among its practitioners. For while the profession was founded as much to alleviate the boredom of middle-class women as to alleviate the social ills of working-class immigrants, the meeting of the two classes was eye-opening. Dock wrote, "I never began to think until I went to Henry Street."[18] Public health nurses' exposure to the problems of urban industrial life led them to develop an agenda for reform, with peace as part of that agenda. Public health nursing was also a springboard for political activism in that it equipped nurses with leadership skills. Nurses' independent work in autonomous agencies like settlement houses and clinics empowered them to take on key positions in the peace movement. In the 1930s and 1940s, public health nursing was absorbed into the medical mainstream. The voluntary agencies run by nurses were replaced by services run by health departments and hospital clinics. With the loss of autonomy and relocation into the hospital, nursing bred acquiescence, not activism.

If immersion in the social problems of the community and experience in managing autonomous agencies did indeed contribute to peace activism among nurses, perhaps we are on the brink of a resurgence. Today, trends in health care are moving nurses out of acute-care settings and back into the community. With the rise of nurse-practitioners, nurses are regaining a base for autonomous practice. Perhaps these changes will produce a new generation of public health nurses like Sanger, Wald, and Dock, who promote peace as the basis for health.

REFERENCES

1. Sanger, M. *An autobiography.* New York: W. W. Norton and Company, 1938, pp. 257, 263.
2. Sanger, M. Woman and war. *Birth Control Review* 1:5, 1917.
3. Sanger, M. *Woman and the new race.* New York: Brentano's Publishers, 1920, pp. 7, 151, 153–162.

4. Muncy, R. *Creating a female dominion in American reform, 1890–1935.* New York: Oxford University Press, 1991, p. 96.

5. *Woman rebel* 1: 56, 1914.

6. Sanger, M. *The pivot of civilization.* New York: Brentano's Publishers, 1922, p. 116.

7. Wald, L.D. *The house on Henry Street.* New York: Henry Holt and Co, 1915, p. 60.

8. Henry Street Peace Committee. Quoted by: Marchand, C.R. *The American peace movement and social reform, 1898–1918.* Princeton: Princeton University Press, 1972, p. 225.

9. Wald, L.D. Seeing red: When militarism comes in at the door, democracy flies out of the window. 1916. Available in: Wald Papers, New York Public Library, New York.

10. Wald, L.D. Address to the Woman's Peace Party. In Coss, C. (ed.), *Lillian D. Wald: Progressive activist.* New York: The Feminist Press at CUNY, 1989, p. 92.

11. *New York Times.* May 9, 1916, pp. 1–2; June 22, 1916, p. 1; June 26, 1916, p. 1; June 27, 1916, p. 7.

12. Link, A.S. *Woodrow Wilson and the Progressive Era, 1910–1917.* New York: Harper and Brothers, 1954, pp. 107–144.

13. Wald, L.D. *Windows on Henry Street.* Boston: Little, Brown, and Company; 1934, pp. 311, 316.

14. Dock, L.L. Some urgent social claims. *American Journal of Nursing* 7:899, 1907

15. Dock, L.L. Foreign department. *American Journal of Nursing* 15:47, 847, 1914; 16:752, 1916; 21:634, 1921.

16. Cott, N.F. *The grounding of modern feminism.* New Haven: Yale University Press, 1987, p. 22.

17. Quoted by Daniels, D.G. *Always a sister: The feminism of Lillian D. Wald.* New York: The Feminist Press at CUNY, 1989, pp. 28,35.

18. Dock, L.L. Self portrait. *Nursing Outlook* 25:24, 1977.

24

Keeping Peace and Preventing War: The Role of the United Nations

MICHAEL RENNER

Since the end of the Cold War, the world has been rocked by a seemingly unending series of new conflicts. Seen individually, events in Somalia, Bosnia, Rwanda, Haiti, and elsewhere pose many perplexing local and regional problems. Taken together, however, they spell nothing less than an epochal watershed: a time that future historians will likely describe as a moment when humanity seized—or failed to seize—the opportunity to replace obsolescent mechanisms for resolving human conflict.

The obsolescent mechanisms are those time-honored methods of maintaining individual nations' security against whatever forces most threaten it: the building, feeding, and conspicuous flaunting of increasingly powerful military forces, whatever the cost. This fundamental rule of security was expressed by the ancient Roman maxim, *"Si vis pacem, para bellum"* ("If you want peace, prepare for war"). This has been a rarely questioned guiding principle of nations for 2,000 years. But in today's global village, economic and environmental interdependencies among nations are now so advanced—and communications so routine—that the ancient Romans' doctrine no longer works. In fact, there is reason to believe we have reached a juncture where either the world consciously rejects this doctrine and systematically replaces it with a new kind of collective security, or the post–Cold-War events begin to gather a dangerous momentum of their own.

In the nearly 20 centuries since Rome began its regime of peace through conquest, the vast bulk of all preparation for war has been concentrated in this century. By the ancient logic, then, the twentieth century should also have produced the most stable peace. Yet, the result has been the opposite: Devising ever more ingenious weapons, governments have acquired unprecedented ability to destroy, but little capacity to

This chapter is adapted and updated from Renner, M. *Critical juncture: The future of peacekeeping.* Worldwatch Paper 114. Washington, DC: Worldwatch Institute, May 1993.

defend. While constituting just five percent of the time that has passed since the rise of Rome, this century has produced 75 percent of all the war deaths inflicted. Within the twentieth century itself, hopes for more peaceful human coexistence were dashed by two world wars and an East-West standoff that drove much of humanity into two armed camps.[1]

The ending of the Cold War at first brought a wave of euphoria—a sense that the "major" risks of global nuclear holocaust had been averted at last. But it soon became obvious that the remaining "minor" conflicts pose serious problems, threatening the violent disintegration of states and regional instability. The international community has responded in different ways to each of these theaters of conflict, reflecting the lack of a consistent strategy for dealing with threats to peace in the post–Cold-War world.

Recognizing that, in a world of increasingly interconnected economies and communications, fortress-based forms of security are becoming increasingly anachronistic, the international community has been edging toward a greater reliance on the promise of "collective security" via the United Nations. The contours of a collective security system are emerging less by design than by ad hoc responses to crises around the globe. The United Nations' moves toward an alternative security system have been tentative, inconsistent, and often lacking in teeth. They have been undermined by lack of agreement on what its powers should be, underfunded by a refusal of key members to pay all their dues, and overwhelmed by demands for services that it is not fully prepared to render. As Robert Johansen of Notre Dame University's Institute for International Peace Studies has noted, the UN "has become essential before it has become effective."[2]

UN Peacekeeping: Promise and Peril

With the ending of the East-West confrontation, tremendous hope arose that the United Nations may finally become what its founders envisioned: an organization at the center of a collective security system. When UN peacekeepers were awarded the Nobel Peace Prize in 1988, Secretary-General Javier Pérez de Cuéllar noted that it marked the first time in history that "military forces have been employed internationally not to wage war, not to establish domination and not to serve the interests of any power or group of powers."[3]

Curiously enough, peacekeeping as presently practiced by the UN "Blue Helmets" is an accident of history. Originally, the Security Council was to have had, on call, a full-strength armed force assembled from national armies of member states, for the purpose of "maintaining international peace and security." But the Cold War rivalry between the United States and the Soviet Union deadlocked the Security Council, and the provisions of Article 43 of the UN Charter were never implemented. An improvised alternative—peacekeeping with no enforcement capability—arose in its place.

Improvisation turned this weakness into a virtue, however. Instead of enforcing the will of the Security Council by simply becoming another combatant trying to outgun any opponent, the UN found that it could succeed by adhering to nonviolent principles. This nonaggressive approach was adopted as a general policy, with peacekeeping troops using their light weapons only in self-defense. Before any peacekeeping forces were dispatched, the combatants first had to agree to cease hostilities and consent to any UN deployment. A crucial element in marshaling the support of both the major powers and the local antagonists has been the UN's reputation for impartiality, its being an "honest broker."

In the first four decades of UN peacekeeping, only 18 operations were undertaken. In recent years, however, the Blue Helmets have been inundated with requests for their services. The period since 1988 has seen a larger number of operations than the previous four decades, including the three largest ever undertaken—in Cambodia (Figure 24-1), Yugoslavia, and Somalia (see Table 24-1).[4,5]

For many years, peacekeeping operations focused narrowly on conflict containment: monitoring borders and buffer zones after ceasefires were signed, as happened on the Golan Heights between Israel and Syria. But since the late 1980s, missions have become far more complex and ambitious: supervising the disarming or disbanding of armed factions (Figure 24-2), establishing protected areas, monitoring elections and human rights records, and repatriating refugees. They have even included—in Cambodia—temporarily taking over the administration of an entire nation torn by war. In such cases, the UN has been asked to reach far beyond its original mission, by facilitating the rebuilding of institutions and infrastructures, and thus the rebirth of civilian society. In effect, peacekeeping is gradually being transformed into peacemaking.

Expenditures for UN peacekeeping operations between 1987 and 1994 grew 14-fold—to $3.4 billion (Table 24-2), as the number, size, and complexity of the missions rapidly increased. Most of the almost $17 billion in outlays from 1947 to 1995 were made in just four years—1992 through 1995. Since the late 1980s, the number of people involved has similarly soared, to 77,783 at the end of 1994, increasing from 11,121 in early 1988.[6–9]

This vast increase of responsibilities, however, threatens to overwhelm the UN's limited resources. An endemic set of problems may not only undermine the organization's effectiveness today but could condemn it to failure in the long run. These include the ad hoc quality of the peacekeeping system and the changing nature of conflicts in the post–Cold-War world.

Having evolved through improvisation, the current system is handicapped in a number of ways. Peacekeeping units are assembled for specific missions only and are composed of national contingents with highly uneven sets of equipment, capabilities, and expertise. They are given virtually no opportunity to form a compatible, cohesive, and coherent whole. Training peacekeepers is left to the contributing governments,

Figure 24-1. A Canadian medic with the United Nations Transitional Authority in Cambodia (UNTAC) examines an elderly man in 1993 (Source/Photographer: United Nations/DPI/159762/ J. Isaac).

resulting in uneven levels of preparation, experience, and competence—particularly the negotiating and mediating skills that successful peacekeeping demands.

Governments are often slow to provide personnel and equipment to peacekeeping missions, which routinely results in delays of several months between the authorization of a mission and its actual dispatch. In the wake of the Somalia mission, in which more than 100 peacekeepers were killed, many governments grew even more reluctant to contribute troops. "A Security Council resolution mandating an operation no longer automatically implies that it will happen as authorized," UN Secretary-General Boutros-Ghali lamented in 1994. Yet, speed can be essential to the success of a mis-

Table 24-1. Budgets and personnel of recent and ongoing UN peacekeeping operations and observer missions

UN Operations in:	Duration	Costs[a] ($ million)	Personnel[b]
Middle East	since 1948	24	178
India/Pakistan	since 1949	8	44
Cyprus	since 1964	43	1,200
Golan Heights	since 1974	32	1,054
Lebanon	since 1978	135	4,568
Afghanistan/Pakistan	1988–90	7	50
Iran/Iraq	1988–91	55	750
Namibia	1989–90	97	6,150
Central America	1989–92	48	625
Angola	since 1989	268	7,138
Cambodia	1991–93	726	22,000[c]
El Salvador	1991–95	26	301
Iraq/Kuwait	since 1991	65	1,179
Western Sahara	since 1991	68	352
Former Yugoslavia	since 1992	1,771	6,145[d]
Somalia	1992–95	827	18,404
Mozambique	1992–95	258	5,760
Rwanda	1993–96	227	688
Georgia	since 1993	19	128
Liberia	since 1993	20	93
Haiti	since 1993	271	2,700
Tajikistan	since 1993	5	44
Chad/Libya	1994	0.4	15

Source: UN Department of Peacekeeping Operations, private communications, October 23 and December 20, 1995 and April 19, 1996.

[a]Costs incurred during 1995 for ongoing missions. For completed missions, costs incurred during the last full year of operations are provided. All figures are rounded to the nearest million dollars.

[b]As at March 30, 1996 for ongoing missions. Last year of operation for completed missions. Data include soldiers, military observers, and civilian police.

[c]Peak authorized strength.

[d]Operations were substantially downsized and altered in terms of their mandate following the Dayton Peace Agreement of late 1995.

sion: Ceasefires are often fragile, and the willingness of all parties to accept outsiders may evaporate quickly.[10]

Perhaps the most serious impediment is that even the financing is ad hoc; there is no regular, permanent budget for peacekeeping, and most member states either fail to pay their assessed share of costs or pay late. Collectively, the members' arrears have grown from $19 million in 1975 to $1.3 billion at the end of 1994. By late 1995, outstanding dues had soared to about $2.5 billion. The United States and Russia are by far the biggest debtors. The UN has had to resort to both internal borrowing—juggling money among different accounts—and delaying reimbursement of governments that contribute personnel and equipment to peacekeeping operations. By August

Figure 24-2. Troops of the United Nations Observer Group in Central America (ONUCA) destroy weapons surrendered by resistance forces as part of the peace process in Honduras in 1990 (Source/Photographer: United Nations/DPI/157589/S. Johansen).

1994, the UN owed troop-contributing countries more than $1 billion. Some 20 countries indicated in 1994 that this unhappy experience posed not only a problem for their continued participation in ongoing operations, but also made them reluctant to commit personnel or equipment to future missions.[11,12]

While the peacekeeping role evolved mainly in response to conflicts between nations, the UN now finds itself increasingly drawn into mediating internal conflicts as well. Of five peacekeeping operations in early 1988, only one was concerned with an internal conflict, compared with 13 of 21 missions established since then, including 9 of 11 operations established in 1992–1994.[13]

Even though Article 2 of the UN Charter specifies that the United Nations is not authorized ''to intervene in matters which are essentially within the domestic jurisdiction of any state,'' the traditional distinction between internal and international affairs is becoming increasingly blurred. Civil strife within a country may have greater repercussions beyond its borders than in the past: Outside powers are often drawn into the conflict because they want to affect the political outcome. Ever larger streams of refugees threaten to destabilize neighboring countries. And today's far greater economic interdependence means that the fighting may have more pronounced effects in other nations.

There is growing support for the argument that the principle of national sovereignty should be superseded in cases of extreme violations of human rights or democratic

Table 24-2.   UN peacekeeping expenditures,
1986–1994, in millions of dollars

Year	Expenditures in Millions of Dollars
1986	242
1987	240
1988	266
1989	635
1990	464
1991	490
1992	1,767
1993	3,059
1994	3,342
1995	3,364

Source: United Nations Department of Peacekeeping
Operations, New York, private communications, October 23, 1995 and December 20, 1995.

principles. But this support is tempered by concern that ostensibly humanitarian motives may turn out to be a convenient pretext for old-style intervention. A discussion concerning the merits of expanded humanitarian intervention flourished in 1993 and 1994, but it quickly disappeared from the international agenda when, following the disastrous events in Somalia, the major powers lost their appetite for such operations.[14]

Restoring the peace inside a country wracked by conflict is a more treacherous undertaking than monitoring international borders. Government troops, insurgents, and factions competing for power confront peacekeepers with a tangle of self-proclaimed authorities. Protagonists may deliberately leave the outside world confused about who controls the acts of militias and other irregular armed groups. Trying to compel some of these groups to adhere to ceasefires, to allow unmolested passage of humanitarian aid convoys ferrying supplies of food and medicine (Figure 24-3), or to permit inspections of prisoner-of-war camps can easily pull peacekeepers into a quagmire.

The traditional peacekeeping model is based on the principles of impartiality, non-violence, consent of all parties, and no deployment without an established ceasefire. It is workable in cases where the UN is called upon by the warring parties themselves to police a ceasefire. But it appears unworkable in the two types of situations in which the UN increasingly becomes involved: (1) those in which it is invited to facilitate a demilitarization but the combatants fail to comply with the terms to which they earlier agreed; and (2) those in which it intervenes against the express wishes of one or more of the contenders, for humanitarian purposes.

In such situations, ceasefires are so precarious that some observers have questioned whether—or to what extent—the UN should use coercion to establish them. Questions have also been raised about whether it is possible to continue practicing impartiality in the traditional way. Until now, impartiality has meant that UN peacekeepers could not act against any of the antagonists, even if they turned belligerent and began violating their own commitments to peaceful conflict resolution. Such restraint will be

Figure 24-3. Ambulances from the British contingent of the United Nations Protection Force (UNPROFOR) drive through Vukovar, Croatia, in 1992 (Source/Photographer: United Nations/ DPI/159206/S. Whitehouse).

difficult to justify in the future. But taking active steps to enforce compliance should not imply that the UN is taking sides in a conflict.

These issues pose a conundrum to the international community, and the key to solving it is to make a clear distinction between peacekeeping and peacemaking. Without a deliberately constructed peacemaking or peace enforcement paradigm—one that establishes guidelines for the organization's activities and provides adequate resources to carry them out—there is a considerable danger that the UN could stumble and fail in its peacemaking attempts.

Collective Security: Making It Work

The international community is still reacting to crises rather than trying to prevent them. This was the only approach feasible during the Cold-War years. Now that the Security Council is no longer permanently deadlocked, however, preventive diplomacy is not only possible but necessary. In the kind of collective security system needed, unlike the ad hoc one that now exists, priority would be given to enabling the UN to identify potential crises and to prevent disputes from escalating into armed conflicts:

- It would be given a greatly strengthened capacity, where conflicts do erupt, to deal with them through reconciliation efforts, in addition to its traditional peace-keeping activities.
- It might also have the capacity to enforce the terms of ceasefire and peace agreements.
- It would have a capability to help with establishing conditions that prevent the resumption of violent conflict at a later stage.

As the UN's capabilities are bolstered, the world community needs to define a set of criteria—in effect, create a kind of trigger mechanism—that would activate appropriate elements of this machinery. In addition to breaches of international peace and security, the criteria could include large-scale human rights violations and human suffering induced by warfare. If a credible mechanism can be established that makes UN intervention a virtual certainty under well-defined circumstances, it would likely help to deter at least some acts of aggression and violence. Areas have been suggested in which criteria could be developed to determine whether any UN intervention should take place, including the number of people affected, the severity of the threat to human life, the generation of substantial flows of refugees, and the demonstrated inability of the government to cope with the magnitude of the crisis.[15]

The successful prevention of conflicts—avoiding the slide toward such levels of savagery and hatred that no peaceful settlement appears even imaginable—requires early and active UN involvement. If it is to have any chance of meeting this challenge, it requires a dedicated, competent staff that is large enough to continuously monitor and analyze developments as they unfold around the world and to alert the Secretary-General and Security Council to impending threats to peace and security. A key task would be to prepare "boundary and ethnic contingency maps," identifying potential "hot spots" where borders may be contested or contending groups may clash. Early warning alerts would then kick into gear the UN machinery for conflict mediation and arbitration.[16]

Adequate early warning is the keystone of any effort to succeed at defusing and preventing conflicts. Its importance—and its difficulty—can hardly be overstated. Signs of impending violent conflict are not always clearly discernible, and observers may disagree in interpreting the significance of particular developments. Therefore, in addition to maintaining an in-house staff to obtain early warnings of possible conflict, it would be sensible for the UN to contract with outside experts, university departments that specialize in regional affairs, and nongovernmental groups such as human rights organizations.

If it is to stay abreast of situations that can change frequently and abruptly, the UN's monitoring capabilities will need to include individuals in the field and airborne monitoring equipment. Ground-based observers are exposed to the complexities and nuances of evolving situations, able to provide the context and feedback indispensable to any meaningful evaluation of events. But they cannot be omnipresent, and they may be prevented from entering certain areas. To complement them, therefore, I believe that the UN may need to acquire an aerial monitoring capability—a fleet of reconnaissance planes and perhaps even a satellite system.

A satellite capability would provide important information to support preventive diplomacy. By confirming or denying alleged border violations, troop movements, or illicit flows of weapons, or by providing warnings against surprise attacks, it could help build trust between opposing parties. It could also play a crucial role in monitoring ceasefires, verifying disarmament agreements, and assisting peacekeeping missions. Initially, at least, the UN could seek to lease planes and buy commercial satellite time while it assesses its needs and begins to build up its own capacity.

At present, the UN's capabilities fall tragically short of needs. In 1987, Secretary-General Javier Pérez de Cuéllar set up an Office of Research and the Collection of Information (ORCI) and gave it primary responsibility for early warning. Although it was only a small undertaking, inadequately staffed and funded, it nevertheless had taken five years to persuade the permanent members of the Security Council to agree to its establishment. After another five years, under a reorganization of the UN Secretariat in early 1992, ORCI was abolished. The UN Department of Political Affairs now is involved in the collection and analysis of information relevant to early warning, but there is no unit dedicated per se to this crucial task.[6]

Once an alert of impending conflict occurs, the UN could take actions to diminish the likelihood that violence will actually break out. Where further clarification is needed, fact-finding missions could be dispatched. The UN can also make fuller use of conflict-resolution techniques. Throughout the organization's existence, the Secretaries-General have offered their help in personally mediating disputes—as, for example, they did in the Afghanistan and Iran-Iraq wars. These interventions are often high-profile, last-ditch efforts to avert the outbreak of hostilities, or to halt fighting where it has already begun. But more routine, low-key efforts could help to defuse tensions and resolve disputes at an earlier stage, long before violent conflict is imminent. Boutros Boutros-Ghali has made much greater use than any of his predecessors of Special Representatives dispatched on preventive diplomacy missions—he had 44 such envoys by the beginning of 1995—but he has complained of a shortage of skilled diplomats available for such tasks.

The conflict-mediation function could be served by mechanisms that allow grievances, both within and among nations, to be heard before impartial forums. David Scheffer of the Carnegie Endowment for International Peace in Washington has suggested that the UN Trusteeship Council be transformed into a clearinghouse for self-determination issues.[17] Robert Johansen of Notre Dame University proposes that the Security Council "establish standing conflict resolution committees for each region of the world."[18]

If an early warning alert or the conclusions of a fact-finding mission warrant it, the UN could decide on the preventive deployment of observers or of lightly armed peacekeepers. Monitors could be dispatched to areas where tensions exist but are still sufficiently far from turning violent, while peacekeepers could be sent where violence seems more imminent. For example, the Security Council decided in 1992 to station a small UN observer force in the former Yugoslav republic of Macedonia. As of this writing (April 1996), this move has helped to prevent the fighting in Bosnia from spilling into Macedonia.

In his landmark 1992 report to the Security Council, *An Agenda for Peace,* Boutros-Ghali proposed that the Council authorize stationing peacekeepers along international borders if requested by one or both countries involved in a dispute (with deployments on either one or both sides of the border), or inside countries plagued by internal conflict (though only with the consent of all parties concerned).[19]

The early deployment of a UN force could discourage acts of aggression by symbolizing the international community's determination to oppose them. However, a determined attacker may simply push the peacekeepers aside. If such defiance of UN authority occurs without penalty, preventive deployments will quickly lose credibility among both aggressors and those to be protected. To be an effective deterrent, a UN deployment would either have to be militarily significant itself (and hence depart from the peacekeeping model) or be backed up by some other military force—effectively making the peacekeeping force a "trip wire."

Reflecting the heightened demand for peacekeeping and peacemaking services since 1988, there has been discussion about the merits of a more permanent UN force. In *An Agenda for Peace,* Boutros-Ghali recommended that UN member states make specially trained contingents of their national armed forces available on a stand-by basis, an option spelled out in Article 43 of the UN Charter, but never implemented. In January 1993, Boutros-Ghali established a special planning team that developed an overall concept and designed standard military and civilian "building blocks" necessary for peacekeeping. By mid-1994, 21 member states (with Britain the only permanent Security Council member among them) had made firm commitments for some 30,000 troops; an additional 27 members promised a similar commitment, raising the number of personnel under stand-by arrangements to about 70,000.[20,21]

Still, this approach has its deficiencies. Commitments of resources in communications, multi-role logistics, engineering, transport, and some other areas remain inadequate. And the commitments do not mean that troops and equipment will be automatically available to the UN. The individual governments still have to give their specific approval. Boutros-Ghali lamented in January 1995 that "when in May 1994 the Security Council decided to expand the UN Assistance Mission for Rwanda (UNAMIR), not one of the 19 governments that at that time had undertaken to have troops on stand-by agreed to contribute."[8]

These problems could be avoided by establishing a permanent peacekeeping force under direct UN authority. Unlike an army, it would be neither equipped nor mandated to use force. The impartiality of such a force—and therefore its acceptability—could be emphasized by directly recruiting, from a broad variety of countries, individuals whose loyalty to the UN is not in question, rather than forces drawn from sometimes reluctant governments. I believe that establishing a standing force would bring several benefits. Logistical and financial arrangements could be standardized, and the diverse tasks of civilian and military personnel better coordinated. A standing force would also avoid the perennial problem of familiarizing new peacekeepers with UN procedures and practices. While not assigned to any mission, peacekeeping units would not be stationed at UN headquarters, but instead throughout the world; for example, military bases slated for closure could be made available to them.

To give the UN sufficient flexibility to deal with the security challenges of the post–Cold-War era, I believe that it may be useful to establish a two-tiered UN force. The first tier would consist of a permanent, directly recruited, and specially trained peacekeeping force that strictly adheres to the principle of nonviolence. The second tier would be composed of more militarily capable stand-by units to deter aggression, truly protect safe havens for civilians, and possibly to enforce ceasefire agreements. It would not be designed to launch offensive military operations. In most cases, the second tier would function as a backup, mobilized only if peacekeeping units faced severe challenges to their authority. Where an act of aggression seems imminent, it could serve as a first recourse. Initially, the UN might set up just a small permanent unit to allow the world's governments to grow accustomed to the idea.

Systematic training is critical. The Scandinavian countries have established joint programs to train volunteers for peacekeeping missions. Their approach has been emulated by Austria, Malaysia, Poland, and Switzerland, and other countries have begun to provide some training. To assure that it has a sufficient reservoir of competence, the international community would be well advised to set up training programs in each region of the world to impart the many unique nonmilitary skills that successful peacekeeping and peacekeeping operations demand.

The smooth functioning of a machinery for peace depends on the availability of sufficient financial resources. UN peacekeeping and peacemaking can be seen as the bargain of the century when their cost is compared with the enormous resources absorbed by the world's larger military machines (see Table 24-3). There is no shortage of ideas on how to solidify UN finances.[22]

Among them are giving the Secretary-General authority to borrow in commercial markets, to charge interest on overdue assessments, to issue bonds, or to levy a tax on military spending or the international arms trade. (In the late 1980s, the General Assembly rejected proposals for borrowing authority and for charging interest.) But most important, there is a need for a regular annual peacekeeping budget, plus a reserve fund to cover start-up costs and any unexpected expenses. To cover start-up expenses, a $150 million start-up fund has been established, but even though this amount is inadequate, UN members have failed to provide sufficient resources.

More than 30 years ago, Adlai Stevenson said at the United Nations: "We do not hold the vision of a world without conflict. We do hold the vision of a world without

Table 24-3.   Comparison of military expenditures and UN peacekeeping assessments, selected countries, 1991

Country	Military Expenditures (million dollars)	Peacekeeping Assessment[a] (million dollars)	Military: Peacekeeping Ratio
Czechoslovakia	723	3.2	223 : 1
Japan	32,100	55.9	574 : 1
Mexico	662	0.9	717 : 1
Germany	39,900	46.0	868 : 1
France	41,400	37.8	1,096 : 1
Nigeria	234	0.2	1,191 : 1
Britain	42,300	29.4	1,441 : 1
United States	304,500	151.0	2,016 : 1
China	12,000	4.8	2,520 : 1
Brazil	4,900	1.4	3,441 : 1
Russia	224,100	60.3	3,714 : 1
India	7,200	0.4	19,816 : 1
Israel	4,500	0.2	21,821 : 1
Pakistan	2,800	0.059	47,522 : 1
Syria	4,500	0.039	114,562 : 1
Ethiopia	896	0.005	182,485 : 1
WORLD	921,500	491.0	1,877 : 1

Source: Adapted from Independent Advisory Group on UN Financing, *Financing an Effective United Nations.* New York: Ford Foundation, February 1993.

[a]Assessment is the amount the UN estimates will be required to carry out existing or new peacekeeping missions. The contribution of each member state to this amount is calculated via an assessment scale. The assessment for a given mission could be somewhat higher or lower than the actual expenditures.

war—and this inevitably requires an alternative system for coping with conflict."[23] Strengthening the UN's capability for preventive diplomacy, peacekeeping, and peace-making would go a long way toward responding to Stevenson's challenge.

Conclusion

The momentum of human conflict in the 1990s is such that for the world's governments, the task of maintaining peace and security cannot simply be carried on in the future as it has been in the past—each nation fending for itself. Either a new mechanism of collective security will be firmly established and financed, or nations will find themselves increasingly embattled—and fractured—by challenges to their economic viability, cultural integrity, and sovereignty.

The question facing the international community now is whether a strengthened UN peacekeeping system can offer a workable and affordable alternative to the use of force by national governments and their adversaries, and, more immediately, whether governments are prepared to vest the UN with the resources and authority to succeed in its difficult task.

It is only realistic to assume that opportunities for peaceful conflict resolution will continue to be missed in the future, that diplomacy will not always be as effective as it could be, and that the antagonists may prefer to fight rather than negotiate. The international community needs to learn—by trial and error, at first—how to employ the tools of preventive diplomacy and peacemaking effectively. Unfortunately, in response to the difficulties encountered in Somalia and Bosnia, the United States and a number of other governments seem prepared to judge peacekeeping a failure and to pull the plug prematurely.

The current era is a watershed. The question is whether the nations of the world are prepared to transform the United Nations from a peacekeeper of last resort to a peacemaker of first, and routine, recourse.

REFERENCES

1. Eckhardt, W. War-related deaths since 3000 B.C. *Bulletin of Peace Proposals,* Vol. 22, 1991.
2. Johansen, R.C. The Reagan Administration and the UN: The costs of unilateralism. *World Policy Journal,* Fall 1986.
3. Lewis, P. UN chief warns of costs of peace. *New York Times,* Dec. 11, 1988.
4. Baratta, J.P. *International peacekeeping: History and strengthening.* Monograph No. 6. Washington, D.C.: The Center for UN Reform Education, Nov. 1989.
5. UN Department of Public Information. *United Nations peacekeeping operations: Information notes.* New York, 1992.
6. UN Department of Peacekeeping Operations. Private communications, Oct. 23, 1995; Dec. 20, 1995; and Apr. 19, 1996.
7. UN Department of Public Information. *United Nations Peacekeeping Information Notes.* New York, 1993.
8. Blechman, B.M. and Vaccaro, J.M. *Training for peacekeeping: The United Nations' role.* Report No. 12, Washington, D.C.: Henry L. Stimson Center, July 1994.
9. Evans, G. *Cooperating for peace: The global agenda for the 1990s and beyond.* St. Leonards, Australia: Allen and Unwin, 1993.
10. Boutros-Ghali, B. *Building peace and development 1994: Annual report on the work of the organization.* New York, UN Department of Public Information, 1994.
11. UN Secretariat. Status of Contributions (issued monthly, document symbol ST/ADM/SER.B, various year-end editions).
12. United Nations. Daily Highlights Press Release DH/1717, Aug. 26, 1994.
13. United Nations. Supplement to an Agenda for Peace: Position paper of the Secretary-General on the occasion of the fiftieth anniversary of the United Nations. General Assembly document A/50/60 and Security Council document S/1995/1. New York: Jan. 3, 1995.
14. Ferris, E.G. (ed.), *The challenge to intervene: A new role for the United Nations?* Conference Report 2. Uppsala, Sweden: Life and Peace Institute, 1992.
15. Minear, L. Testimony before the House Select Committee on Hunger, U.S. Congress. Washington, D.C., July 30, 1991.
16. Childers, E. UN mechanisms and capacities for intervention. In Ferris, E.G. (ed.), *The*

challenge to intervene: A new role for the United Nations? Conference Report 2. Uppsala, Sweden: Life and Peace Institute, 1992.

17. Mouat, L. Broad mission, small budget strain UN effort. *Christian Science Monitor,* July 27, 1992.

18. Johansen, R.C. Lessons for collective security. *World Policy Journal,* Summer 1991.

19. Boutros-Ghali, B. *An agenda for peace: Preventive diplomacy, peacemaking and peace-keeping.* Report of the Secretary-General pursuant to the Statement adopted by the Summit Meeting of the Security Council on January 31, 1992. New York: United Nations, 1992.

20. United Nations. Improving the capacity of the United Nations for peacekeeping: Report of the Secretary-General. General Assembly document A/48/403 and Security Council document S/26450. New York, March 14, 1994.

21. United Nations. Stand-by arrangements for peacekeeping: Report of the Secretary-General. Security Council document S/1994/777. New York, June 30, 1994.

22. Schoettle, E.C.B. UN dues: The price of peace. *Bulletin of the Atomic Scientists,* June 1992.

23. Johansen, R.C. *Toward a dependable peace: A proposal for an appropriate security system.* World Policy Paper No. 8. New York: World Policy Institute, 1983.

25

Conflict Resolution and Mediation for Health Professionals

NICK LEWER

Health professionals may find special opportunities for engagement in conflict resolution and mediation within their own communities and at other sites at which conflict is occurring or threatening to occur. This chapter briefly reviews the history of unofficial conflict resolution and mediation since 1945, describes the process of mediation, and considers applications of conflict resolution and mediation from the perspective of public health professionals.

It is not within the scope of this chapter to delve into the complex history of international and domestic conflict management and resolution mechanisms. Useful reviews of the development of conflict resolution in historical, political, and theoretical contexts can be found in the background readings given at the end of this chapter. However, a summary of the main influences and terminology gleaned from these sources is helpful in setting the context within which this chapter is written, and in illustrating some of the changes that have occurred in conflict resolution and mediation approaches since World War II. A convenient starting point is the formation of the United Nations. The United Nations Charter was drawn up based on the "Law and Order Model," supported by theorists such as Morgenthau:[1]

... world society was, in short, to be constructed and administered along the lines of the single nation-state. Law and order, majority rule, the common good, were among the conceptual notions that made up the political philosophy of the time. What was not brought to the surface was that this policy was a power philosophy: The common good turned out to be, both at the domestic level and at the international level, the common good as interpreted by the powerful. ... The belief was that power and enforcement of power norms could give a stability that was in the common interest.[2]

There are three serious flaws within the United Nations that are relevant to the development of nonviolent conflict resolution methods, such as mediation:

1. The "legitimacy" of governments that represent their peoples at the United Nations is frequently questioned.
2. The United Nations has no jurisdiction over matters that are "internal or domestic" to a UN member nation.
3. The United Nations has no physical (military) forces of its own at its direct disposal to enforce its resolutions and directives.

While these flaws severely limit the UN's effectiveness, it can, through the "good offices" of the Secretary-General, nevertheless make available opportunities for mediation and other types of peacemaking[3] (see Chapter 24).

The role of the United Nations should be viewed in the context of the post–World-War-II era, particularly during the Cold-War years, and attributed to widespread discrediting of the pre–World-War-II liberalism, upon which was blamed the failure of the League of Nations, the global economic depression, and the imperialistic activities of Hitler, Tojo, and Mussolini.[4] After World War II, the "realist" view of international relations was reasserted and little effort was put into the exploration of new avenues of peaceful conflict resolution. By the end of the 1950s, however, these major assumptions were being challenged.

Two schools of thought developed. The first retained an emphasis on the role of power and the state (or other institutions) as the main channels of activity. The second, a more radical school, began to shift the emphasis away from the state and its institutions more toward the individual, formulating concepts of "basic human needs" within the broader theories of conflict and conflict resolution.[5] Some scholars and practitioners began to investigate alternative methods for dispute resolution, ranging from the interpersonal to the international level. It is worth briefly reviewing the main factors prompting this investigation of alternative methods for dispute resolution.

The flaws already noted within the United Nations meant that many of the conflicts, especially post-colonial ones that were occurring throughout the world, could not be dealt with under UN auspices. Traditional methods of peacemaking and diplomacy seemed incapable of dealing with these lethal conflicts. This failure was reflected not only by the UN, but also by other international bodies such as the British Commonwealth. On the domestic scene, society was having difficulty in coping, using the traditional means at its disposal, with increasing levels of community dissatisfaction, such as ethnic and cultural grievances, increasing crime rates, problems with drugs, industrial disputes, and family disputes. Authorities were less able to find settlements, the legal system was becoming clogged, and the economic costs of dealing with and imposing settlements were rising. Nations, organizations, and individuals were becoming less prepared to use the existing mechanisms and opportunities for conflict resolution.

Against this background, the field of nonviolent conflict resolution, and one its strands—nonofficial mediation—has grown and is still developing in both the domestic and international arenas. Fuller accounts of these developments can be found in the background readings at the end of the chapter. Some of the practitioners working in nonofficial mediation talk of a paradigm shift in its theory and approaches, which can in part be traced to advances in the management of industrial relations, in the legal system, in developments pioneered by social psychologists, and in changes in therapeutic techniques. These allowed disputants to explore the real, though often hidden, causes of their conflict and to deal with each other's interests rather than bargaining from fixed positions. This method was explained by Fisher and Ury in their book, *Getting to Yes.*[6]

Perceived advantages of this developing approach to mediation are that it is less expensive, less time-consuming, and less coercive than conventional ways of managing or resolving conflict. Moreover, it is said to be more satisfactory to the adversaries involved and more likely to produce long-lasting solutions to disputes, because these solutions are self-supporting. Practitioners of such methods emphasize the shift from settlement of conflict by authoritative controls to conflict resolution by the parties themselves. Unlike compromise settlements, when conflicts are truly resolved no aspect of the original conflict should remain to restart the conflict cycle at a later time. The aim is for the parties in dispute to establish a new relationship of mutual collaboration, such as by utilizing problem-solving or process-promoting workshops or both.

Relevant Observations

How mediators approach their task is very much a personal matter. Attitudes and approaches obviously depend on where mediators are "coming from" in their own lives, and their motivation—religious, political, academic, or humanitarian. It is important that disputants know why mediators wish to get involved in "their" conflict, particularly when the mediators offer their services, rather than the disputants' calling for their help. The most important ingredient in the mediation dynamic is trust in the mediators by the disputants. Nonofficial mediation is not about peace at any price, and not all conflicts are amenable—or even appropriate—for mediation. For some conflicts there may be such an imbalance of power in favor of one party that it might be more appropriate to work to peacefully empower the weaker side in order to increase its future negotiating effectiveness. In some cases, one side in the conflict may refuse to become involved in a mediation initiative, particularly if it thinks that it has more to lose than gain.

Mediation is most effective if a situation is reached where continuation of hostilities would prove too costly for all involved, and a way out is being sought without loss of face for any of the participants. Mediation work is not based on the naive assumption that simply by managing to bring the disputants together a solution to the conflict will be found. Perhaps a useful role for mediators lies in the area of prevention—

intervening into a potentially violent conflict situation and utilizing peacemaking skills before blood is spilled, at which stage the conflict becomes extremely difficult to resolve peacefully.

A Working Definition

The word *mediator* means different things to different people. So many factors and influences are involved, some of which are not static and depend upon often erratic human behavior, that the most suitable avenue of approach is through some multiple definition, which is the only effective way of describing a complex dynamic process. Mediation can be looked at from four different perspectives:

1. The mediator's history.
2. The mediator's perspective from within the conflict setting.
3. The mediator/disputant dynamic.
4. The construction of mediation contexts.

All of these perspectives are interlinked and can occur concurrently. This approach allows the process of mediation and the activities of mediators to be considered in their interactive complexity.

The first perspective stems from the mediator's personal history and preparation, including factors such as background research, training, personal motivation and commitment, organization of resources and support, and physical and psychological health. Perhaps the most important aspect in this category is the "inner" preparation by the mediator and the personal psychological groundwork that is vital before a mediation intervention is undertaken.

The next three perspectives are illustrated in the following diagrams. Figure 25-1 describes the process from the perspective of the mediator's being truly "in the middle" of the conflict, endeavoring to tackle both the subjective and objective causes. Surrounding the disputants is a fog of subjective factors, such as misperceptions, irrational mistrust, prejudices, and stereotyping, which must be tackled before any resolution of the underlying objective factors can be attempted. The mediator helps the disputants to break out of these constraints so that they can communicate meaningfully. Adam Curle in his book, *In The Middle,*[7] when talking of this perspective of mediation, identifies four stages of a mediator's work when intervening in a conflict:

1. Building, maintaining, and improving communications.
2. Providing information.
3. Befriending.
4. Active mediation.

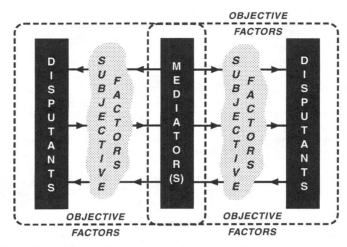

Figure 25-1. The mediator's perspective from within the conflict setting.

Figure 25-2 focuses on the interactive-dynamic relationship between mediator and disputants who are surrounded by these subjective and objective influences. A relationship of mutual trust must be built up within this dynamic by the mediator, in collaboration with the disputants, in order to assist in free dialogue and communication.

Figure 25-3 examines mediation opportunities as being created by mediation contexts. Often mediation flows from other activities such as community projects, training workshops, fact-finding missions, and academic research studies. Although headings are grouped separately around the core of mediation contexts, in real life some of these would be interlinked and others perhaps interdependent.

These four perspectives are connected. For example, a mediator may begin by "shuttling" between the disputants (as in Figure 25-1) before bringing them together for face-to-face talks, when a more facilitative role would be required (Figure 25-2). Either of these two processes could be a result of the mediation contexts described in Figure 25-3. Because of this interactive complexity of the mediation process, the term *mediation* almost defies definition, and many different definitions can be found in the literature. I offer a working explanation for nonofficial mediation:

> Mediation is a process that first aims to remove obstacles such as misperceptions, prejudices, and irrational fears that prevent people in conflict meeting for constructive talks, including the creation of a context in which mediation attempts could be initiated. Should this primary task succeed, the mediator could act as a facilitator allowing the disputants, talking face-to-face, to lay the groundwork that would enable substantive issues to be resolved. The mediator's task is not to negotiate directly, unless requested to do so by disputants; direct negotiation is the job of professional diplomats and politicians.

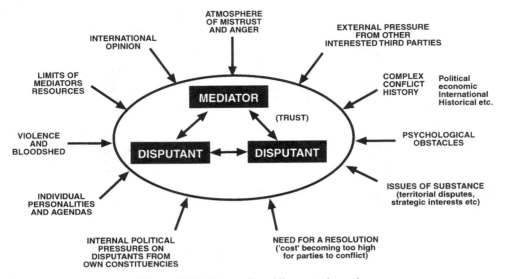

Figure 25-2. The mediator/disputant dynamic.

During any approach by a health professional, the professional should be perceived as an impartial, but interested, third party. This interest is rooted in the traditional humanitarian concerns of medical workers, and in their commitment to the peaceful resolution of conflicts in general.

The terms *mediation* and *mediator* can best be embodied by the phrase *in the middle*. To be effective a mediator must be nonjudgmental, committed, and impartial. He or she must assure confidentiality—without media publicity or the publication of research articles exposing shared confidences. Among the many desired personal qualities are patience, stamina, persistence, imagination, energy, and the ability to listen attentively to those caught up in the conflict spiral. At its simplest, mediation is the ability to form significant interpersonal relationships with the parties in conflict in an evenhanded manner.

Distinction must be made between Track One (T1), or official diplomacy, and Track Two (T2), or nonofficial approaches to conflict resolution and mediation. T2 is also known as citizen diplomacy, supplemental diplomacy, and complementary diplomacy. T2 has been, and still is, viewed with suspicion by the traditional and official T1 diplomats. Whereas T2 diplomacy represents a form of conflict resolution that is nongovernmental, nondirective, nonofficial, and informal, T1 continues the government-to-government, power-based, formal, and official traditional approaches to international interactions. Many T1 diplomats see T2 initiatives as being citizens ''meddling'' in what is considered to be ''government business'' and may ignore or denigrate T2 attempts.

Recently, increasing efforts have been made to develop T2 methods in such a manner as to strengthen and complement T1 rather than compete with T1 activities,

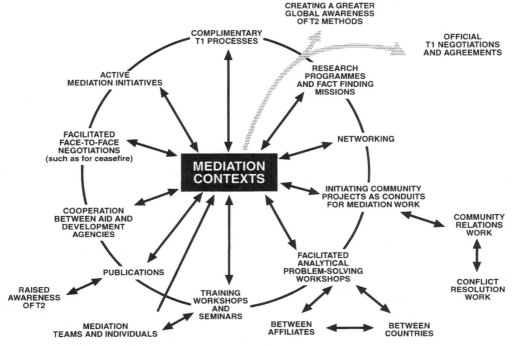

Figure 25-3. The construction of mediation contexts.

which will remain the principal avenue of international relations. Advances in T2 have, in a sense, been inevitable, as rapid development in communications technology and transport systems means greater contact between peoples; more access and debate in many countries regarding government foreign policy mean better informed populations; boundaries between national and international systems are becoming less clear because of environmental and demographic issues; and growth of international, nongovernmental, and transnational organizations means there is increasing cooperation among citizens. All of these factors can combine to put pressure on governments to implement United Nations resolutions, for example, and to moderate or influence national and international decision-makers. Behind all T2 approaches is a determination by people outside official government institutions to influence not only their own countries' affairs, but also those of other nations.

The general assumptions and concepts that underpin nonofficial conflict resolution and mediation work can be summarized by the following ten general propositions developed at the Centre for Conflict Resolution, Department of Peace Studies, University of Bradford, United Kingdom:

1. There are certain basic elements of structure and process that conflict situations, whether they be interpersonal or international, have in common.

2. There are subjective and objective elements to conflict situations, and both of these elements need to be addressed in the resolution process.

3. Problem-solving methods and third-party interventions can be conducive to the peaceful settlement of conflict.

4. For conflict settlements to be longlasting, they should ideally have integrative outcomes so that the interests of the parties can be recognized and combined.

5. Conflicts over interests are easier to resolve peacefully than conflicts over values or identity, although in major social and international conflicts interests and values tend to become enmeshed.

6. Protracted conflicts, those which combine differences of interests and a clash of beliefs or values, are often a source of instability and threat outside of their immediate environment, and so require urgent attention by the international community.

7. Skills and techniques of dialogue and communication, cooperative problem-solving, conflict analysis, mediation, and negotiation can be usefully learned and practiced in workshop settings, and these skills and techniques can then be used at practitioner level.

8. These conflict-resolution skills can be transferred and adapted for use in a variety of contexts, such as in the general interaction of people in family and friendship groups (interpersonally); in various professions where the positive management of human relationships has a high priority; within culturally divided societies; and across cultures and between states to enable a greater degree of global awareness of peaceful conflict resolution and conflict management.

9. Through this range of work we can create a common "conflict language," which facilitates dialogue and communications, in general, between parties in conflict.

10. Despite the wide range of cultural variation that affects the nature of conflict, it is important for communities and states to foster a political culture in which skills and opportunities for conflict resolution are seen as a basic human right.

Implications for Health Professionals

Three main strands to nonviolent conflict resolution and mediation work can be identified: (1) training, preparation, and networking; (2) creating mediation contexts; and (3) active mediation.

Training, Preparation, and Networking

Health professionals wishing to become engaged in mediation and conflict-resolution work should ensure that they undertake thorough training and preparation. At the heart of this are:

- Development and refinement of interpersonal communication skills.
- Knowledge of the dynamics and processes of conflict at intrapersonal, interpersonal, intragroup, intercommunity, and international levels of conflict.
- Understanding of the causes of conflict and conflict resolution theories.
- Knowledge of the history and causes of the conflict for which the intervention is intended.
- A personal humanitarian commitment to the pursuit of peace with justice.

A working knowledge of and practice in good communication skills is essential, not only for effective coping, management, and resolution strategies in conflict situations, but also for caring and empathetic relationships between doctor and patient and between the public health worker and the community.

Conflict resolution skills and methods therefore have importance for physicians, public health professionals, other health professionals, and students who wish to improve their clinical and public health practice and also contribute positively to the peaceful functioning of the communities in which they live. When opportunity arises, they may wish to use their peacemaking skills to promote international conflict resolution, communication and dialogue-building projects, and reconciliation initiatives. In many cases, these skills and strategies are called on when conflict and violence has already broken out. But the greatest potential lies in using them to prevent conflicts from becoming destructive and violent. Preparation is a continuous process that includes the study of other mediation attempts, keeping up-to-date with the current literature, tracking existing and potential conflicts, meeting experienced mediators, gaining experience at the community and the international level, and attending conferences and seminars.

One international nongovernmental organization (NGO) that has been active, through its national affiliates, in organizing training workshops is the International Physicians for the Prevention of Nuclear War (IPPNW) (see Chapter 22). It has facilitated training sessions since 1989 in Bradford, UK; Coventry, UK; the Hague, the Netherlands; Colombo, Sri Lanka; Osijek, Croatia; Belfast, Ireland; Budapest, Hungary; Kampala, Uganda; Kuala Lumpur, Malaysia; and Skopje, Macedonia. The workshops have utilized a blend of theoretical input and experiential techniques, such as roleplay and simulation. Such workshops operate at many levels, for example, by providing basic exposure to mediation and other nonviolent conflict resolution methods and training, thus promoting a greater awareness of such methods; fostering relationships and building up trust between representatives from conflicting communities, thus making contacts for possible future mediation initiatives; and enabling the facilitators to become known as people who are concerned with mediation work, both within local communities and within government institutions. The intention of such workshops is not just to introduce Western-style methods and thinking about conflict resolution into other cultures, but also to attempt to facilitate the adaptation of such concepts to suit the appropriate cultural setting. What is important is a common language or understanding as a starting point for conflict resolution and mediation work.

Creating Mediation Contexts

International opportunities for conflict mediation are most likely to arise within the context of other projects. Such contexts include (see Figure 25-3):

- Conflict-resolution training workshops, as described above.
- Facilitating professional conferences and seminars on "neutral" territory.
- Organizing humanitarian ceasefires and "corridors of tranquility" or "bubbles of peace".
- Delivery of humanitarian aid.
- Remaining in contact with colleagues on all sides of a conflict.

The examples below illustrate some of these mediation contexts.

In 1991, a mediation team from the Medical Association for the Prevention of War (now known as Medical Action for Global Security), the IPPNW affiliate in the United Kingdom, visited Cyprus in an initiative to further rapprochement and bicommunal relations between Turkish and Greek Cypriot health professionals. The group organized a medical seminar to benefit both medical communities in the neutral territory of the UN buffer zone. Over a nine-month period, the team managed to meet with and get clearance from the political and medical leadership of both communities for the seminar to take place. Talks were also held with doctors from both medical communities and with senior personnel of the UN agencies in Cyprus. A program was designed and agreed upon by all parties that reflected a wide range of medical interests. In October 1991, 50 doctors met in a conducive and professional atmosphere, in which an equal number of Greek and Turkish Cypriot doctors presented medical case studies. For some participants, friendships from almost 20 years before were rekindled. It was hoped that this medical initiative, while not overtly a mediation attempt, would act as a conduit for communication between the two communities by creating a mediation context.[8]

The war in former Yugoslavia brought requests from medical colleagues on all sides. In 1991, at the beginning of the Serb-Croat War, health professionals in Zagreb and Belgrade formed Physicians for the Prevention of War (PPW) in an attempt to keep lines of communication and dialogue open; to work for human rights and justice; and to maintain support for, and adherence to, the Geneva Conventions—particularly those pertaining to the rights and duties of medical personnel.[9] Until the war became too intense for PPW to continue its activities, members from IPPNW affiliates attended the PPW meetings to support and show solidarity with these efforts to work for peace. As the war spread to Bosnia-Herzegovina, the activities of IPPNW and many other medical organizations became more intense. IPPNW in Europe organized a series of seminars and conferences in Austria and Hungary to which were invited medical colleagues from all over the Balkan region. These meetings provided a "neutral" forum to keep communication open, at a medical and humanitarian level, between health professionals from the various belligerent parties and other parties related to the conflict. Representatives at these meetings from Western European IPPNW affiliates were in a position to moderate and mediate. Professor Dr. Ulrich Gottstein (IPPNW-Germany), in consultation with doctors from the Balkans, was responsible for the bulk of the energy and organization behind these meetings. Topics covered included the care of refugees, trauma and rape counseling, the special needs of children, mediation and conflict resolution, humanitarian aid delivery, and medical "corridors of peace." The value of keeping alive personal contacts was recognized not only by outsiders to the conflict, but also those engaged in it. There was a need for personal contacts with all peoples of the former Yugoslavia to develop understanding of the situation and to hasten the process of mediation and peacemaking.[10]

In Canada, the Committee for Five Days of Peace has promoted days of peace in war zones to immunize children against the major vaccine-preventable causes of child death and disability and to provide an opportunity for building peace. This idea of humanitarian immunization ceasefires—health as a bridge to peace—was based on initiatives in El Salvador and Lebanon. By linking the campaign to immunize all the children of the world with the perceived movement toward the resolution of regional conflict, it was hoped that the chance for success of both goals would be increased.[11]

Active Mediation

Adam Curle defines active mediation as "the diplomatic activity of mediators, which involves direct mediation between the political and/or military leaderships of conflicting parties."[7] Active mediation is "shuttle-type diplomacy," involving traveling between the disputants, perhaps carrying messages (if appropriate) and information, finding common ground, and attempting to identify common issues. Mediators undertake active mediation with the specific purpose of removing obstacles on the path to peace, while arguing strongly against the misunderstandings and preconceptions that strengthen these obstacles.

Conclusion

Health professionals, who have a long and rich tradition in peacemaking,[12,13] can play an important role in international conflict resolution and mediation, not usually as major political players, but at grassroots levels in areas where their medical and public health knowledge, expertise, and connections can be maximized. By utilizing extensive global medical networks, by communicating with organizations of other professionals, and by speaking up loudly for respect and adherence to international humanitarian law and the Geneva Conventions, health professionals can add a powerful voice to calls for peace, reconciliation, and justice. Conflict resolution, and mediation in particular, are just two of the tools in the peacemaker's "kit bag" that can act as vehicles to promote these aims. These tools must be used to complement other initiatives, some of which have been described in this chapter.

Conflict resolvers and mediators wishing to intervene in conflicts will face ethical dilemmas and must ask themselves some important questions.[14] Interventions by outside "third parties" must be appropriate and sensitive to the needs of the local people. In addition to offering support in the form of skills training workshops, mine clearance, negotiation, human rights protection, medical and food aid, and other assistance, individuals involved at the local level in working to resolve and manage violent conflict must address their own psychological preparation. This includes development of their inner resources of wisdom, courage, and compassionate nonviolence. Otherwise, they will be worn down by those who are less interested in peace than in violence.[15]

Stepping out of their professional roles and into those of being citizen peacemakers is a serious undertaking for health professionals. Intervening nonviolently in other people's personal and political conflicts carries with it great moral and ethical responsibilities and obligations; it should not be undertaken without serious consideration of the motives for and commitment to such an undertaking.

REFERENCES

1. Morgenthau, H. *Politics among nations: The struggle for power and peace.* New York: Knopf, 1948.
2. Burton, J. The history of international conflict resolution. In Azar, E. and Burton, J. (eds.), *International conflict resolution: Theory and practice.* Sussex: Wheatsheaf Books, 1986, p. 42.
3. Osmanczyk, J. *Encyclopedia of United Nations and international agreements.* London: Taylor & Francis, 1985.
4. Banks, M. (ed.). *Conflict in world society: A new perspective on international relations.* Sussex: Wheatsheaf Books, 1984, p. 8.
5. Burton, J. (ed.), *Conflict: Human needs theory.* London: Macmillan, 1990.
6. Fisher, R. and Ury, W. *Getting to yes: How to negotiate without giving in.* London: Arrow Books, 1981.
7. Curle, A. *In the middle: Nonofficial mediation in violent situations.* Leamington Spa: Berg, 1986, pp. 21–48.
8. Lewer, N. Medical mediation in Cyprus. *The Friend,* Dec. 13, 1991, p. 1593. Craig, K. Medical mediation. *Medicine and War* 9(1):62–65, 1993.
9. Baccino-Astrada, A. *A manual on the rights and duties of medical personnel in armed conflicts.* Geneva: ICRC, 1982.
10. Middleton, J. (ed) Wounded healthy cities: Searching for health and human dignity. A report by the Croatian Healthy Cities Network. Compiled by Ivana Eterovic, Selma Segoritch, and Slobadan Lang. Lyndon, West Bromwich, United Kingdom: Sandwell Public Health Publications, 1992.
11. Hay, R. Humanitarian ceasefires: An examination of their potential contribution to the resolution of conflict. Working Paper No. 28. Ottawa: Canadian Institute for International Peace and Security, July 1990.

12. Lewer, N. *Physicians and the peace movement: Prescriptions for hope.* London: Frank Cass, 1992.

13. Ruprect, T. and Jensen, C. (eds). *Askulap oder Mars? Artze geyen den kreig.* Bremen: Geschichte & Frieden, Donat Verlag, 1991.

14. Lewer, N. and Ramsbotham, O. Something must be done. Towards an ethical framework for humanitarian intervention in international social conflict. Peace Research Report No. 33, Department of Peace Studies, University of Bradford, 1993.

15. Curle, A. New challenges for citizen peacemaking. Global Security Study No. 14, Nuclear Age Peace Foundation, June 1993.

Background Readings

Azar, E. *The management of protracted social conflict: Theory and cases.* Aldershot: Dartmouth, 1990.

Azar, E. and Burton, J. (eds.). *International conflict resolution: Theory and practice.* Sussex, United Kingdom: Wheatsheaf Books, 1986.

Bercovitch, J. and Rubin, J. (eds.). *Mediation in international relations: Multiple approaches to conflict management.* London: Macmillan, 1994.

Berman, M. and Johnson, E. (eds.). *Unofficial diplomats.* New York: Columbia Press, 1977.

Burton, J. and Dukes, F. *Conflict: Readings in management and resolution.* London: Macmillan, 1990.

Fisher, R., Kopelman, E. and Schneider, A. *Beyond Machiavelli: Tools for coping with conflict.* Cambridge, Mass.: Harvard University Press, 1994.

Mitchell, C. and Webb, K. (eds.). *New approaches to international mediation.* Westport, CT: Greenwood Press, 1988.

Sandole, J. and Sandole-Staroste, I. (eds.). *Conflict management and problem-solving: Interpersonal to international applications.* New York: New York University Press, 1987.

Sandole, D.J.D. and van der Merwe, H. (eds). *Conflict resolution theory and practice: Integration and application.* Manchester: Manchester University Press, 1993.

Touval, S. and Zartman, W. *International mediation in theory and practice.* Boulder, CO: Westview Press, 1985.

Yarrow, M. *Quaker experiences in international mediation.* New Haven, CT: Yale University Press, 1978.

Young, O. *The intermediaries: Third parties in international crises.* Princeton, NJ: Princeton University Press, 1967.

26

Preventing War and Its Health Consequences: Roles of Public Health Professionals

BARRY S. LEVY and VICTOR W. SIDEL

Like most public health problems, war and its health consequences are preventable.

The contributors to this book have documented the many adverse effects of war and preparation for war, and of the social, economic and psychological atmosphere, usually termed "militarism," that accompanies them. They have provided information on the ways in which these consequences may be prevented or minimized. This chapter is designed to summarize the preventive measures described in earlier chapters of this book, and to provide a unified approach to the subject of prevention.

In this chapter, the use of the word "war" will include not only war itself, but also militarism and preparation for war. There are a number of roles that public health professionals can play in preventing war and its consequences. These roles include the following:

- Participating in surveillance and documentation of the health effects of war and on the factors that may cause war;
- Developing and implementing education and awareness-raising programs on the health effects of war;
- Advocating policies and promoting actions to prevent war and its health consequences; and

• Working directly in actions to prevent war and and its consequences.

Resources and organizations that can facilitate or support these roles are listed in the Appendix.

A number of ethical issues may arise for public health professionals with regard to these roles, especially in war-zone health-related activities that serve to support military efforts (see Chapter 18).

The basic principles of prevention are applicable to the prevention of war, and the minimization of its consequences. In this context, as in Chapter 22, we define:

• *Primary prevention* as preventing war or causing a halt to a war that is taking place;
• *Secondary prevention* as preventing and minimizing the health and environmental consequences of war once it has begun. Once a war has begun, public health professionals can play a number of roles in protecting the public's health and minimizing the consequences of war; and
• *Tertiary prevention* as treating or ameliorating the health consequences of war.

It should be noted that many of the roles for public health professionals in secondary and tertiary prevention take place in the war zone, where there is a narrow line, particularly in direct participation in activities, between protecting and serving people, and enabling the war effort to move forward.

Surveillance and Documentation

Primary Prevention

Public health professionals with access to information on the health and environmental effects of war or militarism, and on factors that may cause war, have the capability—and we believe, the responsibility—to gather these data, to analyze them, and to make them widely available. Such data can be extremely useful, if used by health professionals and others in education and awareness-raising programs, in preventing war or preparation for war, or in causing a halt to a war that is taking place.

Secondary and Tertiary Prevention

Once a war has begun, public health professionals can play important roles in documenting and publicizing the nature and extent of injuries, illnesses (both physical and psychological), disabilities, and deaths—among both civilians and members of the military—occurring as a result of war. These data may be useful for the purposes of limiting the health consequences of the conflict or of bringing about a ceasefire.

Education and Awareness-Raising Programs

Primary prevention

Along with gathering and analyzing relevant data, public health professionals can play important roles in information, education, and communication activities on the health consequences of war—for health professionals, for the public, and for political leaders (see Chapters 21 and 22).

Secondary and Tertiary Prevention

Public health professionals can continue to play these roles even after war has begun. (See Surveillance and Documentation, above.)

Advocacy

Primary Prevention

Public health professionals can play important roles in advocating policies and promoting actions that prevent war or minimize the consequences of war. They can usually do this most effectively by working with or on behalf of public health organizations, such as the American Public Health Association. Another avenue for advocacy is through organizations for specific disciplines such as those for physicians, nurses, environmentalists, social workers, or others, or their labor unions. Such organizations include the American Medical Association, the American Nursing Association, and the National Association of Social Workers. In addition, health professionals can work within groups with broader memberships, such as the local chapters of Physicians for Social Responsibility, other national affiliates of the International Physicians for the Prevention of Nuclear War, and community or national groups, such as Peace Action.

There are a variety of objectives for advocacy work by public health professionals. These include:

- Promoting nonviolent conflict resolution (Chapter 25), both in general and in specific situations;
- Advocating maintenance of public health resources and services;
- Advocating decreases in military spending;
- Advocating decreases in—and ultimately elimination of—the international arms trade;
- Advocating cessation of the development, production, stockpiling, transfer, and testing of nuclear weapons (Chapter 22);
- Advocating ratification of—and then adherence to—the Chemical Weapons Convention (Chapter 7);

- Advocating cessation of the development, production, stockpiling, transfer, and testing of chemical weapons until the Chemical Weapons Convention is ratified by 65 nations and goes into effect;
- Advocating against the use of land mines and for treaties banning their production, transfer, and use (Chapter 10);
- Advocating, strengthening, and promoting adherence to the Biological Weapons Convention (Chapter 8);
- Advocating that economic sanctions with major impact on civilians never be used (see box on pp. 156–58 and Chapter 17);
- Advocating prevention of environmental degradation and overuse of environmental resources in preparation for or in the conduct of war (Chapters 5 and 9); and
- Promoting the United Nations and its activities, by supporting these activities and ensuring their nation's financial support of the UN (Chapter 24).

Secondary Prevention

Even after war has begun, public health professionals can continue to play important roles in advocating policies and promoting activities to minimize the consequences of war, including:

- Promoting public health and medical care activities for the protection of civilians (Chapters 19 and 20);
- Preventing the use of chemical, biological, and nuclear weapons (Chapters 6–8); and
- If these weapons are used, ensuring use by the population affected of appropriate protective devices and medications, such as the use of barrier methods against chemical and biological weapons and the use of thyroid tablets to protect against the concentration of iodine-131 in the thyroid gland after the use of nuclear weapons.

Tertiary Prevention

Health professionals can advocate for effective services for those physically or mentally injured or displaced by war.

Participating Directly in Effective Actions

Primary Prevention

There are a variety of ways in which public health professionals can act. One is participation in nonviolent conflict resolution. Public health professionals can work in their own communities or in other communities in which violence is likely. They can also participate in activities that foster transparency and trust-building in individual relationships (see Chapter 25).

Secondary Prevention

There are at least four ways that public health professionals may involve themselves directly in secondary prevention:

- As part of the armed forces of a nation;
- As part of a United Nations peacekeeping force (Chapter 24);
- As part of another international agency, such as UNICEF (Chapter 2); and
- As part of a nongovernmental organization, such as the International Committee of the Red Cross, the International Rescue Committee, Médecins du Monde, or Médecins Sans Frontières (Chapters 19 and 20).

There are a variety of direct participation roles that public health professionals can play. They can work to protect the health of civilians (especially women and children), including:

- Maintaining public health functions (such as sanitation and water supply);
- Taking special measures to ensure provision of public health services, such as ceasefires for immunization days;
- Maintaining medical—including mental health—services for treatment of victims and their families, including maintaining safe zones for hospitals and other health care facilities; and
- Ensuring prompt burial of the dead.

Health professionals can also work to ensure human rights (Chapter 4):

- Preventing sexual exploitation and other forms of exploitation of women (Chapter 13);
- Preventing child labor and other forms of exploitation of children, including their being forced into military roles (Chapter 12);
- Preventing indentured service and protecting those who refuse to participate in military services (Chapter 18); and
- Protecting the rights of displaced persons (Chapter 14) and prisoners of war.

Protecting the physical environment (Chapters 5 and 9) can be another role for the health professional:

- Preventing the use of weapons that damage the environment;
- Protecting safe water supplies; and
- Ensuring restoration and clean-up if the environment has been damaged.

Tertiary Prevention

Potential roles that public health professionals can play include caring for victims of war (Chapters 19 and 20), including assisting and providing health services for all displaced persons (Chapter 14) and prisoners of war. Health professionals can help to document the dangers that refugees would face if they were forced to return to their home countries.

Tertiary prevention roles of health professionals in caring for victims of war are controversial and have been criticized by some as making war more tolerable (Chapter 18).

Conclusion

War is the most serious threat to public health. Public health professionals can do much to prevent war and its health consequences. Preventing war and its consequences should be in the curricula of schools of public health, on the agendas of public health organizations, and in the practice of public health professionals. Activities by public health professionals to prevent war and its health consequences are, in our view, an essential part of our professional obligations.

VIII

Epilogue

Epilogue

VICTOR W. SIDEL and BARRY S. LEVY

In the years since 1996, when the manuscripts for the first edition were completed, there have been important developments in a number of the topic areas covered in *War and Public Health*. In this Epilogue, we describe the most important and significant of these developments. This information should be reviewed in the context of the relevant information in the first edition.

Human Consequences of War
(See also Chapter 3, pp. 27-38, and Part IV, pp. 149-212)

While the number of wars being fought and the number of people, both military and civilian, killed directly by military action has declined during the 1990s, military actions and civil strife with major public heath consequences have continued or have begun in Africa, Asia, South America, and Europe.[1,2]

In Africa, a genocidal war in Rwanda in 1994 led to a war in the late 1990s in Congo and the nine nations surrounding it, widely known as "Africa's First World War." At the start of 2000, at least 35,000 troops from six countries outside Congo were fighting inside Congo.[3,4] The war in Angola, spilling into Namibia with additional civilian deaths, and armed conflicts in Sudan and Sierra Leone also continued.

In Asia, a referendum in East Timor resulted in a decisive vote for independence from Indonesia, which led immediately to extensive militia violence against the civilian population of East Timor. The violence, which was said to have been incited by Indonesian military forces, led to major casualties and prompted intervention by a military force led by Australia. In Kashmir, military forces from India and Pakistan continued sporadic struggle, complicated by 1998 nuclear test explosions conducted by both countries. In

Chechnya, Russian troops have conducted a fierce and protracted military operation against rebel forces, with massive military and civilian casualties on both sides.

In Colombia, a vicious and bloody civil war has raged for almost 40 years with widespread terror, the involvement of child soldiers, and extensive casualties among civilians. The United States has supported the military forces of the Government of Colombia in this civil war, stating that this support was part of its effort to interdict the supply of illegal drugs entering the United States.[4a,b,c,d]

In Europe, the U.S.-led North Atlantic Treaty Organization (NATO) launched an air assault in 1999 against Yugoslavia. The purpose of the assault, NATO stated, was humanitarian intervention to stop human rights abuses by the Serbian Government against the ethnic Albanian population of Kosovo. This action illustrated the fundamental contradiction, in international law and in the procedures of international governmental organizations, between guarantee of the sovereignty of nations and the guarantee of human rights for all their inhabitants. The United Nations Charter (Article 2(4)) permits military force to be used only under two conditions: (1) "self-defense if an armed attack occurs" against a nation or an allied nation (Article 51); or (2) as part of enforcement action by a United Nations force authorized by the UN Security Council to counter threats to or breaches of international peace (Article 42). The use of military force against a country by another country or group of countries in order to protect the human rights of the people within the borders of another nation would therefore only be legitimate in current international law when the intervention is explicitly authorized by the Security Council. The organization of such a military intervention is difficult to achieve within the current United Nations structure, in which unanimity of the five permanent members of the Security Council is required, but it has been achieved in Somalia, Rwanda, Haiti, and Bosnia.[5] Although the United States Government and the governments of other NATO countries defended the military attack on Serbia as "just and necessary,"[6] authorization by the Security Council had not been given and the NATO action was therefore illegal under international law.

Apart from legality, certain types of military force, even if authorized by the Security Council, may exacerbate the destruction of the rights, the lives, and the health of people in countries against which military force is used, including those whose defense prompted the use of force. The bombing of Serbian targets by NATO forces was not only illegal but also destructive to the health, environment, and infrastructure of the people of both Serbia and Kosovo and ineffective—at least in the short-run—in protecting the human rights of the ethnic Albanian Kosovars.

There is no doubt that the international community has failed to act in recent years to prevent acts of genocide. A report from the Organization of African Unity in the year 2000 detailed the atrocities that killed some 800,000 people in Rwanda in 1994 and declared that the genocide had been preventable.[7] Noting the lack of humanitarian intervention in Rwanda, a number of groups advocated in 1998 humanitarian intervention in Kosovo during the period leading up to and during the reported acts of genocide there in 1998 and 1999. Physicians for Human Rights (PHR) particularly noted the brutal treatment of doctors, other health care workers, and their patients in the former Yugoslavia.[8] PHR, together with other civil society groups, including Human Rights Watch and the International Committee of the Red Cross, and together with some governmental and intergovernmental organizations, tried to stop the escalation of what was termed "ethnic cleansing" of the ethnic Albanian population of Kosovo. Serbian troops under Yugoslav president Slobodan Milosevic were, these groups reported, amassing their forces in Kosovo in early 1999 even as negotiators were working to get the Serbs and representatives of the Kosovo Liberation Army (KLA) to accept the terms of what would come to be known as the Rambouillet Agreement.[8a,b,c] When the failure of the negotiations seemed imminent and ethnic cleansing, if not genocide, loomed on the horizon, PHR and a coalition of human rights and humanitarian groups called upon the international community to deploy a force of peacekeeping troops into Kosovo in order to protect the Kosovar Albanians. When NATO eventually did intervene it was with a three-month campaign of air strikes that inflicted massive damage not only on President Milosevic's military assets, but also on the civilian infrastructure and the environment of Serbia, Kosovo, and neighboring countries.

Whether or not the air strikes triggered the ethnic cleansing that escalated over the next two months, as many opponents of the NATO strategy claimed, they certainly did nothing to prevent it, as President Clinton and other NATO leaders said they were intended to do. By the time President Milosevic capitulated and a cease-fire was declared in early June, more than 700,000 Kosovo Albanians had been driven from their homes. Most were living in refugee camps and with host families in Albania, Macedonia, and Montenegro[9]; hundreds of thousands of others had fled into the mountains as internally displaced persons; tens of thousands had been evacuated to countries outside the region. Atrocities against women, adult men, and the elderly, although difficult to document once Kosovo was sealed off, were widely and credibly reported by refugees as they flooded over the borders. Reports in July 2000, one year after the end of the war, indicated the continuing plight of the Kosovo Albanians who had been forced from their homes during the three-month war and had subsequently returned home.[10] In short, this military intervention appeared to be ineffective for its "humanitarian intervention" purposes.

Given the brutality of President Milosevic's policies, it is not hard to understand why groups such as PHR and Human Rights Watch, which had been extremely reluctant to endorse military intervention in the past, would do so this time, with the failures of Rwanda and Somalia still so fresh in their memories. What they asked the international community to do in response, controversial in itself, was a far cry from the form of intervention the US and NATO chose. Many observers felt the campaign of air strikes was wrong for three principal reasons:[11]

1. War in the nuclear age—even a war with an arguably "just" cause—is no longer a viable option for resolving conflict or dealing with aggression.

2. The means employed by the U.S.-led NATO forces were disproportionate to the stated ends and, therefore, were unacceptable regardless of the outcome.

3. Even if a multinational peacekeeping force was required to prevent ethnic cleansing, that force should have been deployed far sooner and under a UN flag, not by NATO.

Sanctions
(see also pp. 156-158)

If protection of human rights by military intervention is impossible, illegal, destructive, or ineffective economic sanctions—the suspension of customary trade and financial relations with the offending country—have been advocated as a preferable substitute. The United Nations Charter in Article 41 authorizes the Security Council to apply measures such as "complete or partial interruption of economic relations and of rail, sea, air, postal, telegraphic, radio and other means of communication, and the severance of diplomatic relations." There are indeed instances in which international sanctions were useful in leading to the correction of human rights abuses. For example, international sanctions helped to pressure the apartheid government of the Republic of South Africa to relinquish power and were welcomed by many black South Africans who had to endure the economic consequences produced by the sanctions.[12]

Other examples of sanctions imposed by the Security Council were apparently successful, such as the sanctions on former Yugoslavia that were an important incentive for the Dayton Accords and the sanctions in Angola that have been viewed as targeted and protective of human rights. In Cuba, on the other hand, sanctions were unilaterally imposed by the United States without the authorization of the United Nations. These sanctions have led to severe hardship among the Cuban people without any evidence of significant impact on the goals sought by the United States.[13,14]

Sanctions, whether authorized by the UN Security Council or not, have frequently been associated with severe deterioration of the health and welfare of the populations affected, with particular impact demonstrated on women, children and the elderly. Data on the impact of sanctions on the people of nations such as Vietnam (pages 215-237), Nicaragua (pages 238-253), Haiti,[15] and Iraq (pages 254-278),[16,17] while incomplete and difficult to interpret in terms of the extent to which sanctions rather than military action or economic problems cause the human consequences, are of great concern to those working to protect public health.[18-20]

If sanctions are to be used as a substitute for military intervention to protect human rights, it seems clear certain conditions for use of sanctions will have to be met:[20]

1. *Sanctions must be authorized by the United Nations.* The economic blockade of Cuba unilaterally imposed by the United States is an example of sanctions that are

clearly illegal under international law. Sanctions imposed without the authorization of the United Nations, many believe, should be considered an act of war and punished according to international law.

When the Security Council cannot act to authorize sanctions in instances in which most nations or most of the world's people concur and in which prompt action is needed, some observers believe a method should be found to permit the United Nations General Assembly to authorize sanctions.[20] This would allow rapid intervention, would ease the frustration of those concerned about prompt response to human rights abuses, and might deter a country or groups of countries from intervening without United Nations authorization.

2. *Sanctions must protect the human rights of the affected population.* Authorization by the United Nations does not guarantee, as the world has seen in Iraq, that sanctions will be humane. Sanctions should specify that restriction of food, medicine, and other items needed for health and welfare are specifically forbidden.

3. *Sanctions must be accompanied by effective surveillance of the health and well-being of the affected population.* The United Nations Children's Fund (UNICEF), in its ten-point Anti-War Agenda [See Chapter 2, p.23], stated that "Economic sanctions are imposed on the assumption that the long-term benefits of pressure on errant regimes outweigh the immediate cost to children. This may not be the case. There should be a 'child impact assessment' at the point at which any set of sanctions is applied, and constant monitoring thereafter to gauge impact." When it is clear that sanctions are affecting predominantly the poor population of the offending country, methods must be sought to provide food, medicine and medical services despite the sanctions.

4. *Sanctions should concentrate on restrictions that will specifically target the elite and the political and economic leadership of the offending country.* These restrictions might include freezing of assets, denial of international travel, embargoes on goods and services used by the elite, and restrictions on business and profit. While these measures may indirectly affect the disadvantaged population of the country against which they are applied, these secondary efforts should be small compared to the impact on the targeted elite. This was apparently the case in South Africa, but has not been the case in Iraq.

The definition of public health adopted by the Institute of Medicine in its 1988 report *The Future of Public Health*[21] is: "Public health is what we, as a society, do collectively to assure the conditions in which people can be healthy." If this definition is an apt one, those concerned with public health must be concerned about both protection of human rights and the public health consequences of measures used to attempt to protect human rights. That protection of human rights is a necessary condition for assuring public health was strongly asserted during 1998, the 50th anniversary of the adoption of the Universal Declaration of Human Rights.[22-24] Sanctions are clearly an imperfect tool for protecting human rights. But they may be less likely than military intervention to lead to wider conflict or to further loss of rights. To make sanctions more useful, efforts must be made to develop more humane yet effective sanctions and to develop efficient and effective international methods for deciding whether and when to use them. These are public health issues and those concerned about the health of the people have an obligation to contribute to making sanctions more legitimate, more humane, and more effective.

Nuclear Weapons
(See also Chapter 6, pp. 65-83, and Chapter 22, pp. 336-349)

Consequences of nuclear weapons production

The U.S. Department of Energy (DOE) announced in 1999 that "nuclear weapons production during the Cold War may have caused illnesses in thousands of workers" and that legislation would be introduced that would "compensate many of them for their medical care and lost wages." The announcement was based on a study demonstrating that workers were exposed to radiation beyond permissible limits and to chemicals such as beryllium, asbestos, mercury, and uranium. The study, prepared by a panel of the White House National Economic Council with the cooperation of the DOE and other federal agencies, found elevated rates of 22 types of cancer among employees at 14 DOE facilities.[25,26]

Radioactive contamination remains a problem at the sites at which nuclear weapons were produced. At the 560-square-mile Hanford reservation, for example, which produced plutonium for nuclear weapons for more than 40 years, 80% of the spent nuclear fuel in the Department of Energy's inventory—2,100 metric tons in all—is stored in a pair of aging basins, some of their fuel canisters crumbling and corroded. Deteriorating underground tanks a few miles away hold 54 million gallons of radioactive soup that over the years has made its way into the groundwater. In 1999, routine surveys found tritium at concentrations 90 times the federal drinking water standard in a nearby well. The well lies near the Columbia River, the waterway that irrigates 1 million acres of prime farmland in Oregon and Washington State and nurtures 80% of the fall chinook salmon harvested in Alaska and British Columbia. Tests of other wells have shown that the tritium seep has not moved more than a quarter-mile from the burial site, but it is nonetheless estimated that the contamination could reach the river in as little as three years with serious health and environmental consequences. Furthermore, tritium is one of the fastest-moving radionuclides and movement of other, more toxic nuclear wastes may follow.[27]

Consequences of nuclear weapons testing

Recent studies have provided additional information on the health consequences to the U.S. population of nuclear weapons testing in the atmosphere. The U.S. National Cancer

Institute has estimated that the release of iodine-131 in fallout from U.S. nuclear test explosions would by itself be responsible for between 11,200 and 212,000 excess cases (with a central estimate of 49,000 cases) of thyroid cancer among the U.S. population.[28] A study by the International Physicians for the Prevention of Nuclear War (IPPNW) estimated that the strontium-90, cesium-137, carbon-14, and plutonium-239 released worldwide in all nuclear test explosions would be responsible for 430,000 cancer deaths by the year 2000.[29] Previously, a study by IPPNW and the Institute for Energy and Environmental Research (IEER) summarized additional widespread health and environmental effects of nuclear weapons production, with massive contamination of land by radioactive materials and toxic chemicals.[30]

Although nuclear weapons are often thought of as a relatively inexpensive source of military strength, a 1998 Brookings Institute study concluded that since 1940 the cost of the U.S. nuclear arsenal alone was over $5 trillion, larger than the entire U.S. national debt.[31] The Brookings study further estimated that $35 billion continue to be spent annually on nuclear weapons by the U.S. alone, including $4.5 billion per year to maintain existing weapons and develop new weapon designs.[32]

Since 1963, the Limited Nuclear Test Ban Treaty has banned nuclear explosions in the atmosphere, under water, and in space, and attempts have been made to negotiate a Comprehensive Nuclear Test Ban Treaty (CTBT). Underground tests continued, however, and in 1998 a series of Indian and Pakistani nuclear test explosions sparked fears both of a South Asian nuclear war and of an unraveling of global efforts to prevent nuclear proliferation. In 1996 a CTBT was approved by the United Nations General Assembly and submitted to the world's nations for signature and ratification. It would set up an international monitoring system and allow for short-notice, on-site inspections to ensure compliance. By July 2000 a total of 155 countries had signed the CTBT and 60 had ratified it, but the treaty cannot come into force until 44 specifically-named countries, known to possess nuclear weapons or thought capable of developing them, ratify it. Of these 44 specifically-named countries, 30 had ratified the treaty by July 2000. Of the five major nuclear powers, the UK and France had ratified it, and in May 2000 the Federation Council, the upper house of Russia's parliament, confirmed the previous action of the State Duma, the lower chamber, and ratified the treaty. Countries that had not ratified the CTBT by mid-2000 included China, India, Israel, North Korea, and Pakistan. While the United States has signed the CTBT, ratification was debated in the U.S. Senate in 1999 and was defeated by vote of 51-48. The Senate is the first and only legislature of any country to reject the treaty.[33]

Risks of use of nuclear weapons

Since 1945, nuclear strategy has been based on the premise that the only way to deter a nuclear attack is to prepare for the use of nuclear weapons in war. After the Soviet Union disintegrated in 1991, the U.S. unilaterally de-emphasized nuclear weapons, took strategic nuclear bombers off alert, removed launch pins from long-range nuclear missiles, removed tactical nuclear weapons from Europe, and negotiated the START II treaty with Russia to decrease the number of long-range nuclear-tipped missiles.[34] The United States and Russia began negotiation of START III and attempted to limit the spread of nuclear weapons and defuse the threat of nuclear war by helping some of the former Soviet republics rid themselves of nuclear weapons and by pressuring other countries for an extension of the Nuclear Non-Proliferation Treaty (NPT), under which countries without nuclear weapons agree not to acquire them.[35]

Despite some reductions, 35,000 nuclear weapons remain in today's arsenals.[36] Even if all existing U. S.-Russian arms control treaties were fully implemented (by the year 2003), nearly 20,000 nuclear warheads will remain, with an explosive force of 200,000 Hiroshima bombs. Dangerous Cold War launch-on-warning procedures also remain in place. A 1998 study reported that the risk of "accidental" nuclear war was increasing as a result of deterioration in Russian computer and radar systems. The study estimated that an "accidental" or unauthorized nuclear attack by a single Russian submarine would likely cause at least 6.8 million immediate U.S. deaths in urban firestorms, even though concrete steps to eliminate that danger are available.[37] Other risks include the possibility of nuclear terrorism by non-governmental groups.[38-40] Reiterating their opposition to the perpetuation of the "nuclear apartheid" that they believe is the purpose of the NPT, under which the five permanent members of the U.N. maintain their own nuclear arsenals while denying them to other nations, India and other nations have repeatedly called for a serious global commitment to nuclear abolition.[41]]

Although the Cold War has ended, some arms control specialists believe the threat of a nuclear war is actually greater now then ever before. While Russia and the United States continue to decrease their massive strategic nuclear arsenals, the Kremlin in early 2000 approved a shift in military doctrine that *increases* Russia's reliance on nuclear weapons. Rather than threatening to use nuclear weapons only if there is a threat to the existence of Russia, it would now use them "if all other means of resolving the crisis have been exhausted," a seemingly lower threshold.[34]

In addition, the U.S. government continues to debate national policy on nuclear weapons use and has since the 1990s threatened their use in response to a nuclear, chemical, or biological attack—although its policy requires that any response to an attack be proportionate to the attack itself and essential to prevent a further attack. Given these constraints, specialists believe that even a "limited" nuclear response to a biological or chemical attack on the United States would almost certainly violate international law. This is particularly true in the light of the advisory opinion issued by the International Court of Justice in 1996 (see below) that declared the only possible legal justification for the use of nuclear weapons is if a country≠'s very survival is at stake. The apparent lack of a consensus on clarification of the U.S. position means, however, that the current U.S. policy—threatening an "absolutely overwhelming" and a "devastating" response to an unconventional attack—is likely to continue.[34] Public health workers are also concerned about reports of nuclear weapons stockpiles in Israel, about the potential of North Korea, Iraq, and perhaps other countries to acquire nuclear weapons, and about U.S. commitment to maintenance of its Stockpile Stewardship Program.

Finally, attempts by the United States to develop a national ballistic missile defense system were renewed during the late 1990s. Funding for implementation of this system had been reduced, but funds for research and development kept the program alive. Between 1993 and 1998 the United States spent over $39 billion on various forms of a national missile defense system, but the technology needed to demonstrate an effective system continued to be elusive.[42] Deployment of a national system would require modification of the Anti-Ballistic Missile Treaty, one of the bulwarks of nuclear weapons arms control between the United States and the Soviet Union and now Russia.[43] In addition, some forms of missile defense involve placing weapons such as lasers in outer space. The United States has negotiated a multimillion dollar contract with TRW and Boeing to build a Space-Based Laser Readiness Demonstrator. In contrast, on November 1, 1999, the United Nations General assembly voted to reaffirm the Outer Space Treaty, which preserves use of outer space for peaceful purposes, by adopting a resolution entitled "Prevention of an Arms Race in Outer Space." Some 140 countries voted for the resolution; only two nations did not, the United States and Israel, both of which abstained.[44,45]

Prospects for abolition of nuclear weapons

In 1995, Abolition 2000, a consortium of civil society groups, dedicated itself to seek a signed global agreement by 2000, committing the world to the permanent elimination of nuclear weapons within a specified timeframe.[46,47] National medical associations in Germany, Japan, Norway, and Switzerland called for nuclear abolition.[48] In the United States, the American College of Physicians, the American Public Health Association, and Physicians for Social Responsibility (the U.S. affiliate of the International Physicians for the Prevention of Nuclear War) all called for an abolition agreement by 2000.[49-50] In 1996, the American Medical Association called for the abolition of all weapons of mass destruction: nuclear, chemical, and biological.[51] By the year 2000, Abolition 2000 had grown to more than 2,000 co-sponsoring citizens' organizations in 93 countries.[47] Building upon lessons learned from the first 50 years of unsuccessful efforts to achieve a definitive solution to the dangers of nuclear weapons, the Abolition 2000 campaign has integrated global grassroots activities with legal initiatives and collaboration with military, political, and other world leaders, all aiming at a "final common pathway" of a global treaty banning nuclear weapons. Although the initial target date of the year 2000 will not be achieved, important milestones in the past five years have transformed nuclear abolition from a utopian dream to a serious objective.

In 1996, the International Court of Justice in the Hague (the World Court) issued two advisory opinions. In the first, the Court ruled by a majority vote that the use or even the threat of use of nuclear weapons was virtually always illegal under international law. In the second, the Court unanimously ruled that countries have "an obligation to pursue in good faith and to bring to a conclusion negotiations leading to nuclear disarmament in all its aspects," under Article VI of the Nuclear Non-Proliferation Treaty.[52]

Also in 1996, the Canberra Commission on the Elimination of Nuclear Weapons, including military and political experts from all nuclear weapons states, outlined a series of concrete steps toward abolition that could begin immediately and concluded that: "The proposition that nuclear weapons can be retained in perpetuity and never used accidentally or by decision defies credibility. The only complete defense is the elimination of nuclear weapons and assurance that they will never be produced again."[53] In late 1996, 63 generals and admirals from 17 countries issued an unequivocal call for nuclear abolition.[54] In 1997, the U.S. National Academy of Sciences report, *The Future of U.S. Nuclear Weapons Policy*, stated that "increased attention is now warranted to studying and fostering the conditions that would have to be met to make prohibition [of nuclear weapons] desirable and feasible."[55] Subsequently, Mikhail Gorbachev, Jimmy Carter, and 115 other political leaders from 46 countries added their support for nuclear abolition.[56]

A draft Nuclear Weapons Convention has been developed by an international consortium of lawyers, scientists, and disarmament experts and is now a formal U.N. document, available in the six official U.N. languages for consideration and debate.[57] An important precedent is the Chemical Weapons Convention, ratified by the U.S. Senate in 1997, which establishes a timetable for the permanent elimination of all chemical weapons and specifies procedures for unprecedentedly intrusive onsite inspections.

For health professionals, engendering fear of nuclear war is not enough. Concrete steps that individuals or groups can take to mitigate the danger must be identified. If, however, these steps involve only partial solutions, the dangers of nuclear arsenals are likely to resurface in new forms. Today's global dangers of nuclear arsenals require global solutions. The Indian and Pakistani test explosions have cast grave doubt on whether it is even plausible that the world can still maintain a double standard, in which some countries insist that nuclear arsenals are vital to their own security while denying those same arsenals to others. A united global voice of public health and medicine could play a powerful role in establishing for nuclear weapons the single global norm that applies to chemical and biological weapons: zero.

Finally, as was true in the period immediately following Hiroshima and Nagasaki, the current window of opportunity to build global support for nuclear abolition is almost certain to be brief. Although the abolition of nuclear weapons today has stronger support than ever before, dramatically increased efforts will be required of organizations and individuals if the global devastation that today's thermonuclear arsenals threaten are to be definitively prevented. A successful campaign by medical organizations worldwide in support of a verifiable and enforceable Nuclear Weapons Convention would be an extraordinary contribution to safeguarding health in the 21st century.

Nuclear abolition cannot be achieved without U.S. leadership, yet the U.S. has not yet seriously questioned its commitment to maintaining a massive nuclear arsenal. Public health workers and other citizens thus have a special opportunity and responsibility to convince elected leaders to make the abolition (or "prohibition") of nuclear weapons a major national priority, as U.S. officials have advocated since the 1940s[58,59] and as the Nuclear Non-Proliferation Treaty legally requires.[52]

At the NPT Review Conference at the United Nations in New York City in April 2000, the first review conference since the Treaty was indefinitely extended in 1995, major roles were played by non-nuclear-weapon states, especially the "New Agenda Coalition" composed of Brazil, Egypt, Ireland, Mexico, New Zealand, South Africa, and Sweden, who effectively argued for an unequivocal undertaking and next steps on nuclear disarmament. The final document called on India and Pakistan to adhere to UN Security Resolution 1172, adopted after both countries conducted nuclear tests in 1998, and called on the Middle East for a zone free of weapons of mass destruction. Most important, the nuclear powers pledged an "unequivocal undertaking ... to accomplish the total elimination of their nuclear arsenals" and agreed to omit the word "ultimate" that they had previously insisted be included. The NPT Parties underscored the necessity of achieving the early entry into force of the CTBT and prompt negotiations on a fissile material production ban. While supporting full implementation of START II, the parties urged the United States and Russia to conclude START III. There was, however, no discussion in the final document of the proliferation dangers inherent in US plans to deploy national ballistic missile defenses or of the importance of negotiating and concluding a ban on the production of fissile materials for nuclear weapons. While there were useful agreements on nuclear safety and liability, there was incomplete discussion on export controls on nuclear materials and technology. The Review Conference demonstrated the frustration felt by non-nuclear-weapon countries with lack of progress toward abolition despite the increased accountability demanded in 1995 when the NPT was indefinitely extended.[60]

Chemical Weapons
(See also Chapter 7, pp. 84-97)

Although there was no evidence that chemical weapons were used during the Persian Gulf War, there have been problems caused by efforts to protect civilians and troops from the effects of chemical weapons. In Israel, where self-injecting atropine syringes were distributed for civilian use in case of an attack with nerve agents, there were reports of use of the syringes even in the absence of attack. U.S. troops, who were issued autoinjectors filled with atropine and pralidoxime, may have also used them because of fear of attack. In addition, U.S. troops were supplied with pyridostigmine bromide (PB) tablets, which the Department of Defense (DoD) thought might be useful as pretreatment for protection against the effects of nerve agents.[61] PB is a drug licensed by the FDA for treatment of myasthenia gravis, but was viewed by the FDA as experimental when used for protection against nerve agents. The FDA instructed the DoD to secure informed consent from all troops to whom the PB was given, but the DoD failed to do so. The 1999 report of a DoD-sponsored Rand Corporation study concluded that PB cannot be excluded as a potential factor in the etiology of the Gulf War Syndrome.[62] In addition, further evidence has been released that U.S. troops may have been exposed to chemical weapons during the destruction of Iraqi chemical weapons stockpiles.

In part as a result of the use of chemical weapons in the Iran-Iraq War and the threat of use during the Persian Gulf War, the Chemical Weapons Convention (CWC) was negotiated and was opened in Paris for signature in 1992. The CWC was promptly signed by the United States. Five years later, on April 24, 1997, the United States Senate ratified the CWC and on April 29, 1997, the CWC, having been ratified by more than the required 65 nations, entered into force. The provisions of the CWC include (1) a ban on the development, production, acquisition, stockpiling, transfer and use of chemical weapons; (2) elimination of all chemical weapons and their production facilities by 2007, although U.S. military forces are already obligated by U.S. law to do so by 2004; and (3) creation of an Organisation for the Prohibition of Chemical Weapons (OPCW) in the Hague to conduct routine and unannounced inspections of companies using precursor chemicals covered by the treaty.[63]

Now that the CWC has entered into force, a number of tasks remain: The governments of the U.S. and of other countries must support fully the activities of the OPCW and must provide the financial, technical, and administrative assistance necessary to implement the CWC. As of July 2000, a total of 135 nations had ratified or acceded to the CWC. However, Iraq, Libya, and Syria, countries that are alleged to have chemical weapons programs, have not yet even signed the treaty.[63]

Since it is clear that the disposal of chemical weapons required by the CWC may create health and environmental hazards, the CWC must be implemented in a manner that protects health and the environment. As of July 2000, a total of 70,000 metric tons of chemical weapons and more than 8 million munitions and bulk containers have been inspected by OPCW and are subject to a stringent international verification regime. More than a million weapons and 4,000 metric tons of chemical warfare agents have been destroyed.[63] In the United States, approximately 21 percent of the stockpile has been destroyed.[63a]

The United States had planned to use incineration for "demilitarization" of its chemical weapons and this method has actually been used at Johnston Island in the Pacific to demilitarize nerve agents shipped there from Okinawa and from NATO forces in Europe, and in Toole, Utah.[63a] Facilities have been constructed for incineration of stockpiles of chemical weapons at sites in the United States. Russia, on the other hand, plans to use chemical neutralization to dispose of its chemical weapons.[64-66] There remains considerable debate about the safety of the methods of disposal. Incineration leads to the decomposition of the chemical agents into small particles, which are released into the atmosphere through tall smokestacks. Critics contend that the concentration of products of incineration that are released into the atmosphere, which may include dioxins, may be high enough to cause toxic effects. The proponents of chemical neutralization in Russia contend that it would provide a safer means of disposal, but the Russian method leads to a complex organic "soup" that must be mixed with bitumen, a tar-like substance, before disposal in landfills. Opposition to the incineration method at weapons sites in Newport, Indiana, and Aberdeen, Maryland, has led to development of alternative chemical methods of disposal. Scientific and political opposition to the use of these methods must be resolved quickly if the United States, Russia, and other countries are to proceed to timely disposal to meet the deadlines imposed by the CWC.

Biological Weapons
(See also Chapter 8, pp. 98-116)

Use of biological weapons

There has still been no credible evidence of use of biological weapons in war since the end of World War II, and a Biological Weapons Convention (BWC) prohibiting the development, production, and stockpiling of biological and toxin weapons and requiring their destruction entered into force in 1975.[67] Nonetheless, the BWC is a much weaker convention than the CWC and in recent years there has been a major expansion in the perceived threat of the use of biological weapons. The Clinton administration has stated that at least 12 countries have acquired, or are trying to acquire, such weaponry. Allegations have been published, for example, by Ken Alibek, a defector from Russia, about biological weapons development in the USSR and Russia and the presence of stockpiles of weaponized smallpox and anthrax.[68]

In July 2000 it was revealed that the United States was pressuring the Colombian Government to allow the widespread spraying of the fungus *Fusarium oxysporum* as an anti-crop agent against coca, as part of the U.S. military aid package aimed at suppressing Colombian rebel operations. These plans raised concerns about risks posed by uncontrolled spread of Fusarium beyond the coca crop that could destroy basic foodstuffs needed by the Colombian rural population for survival and possibly lead to human infection by the agent.[69]

In December 1997, despite public controversy, the U.S. Department of Defense (DoD) announced that all 2.4 million active duty military personnel and reservists would be inoculated with anthrax vaccine.[70] Anthrax is a highly virulent infectious disease of animals. When transmitted to humans, cutaneous, gastrointestinal or inhalation anthrax can occur. Inhalation is the route by which anthrax might be employed as a biological weapon.

The vaccine that the DoD began using was produced by one supplier, the Michigan Biologic Products Institute (MBPI). First developed during the 1950s, reformulated in the 1960s, and approved by the U.S. Food and Drug Administration (FDA) for general use in 1970, the vaccine has been given to some veterinarians, those who work with livestock or animal products, anthrax researchers, and special deployment troops.

The insistence by the DoD that all military personnel be immunized, regardless of whether they have provided informed consent, has raised issues of public health ethics. Military personnel may ethically require special protection against mandatory treatment or against experimental treatment (see page 286). Several hundred members of the U.S. armed forces are known to have refused inoculation with the anthrax vaccine and many have been subjected to severe punishment, such as demotion or dismissal. In contrast, the United Kingdom has made anthrax immunization voluntary for its armed forces; 70% of U.K. military personnel have refused.[71]

The evidence that the MBPI vaccine will be effective in protecting troops against airborne infection with anthrax remains questionable. The only published human efficacy trial of an anthrax vaccine is a study performed 40 years ago in a mill that processed contaminated raw imported goat hair in which clinical anthrax infections occurred.[72] Some protective value against cutaneous anthrax was noted, but there were not enough cases of inhalation anthrax to reach any conclusions about vaccine efficacy. A controlled trial that involved purposeful exposure of humans to inhalation anthrax would be unethical, but experiments have been done exposing monkeys and guinea pigs to inhalation anthrax. These experiments yielded contradictory results. The Senate Veterans' Affairs Committee examined the issue of efficacy and safety of the vaccine in 1994 and recommended that "the vaccine should be considered investigational when used as a protection against biologic warfare." More recent experiments using rhesus macaques have led to greater conviction by the military that the vaccine may be effective against the strain of anthrax to which the macaques were exposed,[73] but the military cannot predict which strain, if any, will be used. Further complicating the question of efficacy is the evidence that new strains of anthrax may have been developed specifically to defeat the current vaccine.

The potential risks of mass administration of anthrax vaccine to military personnel are still largely unknown. While sufficient small-scale testing had indeed been done in humans to convince the FDA to license the vaccine for use in protecting small numbers of at-risk workers, and while there have been no reports of major adverse consequences from the limited use of the vaccine to protect those exposed to anthrax in the course of their work, there is no reported experience with its use on a scale comparable to the inoculation of 2.4 million people. Many public health workers believe the current passive reporting system for reactions is inadequate.

The Pentagon's record of conducting immunization programs in the past does not inspire confidence. For example, the Presidential Advisory Committee on Gulf War Veterans' Illnesses was sharply critical of the military's poor recordkeeping on immunizations during the Gulf War. More recently, it characterized the Pentagon's efforts to improve its medical recordkeeping in Bosnia, where it used tickborne encephalitis vaccine, as an "abysmal failure."[74,75] Closely related to the question of the safety of anthrax immunization is the failure of the military to maintain adequate records and perform adequate follow-up on the 150,000 U.S. troops who received anthrax vaccine during the Persian Gulf War.

Furthermore, other risks in vaccine policies also loom large, such as the impact that use of vaccines for inoculation of troops will have on the control of biologic weapons. Knowledge that a country is embarking on a program to defend its troops against a specific biologic weapon might be misread as a sign the country has a secret offensive capability or intends to develop one. In a world in which many countries are prepared to believe the worst about the military policies of other countries, information about immunization of the armed forces of a potential enemy may lead to destabilizing suspicions and unnecessary, costly, and risky countermeasures to possible bioattack. Moreover, immunizing troops with a vaccine that may be effective while leaving civilians unprotected comes dangerously close to a violation of the Geneva Conventions, in that such a policy specifically leaves civilians at risk.

In November 1999, the Governing Council of the American Public Health Association adopted a policy statement urging the Department of Defense "to delay any further immunization against anthrax using the current vaccine or at least to make immunization voluntary."[76] In December 1999, the FDA ordered the production of the vaccine by the MBPI halted because of deficiencies in the process.[77] In February 2000, the National Security Subcommittee of the Committee on Government Reform of the U.S. House of Representatives, after a year-long review, issued a report critical of the program and urging its suspension.[78] In July 2000 the Department of Defense sharply reduced the effort to inoculate U.S. military personnel against anthrax because of a shortage of vaccine[79] and, at a hearing before the Senate Armed Services Committee witnesses "described blunder after blunder in the Pentagon's two-and-a-half year program."[80]

Bioterrorism

A greatly expanded effort has been undertaken to protect the U.S. population against what has been called "bioterrorism." Once a hot topic of science fiction, bioterrorism has been cited as a major priority on the agendas of public health agencies.[81] Emergency response drills have been staged or planned in 120 major cities.[82] Scare stories and fictional scenarios about bioterrorism have been plentiful but scientific evaluations and public debate have been scant. Fundamental questions remain unanswered, including whether credible evidence supports the claim that the risks of bioterrorism justify the resources being allocated, and whether the interventions being implemented meet the standards of safety and efficacy for all public health interventions.[83]

Statements of public officials and media coverage seem to suggest that bioterrorism incidents have caused tremendous damage and have increased dramatically in recent years.[84] In fact, documented examples have been very rare. The only cited "bioterrorist" use of a biological agent was in 1984 in Oregon, where a religious cult allegedly contaminated several salad bars with salmonella, with hundreds of people affected but no deaths.[85] (A chemical nerve agent, sarin, was used in 1994 by a religious cult in Japan that killed 7 in the suburb Matsumoto and used again in 1995 in a Tokyo subway killing

12 people and injuring many more (see pp. 93-94). Although presentations about bio-terrorism in the media, at conferences and by government officials repeatedly refer to the above-mentioned episodes as "examples," they are the total sum of documented cases.

The public health burden of these dramatic and deplorable incidents is small compared with that of "ordinary" diseases and accidents such as an estimated 76 million illnesses from foodborne disease each year, with 325,000 hospitalizations and 5,000 deaths.[86] Also each year in the U.S. there are approximately 60,000 chemical spills, leaks and explosions, of which about 8,000 are considered "serious," with about 300-400 deaths.[87]

In order to make a reasonable estimate of risk, it is useful to distinguish between very different types of potential incidents. The most frightening is the use of chemical, biological, or nuclear agents in war, causing massive devastation and tens of thousands or even millions of casualties. But nuclear, biological, and chemical weapons of the kind and amounts that could cause catastrophic casualties are extremely difficult to obtain and still harder to deploy. Only the countries with nuclear weapons and a relatively few others with large military establishments have that capacity. It is extremely unlikely that terrorist organizations, in secret and without government support, could develop a capacity that only a limited number of countries have had the resources to acquire. And even if terrorists were able to obtain such catastrophic weaponry, their use would bring universal condemnation even from those who might otherwise sympathize with their cause.[88, 89]

Furthermore, fear of attack by chemical and biological weapons may lead to preemptive strikes to prevent the feared attack. In 1999, U.S. military forces bombed the Al Shifa pharmaceutical plant in Sudan, alleging that the factory was producing biological or chemical warfare agents. The allegations were later shown to lack substance.[90, 91] The damaged facility is reported to have provided half the medicines for North Africa.[92]

As distinct from catastrophic terrorism, smaller scale incidents—similar to those that occurred in Japan or Oregon—could reasonably be considered within the capabilities of organizations or individuals that might be inclined to use them. While even these have been extremely rare, recurrences cannot be ruled out. Nonetheless, once the scale of potential casualties has been reduced from the tens of thousands of the fictional scenarios to the much smaller numbers that might be seen if smaller scale incidents did reoccur, then the competing benefits and risks of appropriate interventions can be and must be rationally weighed and discussed. So far, however, unwarranted fear has prevailed, and programs with massive budgets and perhaps hazardous implications have been implemented with little discussion.

Some public health authorities have suggested that bioterrorism programs will make more money and expertise available for the public health infrastructure.[93] Spending patterns so far suggest that the programs will be dominated by military and law enforcement spending with little left for non-military and non-law-enforcement programs. In addition to wasting resources, fear of bioterrorism—based as it is on hypothetical and speculative scenarios—can be a handy excuse for many suspect policy recommendations driven by profit and political agendas quite different from the interests of national and international public health. Concerns about the influence of military and law enforcement agencies on public health policy was heightened by the recommendations in June 2000 of the National Commission on Terrorism, which called for greater use of wiretaps, using military personnel instead of civilian law enforcement personnel, and investigating foreign students who change their fields of study to scientific topics.[94]

Multi-billion dollar bioterrorism programs are already underway. The CDC and numerous county and state departments of public health have all become engaged in this campaign. Institutes to study bioterrorism have been established and schools of public health are being encouraged to set up core curricula to study it. This huge coordinated public health intervention has been undertaken with scant evidence, little public debate, and no independent review. Public health and medical professionals should insist that these programs be halted or postponed until there can be a scientific assessment of the risks of bioterrorism and a full and independent examination and public debate on the risks and benefits of proposed interventions.[95, 96] At a minimum, explicit comparison with the benefits of alternative use of these funds for public health efforts must be included in any assessment of the programs.

Much more attention and substantial resources are needed to improve national and international abilities for the surveillance of disease outbreaks and environmental insults. Such outbreaks and insults will continue to occur from natural causes, accidents, and negligence. If adequate systems are in place to prevent these outbreaks and to find and respond to those that occur, then in the unlikely event of bioterrorism the in-place system would likely be able to identify and respond to it adequately. On the other hand, creating a system that is targeted at the rare or phantom case may leave the public vulnerable to the ravages of other preventable diseases and injuries.

Antipersonnel Landmines
(Chapter 10, pp. 137-146)

As a result of pressure from civil society organizations (often termed nongovernmental organizations or NGOs), the Government of Canada convened a conference in 1997 at which governmental representatives negotiated a Convention on the Prohibition of Use, Stockpiling, Production and Transfer of Anti-Personnel Landmines and on Their Destruction. The time from the negotiation of the treaty to its ratification by the requisite number of countries to bring it into force on March 1, 1999, was the shortest in the history of ratification of major arms agreements. The 1997 Nobel Peace Prize was awarded to the International Campaign to Ban Landmines (ICBL) and to its coordinator, Jody Williams. In announcing the Prize, the Norwegian Nobel Committee stated:

"There are at present probably over one hundred million anti-personnel mines scattered over large areas on several continents. Such mines maim and kill indiscriminately and are a major threat to the civilian populations and to the social and economic development of the many countries affected."

The ICBL and Jody Williams started a process which in the space of a few years changed a ban on anti-personnel mines from a vision to a feasible reality. The Convention which will be signed in Ottawa in December this year (1997) is to a considerable extent a result of their important work.

There are already over 1,000 organizations, large and small, affiliated to the ICBL, making up a network through which it has been possible to express and mediate a broad wave of popular commitment in an unprecedented way. With the governments of several small and medium-sized countries taking the issue up and taking steps to deal with it, this work has grown into a convincing example of an effective policy for peace.[97]

By July 2000, 138 countries had signed or acceded to the treaty. Most of the United States' allies have signed, including all NATO countries except Turkey. A total of 41 of sub-Saharan Africa's 48 states have signed, and every country in the Western Hemisphere has signed except the U.S. and Cuba. In addition, China, India, Iraq, Israel, the Koreas, Pakistan, and Russia are among the 57 countries that have not yet signed. In May 1996, President Clinton stated that he would support an international ban on antipersonnel landmines, and ordered the Pentagon to find alternatives to the weapon. Two years later, he issued a policy directive stating that the U.S. would sign the ban by the year 2006 if, and only if, the Pentagon had found suitable alternatives to the weapon's use in Korea and in mixed-mine systems.[98]

In August 2000, the ICBL reported that since the treaty entered into force shipments of landmines have been halted and 22 million of the more than 250 million stockpiled have been destroyed. Nevertheless, landmines have been used in 20 conflicts by 11 governments and 30 non-governmental groups between March 1999 and August 2000.[98a]

During 1999, landmines were used by Yugoslav forces in Kosovo and by Russian forces in Dagestan. In May 1998, the World Health Assembly declared damage caused by the use of anti-personnel mines to be a public health problem. With some one hundred million landmines planted in one-third of the countries of the developing world, hundreds of people are injured each week by uncleared mines. Since the clearing of mines is hazardous and the cost of removing each mine may cost as much as $1,000, the clearing of mines has been extremely slow. Environmental health personnel and other public health workers should be involved in promoting awareness of the problem, in improving services for landmine victims, and in supporting effective efforts to ban future use of landmines.[98b]

Other Developments

Child Soldiers

In 1999, after years of objection to a draft international agreement that would raise the age for conscription and participation in armed conflict to 18, the United States agreed to compromise language allowing the continued recruitment and training of 17-year-olds, but requiring governments to take "all feasible measures" to prevent sending anyone under 18 into combat. Previous international law had established the age for participation, conscription, and recruitment into military forces at 15. United Nations officials estimate that there are approximately 300,000 children under 18 serving as soldiers around the world. The parent treaty for the new agreement is the UN Convention on the Rights of the Child, which the United States as of 2000 had not yet ratified, making it and Somalia the only two countries in the world that have failed to do so.[99]

Conventional Arms

Increasing public health interest is being focused on weapons not considered "weapons of mass destruction"—often termed "conventional arms"—that continue to cause the vast majority of war-related casualties in current wars. With the decline in the importance of Russia as an arms exporter, the United States has become by far the largest supplier of such arms to the other countries of the world. The arms transfer data base maintained by the Stockholm International Peace Research Institute records $20.6 billion (in constant 1990 dollars) as the total for "Major Conventional Weapons Transfers in 1999" by the United States compared to $3.1 billion by Russia.[100] This level of arms sales has been supported by the U.S. government, not only as a method of reducing the U.S. trade deficit but also for the purpose of supporting the U.S. arms manufacturing industries.[101] The availability of enormous numbers of small arms, manufactured in the United States and elsewhere, has been cited as an important factor in the extraordinary amount of gun violence in the United States.[102]

The Geneva Conventions and the Additional Protocol I state that no weapon system should render death inevitable, that weapons should not be indiscriminate in their effects, and that their effects should not inflict superfluous injury nor cause the victim suffering that is unnecessary for the military purpose of the user.[103] Efforts to enforce these restrictions have been proposed by the International Committee of the Red Cross in the ICRC Project on Superfluous Injury and Unnecessary Suffering (SIrUS). Defining what is meant by "Superfluous Injury and Unnecessary Suffering," which would help to define weapons that are illegal under international law, has been extremely difficult. This remains an important task for public health.[104]

Humanitarian Aid
(Chapter 19, pp. 293-307, and Chapter 20, pp. 308-319)

In 1999, the Nobel Prize for Peace was awarded to Médecins Sans Frontières (MSF, Doctors Without Borders). In announcing the award, the Norwegian Nobel Committee stated:

Since its foundation in the early 1970s, (MSF) has adhered to the fundamental principle that all disaster victims, whether the disaster is natural or human in origin, have a right to professional assistance, given as quickly and efficiently as possible. National boundaries and political circumstances or sympathies must have no influence on who is to receive humanitarian help. By maintaining a high degree of independence, (MSF) has succeeded in living up to these ideals.

By intervening so rapidly, (MSF) calls public attention to humanitarian catastrophes, and by pointing to the causes of such catastrophes, (it) helps to form bodies of public opinion opposed to violations and abuses of power.

In critical situations, marked by violence and brutality, the humanitarian work of (MSF) enables (it) to create openings for contacts between the opposed parties. At the same time, each fearless and self-sacrificing helper shows each victim a human face, stands for respect for that person's dignity, and is a source of hope for peace and reconciliation."[105]

MSF has retained its ability to receive invitations to provide humanitarian aid in countries to which other organizations have not been invited by keeping a careful balance between providing direct humanitarian aid and expressing public criticism of human rights violations it finds in the course of its work. MSF has nonetheless spoken out on a number of occasions about human rights abuses. The International Committee of the Red Cross, whose work on the SIrUS Project is described above, has also been careful to maintain its ability to enter into situations in which it can provide humanitarian aid by maintaining a policy of confidentiality and secrecy but has spoken out on a few occasions. Other organizations, such as Physicians for Human Rights and Human Rights Watch, place more emphasis on reporting human rights abuses wherever they are found, often relying on contacts with indigenous observers and informants when organizational access is denied. The work of all of these organizations is important to public health.

Issues related to humanitarian aid are receiving increasing attention in the public health, medical, and broader literature.[106, 107] The role in building peace of health initiatives in zones of conflict was reviewed in July 2000 by members of the Center for Peace Studies at McMaster University.[108]

Prevention of War and Development of a "Culture of Peace"

The Hague Appeal for Peace Civil Society Conference was held in May 1999 on the 100th anniversary of the 1899 Hague Peace Conference. The 1899 conference, attended by governmental representatives, was devoted to finding methods for making war more humane. The 1999 conference, attended by some 1,000 individuals and representatives of civil society groups, was devoted to finding methods to prevent war and to establish a "culture of peace." The document adopted at the 1999 conference, the *Hague Appeal for Peace and Justice for the 21st Century*, has been translated by the United Nations into all its official languages and distributed widely around the world.[109]

The Role of Public Health

Since the original publication of *War and Public Health* in 1997, health problems and problems in provision of public health services associated with war and preparation for war have continued and in some ways intensified. On the other hand, health workers and others have been actively engaged in the search for solutions and have had some limited success. We hope *War and Public Health* has been useful in that effort. This work must continue during the 21st century, since the health and the very future of humankind may depend on its success.

Acknowledgments

The authors are grateful to Meryl Nass and Tod Ensign for use of portions of material published in Sidel VW, Nass M, Ensign T, The anthrax dilemma. ; 5(2):97-104, 1998; to Hillel Cohen and Robert Gould for use of portions of material published in Cohen HW, Gould RM, Sidel VW, Bioterrorism initiatives: Public health in reverse? *Am. J Pub Health* 89:1629-1631, 1999; and in Cohen HW, Sidel VW, Gould RM. Prescriptions on bioterrorism have it backwards. *British Medical Journal* 320:1211, 2000; and to Lachlan Forrow for use of portions of material published in Forrow LF and Sidel VW, Medicine and nuclear war, *JAMA* 280:456-461, 1998.

REFERENCES

1. Department of Peace and Conflict Research. The *Conflict Data Project*. Uppsala, Sweden: Uppsala University, 1996.
2. Carnegie Commission on Preventing Deadly Conflict. *Preventing Deadly Conflict: Final Report with Executive Summary*. New York: Carnegie Corporation, 1997.
3. Fisher, I. and Onishi, N. Many armies ravage rich land in the "First World War of Africa." *New York Times*, February 6, 2000, pp. A1, A10.
4. Crosette, B. Death toll in Congo's 2-year war is at least 1.7 million, study says. *New York Times*, June 9, 2000, pp. A1, A10.
4a. Schmitt, E. Senate approves $1 billion to aid Colombian military. *New York Times*, July 22, 2000.
4b. Rohter, L. With U.S. Training Colombia melds war on rebels and drugs. *New York Times*, July 29, 2000.
4c. Krauss, C. Neighbors fear fallout of aid to Colombians. *New York Times*, August 25, 2000.
4d. Krauss, C. War in Colombia creates a nation of victims. *New York Times*, September 10, 2000.
5. Lobel, J. and Ratner, M. Humanitarian military intervention. *Foreign Policy Focus*; 5(1):1-4, January, 2000
6. Clinton, W.J. A Just and Necessary War. *New York Times,* May 23, 1999, p. WK 17.
7. Crossette, B. Report Says U.S. and others Allowed Rwanda Genocide. *New York Times*, July 8, 2000, p.A4.

8. Burkhalter, H. Facing Up to Genocide: The Obligation to Intervene. *Medicine and Global Survival* 6:51-53, 1999.

8a. Perlez, J. Allies call Kosovo rivals for peace talks in France. *New York Times*, January 30, 1999.

8b. Perlez, J. U.S. starts push to salvage Kosovo talks. *New York Times*, March 5, 1999.

8c. Perlez, J. Kosovo situation worsens as Serbs press offensive. *New York Times*, March 21, 1999.

9. US Agency for International Development. *Kosovo Crisis*. Fact Sheet #68. Washington, DC: USAID. June 9, 1999.

10. Gall, C. In the Hundreds of Thousands, Kosovo Homeless Feel Forsaken. *New York Times*, July 7, 2000, p.1.

11. Loretz, J., Spanjaard, H. and Sidel, V.W. What Should Have Been Done in Kosovo? *Medicine and Global Survival* 6:46-50, 1999.

12. Coovadia, H.M. Economic sanctions and the struggle for health in South Africa. *Am. J. Public Health* 89:1505-1508,1999.

13. Kuntz, D. ed. *The Politics of Suffering: The Impact of the US Embargo on the Health of the Cuban People*. Washington, DC: American Public Health Association, 1993.

14. Garfield, R. and Santana, S. The impact of the economic crisis and the US embargo on health in Cuba. *Am. J. Public Health* 87:15-20, 1997.

15. Gibbons, E. and Garfield, R. The impact of economic sanctions on health and human rights in Haiti, 1991-1994. *Am. J. Public Health* 89:1499-1504, 1999.

16. Garfield, R.. *Morbidity and mortality among Iraqi children from 1990 to 1998: assessing the impact of economic sanctions*. Goshen, Indiana: Fourth Freedom Forum, 1999.

17. McCutcheon R. Assessing Iraqi sanctions. In: *Forum on Economic Sanctions*. Toronto: University of Toronto, 1997, pp. 1-12.

18. Gottstein, U. Peace through sanctions? Lessons from Cuba, former Yugoslavia and Iraq. *Medicine Conflict and Survival* 15:271-285, 1999.

19. Marks, S.P. Economic sanctions as human rights violations: reconciling political and public health imperatives. *Am. J. Public Health* 89:1509-1513, 1999.

20. Sidel VW. Can sanctions be sanctioned? *Am. J. Public Health*; 89:1497-1498, 1999.

21. Institute of Medicine. *The Future of Pubic Health*. Washington, DC: National Academy of Sciences Press, 1988.

22. Health and human rights: a call to action on the 50th anniversary of the Universal Declaration of Human Rights. *JAMA* 280:462-464, 1998.

23. Universal Declaration of Human Rights. *JAMA* 279:469-470, 1998, UN GA Resolution 217 A (III); December 10, 1948. UN document A/810 at 71 (1948).

24. Mann, J., Gostin, L., Gruskin, S., Brennan, T., Lazzarini, Z. and Fineberg, H. Health and human rights. *Health and Hum Rights* 1:6-23, 1994.

25. Wald, M.L. Work on weapons affected health, government admits. *New York Times*. July 15, 1999.

26. National Economic Council, The Link Between Exposure to Occupational Hazards and Illness in the Department of Energy Contractor Workforce. April, 2000. Available at http://www.eh.doe.gov/benefits/nec/nec.html

27. Murphy, K. Radioactive waste seeps toward the greatest river of the American west *Los Angeles Times*, March 12, 2000.

28. *Exposure of the American People to Iodine-131 from Nevada Nuclear-Tests: Review of the National Cancer Institute Report and Public Health Implications*. Institute of Medicine and National Research Council. Washington, DC: National Academy Press, 1999, p. 193.

29. International Physicians for the Prevention of Nuclear War. *Radioactive Heaven and Earth: The Health and Environmental Effects of Nuclear Weapons Testing in, on, and Above the Earth*. New York, NY: Apex Press; 1991.

30. Makhijani, A., Hu, H. and Yih, K., eds. *Nuclear Wastelands: A Global Guide to Nuclear Weapons Production and Its Health and Environmental Effects*. Cambridge, Mass: MIT Press, 1995.

31. Schwartz, S.I. *Atomic Audit: The Costs and Consequences of US Nuclear Weapons Since 1940*. Washington, DC: Brookings Institute Press, 1998.

32. Paine, C.E. and McKinzie, M.G. *End Run: The US Government's Plan for Designing Nuclear Weapons and Simulating Nuclear Explosions Under the Comprehensive Test Ban Treaty*. Washington, DC: Natural Resources Defense Council; 1997. Available at: http://www.NRDC.ORG/nrdcpro/fppubl.html. Accessed July 10, 1998.

33. Current information on nations ratifying the CTBT may be found at http://www.ctbto.org/sg_rat.shto. Accessed July 26, 2000.

34. Miller, J. Nuclear anxieties in a new world. *New York Times*. February 5, 2000.

35. Nolan, J.E. An Elusive Consensus. Brookings Institute Press, 1999.

36. Schell, J. *The Gift of Time: The Case for Abolishing Nuclear Weapons Now*. New York: Henry Holt & Co Inc., 1998.

37. Forrow, L., Blair, B.G., Helfand, I., Lewis G., Postol T., Sidel, V.W., Levy, B.S., Abrams, H. and Cassel, C. Accidental nuclear war: a post-cold war assessment. *N. Engl. J. Med.* 338:1326-1331, 1998.

38. International Physicians for the Prevention of Nuclear War. *IPPNW Global Health Watch Report Number 1: Crude Nuclear Weapons–Proliferation and the Terrorist Threat*. Cambridge, Mass: International Physicians for the Prevention of Nuclear War, 1996.

39. Leventhal, P. and Alexander, Y., eds. *Nuclear Terrorism: Defining the Threat*. Washington, DC: Pergamon-Brassey's, 1986.

40. Allison, G.T., Cote, O.R., Jr., Falkenrath, R.A. and Miller, S.E. *Avoiding Nuclear Anarchy: Containing the Threat of Loose Russian Nuclear Weapons and Fissile Material*. Cambridge, Mass: *MIT Press*, 1996, p.10.

41. We are a nuclear power: interview with Indian Prime Minister Vajpayee. *Newsweek*. May 25, 1998, p. 32D.

42. The Cost of National Missile Defense. *The Defense Monitor* (Center for Defense Information) 29(1):1,6, 2000.

43. Treaty between the United States of America and the Union of Soviet Socialist Republics on the limitation of anti-ballistic missile systems. 1972. Available at:http://www.acda.gov/treaties/abm2.htm. Accessed Dec. 5, 1999.

44. United Nations General Assembly News Service. General Assembly calls for strict compliance of 1972 ABM Treaty, as it adopts 51 disarmament, international security texts. 19991201. Available at: http://www.un.org/News/Press/docs/1999/19991201.ga9675.doc.html. Accessed Dec. 6, 1999.

45. Grossman, K. Master of Space. *The Progressive*. January 6, 2000.

46. Forrow, L., Mutalik, G. and Christ, M., eds. *Abolition 2000:Handbook for a World Without Nuclear Weapons*. Cambridge, Mass: International Physicians for the Prevention of Nuclear War; 1995.

47. Information on Abolition 2000 maybe found at http://www.abolition2000.org. Accessed July 27, 2000.

48. International Physicians for the Prevention of Nuclear War. *Vital Signs* 8:1, 1995.

49. American College of Physicians. Resolution from the Board of Governors, approved by the Board of Regents. Presented at: Meeting of the American College of Physicians; October 1996; Philadelphia, Pa.

50. American Public Health Association. Cessation of nuclear testing and abolition of nuclear weapons: policy statement No. 9605 (adopted by the Governing Council November 20, 1996). *Am. J. Public Health* 87:500, 1997.

51. American Medical Association. House of Delegates Resolution 617 (I-96). Presented at: Meeting of the House of Delegates, American Medical Association; December 1996; Chicago, Ill.

52. International Court of Justice Communique No. 96/3. July 8, 1996. Available at: http://www.web.pgs.ca/pages/wcp0/html. Accessed July 1, 1998.

53. The Canberra Commission Web site. Available at: http://www.dfat.gov.au/dfat/cc/cchome.html. Accessed July 1, 1998.

54. Statement on Nuclear Weapons by International Admirals and Generals. Available at: http://www.stimson.org/zeronuke/index.html. Accessed July 1, 1998.

55. Committee on International Security and Arms Control, National Academy of Sciences. *The Future of US Nuclear Weapons Policy*. Washington, DC: National Academy Press; 1997.

56. Statement on Nuclear Weapons by International Civilian Leaders. Available at: http://www.worldforum.org. Accessed July 1, 1998.

57. Nuclear Weapons Convention. Available at: http://www.ddh.nl/org/ialana/modelin.html. Accessed July 1, 1998.

58. Witnner, L.S. *One World or None: The Struggle Against the Bomb*. Vol 1. Stanford, Calif: Stanford University Press, 1993, pp.250, 254, 277-285.

59. Boyer, P. *By the Bomb's Early Light: American Thought and Culture at the Dawn of the Atomic Age*. Chapel Hill: University of North Carolina Press, 1994, pp.53, 102, 322-328, 353, 355.

60. A report on the 2000 NPT Review Conference is available at http://www.acronym.org.uk.

61. Keeler, J.R., Hurst, C.G., and Dunn, M.A.. Pyridostigmine used as a nerve agent pretreatment under wartime conditions. *JAMA* 266:693-695, 1991.

62. Myers, S.L. Drug may be cause of veterans' illnesses. *New York Times*. Oct. 19, 1999, p. A18.

63. Further information maybe found on the websites of the Federation of American Scientists (http://www.fas.org) and of the Organisation for the Prohibition of Chemical Weapons (http://www. opcw.org) Also, Arms Control and Disarmament Agency. Convention on the Prohibition of the Development, Production, Stockpiling and Use of Chemical Weapons and on their Destruction (CWC). Available at: http://www.acda.gov/treaties/cwctext.html. Accessed Aug. 20, 1999

64. Carnes, S.A. and Watson, A.P. Disposing of the US chemical weapons stockpile: an approaching reality. *JAMA* 262:653-659, 1989.

65. Koplow, D.A. How do we get rid of these things? Dismantling excess weapons while protecting the environment. *Northwestern University Law Review*; 44:57-64, 1995.

66. Brooke, L.J. Chemical neutralization is gaining in war on poison gas. *New York Times*, February 7, 1997.

67. Arms Control and Disarmament Agency. Convention on the Prohibition of the Development, Production and Stockpiling of Bacteriological (Biological) and Toxin Weapons and on their Destruction (BWC). Available at: http://www.acda.gov/treaties/bwc2.html. Accessed August 20, 1999.

68. Alibek, K. *Biohazard*. New York: Random House, 1999.

69. Golden, T. Fungus considered a tool to kill coca in Colombia. *New York Times*, July 6, 2000.

70. Myers, S.L. U.S. armed forces to be vaccinated against anthrax. *New York Times*, December 16, 1997. p. A1.

71. Sidel, V.W., Nass, M. and Ensign, T. The anthrax dilemma. *Medicine and Global Survival*; 5(2):97-104, 1998.

72. Brachman, P.S., Gold, H. and Plotkin, S.A. Field evaluation of a human anthrax vaccine.

73. Friedlander, P.S., Pittman, P.R. and Parker, G.W. Anthrax vaccine: evidence for safety and efficacy against inhalation anthrax. *JAMA* 282:2104-2106, 1999.

74. Presidential Advisory Committee on Gulf War Veterans' Illnesses. 1997. Special Report, October 31, 1997.

75. Sloat, Bill, and Epstein, Keith. 1998. Army Misled Troops Who Got Vaccine in Bosnia. *Plain Dealer* (Cleveland, Ohio), January 25, 1998, pp. 1A, 18A.

76. American Public Health Association policy statement 9930: anthrax immunization, November 10, 1999. *Am. J. Public Health* 90:481-482, 2000.

77. Strong, C. FDA cites 30 deficiencies in anthrax vaccine production. *Associated Press* (National), Dec. 14, 1999.

78. Myers, L.M. Criticizing Pentagon, panel calls for suspension of military's anthrax shots. *New York Times*, February 18, 2000, p. A14

79. Siciolino, E. Shortage forces Pentagon to cut anthrax inoculations. *New York Times*, July 11, 2000.

80. Siciolino, E. Anthrax vaccination program is failing, Pentagon admits. *New York Times*, July 13, 2000.
81. Satcher, D. My Priorities. The Virtual Office of the Surgeon General. Available from: URL: http://www.surgeongeneral.gov/myjob/priorities.html. Accessed: December 3, 1999.
82. Hulse C. Readying emergency teams for terrorist attacks. *New York Times*. July 3, 1999: A9.
83. Guillemin J. Scare campaign about biological weapons is itself a threat. *Boston Globe*. December 2, 1999. A27.
84. Clinton, WJ. Remarks by the President on keeping America secure for the 21st century. The White House, Washington D.C.. Jan. 22, 1999. Available at: http://www.whitehouse.gov/WH/New/html/19990122-7214.html. Accessed August 18, 1999.
85. Toro, T.J., Tauxe, R.V., Wise, R.P., Livengood, J.R., Sokolow, R., Mauvais, S., Birkness, K.A., Skeels, M.R., Horan, J.M. and Foster, L.R. A large community outbreak of salmonellosis caused by intentional contamination of restaurant salad bars. *JAMA* 278(5):389-395, 1997.
86. Mead PS, Slutsker L, Dietz V, McCaig LF, Bresee JS, Shapiro C, Griffin PM, and Tauxe RV. Food-related illness and death in the United States. *Emerging Infectious Diseases*. 5(5):607-650, 1999.
87. Klink, R. Internet posting of chemical 'worst case' scenarios: a roadmap for terrorists. Joint Hearing Before the Subcommittees on Health and Environment and Oversight and Investigations of the Committee on Commerce, House of Representatives. Feb. 10, 1999. Available at http://ww1.access.gpo.gov/GPOAccess/sitesearch/congress/house/ house05ch106.html. Accessed Dec. 5, 1999.
88. Tucker JB. Bioterrorism is the least of our worries. *New York Times*, Oct. 16, 1999, p. A19.
89. Sprinzak E. The Great "Superterrorism" Scare. *Foreign Policy*. 112: 110-124, 1998 (Oct. 1, 1998).
90. Rouhi, M. No trace of nerve gas precursor found at bombed Sudan plant. *Chemical and Engineering News* 77(7):11-12, 1999.
91. Rouhi, M. Analytical credibility. *Chemical and Engineering News* 77(8):37, 1999.
92. Vest, J. The bombing of the Al Shifa pharmaceutical plant in Sudan is one of Clinton's lamest lies, but who cares? *Village Voice* 44(10): 55-59, March 16, 1999.
93. Rosen P. Coping with bioterrorism is difficult, but may help us respond to new epidemics. *BMJ* 320:71-72, 2000.
94. National Commission on Terrorism. Report available at http://www.usinfo.state.gov/topical/pol/terror/00060501.htm
95. Cohen, H.W., Gould, R.M. and Sidel, V.W. Bioterrorism initiatives: public health in reverse? *Am. J. Public Health* 89:1629-1631, 1999.
96. Cohen H.W., Sidel, V.W. and Gould R.M. Prescriptions on bioterrorism have it backwards. *British Medical Journal* 320:1211, 2000.
97. Further information on the 1997 Nobel Peace Prize may be found on the Nobel Prize website, http://www.nobel.se.
98. Further information on the status of the Anti-Personnel Landmine Treaty and on the removal of mines from countries around the world may be found on the website of the Physicians for Human Rights, http://www.phrusa.org.
98a. International Committee to Ban Landmines. *Landmine Monitor Report 2000: Toward a Mine-Free World.* Washington, DC: Human Rights Watch, 2000.
98b. Newman, R. D. and Mercer, M. A. Envrionmental health consequences of landmines. *International Journal of Occupational and Environmental Health* 6:243-248, 2000.
99. United States changes position on child soldiers. The Defense Monitor (Center for Defense Information) 29(1):3,6, 2000.
100. Current information on international arms transfers maybe obtained from the Conventional Arms Transfers Project of the Council for a Livable World Education Fund http://www.clw.org/cat/.
101. Sidel, V.W. The International Arms Trade and Its Impact on Health. *British Medical Journal* 311:1677-1680, 1995.

102. Sidel, V.W. and Wesley, R.C. Violence as a Public Health Problem: Lessons for Action Against Violence By Health Care Professionals from the Work of the International Physicians Movement for the Prevention of Nuclear War. *Social Justice* 22(4):154-170, 1995.
103. Coupland, R.M. The Effect of Weapons: Defining Superfluous Injury and Unnecessary Suffering. *Medicine and Global Survival* 3:1-6, 1996.
104. Coupland, R.M. Abnormal Weapons and "Superfluous Injury and Unnecessary Suffering:" from field surgery to law. *BMJ* 315:1450, 1997.
105. Further information on the 1999 Nobel Peace Prize may be found on the Nobel Prize website, http://www.nobel.se.
106. Allen, R.G., Cherniack, M. and Andreopoulos GJ. Refining War: Civil Wars and Humanitarian Controls. *Human Reports Quarterly* 18:747-781, 1996.
107. Leaning, J., Briggs, S.M. and Chen, L.C., eds. *Humanitarian Crises: The Medical and Public Health Response*. Cambridge, Mass: Harvard University Press, 1999.
108. Riesen, J. Terrorism panel faults U.S. efforts on Iran and 1996 bombing. *New York Times*, June 4, 2000.
109. The *Agenda* and other documents related to the Hague Appeal for Peace are available at http://www.haguepeace.org.

Appendix:
Organizations and Resources

American Public Health Association (APHA)
1015 15th Street, NW, Washington, DC 20005
Tel.: 202 789 5600; Fax: 202 789 5681
Home Page: http://www.apha.org

American Refugee Committee
2344 Nicollet Avenue, Suite 350
Minneapolis, MN 55404
Tel.: 612 872 7060; Fax: 612 872 4309
E-mail: kraus024@maroon.tc.umn.edu

Amnesty International
U.S. Office:
322 Eighth Avenue, New York, NY 10001
Tel.: 212 807 8400; Fax: 212 627 1451
International Secretariat:
One Easton Street, London, England, WC1X 8DJ

Carnegie Endowment for International Peace
2400 N Street, NW, Suite 700
Washington, DC 20037
Tel.: 202 862 7900; Fax: 202 862 2610
E-mail: ceip@ceip.org

The Carter Presidential Center
One Copenhill, Atlanta, GA 30307
Tel.: 404 331 3900; Fax: 404 331 0283
Home Page: http://www.emory.edu/CARTER__
CENTER

Center for Defense Information
1500 Massachusetts Avenue, NW
Washington, DC 20005
Tel.: 202 862 0700; Fax: 202 862 0708
E-mail: info@cdi.org

Centers for Disease Control and Prevention (CDC)
1600 Clifton Road, NE, Atlanta, GA 30333
Tel.: 404 639 3311
Home Page: http://www.cdc.gov

Centre for Conflict Resolution
Department of Peace Studies
University of Bradford
Bradford, West Yorkshire BD7 1DP
United Kingdom
Tel: 44 274 733 466; Fax: 44 274 305 340

Centre for Peace Studies
McMaster University
1280 Main Street West
Hamilton, Ontario L8S 4K1, Canada
Tel.: 905 525 9140 ext. 27592 or ext. 24729
Fax.: 905 529 5845 or 905 570 1167

Center for Strategic and Budgetary Assessments
1730 Rhode Island Avenue, NW, Suite 912
Washington, DC 20036
Tel.: 202 331 7990; Fax: 202 331 8019

Collaborative for Development Action
26 Walker Street, Cambridge, MA 02138
Tel.: 617 661 6310; Fax: 617 661 3805

Commission on Disarmament Education
(co-sponsored by the International Association of
University Presidents and the UN Centre for
Disarmament Affairs)
Tide Mill Landing, Suite 102
2425 Post Road
Southport, CT 06490
Tel.: 203 255 4269; Fax: 203 259 8859

Common Agenda
P.O. Box 31567, Washington, DC 20030
Tel.: 202 388 1535; Fax: 202 269 3944

Council for a Livable World
110 Maryland Avenue, NE, Suite 409
Washington, DC 20002
Tel.: 202 543 4100; Fax: 202 543 6297
E-mail: www.clw.org

Council for Responsible Genetics
5 Upland Road, Suite 3, Cambridge, MA 02140
Tel.: 617 868 0870; Fax: 617 491 5344
E-mail: crg@essential.org

Demilitarization for Democracy
1601 Connecticut Avenue, NW, Suite 600
Washington, DC 20009
Tel.: 202 319 7191; Fax: 202 319 0937;
E-mail: pdd@clark.net
Home Page: http://www.clark.net/pub/dfd

Doctors of the World
(U.S. affiliate of Médecins du Monde)
625 Broadway, New York, NY 10012
Tel.: 212 529 1556 Fax.: 212 529 1571

Doctors without Borders
(Médicins Sans Frontières)
U.S. Office:
11 East 26th Street, Suite 1904
New York, NY 10010
Tel.: 212 679 6800 Fax: 212 679 7016

Educators for Social Responsibility (ESR)
475 Riverside Drive, New York, NY 10115
Tel.: 212 870 3318

Federation of American Scientists
307 Massachusetts Avenue, NE
Washington, DC 20002
Tel.: 202 546 3300; Fax: 202 675 1010
Home Page: http://www.fas.org

François Xavier Bagnoud Center
for Health and Human Rights
Harvard University School of Public Health
651 Huntington Avenue, Building 4
Boston, MA 02115
Tel.: 617 432 0656; Fax: 617 432 4310
E-mail: fxbcenter@igc.apc.org

Friends Committee on National Legislation
245 Second Street, NE, Washington, DC 20002
Tel.: 202 547 6000; Fax: 202 547 6019;
E-mail: fcnl@igc.apc.org

Greenpeace
U.S. Office:
1436 U Street, NW, Washington, DC 20009
Tel.: 202 462 1177; Fax: 202 462 4507
E-mail for information:
sanjay.mishra@green2.greenpeace.org
International Office:
Keizersgracht 174
1016-DW Amsterdam, The Netherlands
Tel.: 31 20 626 1877; Fax: 31 20 622 1272

Human Rights Watch
1522 K Street, NW, Suite 910
Washington, DC 20005
Tel.: 202 371 6592; Fax: 202 371 0124
E-mail: hrwdc@hrw.org

Institute for Defense and Disarmament Studies
675 Massachusetts Avenue
Cambridge, MA 02139
Tel.: 617 354 4337; Fax: 617 354 1450
E-mail: idds@world.org

Institute for Energy and Environmental Research
6935 Laurel Avenue
Takoma Park, MD 20912
Tel.: 301 270 5500; Fax: 301 270 3029
E-mail: ieer@ieer.org
Home Page: http://www.ieer.org

Institute for Human Rights
University of California at Berkeley
460 Stephens Hall, Berkeley, CA 94720
Tel.: 510 642 0965; Fax: 510 643 5284

Institute for Multi-track Diplomacy
1819 H Street, NW, Suite 1200
Washington, DC 20006
Tel.: 202 466 4605 Fax: 202 466 4607
E-mail: imtd@igc.apc.org

International Association of Lawyers
Against Nuclear Arms
U. S. Office:
Lawyers' Committee on Nuclear Policy
666 Broadway, Suite 625, New York, NY 10012
Tel.: 212 674 7790; Fax: 212 674 6199

International Campaign to Ban Landmines
1347 Upper Dummerston Road
Brattleboro, VT 05301
Tel.: 802 254 8807; Fax: 802 254 8808
E-mail: jwlandminees@igc.apc.org

International Center for Technology Assessment
310 D Street, NE, Washington, DC 20002
Tel.: 202 547 9359; Fax: 202 547 9429

International Committee of the Red Cross (ICRC)
Avenue de la Paix 19
CH-1202 Geneva, Switzerland
Tel.: 41 22 734 6001; Fax: 41 22 733 2057
E-mail: webmaster. gva@gwn.icrc.org
Home Page: http://www.icrc.org

International Federation of the Red Cross
Chemin des Crets 17
CH-1211 Geneva, Switzerland
Tel.: 41 22 730 4222; Fax: 42 22 733 0395

International Peace Bureau
41, rue de Zurich
CH-1201 Geneva, Switzerland
Tel.: 41 22 731 6429; Fax: 41 22 738 9418
E-mail: ipb@gn.apc.org

International Physicians for the Prevention
of Nuclear War (IPPNW)
126 Rogers Street, Cambridge, MA 02142
Tel.: 617 868 5050; Fax: 617 868 2560
E-mail: ippnwbos@igc.apc.org
Home Page: http://www.healthnet.org/ippnw/
ippnw.html

International Rescue Committee (IRC)
122 East 42nd Street, New York, NY 10168-1289
Tel.: 212 551 3000; Fax: 212 551 3180;
E-mail: irc.com

The Joan B. Kroc Institute for International
Peace Studies
University of Notre Dame
P. O. Box 639, Notre Dame, IN 46556
Tel.: 219 631 6970; Fax: 219 631 6973
Home Page: http://www.nd.edu/~krocinst

Lawyers Alliance for World Security/Committee
for National Security
1601 Connecticut Avenue, NW, Suite 600
Washington, DC 20009
Tel.: 202 745 2450; Fax: 202 667 0444;
E-mail: laws@earthlink.net

Médecins du Monde (MDM)
International Office:
62, rue Marcadet, F-75018, Paris, France
Tel.: 33 144 92 15 15; Fax: 33 144 92 99 99

Médecins Sans Frontières (MSF)
International Office:
39 Rue de la Tourelle, B-1040 Brussels, Belgium
Tel.: 32 22 80 18 81; Fax: 32 22 80 01 73
U. S. Office:
11 East 26th Street, New York, NY 10010
Tel.: 212 679 6800; Fax: 212 679 7016
E-mail: dwb@Newyork.msf.org

Medical Action for Global Security (MEDACT)
601 Holloway Road, London, England N19 4DJ
Tel.: 44 171 272 2020; Fax: 44 171 281 5717
E-mail: medact@gn.apc.org

National Commission for Economic Conversion
and Disarmament
1601 Connecticut Avenue, NW, Suite 500
Washington, DC 20009
Tel.: 202 234 9382 ext. 214; Fax: 202 319 3558

National Council for International Health
1701 K Street, NW, Suite 600
Washington, DC 20006
Tel.: 202 833 5900; Fax: 202 833 0075
E-mail: ncih@ncih.org

National Priorities Project
160 Main Street, Suite 6
Northampton, MA 01060
Tel.: 413 584 9556; Fax: 413 584 9647
E-mail: natprior@crocker.com

Oxfam America
26 West Street, Boston, MA 02111
Tel.: 617 482 1211; Fax: 617 728 2594
E-mail: oxfamusa@igc.apc.org

Peace Action
1819 H Street, NW, Washington, DC 20006
Tel.: 202 862 9740; Fax: 202 862 9762
Home Page: http://www.webcom.com/peaceact

Physicians for Human Rights
100 Boylston Street, Suite 702
Boston, MA 02116
Tel.: 671 695 0041; Fax: 617 695 0307
E-mail: phrusa@igc.apc.org

Physicians for Social Responsibility (PSR)
1101 14th Street, NW, Suite 700
Washington, DC 20005
Tel.: 202 898 0150; Fax: 202 898 0172;
E-mail: psrnatl@igc.apc.org
Home page: http://www.nucmed.buffalo.edu/PSR

Project on Defense Alternatives
The Commonwealth Institute
186 Hampshire Street
Cambridge, MA 02139
Tel.: 617 547 4474; Fax: 617 868 1267;
E-mail: pda@igc.apc.org

Stockholm International Peace Research
Institute (SIPRI)
Frösunda
171 53 Solna, Sweden
Tel.: (46 8) 655-9700; Fax: (46 8) 655 9733
E-mail: sipri@sipri.se
Home Page: http://www.sipri.se

20/20 Vision
1828 Jefferson Place, NW
Washington, DC 20036
Tel.: 202 833 2020; Fax: 202 833 5307;
E-mail: vision@igc.apc.org
Home page: http://www.2020vision.org

Union of Concerned Scientists
2 Brattle Square, Cambridge, MA 02238-9104
Tel.: 617 547 5552; Fax: 617 864 9405
E-mail: ucs@ucs.usa.org;
Home Page: http://www.ucs.usa.org

United Nations Children's Fund (UNICEF)
Three United Nations Plaza
New York, NY 10017
Tel.: 212 326 7000 Fax: 212 888 7465
Home Page: http://www.unicef.org

United Nations Development Program (UNDP)
One United Nations Plaza, New York, NY 10017
Tel.: (212) 906 5000

United Nations High Commissioner for
Refugees (UNHCR)
Headquarters:
94, Rue de Montbrillant, Case Postale 2500
CH-1211 Geneva, Switzerland
Tel.: (41 22) 739 8111
New York Office:
One United Nations Plaza, Room 2610
New York, NY 10017
Tel.: 212 963 6200

Wisconsin Institute: A Consortium for the
Study of War, Peace and Global Cooperation
University of Wisconsin
2100 Main Street, Stevens Point, WI 54481
Tel.: 715 346 3383

Women's Action for New Directions (WAND)
110 Maryland Avenue, NE,
Washington, DC 20002
Tel.: 202 543 8505; Fax: 202 675 6469;
E-mail: wandwill@clark.net

World Health Organization (WHO)
CH-1211 Geneva, Switzerland
Tel.: (41 22) 791 2111; Fax: (41 22) 791 0816
Home page: http://www.who.ch

Worldwatch Institute
1776 Massachusetts Avenue, NW
Washington, DC 20036
Tel.: 202 452 1999; Fax: 202 296 7365;
E-mail: worldwatch@igc.apc.org;
Home Page: http://www.worldwatch.org

Index